The Journey
From Child to
Scientist

The Journey From Child to Scientist

Integrating Cognitive Development and the Education Sciences

Edited by Sharon M. Carver and Jeff Shrager

American Psychological Association • Washington, DC

KH

Published by
American Psychological Association
750 First Street, NE
Washington, DC 20002
www.apa.org

To order
APA Order Department
P.O. Box 92984
Washington, DC 20090-2984
Tel: (800) 374-2721;
Direct: (202) 336-5510
Fax: (202) 336-5502;
TDD/TTY: (202) 336-6123
Online: www.apa.org/pubs/books
E-mail: order@apa.org

In the U.K., Europe, Africa, and the Middle East,
copies may be ordered from
American Psychological Association
3 Henrietta Street
Covent Garden, London
WC2E 8LU England

Typeset in New Century Schoolbook by Circle Graphics, Inc., Columbia, MD

Printer: United Book Press, Inc., Baltimore, MD
Cover Designer: Mercury Publishing Services, Rockville, MD

The opinions and statements published are the responsibility of the authors, and such opinions and statements do not necessarily represent the policies of the American Psychological Association.

Library of Congress Cataloging-in-Publication Data

The journey from child to scientist : integrating cognitive development and the education sciences / edited by Sharon M. Carver and Jeff Shrager. — 1st ed.
p. cm.
Includes bibliographical references and index.
ISBN-13: 978-1-4338-1138-8 (alk. paper)
ISBN-10: 1-4338-1138-3 (alk. paper)
1. Science—Methodology. 2. Reasoning in children. 3. Science—Psychology. 4. Constructivism (Education) I. Carver, Sharon M. II. Shrager, Jeff.
Q175.32.R45J68 2012
507.1—dc23

2011052352

British Library Cataloguing-in-Publication Data
A CIP record is available from the British Library.

Printed in the United States of America
First Edition

DOI: 10.1037/13617-000

3/15/13

APA Science Volumes

Attribution and Social Interaction: The Legacy of Edward E. Jones

Best Methods for the Analysis of Change: Recent Advances, Unanswered Questions, Future Directions

Cardiovascular Reactivity to Psychological Stress and Disease

The Challenge in Mathematics and Science Education: Psychology's Response

Changing Employment Relations: Behavioral and Social Perspectives

Children Exposed to Marital Violence: Theory, Research, and Applied Issues

Cognition: Conceptual and Methodological Issues

Cognitive Bases of Musical Communication

Cognitive Dissonance: Progress on a Pivotal Theory in Social Psychology

Conceptualization and Measurement of Organism–Environment Interaction

Converging Operations in the Study of Visual Selective Attention

Creative Thought: An Investigation of Conceptual Structures and Processes

Developmental Psychoacoustics

Diversity in Work Teams: Research Paradigms for a Changing Workplace

Emotion and Culture: Empirical Studies of Mutual Influence

Emotion, Disclosure, and Health

Evolving Explanations of Development: Ecological Approaches to Organism–Environment Systems

Examining Lives in Context: Perspectives on the Ecology of Human Development

Gender Differences in Prenatal Substance Exposure

Global Prospects for Education: Development, Culture, and Schooling

Hostility, Coping, and Health

Measuring Patient Changes in Mood, Anxiety, and Personality Disorders: Toward a Core Battery

Occasion Setting: Associative Learning and Cognition in Animals

Organ Donation and Transplantation: Psychological and Behavioral Factors

Origins and Development of Schizophrenia: Advances in Experimental Psychopathology

APA Decade of Behavior Volumes

Chaos and Its Influence on Children's Development: An Ecological Perspective

Child Development and Social Policy: Knowledge for Action

Children's Peer Relations: From Development to Intervention

Cognitive Fatigue: Multidisciplinary Perspectives on Current Research and Future Applications

Commemorating Brown: The Social Psychology of Racism and Discrimination

Computational Modeling of Behavior in Organizations: The Third Scientific Discipline

Couples Coping With Stress: Emerging Perspectives on Dyadic Coping

Developing Individuality in the Human Brain: A Tribute to Michael I. Posner

Emerging Adults in America: Coming of Age in the 21st Century

Experimental Cognitive Psychology and Its Applications

Family Psychology: Science-Based Interventions

Individual Pathways of Change: Statistical Models for Analyzing Learning and Development

Inhibition and Cognition

The Journey From Child to Scientist: Integrating Cognitive Development and the Education Sciences

Measuring Psychological Constructs: Advances in Model-Based Approaches

Medical Illness and Positive Life Change: Can Crisis Lead to Personal Transformation?

Memory Consolidation: Essays in Honor of James L. McGaugh

Models of Intelligence: International Perspectives

The Nature of Remembering: Essays in Honor of Robert G. Crowder

New Methods for the Analysis of Change

On the Consequences of Meaning Selection: Perspectives on Resolving Lexical Ambiguity

Participatory Community Research: Theories and Methods in Action

Personality Psychology in the Workplace

Perspectivism in Social Psychology: The Yin and Yang of Scientific Progress

Primate Perspectives on Behavior and Cognition

Principles of Experimental Psychopathology: Essays in Honor of Brendan A. Maher

The Psychology of Courage: Modern Research on an Ancient Virtue

Every great advance in science has issued from a new audacity of imagination.
—John Dewey, *The Quest for Certainty*

In honor of our mentors
for encouraging us to be bold, inventive, and unconventional
in the pursuit of our passions.

Contents

Contributors

Xornam S. Apedoe, PhD, School of Education, University of San Francisco, San Francisco, CA

Kimberly Brenneman, PhD, National Institute for Early Education Research, Rutgers—The State University of New Jersey, New Brunswick

Sharon M. Carver, PhD, Department of Psychology, Carnegie Mellon University, Pittsburgh, PA

Zhe Chen, PhD, Department of Human and Community Development, University of California, Davis

Kevin Niall Dunbar, PhD, Department of Human Development and Quantitative Methodology, University of Maryland, College Park

Richard A. Duschl, PhD, College of Education, Pennsylvania State University, University Park

Maria Figueroa, PhD, Professor, Universidad de los Andes, Bogotá, Colombia

Erin Marie Furtak, PhD, School of Education, University of Colorado at Boulder

David C. Geary, PhD, Department of Psychological Sciences and Interdisciplinary Neuroscience Program, University of Missouri, Columbia

Rochel Gelman, PhD, Rutgers Center for Cognitive Science and Department of Psychology, Rutgers—The State University of New Jersey, Busch Campus, Piscataway

María Pilar Jiménez-Aleixandre, PhD, Departamento Didactica das Ciencias Experimentais, Universidade de Santiago de Compostela, Santiago de Compostela, Spain

Annette Karmiloff-Smith, Doctorat en Psychologie Genetique et expérimentale, Birkbeck Centre for Brain & Cognitive Development, University of London, England

Frank C. Keil, PhD, Department of Psychology, Yale University, New Haven, CT

David Klahr, PhD, Department of Psychology, Carnegie Mellon University, Pittsburgh, PA

Richard Lehrer, PhD, Department of Teaching and Learning, Vanderbilt University's Peabody College, Nashville, TN

Leona Schauble, PhD, Department of Teaching and Learning, Vanderbilt University's Peabody College, Nashville, TN

Christian D. Schunn, PhD, Learning Research and Development Center, University of Pittsburgh, Pittsburgh, PA

Richard J. Shavelson (Emeritus), PhD, School of Education, Stanford University, Stanford, CA

Jonathan T. Shemwell, PhD, College of Education and Human Development, University of Maine, Orono

Jeff Shrager, PhD, Symbolic Systems Program (consulting), Stanford University, Stanford, CA

Robert S. Siegler, PhD, Department of Psychology, Carnegie Mellon University, Pittsburgh, PA

Eli M. Silk, PhD, Learning Research and Development Center, University of Pittsburgh, Pittsburgh, PA

Foreword

In early 1988, the American Psychological Association (APA) Science Directorate began its sponsorship of what would become an exceptionally successful activity in support of psychological science—the APA Scientific Conferences program. This program has showcased some of the most important topics in psychological science and has provided a forum for collaboration among many leading figures in the field.

The program has inspired a series of books that have presented cutting-edge work in all areas of psychology. At the turn of the millennium, the series was renamed the Decade of Behavior Series to help advance the goals of this important initiative. The Decade of Behavior is a major interdisciplinary campaign designed to promote the contributions of the behavioral and social sciences to our most important societal challenges in the decade leading up to 2010. Although a key goal has been to inform the public about these scientific contributions, other activities have been designed to encourage and further collaboration among scientists. Hence, the series that was the "APA Science Series" has continued as the "Decade of Behavior Series." This represents one element in APA's efforts to promote the Decade of Behavior initiative as one of its endorsing organizations. For additional information about the Decade of Behavior, please visit http://www.decadeofbehavior.org.

Over the course of the past years, the Science Conference and Decade of Behavior Series has allowed psychological scientists to share and explore cutting-edge findings in psychology. The APA Science Directorate looks forward to continuing this successful program and to sponsoring other conferences and books in the years ahead. This series has been so successful that we have chosen to extend it to include books that, although they do not arise from conferences, report with the same high quality of scholarship on the latest research.

We are pleased that this important contribution to the literature was supported in part by the Decade of Behavior program. Congratulations to the editors and contributors of this volume on their sterling effort.

Steven J. Breckler, PhD
Executive Director for Science

Virginia E. Holt
*Assistant Executive Director
for Science*

Preface

This celebratory publication honors the scientific and educational contributions of David Klahr, the Walter van Dyke Bingham Professor of Cognitive Development and Education Sciences in the Department of Psychology at Carnegie Mellon University. Throughout his career, Klahr has pioneered research to strengthen the reciprocal contributions of cognitive development, scientific reasoning, and education. During that time, he has mentored and inspired undergraduates, graduate trainees, postdoctoral fellows, and other leading researchers in the field, many of whom participated in the 37th Carnegie Symposium on Cognition, "From Child to Scientist: Mechanisms of Learning and Development," held in October 2009 to commemorate Klahr's 70th birthday and 40th year at Carnegie Mellon. The chapters herein are based on that symposium.

The symposium connected leading researchers whose work bridges theory and practice to advance both our understanding of scientific and mathematical development and our research regarding strategies for formal and informal education.

The title of the symposium has a dual meaning: Whereas we explicitly considered Klahr's own journey from child to scientist during his first 70 years, we were more centrally concerned with his impact on the field's understanding of the learning and development mechanisms that propel children to become more scientific thinkers, together with ways that educators might facilitate these important changes.

Sharon Carver's introductory tribute briefly traced Klahr's life journey from inquisitive child to prominent—and still inquisitive—scientist, describing the ways in which his family foundations of hard work, collaboration, and passion for understanding how things work contributed to his undergraduate MIT engineering training in computer programming, which in turn supported his graduate business school computer simulations of complex decision making, that led fortuitously to the defining moment of his journey—linking this "artificial intelligence" to Piaget's theory of children's developing cognition. Symposium attendees were treated to Klahr's own version of this somewhat meandering, cross-disciplinary story,[1] during which he stressed the importance of taking risks that may not seem sensible to those on the traditional academic path and of seeking a professional context that is prepared to support such risks, especially with respect to interdisciplinary inquiry. Carver applauded Klahr as a self-described "learning engineer" before the field of learning sciences was so named, and she heralded his pioneering research, broad collaboration, influential publications, and generous service on behalf of the psychology

---

[1]The full video clip, entitled *From AI to Piaget,* which was shown at the October 2009 conference, is available at http://www.4researchers.org/articles/2179, along with many other interesting clips from the same interview.

department at Carnegie Mellon University, and the fields of cognitive development and education sciences.

On the basis of her experience as Klahr's graduate student, postdoctoral fellow, collaborator, and colleague, Carver also highlighted Klahr's genuine respect for children, as has been evident in his stories about his own children, some of which have led to important leaps in theorizing that prompted new research agendas (e.g., Klahr, 1978). She identified Klahr's central focus on how children's thoughts and actions are driven by the ways in which they are processing the information available to them—usually in ways that make sense given their prior knowledge and foundational strategies. Similarly, Klahr's respect for his students resulted in a collegial approach characterized by high expectations, honest feedback, and support for each student's pursuit of his or her unique interests, which in Carver's case meant applying cognitive and developmental theories to the design of educational interventions long before that approach was an accepted focus for psychology dissertations (e.g., Klahr & Carver, 1988). Carver also expressed appreciation for Klahr's model of respect for family, one that continually offers a healthy perspective on balancing diligent and focused work with pursuit of personal passions.

Numerous diverse tributes throughout the symposium echoed Carver's themes regarding Klahr's professional and personal impact; however, when discussing plans for the symposium with us, he insisted that no one should be pressured to suspend scientific critique in favor of praise and thus subvert the academic integrity of the symposium. As is shown in the Introduction, the scientific contributions to this volume exemplify the ways that Klahr's interdisciplinary approach has shaped the field of cognitive development, nurtured the blossoming field of education sciences, and encouraged their integration without sacrificing experimental rigor or sound theorizing. Klahr's walking the less traveled road has engendered critique and debate but has also set the course for investigators to explore new questions, using novel methodologies, all to continue the process of advancing our understanding of development and learning, even beyond what Klahr himself could have imagined.

The volume culminates with Klahr's reflection on his own journey from child to scientist and on the scientific journey related to one of his earliest research questions regarding children's developing understanding of number conservation. Both aspects of the reflection exemplify the type of colleague and mentor Klahr has been throughout his career to so many individuals—one whose sharp theorizing catalyzes others' investigations and one whose willingness to share of himself inspires others to do the same.

Carl Jung (1942/1954) once observed, "One looks back with appreciation to the brilliant teachers, but with gratitude to those who touched our human feelings." Throughout Klahr's career, he has been a generous and gracious mentor, colleague, and friend to many. We hope to continue his legacy by extending such support to those within our spheres of influence. By publishing this volume, we invite a broader range of scholars interested in cognitive development and education sciences to benefit from Klahr's own contributions and those he inspired, as well as to engage their best efforts in our shared endeavor of understanding the journey from child to scientist.

Acknowledgments

The symposium that is the basis for the chapters in this volume was generously funded by the American Psychological Association, the Department of Psychology and Program in Interdisciplinary Education Research at Carnegie Mellon University, and private donations. This funding enabled us to offer the symposium free of charge to all interested attendees. The Children's School at Carnegie Mellon University also supported the conference in diverse ways. We thank Kevin Dunbar and Bob Siegler for their assistance in organizing the conference and Audrey Russo, David Klahr's long-time administrative and research assistant, for handling many organizational details prior to the conference and for gracious hospitality throughout the event.

We extend our deep appreciation to each of the symposium participants for their active engagement in constructive dialogue throughout the event. We are grateful to those participants, and to several colleagues whose schedules precluded participation, who have contributed chapters to this Festschrift. Their timely preparation and thorough response to feedback made our jobs easier. John Anderson, Judy DeLoache, and Micki Chi contributed significantly to the symposium by means of presentations that are, unfortunately, not represented in this volume. We appreciate the scholars who enhanced the event with written and spoken tributes, each of which demonstrated that Klahr's positive influence on colleagues, from graduate school days to the present, has been both professionally challenging and personally enriching.

We extend our thanks also to the Junior Fellows who both demonstrated Klahr's effect on the rising stars in the learning sciences and contributed their own novel perspectives to the symposium dialogue: Christa Asterhan (Learning Research and Development Center, University of Pittsburgh), Jodi Davenport (WestEd, Oakland, CA), Jamie Jirout (Carnegie Mellon University), Jordan Lippman (University of Illinois at Chicago), Bryan Matlen (Carnegie Mellon University), and Andrew Young (University of Wisconsin—Madison). The impressive extent of Klahr's impact on the learning sciences field is evident in the breadth of the Junior Fellows' research topics, which range from studies of preschoolers to college students learning in diverse domains, and from scientific curiosity to psychological argumentation, chemical equilibrium, assistance dilemma, understanding the role of achievement goals, and peer agreement and the evaluation of evidence.

We also thank David Penner, a graduate student of Klahr's who turned his ingenuity to the arts, for creating a unique Festschrift gift that we presented to David after his keynote address. Penner's intriguing "meandering box" was designed to symbolize Klahr's approach to the study of scientific reasoning and, while physically meandering in response to gentle prods, to engage Klahr's delight in discovering the mysteries of the unusual gift.

We are grateful to the *Mind in the Making* producers, Ellen Galinsky, Hank O'Karma, and Amy McCampbell, for graciously sharing a prepublication video clip about David's scientific reasoning research for debut at the symposium.

Each of us, the editors, Sharon Carver and Jeff Shrager, would like to publicly express to the other a word of thanks for being such a supportive collaborator throughout this project. We also acknowledge our development editor, Tyler Aune, and our production editor, Jessica Kamish, from APA Books for significantly enhancing the final product by their diligent efforts and insightful coaching. We both appreciate the opportunity to contribute our best to this productive Festschrift symposium and the present resulting volume. We hope that it will provide readers with a deeper knowledge of Klahr's life and work and that it will prompt personal reflection on readers' own scientific journeys, inspiring them to think and work in ways that will support even more progress in theory, research, and practice in the many fields related to cognitive development and education science.

In addition, Sharon Carver is grateful to Carnegie Mellon University and The Children's School for daily occasions to support staff, children, families, and researchers in training as they continue their journeys from child to scientist. More important, she values her husband, Dave, and daughter, Ariel, as fellow intrepid travelers on life's journey.

The symposium came at an especially poignant time for Jeff Shrager in that his first child, Leonardo Simon, was only about 6 months old when it occurred. Over the next 9 months, while helping Sharon assemble the volume, Jeff thought of Klahr daily as he watched Leo unfold in ways that, even as a PhD developmental psychologist, amazed and surprised him. Leo learned to count up to 10 objects, to subitize to 3, and many other impressive skills by exploring his environment in incredible detail. Jeff is looking forward to watching his son take the journey from child to scientist that Klahr took and described so well through his life's work.

References

Jung, C. G. (1954). The gifted child. In *The collected works of C. G. Jung: Vol. 17. The development of personality* (G. Adler and R. F. C. Hull, Trans.). Princeton, NJ: Princeton University Press.

Klahr, D. (1978). Goal formation, planning, and learning by pre-school problem solvers, or: "My socks are in the dryer." In R. S. Siegler (Ed.), *Children's thinking: What develops?* (pp. 181–212). Hillsdale, NJ: Erlbaum.

Klahr, D., & Carver, S. M. (1988). Cognitive objectives in a LOGO debugging curriculum: Instruction, learning, and transfer. *Cognitive Psychology, 20,* 362–404. doi:10.1016/0010-0285(88)90004-7

The Journey
From Child to
Scientist

Introduction: The Journey From Child to Scientist—The Psychology of Science, Science Education, and the Impact of David Klahr

Sharon M. Carver and Jeff Shrager

> Every great advance in science has issued from a new audacity of imagination.
>
> —John Dewey, *The Quest for Certainty* (1929/1960)

Anyone with even cursory experience of children recognizes their active engagement in exploring the world around them while coming to understand it. This practice also describes scientists. As far back as Piaget, this general observation has led to complementary aphorisms that bookend our understanding of cognitive development as regards science: "child as scientist" and "scientist as child." David Klahr (1999) traced the child-as-scientist view back at least to Piaget's investigations of children's exploration and understanding of fundamental scientific entities (e.g., Piaget, 1952). Klahr then attributed the scientist-as-child view to most adults' putative decline in curiosity about the world, stating that this exploration is retained only by "the fortunate few who wind up as scientists."

There are both subtle and sophisticated ways to understand these commonplace phrases—either as metaphors or as serious scientific hypotheses. As Sloman (2005) indicated, the child-as-scientist view is often reinvented, but it is also "obviously false if taken literally, for instance, because there are many conceptual, representational and mathematical tools used by scientists that are not available to a child" (Slide 4). However, Carey (1985) argued that the mechanisms underlying conceptual change in childhood can be understood as analogous to those that underlie global conceptual change, such as those that occur in scientific revolutions. More recently, Gopnik and her colleagues have suggested that young children's causal inferences are consistent with conditional probabilities in a way analogous to causal Bayesian statistics (e.g., Sobel, Tenenbaum, & Gopnik, 2004), a statistical view that is currently popular in theories of scientific reasoning as well (e.g., Howson & Urbach, 1989). Gopnik (1996) also examined the other end of the spectrum, the scientist as child. These positions have been critiqued (especially Gopnik's, e.g., Solomon, 1996) on the basis of the observation that science takes place in a world that is occupied by the scientist, by the instruments and physical system under study, and by other agents, and that this world has indefinite richness of physical structure and constraint (Shrager & Langley, 1990). Evidence is often very difficult for scientists to obtain, and the global veridicality of the large-scale scientific process is critical. Toward this end, scientific resources and social structures have become organized so as to support the effective and efficient generation and communication of evidence, methods, and theories (Solomon, 1996). The assertion of these researchers is that scientific thinking cannot be understood solely in terms of the cognitive mechanisms of individuals, whereas presumably children's thinking can be so understood. Shrager and Langley (1990) called this systems view the "embedding and embodiment" of science.

The present volume's focus is closely related to the embedding and embodiment of science; that is, regardless of whether one thinks of the twin tropes of child as scientist and scientist as child as specific hypotheses or mere metaphors, one point is clear: Every scientist was once a child and has, therefore, engaged in a journey from child to scientist. Science is dynamic in all of its embeddings, and is, moreover, cognitively dynamic—that is, it develops both in individuals and in the community, as nascent and professional scientists interact. Over time, the relationships that a scientist-in-training has initially with parents and caretakers, then with the formal educational system, and eventually with mentors and the larger scientific community operate in an ongoing interplay with each child-becoming-scientist's development. Shrager and Langley (1990) foreshadowed the present volume, predicting that an important source for models of embedding and embodiment in science will come from "the developmental psychology of socialization," which studies the ways in which children learn to become part of their culture, and furthermore that this investigation will provide a way of understanding the paths and mechanisms through which graduate students and junior scientists become members of their scientific community, "mastering the ways of thinking, operating, and communicating that constitute the institution of science" (p. 20). Indeed, the 1999 symposium organized by Klahr was entitled "Beyond the Child as Scientist or Scientist as Child: The Development of Scientific Reasoning Processes" (Klahr, 1999). In that symposium, Klahr established the goals of characterizing exactly what scientific reasoning entails, charting the developmental course of its components, and specifying the components' integration into the overall scientific discovery process.

Concentrating on the developmental journey from child to scientist, rather than just on its starting and ending-points, focuses the role of science education[1] on teaching the sophisticated methods and models that scientists use, together with the relevant underlying knowledge, skills, and dispositions, as well as on establishing mentorships to guide scientists-in-training through the relevant social, physical, and even political contexts. As Lehrer and Schauble eloquently

---

[1]We use the term *science education* to include what many term the *STEM disciplines:* science, technology, engineering, and mathematics.

explain in Chapter 9 of the present volume: "Disciplinary dispositions are forged only over extended periods and perhaps only when people are continually in contexts where those forms of thinking and reasoning are needed and valued" (p. 204). Whereas in regard to the endpoints one must question the psychological content, mechanisms, and context that constitute children's and adults' science (in whatever form), about the journey one must question further *how* these contents, mechanisms, and contexts change and *what* experiences and education (formal and informal) enable children to muster and nurture the childhood forms of these mechanisms into adult science. Phrased another way, we must ask not only where to plant each foot on the journey but also how to take each step—or, in more typical developmental terms, we must move beyond stage descriptions to explain the mechanisms of change. Only then will we be able to usefully decide what we must teach in school, what experiences we must offer our children in order to encourage them to embark on this journey, and how to most constructively support them along the way.

The chapters in this book address these interesting, important, and expansive questions, with a specific focus on one influential giant in the fields of psychology of science and science education: Klahr, in honor of his 70th birthday and contemporaneous 40th year at Carnegie Mellon University (see Preface). Understanding the detailed cognitive mechanisms underlying children's reasoning and skill acquisition, as well as the role of education in influencing and facilitating the process, has occupied Klahr throughout his long and productive scientific career. According to Frank Keil (quoted from his symposium tribute), Klahr is "the clear leader of his generation in the study of scientific reasoning in both adults and children," "the pioneer who brought information processing approaches to cognitive development," and "the key person to bring experimental rigor and theoretical sophistication to science education research" (F. Keil, personal communication, October 9, 1999). In the preface to Klahr's (2000) book on the development of scientific reasoning, Nobel laureate Herbert A. Simon highlighted the importance of Klahr's scientific contributions:

> It is this hypothesized kinship between children (more generally, young people) and scientists that David Klahr and his colleagues have sought out in the innovative and exciting experiments described in this book. They find similarities between children and adults, but also clear differences, leading them to qualify and sharpen the hypothesis of "child as scientist" and its reciprocal of "scientist as child." We see them arriving at a theory of discovery that describes in closely similar terms much of the seeking and learning behavior of both youngsters and mature scientists, thereby enriching our understanding of both. We see them also illuminating the differences between child and adult that the education and experiences we provide to our children must aim at closing. (Klahr, 2000, p. x)

Klahr's career also demonstrates his abiding concern with enriching the scientific community through publication and mentorship; he has influenced hundreds of researchers through direct collaboration and the indirect impact of his writings and the writings of his collaborators and students. This book, and the symposium on which it is based, brought together many of these collaborators, students, and others who have been touched by the influence of Klahr's work. In the remainder of this Introduction, we examine how the subsequent chapters address the above questions. In keeping with the overall theme, each chapter addresses both science and science education in some balance, while highlighting Klahr's impact. Although each chapter explains its author's or authors' unique scientific goals, conceptual focus, and methodologies, the overarching themes of understanding the journey from child to scientist, of thinking about how we can support and guide children and young scientists along the way, and of the contribution of Klahr to these issues are clearly represented in every contribution.

The variety and integration represented by the breadth and depth of these contributions mirror the breadth and depth of the conceptual space of the motivating questions and the breadth and depth of Klahr's influence on the related fields.

Basic Components of Scientific Reasoning and Their Development

Klahr (1999), quoted above, admonished researchers to better characterize scientific reasoning and how it develops, so this book begins with chapters that examine the development of basic processes that contribute to scientific exploration. Of course, nearly all of the chapters in this volume study basic processes—for example, Karmiloff-Smith's analysis of representation change in Chapter 6 and Duschl and Jiménez-Aleixandre's analysis of conceptual change in Chapter 12—and we could well have included them all under this heading, but these two contributions in particular take as their central focus two largely irrefutable components: (a) numerical representation and (b) analogical reasoning.

We begin this volume with possibly the most basic of formal scientific component skills: arithmetic. Both children and scientists use arithmetic (more generally, mathematics). Even infants may have natural arithmetic abilities (e.g., McCrink & Wynn, 2008), and children, driven by their caregivers and teachers, are exposed to numbers from a very young age. Bob Siegler, a long-term close colleague of Klahr's, has been a leader in the study of developing reasoning, especially of arithmetic skills, so it is appropriate that we begin the volume with his demonstration that playing a linear board game (vs. a circular analog of the same game, or merely learning number facts) promotes mathematical understanding (Chapter 1). True to what Kevin Dunbar (Chapter 5) has called the *Klahrian method* of taking complex issues and specifying the underlying mechanisms, Siegler suggests several mechanisms that might underlie this phenomenon, including the analogous linearity of numerical magnitude representations, the automaticity of numeral identification, the encoding of numerical magnitudes, or simply improved counting skill. This project is also eminently applied; board games such as the ones studied in Chapter 1 are easy to create cheaply from commonplace materials, so they are promising candidates for broad adoption. Siegler's contribution illustrates the bidirectional benefits to be gained by following Klahr's example of applying cognitive developmental theories to real educational problems, and using the outcomes of the applications to refine and improve the theories, as well as Klahr's efforts to integrate the fields of cognitive development and education such that their reciprocal influence improves both theory and practice.

Analogical reasoning has long been recognized as an important mechanism of scientific theory change (e.g., Nersessian, 1988). In Chapter 2, developmentalist Zhe Chen, who did postdoctoral work with Klahr, reports on his extended research on young children's understanding of the fundamental scientific principles to more precisely identify the developmental differences in their use of analogy as a mechanism of learning about science. Chen and his colleagues have demonstrated that analogy can be a powerful tool for children's learning and transfer of domain-general scientific investigation strategies, in addition to its already-well-understood power to support specific knowledge acquisition and specific problem-solving structures. In thinking about how to apply these results, Chen observes that

> direct instruction can be highly effective and efficient in teaching children scientific reasoning strategies inasmuch as it provides explicit feedback about children's correct and incorrect responses, systematic explanations of the scientific principles involved, and/or positive (correct) and negative (incorrect) illustrations of the principles. (p. 62)

On the other hand, strategy learning also benefits from exploration, especially when it is guided by "probe questions, self-generated explanations, implicit feedback from children's own strategies, and/or manipulation of experimental materials in hands-on tasks" (p. 62).

The Importance of "Folk Science" and the Evolution of Scientific Thinking

The replacement of "folk" scientific theories in favor of more "correct" scientific ones is considered by many to be one of the most important transitions between childhood theories of the world and those of formal science. Two very insightful contributions by Keil and Geary address this putative transition, and both demonstrate the subtlety of the folk science concept, its importance in understanding the ways of thinking throughout science, and how studying the evolution and cultural embeddedness of knowledge and reason reveals new insights both to our understanding of the psychology of science and to our thinking about science education. Both offer a broader evolutionary systems perspective that might be productively pursued by Klahr and others interested in better integrating the fields of cognitive development, scientific reasoning, and science education in order to enrich both theory and practice.

In Chapter 3, Keil stresses the importance of learning from children's developing understanding of folk science (vs. formal science), in particular with regard to the human propensity for sensing causal patterns in ways other than by learning rules. He emphasizes human reliance on the social infrastructures in which folk sciences are embedded. Keil describes a broad view of folk science that includes our "emerging understanding of discovery and induction processes, an area where the work of Klahr has been so pioneering and pivotal"

(p. 83). This view also includes different ways of characterizing how individuals track causal structure and relations. Keil observes that children deploy "a rich array of causal patterns," often without an understanding of the mechanistic details. For Keil, development of such reasoning consists of progressing to more detailed levels of analysis while staying above the mechanistic. He concludes that all of these components are dramatically improved in the elementary through middle school years and notes that the child's social infrastructure also undergoes a great deal of restructuring during this time. Moreover, Keil indicates that many common scientific practices, such as making idealizations, are not explicitly taught. He posits that folk and formal science influence one another through "intricate cycles" instead of the simple replacing of misconceptions with correct ones, and he concludes that by studying how folk sciences develop, and the surrounding social infrastructure, we will learn much about formal science.

Geary takes a neurological and evolutionary approach to a similar set of questions, emphasizing the role of culture and context. In Chapter 4, he explores implications of the interrelated evolution of culture and folk knowledge, in particular as they concern the demands we make on children for learning about scientific discoveries in school. He emphasizes the difference between the domains in which folk knowledge originally developed, and what he calls *evolutionarily novel* domains, highlighting the difficulty of separating the core folk knowledge from cultural influences and concluding that a study of folk knowledge should include anthropological studies of knowledge development in cultures that are similar to those in which the folk domains evolved. He observes that moving beyond the constraints of folk knowledge requires extended experience in evolutionarily novel domains and that even professional scientists sometimes defer to folk biases. Turning to the cognitive mechanisms that are used during scientific problem solving, Geary posits that evolved systems support mental model creation and goal-directed problem solving. These, he argues, are necessary but not sufficient for discovery in evolutionarily novel domains and are most likely to be engaged when natural (i.e., folk) heuristics do not provide a satisfactory explanation for the phenomena under study. One requirement for education is, accordingly, to teach students how and when to engage these different systems. Though based on a distinctly different perspective from Klahr's investigations of the cognitive mechanisms underlying scientific reasoning, Geary's theoretical views could prompt novel considerations in science education that would spur new research in Pasteur's Quadrant.

New Directions in Educational Neuroscience and Computer Simulation

Rapid scientific and technological advances in genomics, neuroscience, and computation are significantly influencing research in the psychology of science and science education. Geary's theoretical contribution, just described, represents a contribution to the growing trend that Dunbar calls *educational neuroscience* and that is represented by several other chapters, especially Chapter 6 by Karmiloff-Smith. In this section, we also discuss a chapter by Shrager on a novel use for computer simulation, and we conclude with a brief discussion of a talk by John Anderson that was given at the symposium but that is not represented by a chapter herein.

In Chapter 5, developmental neuroscientist Kevin Dunbar, who did postdoctoral work with Klahr, explicitly explains the Klahrian method of beginning with detailed qualitative descriptions of cognitive processes that are then progressively specified in precise models of the mechanisms underlying development, sometimes to the point of computational models. The goal of Dunbar's current work is similar to Klahr's in that it seeks to understand underlying mechanisms in ways that advance both theory and practice. Dunbar introduces the concept of educational neuroscience and asks what it means for science education, answering that we must move beyond the metaphor of building bridges between disciplines and instead use multiple methods, theoretical stances, population groups, and cultures to build a "mosaic of knowledge." He exemplifies this mosaic through his own integration of naturalistic inquiry in scientists' laboratory meetings with laboratory neuroimaging to better understand the use of analogy in science.

Karmiloff-Smith is concerned with the mechanisms that underlie representational change. Originally inspired by a number of Klahr's classic, child-friendly problem-solving tasks (e.g., Klahr & Wallace, 1976), she has elsewhere hypothesized that the ability to re-represent, in an explicit form, information that was initially embodied in procedural knowledge is a critical aspect of human development. Such representations enable the reasoner to be more flexible because information in explicit form can then be transported to other domains, which is much more difficult to do with the initial procedural knowledge. In Chapter 6, Karmiloff-Smith takes a genetic and neuroscientific approach, using data from individuals with Williams syndrome and Down syndrome, supplemented by precise modeling of cognitive processing. She proposes an alternative to the traditional domain-general versus domain-specific dichotomy by suggesting domain-relevant skills as a developmental specialization from domain-general precursors. According to Karmiloff-Smith, once we understand the basic cognitive architecture and abilities of individuals with Williams syndrome and Down syndrome (as well as other developmental disorders), we can study their problem-solving activities in cases where representational changes may or may not occur. She posits that difficulties with representational change may be one of the sources of the atypical development observed in these children. The newly emerging field of educational neuroscience may well integrate the study of typical and atypical cognitive development.

Computer simulation has already become one of the most important tools of modern science. Klahr's first publication was a computer simulation of a political paradox (Klahr, 1966), and his major early contribution to developmental science was to apply computer simulation to explaining children's progression on Piagetian developmental tasks (Klahr & Wallace, 1976). Not only does a working simulation provide a powerful experimental test bed, but also, in accord with the Klahrian method, building such a simulation requires one to be very precise in explicating the underlying mechanisms. In Chapter 7, Shrager, a former graduate student of Klahr's, addresses broad questions about the workings of the scientific community and the value of scientific education to scientific progress. Whereas one could muster general economic arguments in these regards, or perhaps use comparative natural experiments, Shrager applies multiagent computer simulation, showing how computer simulation can be used to explore the ramifications of multiple scientists communicating in an open and continuous web-based system of sharing results, including the trade-offs involved in gaining quicker access to potentially relevant data while having to search a huge experiment space of uncertain quality.

At the symposium, John Anderson combined cognitive neuroscience and computer simulation in a tour de force demonstration that it is possible to use neuroimaging data of students learning algebra in a computer tutoring context to provide a very precise diagnosis of what the student is thinking, and when (see Stocco & Anderson, 2008). Could such a tool eventually enable us to teach in a much more personalized manner, reaching, as it were, into the thoughts of the student as though the tutor were able to read the individual's mind? For the moment, Anderson is interested primarily in the theoretical aspects of this methodology, and he noted the lack of theoretical models for making predictions that imaging data could be used to test.

The Concepts and Practice of Science Education

Sharing Klahr's skepticism that young children can effectively learn to reason like scientists on their own, Gelman and Brenneman (Chapter 8) introduce the Preschool Pathways to Science program as a way of promoting STEM skills in the youngest schoolchildren, beginning with explicit instruction in observation. Gelman and Brenneman find that "young children's inquisitiveness fits well with a program that teaches them to make systematic observations about questions of interest, using the tools and practices of science" (p. 167). By encouraging the use of these tools, processes, and their technical names across a variety of content lessons, children acquire science terms as they practice using the skills and tools to which they refer. It is clearly possible to encourage young scientists-in-waiting to start to become scientists. In addition to their basic results, Gelman and Brenneman offer in their conclusion an interesting anecdote about children remembering key vocabulary, goals, and conditions of an experiment:

> The conversation was also extremely animated and full of positive affect. This is quite typical of most of the children this age with whom we have worked. They pay attention, listen, and participate in lessons that occur during group time—even if these go on for 20 minutes. Many children and/or their parents tell us that the school activities led to at-home discussions about what they the children had done during the school day, taking science out of the classroom and into the rest of their lives. (p. 168)

The inclusion of opportunities to do classroom science builds on children's natural proclivities, extends these to incorporate the practices and tools of science, and—we hope—helps ensure that science continues to be an enjoyable and positive experience that is considered an integral part of everyday experience. By providing repeated opportunities to engage productively with both the content and processes of science, educators foster the promise in each young scientist-in-waiting, providing critical support as he or she grows from child to scientist.

Lehrer and Schauble (Chapter 9) articulate the foundations of evolutionary thinking, both in terms of the goals of science education and of the developmental underpinnings, or trajectories, for understanding evolution. In the context of elementary science classes, they reflect on children's use of models as forms of analogy and on their representational practices. In previous work they have explored modeling as a representational practice explicitly (Lehrer & Schauble, 1999), explaining that scientists often participate in such representational practices. Scientists' models evolve over extended research programs, and there are alternative ways of modeling the same situation. Lehrer and Schauble discuss the development of modeling practices in elementary school students and argue that an adequate account of the development of scientific reasoning must include an understanding of the contexts and practices whereby such modeling is supported and fostered. Their chapter specifically addresses educational practices that involve and engender such modeling activities. This extended quotation from their chapter clarifies the active, dynamic aspect of the journey from child to scientist:

> The teachers and we plan together for sequences of investigations of this kind, beginning with those that require simple tools and little content knowledge. As occurs with practicing scientists, outcomes of initial investigations provoke new questions and, over time, new investigations that are increasingly challenging, both biologically and mathematically. Our goal is that, across years of this work, students develop a repertoire of inscriptions (graphs, tables, diagrams) and models (difference, rates, and logistic curves to describe the growth of organisms or populations; distributional change; chance models of choice) that were formulated to address current investigations but will continue to have extended utility beyond them. In addition, we expect students to build coherent and structured knowledge about specific parts of the biological world that were identified by researchers and teachers for their potential to make concepts and principles of broad scope visible and accessible to students. By the time they reach high school and encounter formal study of evolution, these students will have received repeated opportunities to investigate change and variability in local ecologies; to struggle with challenges of method and measure; and to structure, interrogate, and draw conclusions from data. Moreover, students will have repeatedly considered and revised their criteria for what serves as an interesting biological question and for the qualities of evidence that are convincing in defense of an explanation. We suspect that disciplinary dispositions are forged only over extended periods and perhaps only when people are continually in contexts where those forms of thinking and reasoning are needed and valued. (p. 203)

Lehrer and Schauble explicitly note that the questions they raise closely parallel those that have occupied Klahr, including in what sense children can be said to reason scientifically; how children base their reasoning on evidence, whether children understand how to design experiments and other sorts of studies; how they use models and other sorts of representations for problem solving problems and communication; and how children think about statistical concepts such as variability, error, and uncertainty.

Continuing into secondary education, and considering the engineering domain, Schunn, Silk, and Apedoe (Chapter 10) detail the underlying processes shared by science and engineering to build a middle school curriculum that capitalizes on the motivational aspects of engineering tasks to teach basic scientific reasoning skills. They present a detailed analysis of science and engineering, ands describe both important differences in overall goals and storyline, and important similarities in underlying processes. Moreover, they show that engagement in engineering design activities can result in gains in scientific knowledge and reasoning skills. Their explanation for this effect is that work on the subsystems in engineering problems requires that students engage in scientific reasoning activities to develop a better understanding of the science that supports the subsystems. Thus, although Schunn et al. are clear about the distinctions between the knowledge and skills of scientific discovery versus engineering design, they encourage their connections. But the differences in goals and storylines between engineering and science can produce differences in learning. In particular, design involves different strategies that can influence which scientific content knowledge is acquired. Moreover, Schunn et al. stress that students who traditionally show poor performance in science classrooms may find design activities more interesting and motivating, which might in turn mean that engineering design activities could foster gains in science knowledge and skills.

The Sociopolitics and Epistemology of Science Education in Context

At the outset of this Introduction, we mentioned the importance of the social, cultural, and indeed the political embedding of science. Many of the chapters in this book deal with aspects of the sociocultural embedding of science: Children interact with caregivers and, later, teachers; professional scientists interact in the scientific community; and science and its underpinnings evolved in complex ways to operate within specific cultures. Chapters 11 and 12 stretch by example beyond the sociocultural context into the larger sociopolitical and contextual aspects of the journey from child to scientist. In Chapter 11, Furtak, Shavelson, Shemwell, and Figueroa examine a theoretical debate regarding inquiry teaching and learning, which is sometimes also described as *self-guided, discovery,* or *exploratory* learning. In Chapter 12, Duschl and Jiménez-Aleixandre contrast distinct epistemic views regarding the nature of science itself, along with their implications for science education.

Inquiry teaching has been a touchstone of modern science education. Indeed, we have seen inquiry teaching dealt with explicitly in other chapters in this volume (e.g., Chapters 2, 8, and 10), and it is at least peripherally important, if not explicit, in many of the other contributions, although perhaps described with other labels. Unfortunately, the theoretical underpinnings that would enable us to decide under what circumstances, and in what specific manner one should (or should not) promote inquiry learning have been lacking. Recently, Klahr and Nigam (2004) demonstrated that in some circumstances inquiry approaches lead to poorer performance on science-related tasks than does direct instruction. Moreover, they showed that, in some circumstances, children who learned about experimental design from direct instruction performed as well in making broader scientific judgments as those who discovered the method through self-directed exploration. These results challenged the presumed superiority of discovery approaches in science education. Policymakers eagerly seized on Klahr and Nigam's apparently strong evidence in support of direct instruction and ignited a "science war" in the education research community.

In Chapter 11, Furtak et al. use the setting of this science war regarding discovery learning to discuss the challenge of a theory's operational definitions in politically charged arenas. They emphasize the danger of getting mired in even commonly accepted labels and instructional jargon to describe global teaching approaches, and they implore us to focus on detailed analyses of teaching–learning interactions. Instead of the name given to a particular instructional paradigm, it is the detailed way in which the instructional condition is implemented, based on individual teachers' interpretations of curriculum materials and the teaching context, that carries the weight of the instructional effect. While acknowledging Klahr and Nigam's (2004) terminology choices as provoking the debate, Furtak et al. affirm Klahr as a model of transparency with respect to his scientific methods and data, such that colleagues could more clearly understand the contrasting experimental conditions and compare them with those used in others' studies.

In Chapter 12, Duschl and Jiménez-Aleixandre raise similar issues about clarifying the epistemological roots of science education approaches, explicitly contrasting Klahr's hypothetico-deductive experimental science with alternate approaches driven by conceptual change theory and model-based approaches. Like Geary, Keil, and Lehrer and Schauble, they advocate studying the conceptual ecology of science learning environments as educators seek to promote students' enculturation into scientific communities. They view science as practice with cognitive, social, and epistemological dynamics that are critical to engaging in the discourse and dialogical strategies that are at the core of what it means to do scientific inquiry. They focus on approaches that involve groups of scientists rather than individuals, the evolution rather than explicit instruction of claims, greater focus on tools and technologies for inquiry, and overall more situated scientific practices. They propose six design principles and seven tenets toward an enhanced model of what we communicate to students as scientific methods, all with the goal of increasing the focus on the epistemology of science.

Klahr's Reflection on His Own Journey From Child to Scientist

In a symposium tribute, Klahr's department chair and long-term colleague Mike Scheier foreshadowed Klahr's personal reflection on the impact of his childhood exploration experiences on his development as a scientist:

> This phrase "from child to scientist" suggests a normal progression of development that leaves more childish thought behind. Yet, I think the most creative people never leave behind the joy of discovery and wonder of insight

that is so much a part of childhood. David Klahr is such a person. He takes true delight in learning new things, or turning the world upside down to see things from new perspectives. (M. Scheier, personal communication, October 9, 1999)

Paul Thagard's (2005) analysis of factors that make some scientists highly successful is even more useful in understanding the roots of Klahr's remarkable impact. Thagard based his analysis on a small survey of psychologists of science, including Klahr himself, and on published advice from several distinguished Nobel laureates. He organized these success factors into six broad categories:

1. Make new connections: Broaden yourself to more than one field. Read widely. Use analogies to link things together. Work on different projects at the same time. Use visual as well as verbal representations. Don't work on what everyone else is doing. Use multiple methods. Seek novel mechanisms. 2. Expect the unexpected: Take anomalies seriously. Learn from failures. Recover from failures. 3. Be persistent: Focus on key problems. Be systematic and keep records. Confirm early, disconfirm late. 4. Get excited: Pursue projects that are fun. Play with ideas and things. Ask interesting questions. Take risks. 5. Be sociable: Find smart collaborators. Organize good teams. Study how others are successful. Listen to people with experience. Foster different cognitive styles. Communicate your work to others. 6. Use the world: Find rich environments. Build instruments. Test ideas. (p. 161)

Note the active nature of the factors that promote scientific productivity: *make, read, use, link, seek, pursue, organize, foster, communicate.* Thagard's compilation of advice highlights constructive aspects of the scientific *journey* instead of simply describing outcomes or milestones along the way.

Klahr's concluding autobiographical reflection on his developmental progress from child to scientist in Chapter 13 enables us to see all of Thagard's (2005) principles in action throughout the journey of a highly productive scientist. Klahr reveals his understanding of evolution in context. He identifies the sorting he did for his father's watch hospital as yielding skills in perceiving patterns and forming categories, as well as the importance of social support; the surveying involved in his adolescent employment as instrumental in developing abstract representations of reality; the satellite detection programs he wrote for the North American Aerospace Defense Command's cold war effort as knowledge-driven search; and his serendipitous meeting with Iain Wallace and subsequent related events as evidence of emergence instead of rule-based learning. It is not surprising that many of Thagard's principles are likewise evident in the research and careers of those mentored and influenced by Klahr, as demonstrated in part by the chapters in this volume. Similarly, Klahr's explication of children's path to number conservation and suggested next steps for scientific investigation are consistent with other symposium participants' approaches. He posits statistical learning mechanisms as potential explanations for very young children's abilities to parse continuous streams of visual information about physical actions to learn about number (cf. Keil's pattern sensing; see Chapter 3), and he emphasizes the need to "see what they see as they encounter the real world" (i.e., in vivo research in context, cf. the approaches to education research discussed in Chapters 8, 9, and 12).

The chapters in this volume illuminate a small number of important areas in the vast theoretical space that is the psychology of science and its development and the practice of science education. In doing so, each author relates his or her work to the perspective offered by one of the field's guiding lights, David Klahr, and represents some of the best work of his numerous students and colleagues. In many ways, the scientists participating in this Festschrift have challenged Klahr's theories and methods as limited in one way or another. We have seen this clearly in the work of Furtak et al. (Chapter 11), and at the symposium Klahr's very first graduate student, Micki Chi, emphasized that not all scientific processes operate in a logical, goal-oriented, hierarchical manner, as is assumed by Klahr's models. Such challenges to a leading scientist's ideas have as their goal the ongoing refinement of science, so any influence of the symposium and resulting Festschrift volume on the field's future theory, research, and practice is itself honoring Klahr's continuing impact on the field.

Just as Klahr encourages reciprocal influence as the fields of cognitive development and education sciences become better integrated, he demonstrates the reciprocal influence of colleagues from different disciplines, collaborators with different strengths, and even of mentors and their protégés. The impact of a single, highly productive researcher and mentor such as David Klahr is multiplied by colleagues and students whose work is similarly inventive, applying foundational concepts and methodologies wheresoever their own passions lead them, illuminating exponentially more and more of that vast space. The diversity of chapters in this volume—science education, biomedicine, evolutionary theory, computational modeling, educational neuroscience—serve both to more clearly explicate the journey from child to scientist and at the same time to provide strong evidence of the continuing expansion of the ripples created by scientists such as David Klahr.

References

Carey, S. (1985). *Conceptual change in childhood.* Cambridge, MA: MIT Press.

Dewey, J. (1960). *The quest for certainty: A study of the relation of knowledge and action. The Gifford Lectures.* New York, NY: Capricorn. (Original work published 1929)

Gopnik, A. (1996). The scientist as child. *Philosophy of Science, 63,* 485–514. doi:10.1086/289970

Howson, C., & Urbach, P. (1989). *Scientific reasoning: The Bayesian approach.* Chicago, IL: Open Court.

Klahr, D. (1966). A computer simulation of the paradox of voting. *American Political Science Review, 60,* 384–390. doi:10.2307/1953365

Klahr, D. (Chair). (1999, October). *Beyond the child as scientist or scientist as child: The development of scientific reasoning processes.* Symposium conducted at the meeting of the Cognitive Development Society, Chapel Hill, NC. Retrieved from http://www.cogdevsoc.org/eventabs.php

Klahr, D. (2000). *Exploring science: The cognition and development of discovery processes.* Cambridge, MA: MIT Press.

Klahr, D., & Nigam, M. (2004). The equivalence of learning paths in early science instruction: Effects of direct instruction and discovery learning. *Psychological Science, 15,* 661–667. doi:10.1111/j.0956-7976.2004.00737.x

Klahr, D., & Wallace, J. G. (1976). *Cognitive development: An information processing view.* Hillsdale, NJ: Erlbaum.

Lehrer, R., & Schauble, L. (1999, October). *Scientific reasoning as modeling: The development of representational competence*. Paper presented at the meeting of the Cognitive Development Society, Chapel Hill, NC. Retrieved from http://www.cogdevsoc.org/eventabs.php

McCrink, K., & Wynn, K. (2008). Mathematical reasoning. In M. Haith & J. Benson (Eds.), *Encyclopedia of infant and early childhood development* (Vol. 2, pp. 280–289). New York, NY: Elsevier. doi:10.1016/B978-012370877-9.00098-0

Nersessian, N. J. (1988). Reasoning from imagery and analogy in scientific concept formation. In J. Leplin, A. Fine, & M. Forbes (Eds.), *Proceedings of the Biennal Meeting of the Philosophy of Science Association* (Vol. 1, pp. 41–47). Chicago, IL: University of Chicago Press.

Piaget, J.-P. (1952). *The origins of intelligence in children*. New York, NY: International Universities Press.

Shrager, J., & Langley, P. (Eds.). (1990). *Computational models of scientific discovery and theory formation*. San Mateo, CA: Morgan Kaufmann.

Sloman, A. (2005). *Two views of child as scientist: Humean and Kantian*. Retrieved from http://cs.bham.ac.uk/research/projects/cosy/presentations/child-as-scientist.pdf

Sobel, D. M., Tenenbaum, J. B., & Gopnik, A. (2004). Children's causal inferences from indirect evidence: Backwards blocking and Bayesian reasoning in preschoolers. *Cognitive Science, 28*, 303–333.

Solomon, M. (1996). Commentary on Alison Gopnik's "The Scientist as Child." *Philosophy of Science, 63*, 547–551. doi:10.1086/289975

Stocco, A., & Anderson, J. R. (2008). Endogenous control and task representation: An fMRI study in algebraic problem solving. *Journal of Cognitive Neuroscience, 20*, 1300–1314. doi:10.1162/jocn.2008.20089

Thagard, P. (2005). How to be a successful scientist. In M. E. Gorman, R. D. Tweney, D. C. Gooding, & A. P. Kincannon (Eds.), *Scientific and technological thinking* (pp. 159–171). Mahwah, NJ: Erlbaum.

1

From Theory to Application and Back: Following in the Giant Footsteps of David Klahr

Robert S. Siegler

Although many people know David Klahr's research, far fewer know that he wears size 14 shoes, has the height (if not the coordination) of a Division I college basketball player, walks unusually quickly, and takes exceptionally long strides. All of these seem fitting, given the giant contribution that Klahr has made toward integrating the fields of cognitive development and education. Over nearly 4 decades, Klahr has organized symposia to encourage integrating the study of cognition and instruction (Carver & Klahr, 2001; Klahr, 1976); served on three National Research Council committees aimed at improving educational assessment, scientific research in education, and science learning, respectively; played leading roles in program project grants from the Mellon Foundation and the National Science Foundation on improving the science of learning; created the Program in Interdisciplinary Education Research to encourage graduate students from diverse disciplines to focus on educational issues; and generated countless journal articles, chapters, and lectures advocating the integration of the two fields and illustrating the benefits of doing so.

People outside of the fields of cognitive development and education probably would find it strange that there is a need to integrate the fields of cognitive development and education, given their inherent interconnections. Regardless of whether the field in question is education or cognitive development, the key questions are how children learn and remember concepts and procedures, how they become increasingly skillful in solving problems, how they transfer knowledge across domains, and how they respond to different types of conditions intended to promote learning. Nonetheless, the disciplines of cognitive development and education are surprisingly segregated; people in them read and publish in different journals, cite different research, rely on different types of evidence, take seriously different theories, attend different conferences, are funded by different agencies, and so on.

The research described in this chapter was funded in part by Grants R305A080013 and R305H050035 from the Institute of Education Sciences as well as by support from the Teresa Heinz Chair at Carnegie Mellon University.

One of Klahr's contributions has been to popularize Stokes's (1997) idea of *Pasteur's Quadrant* as a way of thinking about the relation between psychological theory and educational practice. The insight is that although we often view theoretical and applied research as two ends of a continuum, their relation is better described within a 2 × 2 matrix in which research can be theoretically important, practically important, both, or neither. As the name suggests, Pasteur's Quadrant refers to the cell in which research is important both theoretically and practically. Klahr, like Stokes, has advocated pursuing research of this type. This approach makes sense not only because it is better to be important in two ways than one but also because applying theories to solving practical problems benefits both theory and practice. The advantages to practice are well known: Applying theoretical insights can improve health, education, and welfare. The advantages to theory, though less appreciated, are equally important: Applications often increase one's understanding of the boundary conditions of theories, lead to revisions of theories in light of different types of evidence than would usually be used to test the theory, and result in new theoretical predictions. Klahr's research on scientific reasoning provides one illustration of these benefits; my own research on applying theoretical analyses of numerical representations to improving the mathematical understanding of children from low-income backgrounds provides another; specifically, my colleagues and I have investigated the role of playing linear number board games in the pervasive social class and individual differences in young children's numerical knowledge and the potential impact of enhancing such board game play for reducing those differences (e.g., Ramani & Siegler, 2008; Siegler & Ramani, 2009).

Theories of Numerical Representation

How people represent numerical magnitudes has been a hotly contended theoretical issue in cognitive psychology. One group of investigators has contended that the relation between numbers and their internal representations follows *Fechner's* (1869/1987) *law;* that is, subjective representations of numerical magnitudes are a logarithmic function of the numbers presented. Consistent with the implications of Fechner's law, both children's and adults' speed in comparing numerical magnitudes decrease logarithmically as the ratio of the numbers approaches 1 and the distance between them approaches 0 (Dehaene, Dupoux, & Mehler, 1990; Sekuler & Mierkiewicz, 1977). Similar distance effects have been shown by infants in habituation experiments and by a variety of nonhuman animals in conditioning paradigms designed to parallel numerical estimation (Washburn & Rumbaugh, 1991; Xu & Spelke, 2000). To explain these and other data, Dehaene (1997) proposed the *logarithmic ruler model*, claiming that "our brain represents quantities in a fashion not unlike the logarithmic scale on a slide rule, where equal space is allocated to the interval between 1 and 2, between 2 and 4, and between 4 and 8" (p. 76). Dehaene proposed that use of this representation "occurs as a reflex" (p. 78) and cannot be inhibited.

An alternative theoretical model of how people represent numerical magnitudes is the *accumulator model* (Gibbon & Church, 1981). Within this model, people and other animals represent quantities, including numbers, as equally spaced, linearly increasing magnitudes with scalar variability. Gallistel and Gelman (2000) explained that "scalar variability means that the signals encoding these magnitudes are 'noisy'; they vary from trial to trial, with the width of the signal distribution increasing in proportion to its mean" (p. 59). Although advocates of the accumulator model disagreed with Dehaene (1997) about the form of the representation, they followed him in rejecting the idea that people might use multiple representations, as reflected in Brannon, Wusthoff, Gallistel, and Gibbon's (2001) statement, "We view the idea that number is represented both linearly and logarithmically as unparsimonious" (p. 243).

A third theory of numerical representation, the *linear ruler model*, was proposed by Case and Okamoto (1996). As shown in Figure 1.1, this model is like the accumulator model in proposing that, from age 6 onward, subjective representations of numerical magnitudes increase linearly as a function of objective numerical size, but they differ from that model in that they do not hypothesize scalar variability.

A fourth theory of numerical representation, based on *overlapping waves theory* (Siegler, 1996), posits that children use different representations at different ages, with the representations becoming increasingly adequate as children gain experience with numbers in different ranges. Such developmental progressions have been observed in many other domains, including other tasks within the numerical domain; there seemed to be no obvious reason why people should use the same numerical representation at all ages, regardless of the numbers involved.

The number line task provides a means for testing these hypotheses in a straightforward manner. As shown in Figure 1.2, this task involves presenting lines with a number at each end (e.g., 0 and 100) and no other numbers or marks in between, and asking participants to locate a third number on the line (e.g., "Where does 74 go?"). After the participant estimates the position, a new number line is presented, and the task is to estimate the position of a different number on that line. The procedure continues until participants have estimated the positions of numbers from all parts of the numerical range.

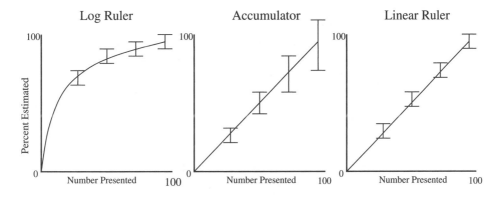

Figure 1.1. Number line estimate means and variability predicted by three theories of numerical representation.

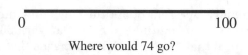

0   100

Where would 74 go?

Figure 1.2. A number line estimation problem.

The four theories of numerical representation predict distinct patterns of data on the number line task depicted in Figure 1.2. The logarithmic ruler hypothesis predicts that, at all ages and with all numerical ranges (e.g., 0–100, 0–1,000), mean number line estimates would fit a logarithmic function. The accumulator hypothesis predicts that, at all ages and with all numerical ranges, mean number line estimates would fit a linear function and variability would increase linearly with numerical size. The linear ruler hypothesis predicts that, at age 6 and beyond, mean number line estimates would increase linearly; it does not make any predictions regarding variability of estimates. Finally, the overlapping waves hypothesis predicts that, with age, children will progress from the less accurate logarithmic pattern of estimates to the more accurate linear pattern, with the estimates increasingly fitting the ideal function $y = x$ and that the transition will occur earlier with smaller numerical ranges.

To test these hypotheses, Siegler and Opfer (2003) presented the number line task to second, fourth, and sixth graders as well as adults. Each participant received one block of trials with the numbers 0 through 100 and another block with the numbers 0 through 1,000.

At all ages, the majority of children generated a linearly increasing pattern of estimates on 0–100 number lines. On 0–1,000 estimates, adults and sixth graders performed similarly, but the large majority of second graders and about half of fourth graders generated a logarithmically increasing pattern of estimates (Siegler & Opfer, 2003; see Figure 1.3). Thus, the results fit the overlapping waves hypothesis and not the other three, all of which predict that children of different ages and adults would generate the same pattern of estimates regardless of the age and numerical scale.

Subsequent studies have expanded these findings using a wider variety of age groups, numerical ranges, and tasks designed to assess children's numerical representations. The story that has emerged is straightforward but moderately complex. Many preschoolers, in particular those from low-income backgrounds, do not even know the rank order of the magnitudes of the numbers from 1 through 10 (Ramani & Siegler, 2008). By kindergarten, most children from middle-income backgrounds generate linear patterns of estimates in the 0–10 range but logarithmic patterns of estimates in the 0–100 range (Siegler & Booth, 2004). Even at these young ages, the numerical representations of children from low-income backgrounds are less advanced, and those of Chinese children more advanced, than those of children from middle-income backgrounds within the United States (Siegler & Mu, 2008; Siegler & Ramani, 2008). Between kindergarten and second grade, the large majority of children progress from logarithmic to linear representations in the 0–100 range; between second and fourth or fifth grade, the large majority of children do the same in the 0–1,000 range; between third and sixth grade, the same pattern is seen with the 0–10,000 range (Booth & Siegler, 2006; Laski & Siegler, 2007; Opfer & Thompson, 2008).

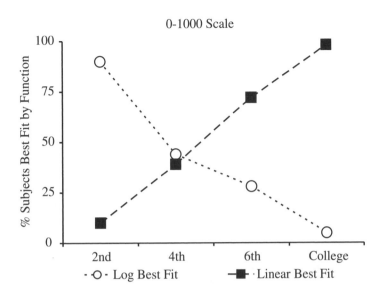

Figure 1.3. Percentage of participants in each age group whose estimates on 0–1,000 number lines were best fit by linear and logarithmic patterns. From "The Development of Numerical Estimation: Evidence for Multiple Representations of Numerical Quantity," by R. S. Siegler and J. E. Opfer, 2003, *Psychological Science, 14,* p. 240. Copyright 2003 by the Association for Psychological Science. Reprinted with permission.

Deviations from a linear representation of numerical magnitudes are predicted to have serious consequences for children's number sense, estimation skill, and learning of answers to arithmetic problems. Without a linear representation of numerical magnitudes, children's number sense and estimates will be distorted, not just on the number line task but on other tasks as well. Children will think that the magnitudes represented by small numbers are more different than they actually are and that the magnitudes represented by large numbers are less different than they actually are. The same compression of numerical magnitudes beyond those at the beginning of the range is predicted to interfere with learning of answers to arithmetic problems, because of the representations of the answers' magnitudes are less distinctive.

Consistent with this perspective, children's performance undergoes the same types of change, from nonlinear to linear estimation patterns, on at least two estimation tasks in addition to number line estimation: (a) numerosity estimation (after seeing a beaker with one dot and a beaker with 1,000 dots on a computer screen, participants were asked to hold down a mouse and to "Put about N dots on the computer screen") and (b) measurement estimation (after seeing a very short line, described as being 1 zip long, and a much longer line, described as being 1,000 zips long, participants were asked to "Draw a line about N zips long"; Booth & Siegler, 2006). Consistent individual differences are also present, with most children within each grade from kindergarten through fourth either producing linear estimation patterns on number line, numerosity, and measurement estimation tasks or not producing such patterns on any of the three tasks (Booth & Siegler, 2006). Perhaps most striking is that linearity of estimates on all three tasks correlates positively—and quite strongly—with scores on tests of arithmetic and standardized mathematics achievement tests (Booth & Siegler, 2006; Geary, Hoard, Byrd-Craven, Nugent, & Numtee, 2007; Geary, Hoard, Nugent, & Byrd-Craven, 2008; Siegler & Booth, 2004).

These findings led to the following question: How do children form a linear representation of numerical magnitudes in the first place? Counting experience during the preschool period seems very likely to contribute; however, such experience also seems to be insufficient to create linear representations of the numbers' magnitudes. Children can often count perfectly in a numerical range more than a year before they generate linear representations of numerical magnitudes in that range (Le Corre, Van de Walle, Brannon, & Carey, 2006; Schaeffer, Eggleston, & Scott, 1974).

If counting experience is insufficient to yield linear numerical magnitude representations, what experiences might contribute? One common activity that seems ideally designed for helping children generate linear representations of numerical magnitudes is playing linear, number board games—that is, board games with linearly arranged, consecutively numbered, equal-size spaces (e.g., Chutes and Ladders, also known as Snakes and Ladders). These board games provide multiple cues to numbers' magnitudes. The greater the number in a square, the greater the likelihood of one or more of the following: the distance that the child has moved the token, the number of discrete moves the child has made, the number of number names the child has spoken, the number of number names the child has heard, and the amount of time since the game began. The linear relations between numerical magnitudes and these visual–spatial, kinesthetic, auditory, and temporal cues provide a broadly based, multimodal foundation for a linear representation of numerical magnitudes.

This theoretical analysis, together with the data on developmental and individual differences in estimation, suggests that providing numerical board game experience to children who had little or no such experience might improve their number sense and their performance on a wide range of numerical tasks. This reasoning led Geetha Ramani and me to investigate the numerical knowledge of children from low-income backgrounds and whether that knowledge could be improved by playing numerical board games that were designed to inculcate a linear representation of numerical magnitudes.

Mathematical Knowledge of Children From Low-Income Backgrounds

Even before children begin school, their numerical knowledge varies greatly. These large individual differences in preschoolers' mathematical knowledge seem to have substantial long-term consequences. Proficiency in mathematics at the beginning of kindergarten is strongly predictive of mathematics achievement test scores years later: in elementary school, in middle school, and even in high school (Duncan et al., 2007; Stevenson & Newman, 1986). This phenomenon can be viewed as an instance of the common finding that initial knowledge is positively related to learning (Bransford, Brown, & Cocking, 1999), but the relations in math are unusually strong and persistent. For example, in a meta-analysis of six long-term, longitudinal studies, Duncan et al. (2007) found that early and later mathematical knowledge were considerably more closely related than were early and later reading proficiency.

Given the strong and persistent relation between early and later mathematical achievement, it is especially unfortunate that preschoolers and kindergartners from low-income families enter school with far less mathematical knowledge than peers from more affluent families. Differences have been demonstrated on a wide range of foundational tasks: reciting the counting string, counting sets of objects, counting up or down from a given number other than 1, recognizing written numerals, adding, subtracting, and comparing numerical magnitudes (Ginsburg & Russell, 1981; Griffin, Case, & Siegler, 1994; Jordan, Kaplan, Olah, & Locuniak, 2006; Jordan, Levine, & Huttenlocher, 1994; Saxe, Guberman, & Gearhart, 1987; Starkey, Klein, & Wakeley, 2004; Stipek & Ryan, 1997). The early differences in numerical proficiency tend to become even more pronounced as children progress through school (Alexander & Entwisle, 1988; Geary, 1994, 2006).

These differences in numerical proficiency are directly attributable to differences in environmental support for mathematics learning. Parents who more frequently engage their children in numerical activities generally have children with greater mathematical knowledge (Blevins-Knabe & Musun-Miller, 1996). Middle-income parents report presenting numerical activities more often than do parents in low-income families (Clements & Sarama, 2007; LeFevre et al., 2009; Starkey et al., 2004). The absolute amount of exposure to explicitly numerical information is extremely low in many low-income families; in an observational study of children's exposure to mathematical activities in their own homes, other people's homes, and early childhood centers, most children from working-class backgrounds were observed engaging in mathematical play or mathematical lessons in 0 of 180 observations (Tudge & Doucet, 2004). Similar findings were obtained in the United Kingdom (Plewis, Mooney, & Creeser, 1990).

Does Playing Numerical Board Games Improve Low-Income Preschoolers' Number Sense?

As an initial test of our hypothesis that differences in numerical magnitude representations play a role in social class differences in mathematical understanding, Siegler and Ramani (2008) compared the number line estimation proficiency of 4-year-olds from low- and middle-income backgrounds. The children were asked to indicate the position of each number between 1 and 9 on a number line with 0 at one end and 10 at the other. The results indicated that the number line estimates of children from middle-income backgrounds were considerably more accurate and linear (Siegler & Ramani, 2008, Experiment 1). The best-fitting linear function accounted for an average of 60% of the variance in the estimates of individual children from middle-income backgrounds, versus an average of 15% for individual children from low-income backgrounds.

The next step was to test whether playing a linear number board game with children from low-income backgrounds would reduce the gap in number sense between them and children from middle-income backgrounds. In Experiment 2, Siegler and Ramani (2008) randomly assigned 36 four-year-olds from low-income backgrounds to play either a number board game, similar to the first row of Chutes and Ladders, or a color board game, similar to Candy Land; children in both conditions were told that the name of the game was "The Great Race." The children attended Head Start or early childhood centers that served impoverished populations. The sample was 58% African American and 42% Caucasian. The number boards and the color boards used to play the games were the same size and shape, and both included 10 horizontally arranged squares of equal size but different colors, with the word *Start* at the left end and the word *End* at the right end. The only difference between the boards was that the one used in the number board game had the numbers 1 through 10 listed consecutively from left to right in the squares, and the one used in the color board game did not. Spinners were used in the board games to determine how far the child or experimenter would move the token on each move. The spinner used in the number board game had a "1" half and a "2" half; the spinner used in the color board game had colors that matched the ones in the squares on the board. Children in both conditions chose a rabbit or a bear token and moved it to mark their progress on the board.

At the beginning of each session, the experimenter told the child that in The Great Race, players take turns spinning the spinner and that whoever reaches the end first wins. Children in the number board condition were told that on each turn, they would move their token the number of spaces indicated on the spinner. Children in the color board condition were told that on each turn, they would move their token to the nearest square with the same color as the one to which the spinner pointed. The experimenter also told children to say the number (color) that they spun and the numbers (colors) on the spaces through which they moved. Thus, children in the number board group who were on a 3 and spun a 2 would say "4, 5" as they moved their token. Children in the color board group who spun a "blue" would say "Red, blue."

If a child erred or could not name the numbers or colors, the experimenter correctly named them and then had the child repeat the names while moving the token. One common error involved children not naming the numbers in the spaces as they moved their token and instead counting the number of spaces they moved their token forward. This led to their always saying "1" or "1, 2" instead of saying the numbers in the spaces (e.g., "5, 6"). If children made this error, the experimenter would first remind them to name the numbers in the spaces as they moved. If children could not do so, the experimenter would point and name the numbers in the spaces and then have the children repeat the number or color names as the experimenter pointed to the spaces.

Over the four sessions, each lasting about 15 minutes, the preschoolers played the number game or the color game about 20 times, with each game lasting 2 to 4 minutes. At the beginning of Session 1 and at the end of Session 4, children were presented the 0–10 number line estimation task as a pretest and posttest. This provided a measure of whether the children's representations of the numerical magnitudes of integers in that range improved as a result of playing the number board game.

Playing the numerical version of the board game led to dramatic improvements in the low-income preschoolers' number line estimates. Before playing the number board game, the best-fitting linear function accounted for an average of 15% of the variance in individual children's number line estimates. After playing the game, the best-fitting linear function accounted for an average of 61% of the variance. In contrast, playing the color board game did not affect the low-income children's number line estimates.

The accuracy of the children's estimates confirmed these findings. The measure of accuracy (or, more specifically, inaccuracy), was *percentage absolute error* (PAE), defined as follows:

PAE = [| (estimate − number estimated) / scale of estimates |] × 100.

Thus, if a child marked the location of 7 on a 0–10 number line when 9 was presented, the PAE would be 20% [(| 7 − 9) / 10 |) × 100)]. In the number board game condition, PAE decreased from 28% on the pretest to 20% on the posttest. In contrast, experience with the color board version had no effect (27% deviation on the pretest and 28% on the posttest). Thus, playing the number board game for four 15- to 20-minute sessions over a 2-week period produced substantial improvements in low-income children's number line estimation and, presumably, their sense of numerical magnitude (Siegler & Ramani, 2008).

Generality and Stability of Effects

These encouraging results led the authors to pursue three new goals in a larger, more ambitious study (Ramani & Siegler, 2008). The first goal was to examine the generality of the benefits of playing the number board game across tasks and types of knowledge. Ramani and Siegler (2008) examined four measures of knowledge of the numbers 1 through 10: (a) number line estimation, (b) numerical magnitude comparison ("Which number is bigger: N or M?"), (c) counting, and (d) identifying printed numerals. Both number line estimation and numerical magnitude comparison measured knowledge of numerical magnitudes; the authors expected that if playing the game improved children's representations of numerical magnitudes, performance on both tasks would improve. Playing the number board game also required children to count and read the numerals 1 through 10; therefore, they expected that playing it would improve these skills as well.

A second goal of the study was to examine the stability of learning over time. If playing the number board game increased knowledge of numerical magnitudes, counting, and number identification, then gains in proficiency should be stable over time. The authors tested these predictions by presenting all four tasks both immediately after the final game playing session and again 9 weeks later.

A third goal was to determine whether different subgroups of children— ones who are older or younger, African American or Caucasian, or above average or below average in initial knowledge—learn comparable amounts from playing the number board game. Children who were initially more knowledgeable might be expected to learn more because they generally learn mathematical tasks more quickly than less knowledgeable children (Geary, 2006); however, less knowledgeable children might learn more in this particular case because they might have had less exposure to number board games and therefore derive greater benefits from experience with them. Yet another possibility was that the benefits would be equal.

The participants in the experiment were 124 children (mean age: 4 years, 9 months), all of whom attended Head Start classrooms. Slightly more than half of the children (52%) were African American; almost all of the rest (42%) were Caucasian. The criteria for participating in Head Start meant that all of the children's families were extremely poor; for example, the income limit for a family of three in 2005–2006, the year in which the study was conducted, was $16,600.

All children were given a pretest, a posttest, and a follow-up test on the four tasks described above. The pretest was given at the beginning of Session 1; the posttest at the end of Session 4; and the follow-up test in Session 5, 9 weeks after the posttest. In between the pretest and posttest, the preschoolers played either the number board game or the color board game in four 15- to 20-minute sessions over a 2-week period. In the pretest, posttest, and follow-up, children were presented the four tasks in random order. On the number line task, the procedure was the same as the one followed in the earlier study (Siegler & Ramani, 2008) study. On the counting task, children were asked to count from 1 through 10. Counting was coded as correct up to the point of the first error (e.g., if a child counted "1, 2, 3, 4, 5, 6, 7, 9, 10," the score was 7). On each of the 10 trials of the numeral identification task, children were presented a card with a number from 1 through 10 on it and were asked to identify the number. Finally, on the numerical magnitude comparison task, children were presented a 20-page booklet, in which each page displayed two numbers from 1 to 9, side by side, and they were asked to choose the bigger number from each pair.

As shown in Figure 1.4, playing the number board game produced significant gains on all four tasks. Moreover, the benefits on all four tasks continued to be evident at the 9-week follow-up.

To examine the effects of playing the number board game on children from different backgrounds, Ramani and Siegler (2008) contrasted the learning of older and younger children, of children with above-average and below-average knowledge, and of African American and Caucasian children. In all cases, learning was highly comparable. Not surprisingly, older children exhibited greater knowledge on both the pretest and posttest than did younger children, and children with above-average initial knowledge showed greater proficiency on both the pretest and posttest than those whose initial knowledge was below average. Amounts of learning were quite comparable, however, except for the gains of children with below-average pretest performance, which tended to be somewhat greater than those of children with above-average pretest performance.

African American and Caucasian preschoolers also showed comparable learning. On three of the four tasks, there were no differences between them on pretest, posttest, or at the follow-up. The one exception was that Caucasian

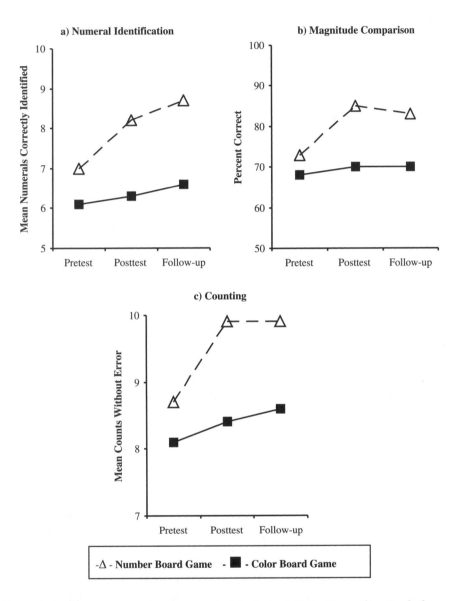

Figure 1.4. Percentage variance accounted for by best-fitting linear function before and after playing the number or color board game (data are from Siegler & Ramani, 2008).

(continued on next page)

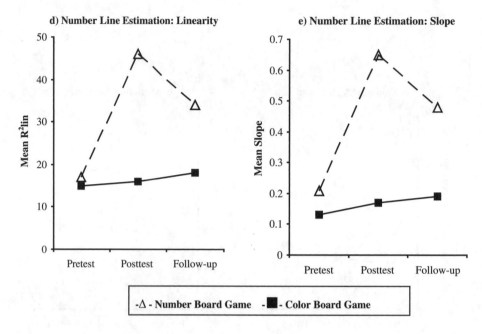

Figure 1.4.   *(Continued).*

children showed somewhat greater number line proficiency at all three times of measurement. On all four tasks, however, the increase in knowledge from pretest to posttest to follow-up was comparable for African American and Caucasian children (Ramani & Siegler, 2008).

Is Board Game Playing in the Everyday Environment Related to Numerical Knowledge?

The analysis suggested that children from middle-income backgrounds should have had more board game experience than children from low-income backgrounds and that board game play outside of the laboratory should be related to preschoolers' numerical knowledge (Ramani & Siegler, 2008). It also seemed plausible that playing card games might enhance early numerical knowledge. For example, in the card game War, the player with the higher card wins the other player's card. For cards with values from 2 through 10, children can determine the winner by identifying the numerals on the pair of cards and comparing their magnitudes, two of the basic numerical skills measured in Experiment 1 of Ramani and Siegler's (2008) study. It also seemed possible, but less likely, that playing video games would promote preschoolers' numerical knowledge. Some video games are designed to teach young children counting, arithmetic, and other number skills, but they comprise a small percentage of video games and are not among the most popular.

To test these hypotheses, in Experiment 2, Ramani and Siegler (2008) obtained data about preschoolers' experiences outside the laboratory with board games, card games, and video games. The participants were 115 children from low-income families who had participated in Experiment 1 as well as 36 age peers from middle-income families. The experimenter asked the preschoolers whether they had ever played board games, card games, and video games at their homes or at other family members' or relatives' homes. If children answered "Yes" to any of these questions, they were asked whether they played that type of game "All the time," "Sometimes," or "Hardly ever" and were asked to name each board game, card game, and video game they had played outside of preschool.

As expected, a higher percentage of children from middle-income backgrounds reported having played at least one board game (80% vs. 47%). Similarly, a higher percentage of children from middle-income families reported having played one or more card games at their home or at friends' or relatives' homes (87% vs. 61%). An unexpected difference in the opposite direction was found for video games: Sixty-six percent of the children from low-income backgrounds reported having played video games outside of preschool, but only 30% of the children from middle-income backgrounds did. This last finding argues against the possibility that the first two differences reflected middle-income children better remembering their game playing experience or being more willing to report their experience to a stranger. Why would such differences in memory or willingness to report their experience be present for board games and card games, but differences in the opposite direction be present for video games?

Table 1.1 lists the percentages of children from low- and middle-income backgrounds who reported playing the most common games in each of the three

Table 1.1.   Percentage of Children Who Reported Playing Specific Board Games and Card Games, and Types of Video Games

Game	Percent children who named the game	
	Low-income	Middle-income
Board games		
Candy Land	29	63
Chutes and Ladders	17	37
Checkers	9	10
Card games		
Go Fish	30	37
Uno	9	33
Old Maid	11	20
Memory	8	10
Video games		
Action/adventure	38	13
Education	22	17
Sports	17	3

Note. Data are from Ramani and Siegler (2008). Candy Land is a game in which players move along squares of different colors.

categories. Children from both groups most often reported playing the same specific board games and card games outside of school, but their amount of experience with them differed. The situation differed somewhat for the video games, because children named a far greater variety of them (65) than board games or card games. This necessitated dividing the video games into three main genres: (a) action/adventure, (b) educational, and (c) sports. As can be seen in Table 1.1, the absolute percentages for all three genres of video games were higher for children from low-income backgrounds.

To determine whether low-income preschoolers' number knowledge was related to their game playing activities outside of school, Ramani and Siegler (2008) correlated their pretest performance in Experiment 1 with their experience playing different types of games in the home environment. The number of board games that the low-income children named was positively and significantly correlated with measures of numerical knowledge on all four tasks. In contrast, the numbers of card games and video games that children named were correlated with performance on only one task apiece (magnitude comparison accuracy for card games and number line linearity for video games).

One number board game, Chutes and Ladders, was named by a fairly high percentage of preschoolers (17%). Because we hypothesized that linear number board games like this one are especially important for gaining numerical knowledge, we tested whether children who reported having played this game had greater numerical knowledge than those who did not report having played it. Whether children reported having played Chutes and Ladders proved to be significantly correlated with pretest numerical knowledge on three of the four tasks from Experiment 1. This provided naturalistic evidence for the hypothesis that playing numerical board games contributes to early numerical knowledge. In contrast, not one child in the sample reported playing the card game War, which might account for the lack of relations on three of the four tasks between card game experience and initial numerical proficiency (Ramani & Siegler, 2008).

What Features of Numerical Board Games Are Crucial for Success?

Given the large, positive effects of playing the number board game, it seemed worthwhile to identify features that contribute to its success. Two studies tested the importance of a pair of features that seemed likely to contribute to learning.

Linear Boards

In the first study, Siegler and Ramani (2009) examined whether the linearity of the board was important for learning. A great deal of evidence, both behavioral and neural, suggests that numerical magnitudes are typically represented within a linear spatial array (Ansari, 2008; Dehaene, Izard, Spelke, & Pica, 2008). If something akin to a mental number line is the natural way to represent numerical magnitudes—that is, one that is easier to learn than alternative representations—then playing the game on a linear board should promote greater learning of numerical magnitudes than playing the game on a circular board.

On the other hand, it clearly is possible to represent numerical magnitudes in circular formats; we do so with analog clocks, speedometers, odometers, scales for weighing food, and so on. Moreover, people can use imaginary circular representations of numerical magnitudes if asked to do so (Bächtold, Baumüller, & Brugger, 1998). The typical use of linear representations may simply reflect exposure to cultural tools for representing numerical magnitudes, such as physical number lines, instead of linear representations being easier to learn.

To distinguish between these hypotheses, Siegler and Ramani (2009) randomly assigned preschoolers from low-income backgrounds to a linear board game condition or a circular board game condition. The linear condition was identical to that used in the previous studies (e.g., Ramani & Siegler, 2008). The circular condition was identical except that the 10 spaces and numbers on the board were arranged in a circular pattern (clockwise for half the children and counterclockwise for the other half). Playing the linear board game was expected to produce greater improvements in numerical magnitude representations, as indicated by number line estimation and numerical magnitude comparison performance. On the other hand, the two game boards were expected to produce similar effects on the number identification and counting tasks, because the counting and number identification activities were identical in the two conditions.

Each of these predictions proved accurate. Preschoolers who played the linear board game improved their linearity of number line estimates and accuracy of magnitude comparisons more than peers in the circular board condition. In contrast, pretest–posttest changes in numeral identification and counting did not differ between children in the two conditions. Thus, the linear arrangement of the board appears to be a crucial feature for the success of the board game in improving numerical magnitude representations.

Counting On

In all of the number game experiments described thus far, children were required to count on from the number where their token was located, rather than beginning at the number 1. Thus, if the token was on the 6 and the child spun a 2, the child needed to count "7, 8" rather than "1, 2." The reason for requiring children to count on was that doing so requires encoding of the number associated with each square. In contrast, children who counted "1, 2" might ignore the numbers on the squares and just treat them like unnumbered locations. If children do not encode the numbers in the squares, they will be unable to detect the correlations between the magnitude cues and the numbers (other than 1 and 2).

This analysis implies that counting on should be crucial to the effectiveness of playing the game, a hypothesis tested by Laski and Siegler (2011). Kindergartners were presented a 0–100 game board, with the 100 squares arranged in a 10 × 10 grid, with the numbers proceeding from 1 through 10 in left-to-right order in the bottom row, from 11 through 20 in left-to-right order in the second row, and so on. Children spun a spinner with the numbers 1 through 5. Some children were instructed to count on; if they were on 38 and spun 4, they needed to count "39, 40, 41, 42." Other children were instructed to count "1, 2, 3, 4" in the same situation.

As predicted, children who counted on from their current location on the board improved their 0–100 number line estimates more than children who counted from 1. The improvement was mediated by changes in encoding. To be specific, participation in the counting-on condition led to greater improvements in accuracy in indicating the locations of specific numbers on a board that had 100 squares but no numbers (the measure of encoding), which in turn was related to greater improvements in number line estimation. Counting on from the current board location also contributed to the effectiveness the board game, apparently through improving encoding of the numbers and their locations. Thus, playing the game on a linear board instead of on a circular one and counting on instead counting from 1 improved children's ability to detect the correlations between numerical magnitudes and the spatial, verbal, temporal, and kinesthetic information involved in progressing from number to number and thus helped children improve their numerical proficiency (Laski & Siegler, 2011).

Conclusions and Future Directions

In this chapter, I have examined whether experience playing linear number board games is (a) a source of social class and individual differences in young children's numerical knowledge and (b) a potential means for reducing those differences. The results indicated that both are true. Children from low-income backgrounds reported only half as much experience playing board games as age peers from middle-income backgrounds; indeed, a small majority of children in the low-income sample reported never having played a board game at home or at the homes of friends or relatives (Ramani & Siegler, 2009). The amount of board game experience that preschoolers reported having was positively correlated with their numerical knowledge. Comparable correlations were not present for card game and video game experience. Especially important is that playing a linear number board game with children from low-income backgrounds for four 15- to 20-minute sessions led to large, broad-based, and enduring gains in the children's numerical knowledge (Ramani & Siegler, 2009). Among the features of such a game that have been found to influence its effectiveness are the board's linearity and counting on from the number of the square on which the token currently sits.

Teaching other numerical skills, such as counting and numeral identification, is useful, but its effects are not as large and broad as those of playing the number board game. Malofeeva, Day, Saco, Young, and Ciancio (2004) presented children at Head Start centers with instruction, practice, and feedback regarding how to count and identify numbers. That intervention led to improvements in counting and numeral identification but not to improvement on tasks that assessed understanding of numerical magnitudes, including numerical magnitude comparison. In a direct comparison, Siegler and Ramani (2009) found that playing the linear number board game produced greater gains in number line estimation and magnitude comparison than did counting and identifying numerals for the same amount of time.

Siegler and Ramani's (2009) study also yielded evidence that playing the linear board game (but not the circular one) improves subsequent learning of answers to arithmetic problems. After the four sessions in which they played the board games, the preschoolers were brought back for a fifth session in which they were presented two addition problems that they had answered incorrectly on the pretest. On each trial, the experimenter said, for example, "Suppose you have two oranges and I give you two more; how many oranges would you have then?" After the child stated an answer, the experimenter would say, for example, either "That's right; 2 + 2 is 4" or "No, 2 + 2 is 4." Each pair of problems was presented three times; then the experimenter tested the child's knowledge by asking him or her to answer each problem without feedback.

Children who earlier had played the linear board game generated a higher percentage of correct addition answers than did children who earlier had played the circular board game or who had engaged in counting and numeral identification: 45% versus 30% versus 28%. Even more striking is that the addition errors of children who had played the game on the linear board were closer in magnitude to the correct sum than were the errors of children in the other two conditions (Ramani & Siegler, 2009). These results support the interpretation that the linear board game facilitated acquisition of a linear representation of numerical magnitudes and that this linear representation made it easier to learn the answers to arithmetic problems. Also consistent with this interpretation is the fact that arithmetic learning was positively correlated with linearity of numerical magnitude representations.

Several mechanisms seem likely to be involved in how playing the linear board game promoted arithmetic learning. One is linearity of numerical magnitude representations. Linear representations seem to help children differentiate among numbers that otherwise are difficult to differentiate. Evidence for the importance of linear representations comes from positive correlations between the linearity of first graders' number line estimates and their arithmetic proficiency and from experimental data demonstrating that providing randomly chosen first graders with pictorial linear representations of addends and sums improves the children's recall of the sums when the physical representations are no longer present (Booth & Siegler, 2008).

A second likely mechanism is automaticity of numeral identification. Playing the board game improves numeral identification, and efficient numeral identification reduces working memory load on numerical problems, including arithmetic problems. Consistent with this analysis is the fact that positive correlations have been found between young children's efficiency of numeral identification and arithmetic proficiency (e.g., Geary, 2006). A third likely mechanism is improved counting skill, which is essential for efficient execution of arithmetic strategies, such as counting from 1 and counting on from the larger addend. Consistent with this interpretation is that individual differences in first graders' counting skill correlate positively with individual differences in their arithmetic proficiency (Geary, Fan, & Bow-Thomas, 1992).

A third likely mechanism is encoding of numerical magnitudes. Laski and Siegler (2011) found that requiring children to encode the numbers in the boxes through reading those numbers aloud led to greater learning than did counting from 1 to move one's token. In preschool and early elementary school, encoding of numbers is not automatic, and learning of numerical magnitudes from board games depends on the children encoding the numbers so that they can learn the correlations between them and visual–spatial, auditory, kinesthetic, and temporal cues.

Number board games such as The Great Race are promising candidates for broad adoption in early childhood centers and individual homes. They cost little or nothing; anyone with a pencil and large piece of cardboard, or even paper, can create a board. No special skills are required for parents or teachers or teachers' aides at early childhood centers to play such games with children. An additional advantage is that children enjoy playing these games, as indicated both by my and my colleagues' observations and the enduring popularity in diverse societies of games such as Chutes and Ladders and Snakes and Ladders.

There is no reason to believe that the present version of The Great Race (and those of Chutes and Ladders and Snakes and Ladders) cannot be improved. Many features of the interventions described in this chapter were based on hunches and guesses instead of on empirical research. One such feature is amount of game playing experience. The decision to have children play the game in four sessions was arbitrary. Varying the number of sessions would indicate whether children could derive greater benefits from playing the game for more sessions or, conversely, whether the same benefits could be realized in fewer sessions. Related issues include whether the game produces comparable learning if played in small groups, whether it produces comparable gains if played by teachers' aides in Head Start programs and early childhood centers, and whether playing the game in an interactive DVD format produces as much learning as playing it with an adult or more knowledgeable child. Addressing these issues should increase researchers' theoretical understanding of numerical development, as well as identify ways of reducing or eliminating the gap in mathematical knowledge with which children from different backgrounds typically enter school. More generally, the research illustrates the bidirectional benefits to be gained by following David Klahr's example of applying cognitive developmental theories to addressing serious educational problems and using the outcomes of the applications to refine and improve the theories.

References

Alexander, K. L., & Entwisle, D. R. (1988). Achievement in the first 2 years of school: Patterns and processes. *Monographs of the Society for Research in Child Development, 53*(2, Serial No. 157).

Ansari, D. (2008). Effects of development and enculturation on number representation in the brain. *Nature Reviews Neuroscience, 9,* 278–291. doi:10.1038/nrn2334

Bächtold, D., Baumüller, M., & Brugger, P. (1998). Stimulus–response compatibility in representational space. *Neuropsychologia, 36,* 731–735. doi:10.1016/S0028-3932(98)00002-5

Blevins-Knabe, B., & Musun-Miller, L. (1996). Number use at home by children and their parents and its relationship to early mathematical performance. *Early Development and Parenting, 5,* 35–45. doi:10.1002/(SICI)1099-0917(199603)5:1<35::AID-EDP113>3.0.CO;2-0

Booth, J. L., & Siegler, R. S. (2006). Developmental and individual differences in pure numerical estimation. *Developmental Psychology, 42,* 189–201. doi:10.1037/0012-1649.41.6.189

Booth, J. L., & Siegler, R. S. (2008). Numerical magnitude representations influence arithmetic learning. *Child Development, 79,* 1016–1031. doi:10.1111/j.1467-8624.2008.01173.x

Brannon, E. M., Wusthoff, C. J., Gallistel, C. R., & Gibbon, J. (2001). Numerical subtraction in the pigeon: Evidence for a linear subjective number scale. *Psychological Science, 12,* 238–243. doi:10.1111/1467-9280.00342

Bransford, J. B., Brown, A. L., & Cocking, R. R. (Eds.). (1999). *How people learn: Brain, mind, experience, and school.* Washington, DC: National Academy Press.

Carver, S. M., & Klahr, D. (Eds.). (2001). *Cognition and instruction: 25 years of progress.* Mahwah, NJ: Erlbaum.

Case, R., & Okamoto, Y. (1996). The role of central conceptual structures in the development of children's thought. *Monographs of the Society for Research in Child Development, 61*(1–2, Serial No. 246).

Clements, D. H., & Sarama, J. (2007). Effects of a preschool mathematics curriculum: Summative research on the Building Blocks project. *Journal for Research in Mathematics Education, 38,* 136–163.

Dehaene, S. (1997). *The number sense: How the mind creates mathematics.* New York, NY: Oxford University Press.

Dehaene, S., Dupoux, E., & Mehler, J. (1990). Is numerical comparison digital? Analogical and symbolic effects in two-digit number comparison. *Journal of Experimental Psychology: Human Perception and Performance, 16,* 626–641. doi:10.1037/0096-1523.16.3.626

Dehaene, S., Izard, V., Spelke, E., & Pica, P. (2008, May 30). Log or linear: Distinct intuitions of the number scale in Western and Amazonian indigene cultures. *Science, 320,* 1217–1220. doi:10.1126/science.1156540

Duncan, G. J., Dowsett, C. J., Claessens, A., Magnuson, K., Huston, A. C., Klebanov, P., . . . Japel, C. (2007). School readiness and later achievement. *Developmental Psychology, 43,* 1428–1446. doi:10.1037/0012-1649.43.6.1428

Fechner, G. T. (1987). My own viewpoint on mental measurement (1887). *Psychological Research, 49,* 213–219. (Original work published 1869) doi:10.1007/BF00309029

Gallistel, C. R., & Gelman, R. R. (2000). Non-verbal numerical cognition: From reals to integers. *Trends in Cognitive Sciences, 4,* 59–65. doi:10.1016/S1364-6613(99)01424-2

Geary, D. C. (1994). *Children's mathematics development: Research and practical applications.* Washington, DC: American Psychological Association. doi:10.1037/10163-000

Geary, D. C. (2006). Development of mathematical understanding. In W. Damon & R. M. Lerner (Series Eds.) & D. Kuhn & R. S. Siegler (Vol. Eds.), *Handbook of child psychology: Vol. 2. Cognition, perception, and language* (6th ed., pp. 777–810). Hoboken, NJ: Wiley.

Geary, D. C., Fan, L., & Bow-Thomas, C. C. (1992). Numerical cognition: Loci of ability differences comparing children from China and the United States. *Psychological Science, 3,* 180–185. doi:10.1111/j.1467-9280.1992.tb00023.x

Geary, D. C., Hoard, M. K., Byrd-Craven, J., Nugent, L., & Numtee, C. (2007). Cognitive mechanisms underlying achievement deficits in children with mathematical learning disability. *Child Development, 78,* 1343–1359. doi:10.1111/j.1467-8624.2007.01069.x

Geary, D. C., Hoard, M. K., Nugent, L., & Byrd-Craven, J. (2008). Development of number line representations in children with mathematical learning disability. *Developmental Neuropsychology, 33,* 277–299. doi:10.1080/87565640801982361

Gibbon, J., & Church, R. M. (1981). Time left: Linear versus logarithmic subjective time. *Journal of Experimental Psychology: Animal Behavior Processes, 7,* 87–107.

Ginsburg, H. P., & Russell, R. L. (1981). Social class and racial influences on early mathematical thinking. *Monographs of the Society for Research in Child Development, 46*(6, Serial No. 69).

Griffin, S., Case, R., & Siegler, R. S. (1994). Rightstart: Providing the central conceptual prerequisites for first formal learning of arithmetic to students at risk for school failure. In K. McGilly (Ed.), *Classroom lessons: Integrating cognitive theory and classroom practice* (pp. 25–49). Cambridge, MA: MIT Press.

Jordan, N. C., Kaplan, D., Olah, L. N., & Locuniak, M. N. (2006). Number sense growth in kindergarten: A longitudinal investigation of children at risk for mathematics difficulties. *Child Development, 77,* 153–175. doi:10.1111/j.1467-8624.2006.00862.x

Jordan, N. C., Levine, S. C., & Huttenlocher, J. (1994). Development of calculation abilities in middle- and low-income children after formal instruction in school. *Journal of Applied Developmental Psychology, 15,* 223–240. doi:10.1016/0193-3973(94)90014-0

Klahr, D. (Ed.). (1976). *Cognition and instruction.* Hillsdale, NJ: Erlbaum.

Laski, E. V. (2008). *Internal and external influences on learning: A microgenetic analysis of the acquisition of numerical knowledge from board games* (Unpublished doctoral dissertation). Carnegie Mellon University, Pittsburgh, PA.

Laski, E. V., & Siegler, R. S. (2007). Is 27 a big number? Correlational and causal connections among numerical categorization, number line estimation, and numerical magnitude comparison. *Child Development, 78,* 1723–1743. doi:10.1111/j.1467-8624.2007.01087.x

Laski, E. V., & Siegler, R. S. (2011). *Making number board games even better.* Manuscript submitted for publication.

Le Corre, M., Van de Walle, G., Brannon, E. M., & Carey, S. (2006). Re-visiting the competence/performance debate in the acquisition of the counting principles. *Cognitive Psychology, 52,* 130–169. doi:10.1016/j.cogpsych.2005.07.002

LeFevre, J., Skwarchuk, S., Smith-Chant, B., Fast, L., Kamawar, D., & Bisanz, J. (2009). Home numeracy experiences and children's math performance in the early school years. *Canadian Journal of Behavioural Science, 41,* 55–66. doi:10.1037/a0014532

Malofeeva, E., Day, J., Saco, X., Young, L., & Ciancio, D. (2004). Construction and evaluation of a number sense test with Head Start children. *Journal of Educational Psychology, 96,* 648–659. doi:10.1037/0022-0663.96.4.648

Opfer, J. E., & Thompson, C. A. (2008). The trouble with transfer: Insights from microgenetic changes in the representation of numerical magnitude. *Child Development, 79,* 788–804. doi:10.1111/j.1467-8624.2008.01158.x

Plewis, I., Mooney, A., & Creeser, R. (1990). Time on educational activities at home and educational progress in infant school. *British Journal of Educational Psychology, 60,* 330–337. doi:10.1111/j.2044-8279.1990.tb00949.x

Ramani, G. B., & Siegler, R. S. (2008). Promoting broad and stable improvements in low-income children's numerical knowledge through playing number board games. *Child Development, 79,* 375–394. doi:10.1111/j.1467-8624.2007.01131.x

Saxe, G. B., Guberman, S. R., & Gearhart, M. (1987). Social processes in early number development. *Monographs of the Society for Research in Child Development, 52*(2, Serial No. 216).

Schaeffer, B., Eggleston, V. H., & Scott, J. L. (1974). Number development in young children. *Cognitive Psychology, 6,* 357–379. doi:10.1016/0010-0285(74)90017-6

Sekuler, R., & Mierkiewicz, D. (1977). Children's judgments of numerical inequality. *Child Development, 48,* 630–633. doi:10.2307/1128664

Siegler, R. S. (1996). *Emerging minds: The process of change in children's thinking.* New York, NY: Oxford University Press.

Siegler, R. S., & Booth, J. L. (2004). Development of numerical estimation in young children. *Child Development, 75,* 428–444. doi:10.1111/j.1467-8624.2004.00684.x

Siegler, R. S., & Mu, Y. (2008). Chinese children excel on novel mathematics problems even before elementary school. *Psychological Science, 19,* 759–763. doi:10.1111/j.1467-9280.2008.02153.x

Siegler, R. S., & Opfer, J. E. (2003). The development of numerical estimation: Evidence for multiple representations of numerical quantity. *Psychological Science, 14,* 237–243. doi:10.1111/1467-9280.02438

Siegler, R. S., & Ramani, G. B. (2008). Playing linear numerical board games promotes low-income children's numerical development. *Developmental Science, 11,* 655–661. doi:10.1111/j.1467-7687.2008.00714.x

Siegler, R. S., & Ramani, G. B. (2009). Playing linear number board games—but not circular ones—improves low-income preschoolers' numerical understanding. *Journal of Educational Psychology, 101,* 545–560. doi:10.1037/a0014239

Starkey, P., Klein, A., & Wakeley, A. (2004). Enhancing young children's mathematical knowledge through a pre-kindergarten mathematics intervention. *Early Childhood Research Quarterly, 19,* 99–120. doi:10.1016/j.ecresq.2004.01.002

Stevenson, H. W., & Newman, R. S. (1986). Long-term prediction of achievement and attitudes in mathematics and reading. *Child Development, 57,* 646–659. doi:10.2307/1130343

Stipek, D. J., & Ryan, R. H. (1997). Economically disadvantaged preschoolers: Ready to learn but further to go. *Developmental Psychology, 33,* 711–723. doi:10.1037/0012-1649.33.4.711

Stokes, D. (1997). *Pasteur's quadrant: Basic science and technological innovation.* Washington, DC: Brookings Institution.

Tudge, J., & Doucet, F. (2004). Early mathematical experiences: Observing young Black and White children's everyday activities. *Early Childhood Research Quarterly, 19,* 21–39. doi:10.1016/j.ecresq.2004.01.007

Washburn, D. A., & Rumbaugh, D. M. (1991). Ordinal judgments of numerical symbols by macaques (*Macaca mulatta*). *Psychological Science, 2,* 190–193. doi:10.1111/j.1467-9280.1991.tb00130.x

Xu, F., & Spelke, E. S. (2000). Large number discrimination in 6-month-old infants. *Cognition, 74,* B1–B11. doi:10.1016/S0010-0277(99)00066-9

2

The Learning of Science and the Science of Learning: The Role of Analogy

Zhe Chen

One significant, ongoing contribution of David Klahr's work in both basic research and applied classroom studies is in the area of children's understanding of the fundamental principles of scientific reasoning. In this chapter, I present a summary of three studies on which I had the good fortune to collaborate with David Klahr: Klahr and Chen (2003), Chen et al. (2011), and Chen and Klahr (1999). The studies examined how analogy functions as a learning mechanism in children's acquisition of scientific reasoning strategies and transfer of their application from one learning situation to another. They explored the following three central issues: (a) young children's ability to use analogy in learning science, (b) factors that facilitate children's analogical transfer at different ages, and (c) implications for the science of learning and for classroom science education.

Analogy involves using what one knows in one situation to reason about or solve problems in another situation (e.g., Gentner, 1989; Holyoak & Thagard, 1995; Singley & Anderson, 1989). Analogical reasoning, or problem solving, is a powerful process that involves mapping structures between problems and generalizing learned strategies from one task to another (e.g., Dunbar, 2001; Goswami, 1996); however, there has been extensive debate concerning the abilities of children and adults alike to solve problems by analogy (e.g., Detterman & Sternberg, 1993; Dunbar, 2001), and the evidence for transfer is mixed (e.g., Detterman, 1993; Halpern, 1989). For example, even in studies in which children or adults seem to demonstrate successful transfer, the results are often counterintuitive, showing narrowness of learning and a lack of consistent transfer (e.g., Bransford, Brown, & Cocking, 1999; Cognition and Technology Group at Vanderbilt, 1997).

One issue in the ongoing debate about analogical reasoning concerns the phenomenon of *inert knowledge* (Brown & Campione, 1981; Whitehead, 1929), defined as "knowledge that is accessed only in a restricted set of contexts even though it is applicable to a wide variety of domains" (Bransford et al., 1999, p. 472). There are enduring questions as to whether children are even

---

I thank David Klahr for his mentorship and for the opportunity to collaborate with him on the studies summarized herein.

capable of drawing and activating the analogies needed for successful analogical problem solving. The traditional Piagetian account of analogical reasoning (Inhelder & Piaget, 1958) suggests that this is a late-developing ability. On the other hand, more recent findings indicate that if the analogical relations are relatively simple, and if children possess adequate knowledge, then even very young children are able to think analogically (e.g., Brown, 1989; Halford, 1993; Goswami, 1996).

Part of the uncertainty regarding children's analogical reasoning is no doubt attributable to the fact that, until fairly recently, children's transfer received little sustained and systematic attention in child development research. Over the past couple of decades, however, children's analogical problem solving has become an important focus within the literature and has been examined in numerous domains, including memory strategies (Blöte, Resing, Mazer, & Van Noort, 1999; Coyle & Bjorklund, 1997), mathematical reasoning (e.g., Alibali, 1999; Goldin-Meadow & Alibali, 2002; Rittle-Johnson, 2006; Siegler, 2002; Siegler & Opfer, 2003), conservation (e.g., Gelman, 1969; Siegler, 1995), tool use and causal reasoning (Brown & Kane, 1988; Chen & Siegler, 2000), computer programming (Klahr & Carver, 1988), symbolic understanding (Chen, 2007; DeLoache, 2004), transitive inference (e.g., Goswami, 1995), and theory of mind (Flynn, O'Malley, & Wood, 2004). These studies are significant inasmuch as they have largely quieted the debate as to whether children have the capacity to think analogically; despite the varied domains from which they emerge, these studies offer compelling evidence that children are in fact capable of solving relatively simple insight problems by transferring analogous solution strategies. One question that remains largely unaddressed in the current literature, however, is whether and how children can use analogy as a means for learning scientific reasoning strategies.

Sound scientific reasoning requires the ability to make a series of basic but fairly complex inferences to form bounded hypotheses, to design unconfounded experiments to test these hypotheses, to distinguish determinate from indeterminate evidence, and to interpret results correctly as supporting or refuting the hypotheses. Studies conducted over the past 2 decades indicate that children and adults demonstrate considerable competency in acquiring basic scientific process skills (e.g., Klahr, 2000; Kuhn, Garcia-Mila, Zohar, & Andersen, 1995; Kuhn, Schauble, & Garcia-Mila, 1992; Schauble, 1990, 1996). Although these studies are significant in that they demonstrate older children's and adults' capacity for acquiring scientific reasoning strategies, they do not focus on younger children's learning and transfer of scientific reasoning strategies. The studies summarized in this chapter examined whether and how preschool and elementary school children learn scientific reasoning strategies, maintain the strategies acquired in an initial learning situation, and apply them to solve analogous problems across time and across tasks.

The general approach of the studies summarized in the following sections involved presenting children with a series of isomorphic tasks that shared the same problem structure and required the same general solution strategy. The basic paradigm involved either a training or control condition, followed by a series of analogous target tasks that could be solved by transferring the strategies learned in the training or control conditions. In the training conditions, children encountered a novel task in several highly analogous iterations and received direct instruction and/or explicit feedback to help guide their learning of the appropriate problem-solving strategies. In the control conditions, children encountered the same novel task and proximate iterations as those in the training conditions but received, at most, implicit feedback based on their problem-solving experiences. Analogical transfer performance was then measured by comparing children's performance on the task in the training and control conditions with their subsequent performance on the more analogically distant tasks of the posttraining condition.

The key measures of the studies summarized next focused on two primary areas. First, because the usefulness of analogy depends in part on how well children acquire the scientific reasoning strategies in the original learning context, children's performance on the analogous tasks within the various training and control conditions was analyzed to assess how completely or partially they had acquired the necessary strategies. Thus, at a micro level (e.g., Siegler, 2006; Siegler & Crowley, 1991), children's strategies were assessed on a trial-by-trial basis so as to pinpoint their learning patterns and processes. Second, because the ongoing usefulness of a particular analogy depends on how well children are able to generalize the acquired strategy across both task and time, children's remote transfer was examined. *Remote transfer* refers to the application of concepts and strategies to analogous tasks that differ substantially from the original task in terms of their superficial features, the experimental context in which the tasks are encountered, and the timing of their presentation (Chen & Klahr, 2008; Chen, Mo, & Honomichl, 2004). Most previous studies on the impacts of these various dimensions of distance on children's and adults' analogical transfer involved asking participants to solve analogous problems over the course of minutes, hours, or days, but manipulation of the time interval over a longer term is rare (see Barnett & Ceci, 2002). At a macro level, then, the studies explored the robustness of children's remote transfer by examining the application of the originally acquired strategies to more distantly analogous isomorphic problems presented in a substantially different experimental setting after a delay of a week and of several months.

In the sections that follow, I summarize three studies done in collaboration with David Klahr to explore the role of analogy in children's learning of scientific process strategies: (a) Klahr and Chen (2003), (b) Chen et al. (2011), and (c) Chen and Klahr (1999). Each study focused on children's learning of a different domain-general process strategy and their generalization of the strategy across various tasks in different contexts. Together, these studies addressed three fundamental and ongoing issues in younger children's acquisition and transfer of scientific reasoning strategies: (a) children's ability to use analogy in learning science; (b) facilitating factors, cognitive processes, and developmental differences in scientific learning by analogy; and (c) implications for the science of learning and for classroom science education.

The Ability to Learn Scientific
Reasoning Strategies by Analogy

As noted earlier, each experiment summarized in the following sections examined children's acquisition and transfer of a particular domain-general scientific process strategy. The first study focused on how 4- and 5-year-old children learn to recognize and distinguish between determinate and indeterminate evidence (Klahr & Chen, 2003; hereinafter the *Distinguishing Determinacy Study*), the second study examined the processes by which 6- to 8-year-olds learn to test hypotheses (Chen et al., 2011; hereinafter the *Testing Hypotheses Study*), and the third addressed 7- to 10-year-olds' learning and transfer of the control-of-variables strategy (CVS) in designing valid experiments (Chen & Klahr, 1999; hereinafter the *Designing Experiments Study*).

The Distinguishing Determinacy Study

The ability to distinguish between determinacy and indeterminacy is a foundational aspect of higher order cognition in many domains, including causal reasoning, decision making, and scientific discovery. In each domain, it is necessary to distinguish between situations in which evidence is sufficient for drawing conclusions and situations in which it is not. Young children have particular difficulty in reasoning about determinate and indeterminate evidence. For example, Fay and Klahr (1996) studied preschoolers' understanding of indeterminacy by presenting them with a target object (e.g., a necklace made from red beads) and a set of three boxes, each of which contained only one type of bead. At the outset of each trial, all the boxes were closed. They were then opened sequentially. Prior to the opening of each box, children were asked whether and why they either "knew for sure" or "would have to guess" which box contained the beads that had been used to construct the necklace. Children's difficulty in recognizing ongoing indeterminacy was particularly evident when they encountered the "Positive & Hidden" evidence type, in which a single instance was positive (e.g., a box containing a red bead) and at least one of the boxes still remained closed. On such problems, children typically and incorrectly responded that they "knew for sure" from which box the necklace's beads had come when they should have said "guess" because one or both of the remaining closed boxes might also contain matching (red) beads from which the necklace had been made. Fay and Klahr called this the *positive-capture strategy* because the single positive instance seemed to capture children's attention and, in effect, blind them to the fact that the unexplored option(s) might yet render the problem indeterminate.

Given the consequences of failing to recognize indeterminate situations in scientific reasoning, it is important to investigate whether and how young children eventually replace the positive-capture strategy with a more advanced strategy after experience. Using an analogy approach, Klahr and Chen (2003) examined 4- and 5-year-old children's acquisition and transfer of the indeterminacy concept by presenting young children with various isomorphic tasks designed with different materials (e.g., box, stamp, and marker tasks; Figure 2.1 illustrates the box and stamp tasks as examples of the isomorphic problems). Children's scientific reasoning strategies were assessed on all evidence pattern types over several days and several phases, including a pretest, two learning phases, a posttest, and a delayed transfer test 7 months later. Children were assigned to two learning conditions. In the training condition, correct and incorrect responses were identified, and the rationale for the correct answer was pro-

A   B

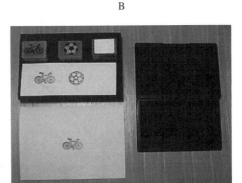

Figure 2.1. Example of isomorphic tasks used in the Distinguishing Determinacy Study. Panel A depicts the box task: The goal was to determine which of the three boxes contained the materials used to construct the necklace in front of the boxes. In this example, all boxes are opened, revealing a − − + evidence pattern: Only the right-most box could have been used. Panel B depicts the stamp task: The goal was to determine which of the three boxes contained the stamp used to make the picture shown on the large sheet at the bottom of the figure. The contents of each box are indicated both by the design on the box lid and the stamped pattern in front of each box. All boxes start out with the design on the box lid obscured by a piece of paper. In this example, the contents of the first two boxes, but not the third, have been revealed, yielding a + − ? pattern. From "Overcoming the Positive-Capture Strategy in Young Children: Learning About Indeterminacy," by D. Klahr and Z. Chen, 2003, *Child Development, 74,* pp. 1275–1296. Copyright 2003 by Wiley-Blackwell. Reprinted with permission.

vided immediately after the child responded to each question; that is, children received immediate, explicit, and systematic feedback after each box was opened (e.g., "This is a time when you have to guess. Even though you see a box with [target] in it, there could be [targets] in these boxes also, and I could have used one of these boxes when I made this [target]"). In the control condition, children received no explicit feedback from the experimenter about whether their response was correct or incorrect; however, even in the control condition children received implicit and subtle feedback in that the opening of subsequent boxes within a problem either validated or invalidated a previous answer about that problem.

One key issue addressed in Klahr and Chen's (2003) study is young children's competencies in learning a general strategy and transferring it across analogous tasks. Children demonstrated impressive analogical transfer in the learning of scientific process strategies. Both 4- and 5-year-olds initially experienced difficulty in solving the tasks, especially when experiencing the Positive & Hidden pattern, but they improved their performance after experiencing an analogous source task, as shown in Figure 2.2. Although the positive-capture strategy is a robust phenomenon in young children's reasoning, 5-year-olds— and, to a lesser extent, 4-year-olds—were capable of learning from their problem-solving experience and transferring the reasoning strategy acquired in the

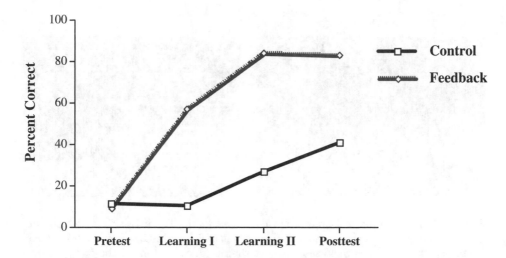

Figure 2.2. Basic evidence for analogical transfer in the Distinguishing Determinacy Study (data is from Klahr & Chen, 2003).

original learning context (Learning Phases I & II; see Figure 2.2). Children's strategy use benefited more from the explicit feedback of the training condition than from the implicit feedback of the control condition. The role of analogy in fostering scientific reasoning is evident in the children's improved performance on indeterminacy problems on the learning and posttest tasks. Note that these patterns are based on children's correct responses when evaluating an evidence pattern involving a single positive instance and an unexplored source of evidence (when only positive capture is possible). Converging findings were also evident from children's overall correct responses to all problems.

The Testing Hypotheses Study

Children's ability to transfer learned strategies across tasks and situations is impacted by the complexity of the tasks that they face. In the Distinguishing Determinacy Study, 4- and 5-year-olds demonstrated an impressive ability to transfer the acquired strategy across isomorphic determinacy versus indeterminacy tasks (e.g., from boxes to markers), but how well would children be able to learn and transfer the more complex scientific process strategy of testing hypotheses? The ability to generate a conclusive test for a hypothesis is a critical component of the scientific reasoning process (e.g., Klahr & Dunbar, 1988; Klayman & Ha, 1987). Early investigations of children's ability to understand hypotheses and evidence suggest that it is not until they reach the age of 11 or 12 that they start to master the conceptual and procedural strategies required to seek and evaluate evidence that can confirm or disconfirm hypotheses (e.g., Kuhn, Amsel, & O'Laughlin, 1988); however, other studies indicate that when presented with two relatively simple and mutually exclusive hypotheses, even young elementary school children can correctly choose which of two "experiments" will conclusively determine which hypothesis is correct (e.g., Ruffman, Perner, Olson, & Doherty, 1993; Sodian, Zaitchik, & Carey, 1991).

Sodian et al. (1991) told first- and second-graders a story in which they had to determine whether a big or small mouse was eating food in the kitchen each night. The children were told that they could place food in either of two houses: (a) one with a big door that could accommodate either a large or small mouse or (b) one with a small door that could accommodate only a small mouse. Most children correctly reasoned that they should put the food in the house with the small door: If the food was gone in the morning, then the small mouse must have gained entry and eaten it. In a second task, children needed to figure out how to determine whether a pet aardvark had a poor or good sense of smell. More than one quarter of the children in both grades generated spontaneous hypothesis tests (e.g., placing the food far away from the aardvark), suggesting they had some nascent understanding of the fundamental logic of hypothesis testing. Because the two tasks were presented one after another, children's apparently spontaneous hypothesis tests may in fact have been more the result of their learning from the guided experience of the first task.

To extend Sodian et al.'s (1991) findings and examine young children's acquisition of strategies in testing hypotheses, Chen et al. (2011) created a series of more complex tasks to examine how 6- to 8-year-old children learn a hypothesis testing strategy by analogy. The basic task involved listening to a story problem, then designing a way to test a simple hypothesis and solve the story problem by choosing the correct solution item from among three options. For example, in one of the isomorphic problems—the "Who sank the boat?" task—children were presented a story in which a fisherman needed to test whether the bear who left footsteps around his pond at night was a big or small one. The solution involved leaving one of his three boats in the water (the one that a big bear, but not a small bear, could sink). If the boat were sunk in the morning, it must have been a big bear that did it. Three isomorphic tasks were presented (see Figure 2.3) that shared a parallel problem structure and logic but involved different objects, protagonists, and storylines. The two trials

Figure 2.3. Example of isomorphic tasks used in the Testing Hypotheses Study (stimuli are from Chen et al., 2011).

within a task differed in the relations between the bear and boats. For example, on the first trial, a big bear could sink the medium boat but not the big boat, and a small bear could sink only the small boat; on the second trial, a big bear could sink only the big boat, and a small bear could sink the medium and small boats. The early tasks served as analogues for later tasks.

Children at each age level were assigned to one of three conditions. At the end of each trial in the verbal-and-physical feedback (explicit) condition, the children received verbal instruction and a physical demonstration with props that a big bear, but not a small one, would sink a particular boat. The verbal instruction illustrated how and why a correct choice would allow one to test the hypothesis conclusively:

> If the fisherman chooses the biggest boat that the big bear can sink but the small bear cannot sink, and if the biggest boat is sunk in the morning, then the fisherman will know that . . . the big bear sank it. If he chooses a smaller boat that either bear can sink, the fisherman will not be able to find out whether a big or small bear sank the boat.

In the physical feedback-only (intermediate) condition, children viewed a physical demonstration of possible solutions but no verbal explanation. Physical demonstration involved showing a correct choice and then an incorrect choice with the props, and asking questions about why it was a good or bad choice. For example, to demonstrate in the largest boat as the correct choice, the experimenter might say,

> Let's see what happens if the fisherman chooses this big boat. See? If the big bear steps in it, the boat sinks. If the small bear steps in, the boat doesn't sink. If the fisherman finds the big boat is sunk in the morning, would he be able to tell whether it was the big bear that sank it? Why?

In the implicit-feedback condition, children received no explicit feedback, but the experimenter's very specific questions served as implicit feedback.

Children's strategies for testing a hypothesis were assessed at three levels across three isomorphic tasks. Short- and long-term analogical transfer was assessed when children's strategy use during the initial and learning phases together was compared with their performance on a posttest given 12 months after the learning phase. During the posttest, only kindergartners and first graders who had participated in the verbal-and-physical feedback and physical feedback-only conditions were tested in three trials 1 year after the learning phase. Classmates who did not participate in any condition of the original study served as a control group.

Although the results as described in the original article examined children's understanding of hypothesis testing on several levels, the results summarized here focus on children's self-generation of a conclusive hypothesis test by spontaneously selecting the appropriate item from among the three available (e.g., leaving the appropriately sized boat in the water). Few children were able to generate an appropriate test for the hypothesis on the first task, especially on the first trial. Children used various strategies in solving the prob-

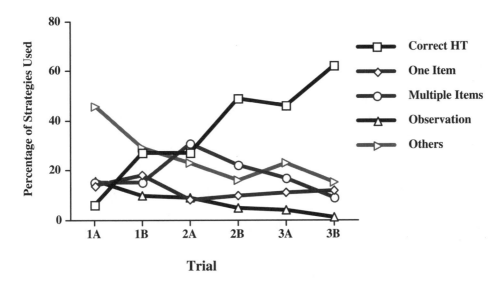

Figure 2.4.   Basic evidence for analogical transfer: Percentages of strategies used in solving the problems in the Testing Hypotheses Study. HT = hypothesis test (data are from Chen et al., 2011).

lems, including selecting the correct item (the correct strategy), selecting an incorrect item, and selecting multiple items, among others. However, they improved their performance in generating a valid hypothesis test across the isomorphic tasks (see Figure 2.4). These results indicate that 6- to 8-year-olds demonstrate the ability to learn by analogy and can learn to understand the fundamental principle of testing a hypothesis by mapping the isomorphic problems and generalizing the strategy from one task to another.

The Designing Experiments Study

The ability to distinguish determinate from indeterminate evidence is essential to testing hypotheses successfully, and the concept of hypothesis testing serves in turn as a foundation for understanding confounded versus unconfounded experimental designs. Chen and Klahr (1999) examined whether and how older children learn and transfer a more complex scientific process strategy—the CVS—in designing valid experiments across analogous tasks. CVS involves making appropriate inferences from the outcomes of unconfounded experiments as well as understanding the inherent indeterminacy of confounded experiments. In a procedural sense, CVS is a method for designing experiments in which a single contrast is made between experimental conditions. The strategy involves not only creating such contrasts but also being able to distinguish between confounded and unconfounded experiments. Previous studies (Bullock & Ziegler, 1999; Kuhn et al., 1995) have indicated that elementary school children have a very limited understanding of CVS, with a majority of fifth and sixth graders producing mainly confounded experimental designs.

Given that CVS is a foundational scientific reasoning strategy, and given that few elementary school children spontaneously use it when they should, it is important to identify effective ways to teach CVS, ways that will have a lasting benefit on children's scientific thinking. Hence, one aim of Chen and Klahr's (1999) study was to determine the extent to which children can learn CVS and then transfer the strategy to situations beyond the original learning context and after a long delay. For example, after learning how to design unconfounded experiments to determine various factors in the stretching of springs, would 7- to 10-year-old children prove able to use CVS to create valid experiments dealing with balls rolling down ramps, a task that shared few superficial similar features with the previous one?

With hands-on devices for each task, children were asked to design experiments to test the possible effects of different variables. Several isomorphic tasks were designed to help children master CVS. The tasks were physics based and involved springs, slopes, and sinking designs. In each task, there were four variables that could assume either of two values, and for each task children were asked to focus on a single outcome that might be affected by all four variables. For example, in the slope task (see Figure 2.5), children had to generate test comparisons to determine how different variables affected the distance that objects traveled after rolling down a ramp. Children could vary

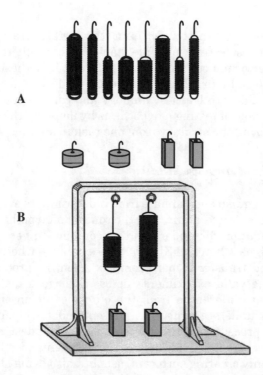

Figure 2.5. Example of isomorphic tasks used in the Designing Experiments Study. From *Cognition and Instruction: 25 years of Progress* (p. 86), by S. M. Carver and D. Klahr, 2001, Mahwah, NJ: Erlbaum. Copyright 2001 by Taylor & Francis. Reprinted with permission.

the steepness of the downhill ramps (either steep or low) using wooden blocks that fit under the ramps. Children could also change the surface of the ramps (either rough or smooth) by placing on the downhill ramps inserts surfaced with carpet or smooth wood. They could also determine how far the balls rolled on the downhill ramp by placing starting gates at two different distances from the top of the ramp (long or short run). Finally, children could choose from two kinds of balls: either rubber squash balls or golf balls.

To test learning and transfer, children were assigned to different instructional conditions, which differed in whether children received explicit instruction in CVS and whether they received systematic probe questions concerning why they designed the tests as they did and what they learned from the tests. Children in the training probe condition received explicit training instructions for the first comparison and were asked systematic probe questions about why they had designed the test they did for each trial. Training included an explanation of the rationale behind controlling variables as well as examples of how to make unconfounded comparisons. After the test was executed, children were asked if they could "tell for sure" from the test whether the variable they were testing made a difference and why they were sure or not sure. During training, the children were given both negative (confounded) and positive (unconfounded) examples and were asked to make a judgment of whether each example was a good or bad comparison and to explain why. The experimenter then provided the rationale for why it was or was not a good comparison. In the no-training-probe condition, children received no explicit training, but they did receive the same series of probe questions surrounding each comparison as were used in the training probe condition. Children in the no training–no probe condition received neither training nor probes.

Using three analogous tasks that shared the same underlying structure but different superficial features, Chen and Klahr (1999) asked children to make a series of four paired comparisons to test particular variables of each problem in four phases of the study: (a) Exploration (e.g., the slope task), (b) Assessment (e.g., different variables of the slope task), (c) Transfer 1 (e.g., the sinking task), and (d) Transfer 2 (e.g., the spring task). The order of the tasks was counterbalanced. Children were presented with materials in a source task, and their initial CVS was examined. Their learning was assessed on the same initial task in the Assessment phase. This assessment measured children's analogical transfer across the isomorphic tasks.

To examine children's ability to transfer CVS from the original learning context to remote situations, a posttest with paper-and-pencil problems was given after a 7-month delay. Third graders and fourth graders who had participated in the original learning experience and their classmates who had not previously participated were given a posttest on which they were asked to solve problems in various novel domains. The posttest tasks involved evaluating whether each of a series of paired comparisons was a good or bad test of the effect of a specific variable (an example of one of the posttest tasks is illustrated in Figure 2.6). Chen and Klahr (1999) considered the application of the general strategy, CVS, in the posttest as remote transfer, for several reasons. The tasks differed from the early learning tasks in several aspects, including the format (generating tests in the hands-on tasks of the learning phase vs. evaluating tests on paper in the posttest),

Plane A   Plane B

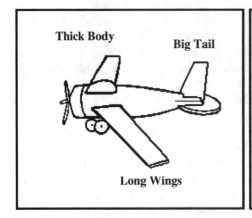
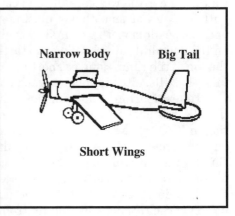

Good Test

Bad Test

Figure 2.6. Sample page from experiment evaluation assessment booklet used in the airplanes test of the Designing Experiments Study. For this test, children were asked to compare the two pictures and assess whether they showed a good way to test if the length of the wings makes a difference in how fast a model plane flies. This example has a single confound because the body type is confounded with the focal variable (wing length); (data are from Chen & Klahr, 1999).

content (mechanical vs. other types of domains), context (working with an experimenter in the laboratory vs. their science teacher in the science classroom), and time elapsed (immediacy of subsequent tasks in learning phase vs. 7-month delay between the learning phase tasks and posttest tasks).

To determine whether and how children in the different conditions transferred CVS and adapted their strategies in designing experiments across the isomorphic tasks, the frequency of CVS use in each phase was examined. Children's performance in designing valid experiments in each phase is illustrated in Figure 2.7. The analyses indicate that children in the training probe condition increased their performance over phases: They increased their use of CVS from about one third of the trials in the Exploration phase (before training) to nearly two thirds of the trials on the Assessment, Transfer 1, and Transfer 2 phases. Children in the no-training-probe condition also somewhat outperformed those in the no training–no probe condition, who did not significantly improve in their use of CVS over phases.

The three studies just summarized were designed to examine the learning and transfer of various scientific reasoning strategies at different age levels. In each study, one key issue the researchers hoped to address was the following: After learning how to distinguish determinate from indeterminate evidence, to test hypotheses, or to design unconfounded experiments, would children be able to use the specific learned strategies to solve problems in different contexts with

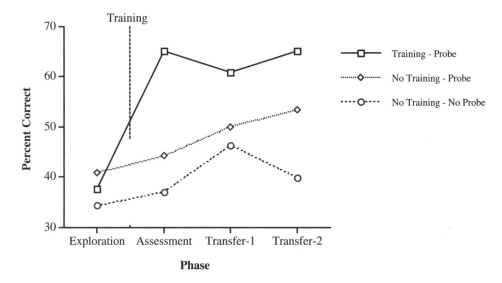

Figure 2.7. Basic evidence for analogical transfer in the Designing Experiments Study From "All Other Things Being Equal: Acquisition of the Control of Variables Strategy," by D. Klahr and Z. Chen, 1999, *Child Development, 70,* pp. 1098–1120. Copyright 1999 by Wiley-Blackwell. Reprinted with permission.

different materials, or would they apply the strategy only to situations sharing very similar features? The data analyses indicated that once children were trained in the original learning phases to use a given scientific strategy, they demonstrated an impressive ability to apply the learned strategies across analogous problems sharing a common task structure and strategy but having different superficial features. Thus, the results signal that analogy is an effective way for children to learn the principles of scientific reasoning. Perhaps even more significant, these studies clearly demonstrate that children can learn and transfer scientific process strategies previously assumed to be beyond their abilities.

Facilitating Factors and Developmental Differences in Analogical Transfer

I turn now to a consideration of the factors promoting the learning and transfer of scientific reasoning strategies by analogy. Whether, how, and when children acquire scientific reasoning strategies are critical issues whose resolution will have important implications for both cognitive development and instruction. In all three studies, the researchers explored factors facilitating the analogical transfer of scientific process strategies by presenting analogous tasks and assessing children's strategy use in various phases under different learning conditions. They focused on two general types of instruction: (a) explicit training via direct instruction (using examples and providing an explicit rationale to teach the general strategy) and (b) implicit training via probes (providing systematic questions or asking children to generate self-explanations following their own activities).

Another common feature among these three studies is the presentation of multiple isomorphic tasks with multiple within-task trials. Two of the studies also included a follow-up posttest with a remote task that required the same reasoning strategies as, and shared the same basic structures but few superficial similarities with, the original learning situations. Such a design allowed both micro- and macroanalyses of children's strategy use and change in order to pinpoint the processes involved in analogical transfer of scientific reasoning strategies under various instructional conditions.

At the microanalysis level, researchers analyzed children's analogical transfer trial by trial using a microgenetic method. Microgenetic methods offer an effective approach for exploring the change process by providing detailed data concerning how new approaches are discovered and how children generalize the new strategies after their initial discovery (Siegler, 2005, 2006; Siegler & Crowley, 1991; Siegler & Jenkins, 1989). The microgenetic approach typically involves a span of observation from the initial use of a strategy to its consistent use, as well as intense analyses of qualitative and quantitative changes (Bjorklund, Coyle, & Gaultney, 1992; Siegler, 1996). Because the method uses trial-by-trial assessments of ongoing cognitive activities, it facilitates precise analyses of how children change their strategies with experience and with instruction. Using the microgenetic approach in these studies allowed detailed analyses of how children learned and transferred. The macroanalysis allowed the researchers to examine how long children maintained the learned strategies and how widely and flexibly children were able to generalize them across situations.

The Distinguishing Determinacy Study

One goal of the Distinguishing Determinacy Study (Klahr & Chen, 2003) was to explore the conditions under which the positive-capture strategy comes to be replaced with a more advanced strategy for evaluating evidence. The authors provided extensive problem-solving experience and explicit feedback to facilitate learning. As indicated in Figure 2.8, both 4- and 5-year-olds initially experienced difficulty in solving Positive & Hidden pattern problems but improved their performance after receiving feedback. Children were assigned to each condition after consistently making errors on Positive & Hidden pattern problems, and children at both ages were equally likely to use the positive-capture strategy. However, 4- and 5-year-olds responded differently to the repeated problem-solving experience in the control condition and to the explicit feedback in the training condition. As noted earlier, the problem-solving experience of the control condition provided subtle and implicit feedback on each trial. Five-year-olds proved more sensitive to such implicit feedback and learned somewhat from it, whereas 4-year-olds failed to do so. Developmental differences in the training condition were evident in several aspects: Older children learned more readily from feedback, improved their performance to a greater extent, and more effectively transferred the correct strategy across tasks (e.g., from boxes to markers).

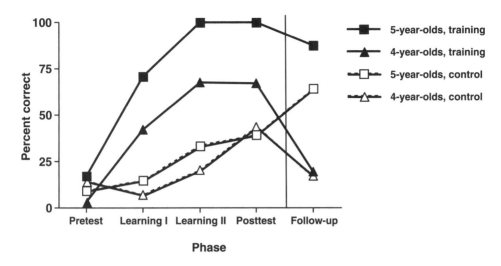

Figure 2.8.   Percentage of correct responses to Positive and Hidden type of evidence over phase by conditions and age in the Distinguishing Determinacy Study. From "Overcoming the Positive-capture Strategy in Young Children: Learning About Indeterminacy," by D. Klahr and Z. Chen, 2003, *Child Development, 74,* pp. 1275–1296. Copyright 2003 by Wiley-Blackwell. Reprinted with permission.

Microgenetic analyses (see Figure 2.9) showed that 5-year-olds in the training condition significantly and readily improved their performance during the learning phase. The positive-capture misconception was overcome, and they started using a correct strategy (as evident in both their answers and explanations) on the third trial of the Positive & Hidden pattern during the learning phase, and their performance remained nearly perfect throughout the learning phase. When they encountered the follow-up task 7 months later, however, their performance on the first trial was far from perfect. This pattern suggests that the children did not readily map the structures from the follow-up to the original tasks and implement the learned strategy on the second and third trials. By contrast, by the follow-up phase, 4-year-olds' performance regressed almost to pretest levels. Five-year-olds in the training condition also increased their scores from pretest to the learning phases, whereas their peers in the control condition did not improve their scores until the follow-up phase.

The Distinguishing Determinacy Study showed that 5-year-olds were able to learn from problem-solving experience, especially from explicit feedback, whereas 4-year-olds' performance on indeterminacy problems benefited somewhat from explicit feedback but not from implicit feedback. Older children's learning proved more effective in magnitude, rate, and generalization. Although 5-year-olds initially used the positive-capture strategy spontaneously in solving indeterminacy patterns, they learned readily from feedback to recognize and explain correctly both determinate and indeterminate situations, and they effectively generalized the acquired strategy across different tasks without a long delay. Thus, compared with 4-year-olds, 5-year-olds improved their performance to a greater extent, learned faster, and generalized the

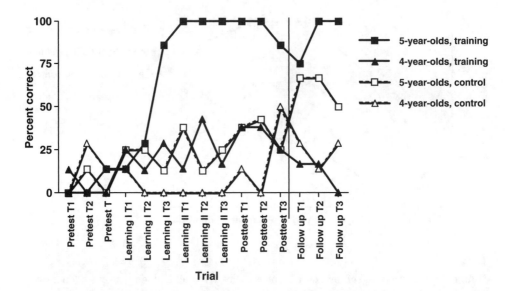

Figure 2.9. Trial-by-trial analyses of children's responses and explanation on each of the Positive and Hidden type in the Distinguishing Determinacy Study. T1 = Transfer 1; T2 = Transfer 2; T3 = Transfer 3. From "Overcoming the Positive-capture Strategy in Young Children: Learning About Indeterminacy," by D. Klahr and Z. Chen, 2003, *Child Development, 74,* pp. 1275–1296. Copyright 2003 by Wiley-Blackwell. Reprinted with permission.

newly acquired strategy to a broader range of indeterminacy tasks and to more remote situations.

The Testing Hypotheses Study

In the Testing Hypotheses Study, Chen et al. (2011) conducted micro- and macro-analyses to examine how different instructional conditions affect children's acquisition and transfer of hypothesis testing strategies across isomorphic tasks at different ages. As shown in Figure 2.10, during the learning phase, first and second graders learned more effectively than kindergartners to generate spontaneously a hypothesis-testing strategy. Few children generated an appropriate test for the hypothesis on the first trial of the first task; however, even kindergartners improved their performance on the second trial and the subsequent tasks. Older children learned more effectively: Across conditions, more than four fifths of the second graders and nearly two thirds of the first graders generated an appropriate test, but only about one fourth of kindergartners did so on the last task.

Different types of feedback, from implicit to explicit (from the specific questions that an experimenter asked, to physical demonstrations, to specific and systematic verbal explanations in tandem with physical demonstrations), have differential effects on learning at different age levels. Effects of condition were evident especially for kindergartners. Kindergartners in the verbal-and-physical

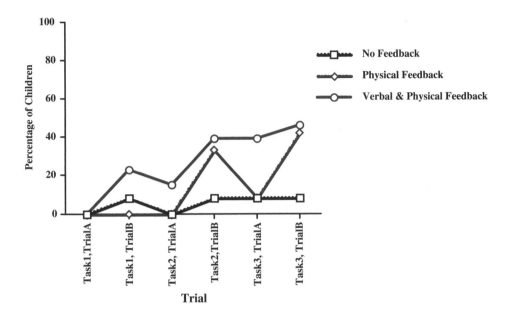

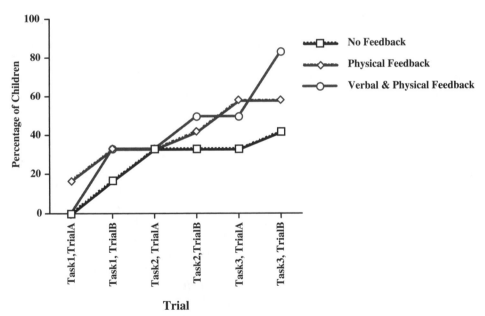

Figure 2.10. Trial-by-trial analyses of children's hypothesis testing strategies in the Testing Hypotheses Study (first grade, and second grade, respectively; data are from Chen et al., 2011).

(continued on next page)

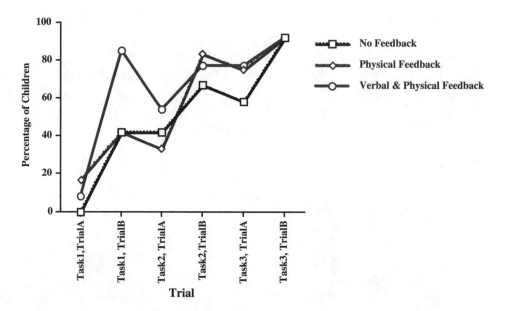

Figure 2.10. *(Continued).*

feedback condition outperformed those in the physical-feedback-only condition, who in turn outperformed those in the implicit-feedback condition. Although these results indicate the greater effectiveness of the combined verbal and physical feedback, they nonetheless signal that even implicit feedback can facilitate learning in early elementary school children.

One central aim of the Testing Hypotheses Study was to examine whether children who experienced the initial learning tasks outperformed their peers who were not exposed to the initial tasks in solving posttest problems. As shown in Figure 2.11, when encountering the posttest task, few first graders in either condition spontaneously came up with correct hypothesis tests on the first trial of the posttest. By contrast, about one third of the second graders in the experimental condition used a correct hypothesis-testing strategy on the first trial, as compared with only a few of their peers in the control group. Note that children in the experimental and control conditions on the posttest received both verbal and physical feedback on each trial, and thus their performance was predicted to improve over trials on the posttest. Children's performance was also examined when correct strategy use was combined over the three posttest trials, yielding main effects of grade and of condition. These findings suggest that first graders were less effective than second graders in learning the hypothesis-testing strategies and transferring the strategies when they encountered an isomorphic problem in a different context after 1 year.

The Designing Experiments Study

The Designing Experiments Study (Chen & Klahr, 1999) was intended to examine which approaches (i.e., training probe, no training probe, and no training–no

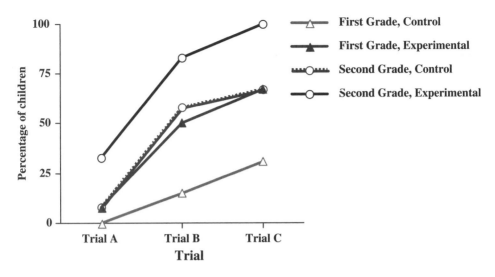

Figure 2.11. Children's performance in generating a correct hypothesis test on the posttest after a 12-month delay in the Testing Hypotheses Study (data are from Chen et al., 2011).

probe) work best in facilitating children's acquisition of CVS and to determine the extent to which children transfer CVS to situations beyond the original learning context and after a substantial delay. As illustrated in Figure 2.12, older children outperformed younger children, and children's performance patterns in different grades differed in each training condition. Only the third graders and fourth graders in the training probe condition improved their performance over phases. The second graders' performance somewhat improved between the Assessment and Exploration phases; however, their transfer performance was not higher than the exploration performance. A similar pattern in age differences was also found in the no-training probe condition in that the third and fourth graders, but not the second graders, showed some improvement over phases. Children in the no training–no probe condition showed no performance increases over phases for any grade level.

To examine the detailed time course of the acquisition and use of CVS, Chen and Klahr (1999) analyzed, on a trial-by-trial basis, the proportion of participants who generated a robust use of CVS with appropriate explanations on each trial (see Figure 2.13). Children in the no training–no probe condition were not included in this analysis because they did not receive probe questions and thus could not be expected to mention CVS. The majority of children started with poor robust-use scores; however, immediately after training, children showed substantial improvement in the robust use of CVS (from about 15% to over 50%), and this level of performance remained throughout the transfer phases. By contrast, children in the no-training probe condition continued to perform at their initial low levels; however, even this fine-grained analysis conceals the fact that the pattern of strategy change varied considerably in both conditions.

One central issue in the posttest was whether children are capable of transferring the learned strategy to remote problems after a long delay. The main

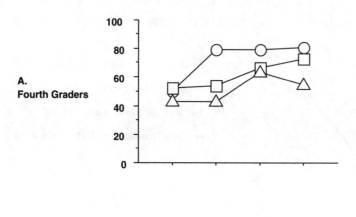

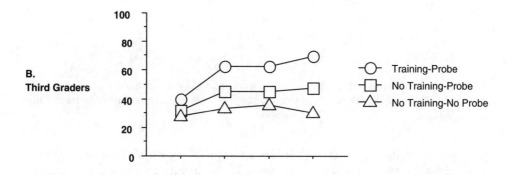

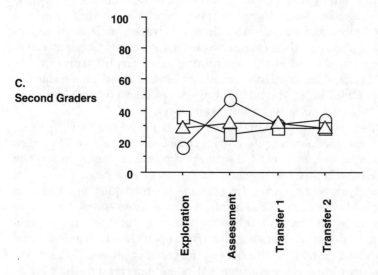

Figure 2.12. Percentage of correct CVS usage by phase, grade, and condition in the Designing Experiments Study. From "All Other Things Being Equal: Acquisition of the Control of Variables Strategy," by D. Klahr and Z. Chen, 1999, *Child Development, 70,* pp. 1098–1120. Copyright 1999 by Wiley-Blackwell. Reprinted with permission.

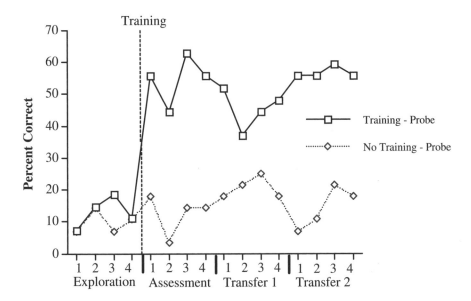

Figure 2.13. Percentage of children in training probe and no-training probe groups who both mentioned and used the control-of-variables strategy (robust use of the strategy) on each trial in the Designing Experiments Study. From "All Other Things Being Equal: Acquisition of the Control of Variables Strategy," by D. Klahr and Z. Chen, 1999, *Child Development, 70,* pp. 1098–1120. Copyright 1999 by Wiley-Blackwell. Reprinted with permission.

dependent measure in the posttest was the number of correct responses to the posttest problems. As indicated in Figure 2.14, fourth graders in the experimental conditions (who participated in the original learning phases) outperformed those in the control condition (who had never been exposed to the learning tasks); however, conditions did not differ significantly for third graders, suggesting that younger children's reasoning did not benefit from the early learning experiences with analogous tasks. Chen and Klahr's (1999) study thus revealed developmental differences in learning and transfer of scientific reasoning skills. Second graders, like older children, showed within-task transfer; that is, they used CVS within the same task and domain as the initial training. Third graders demonstrated the ability to transfer CVS across problems within the domain of mechanics; they were able to apply CVS not only within the slope problems, for example, but also could generalize the strategy to spring and sinking tasks and could do so despite a short-term delay of 1 week. Only fourth graders displayed effective remote transfer across time, context, and task.

Conclusions

I wrote this chapter with the aim of illustrating some of the fundamental issues involved in younger children's acquisition and transfer of scientific reasoning strategies. The three studies summarized share an analogous design in that

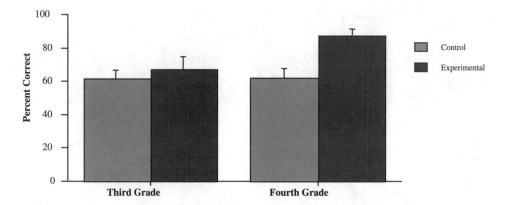

Figure 2.14. Percentage of correct answers at posttest in the Designing Experiments Study. From "All Other Things Being Equal: Acquisition of the Control of Variables Strategy," by D. Klahr and Z. Chen, 1999, *Child Development, 70,* pp. 1098–1120. Copyright 1999 by Wiley-Blackwell. Reprinted with permission.

each one examined various facets of children's reasoning strategies by presenting children at different ages with analogous tasks of differing levels of complexity. The results indicate that, as in other areas of children's learning, analogy plays a key role in children's learning of scientific reasoning strategies. Without such structured experience, instruction, and probing questions, children consistently showed misconceptions in their scientific reasoning across tasks and contexts. In view of these findings, in this section, I offer some conclusions, focusing on the role of analogy in learning scientific process strategies, developmental differences that affect the learning of scientific reasoning strategies, and educational implications and applications. In the next section, I address outstanding issues for future research.

Role of Analogical Transfer in Learning Scientific Process Strategies

Whether and how children retrieve relevant information and use examples acquired in the past to solve analogous problems is a central issue in human cognition and children's thinking. Despite the large number of studies that have examined children's competencies in solving classic analogies or simple insight problems by mapping the source and target (transfer) problems (e.g., Gentner, 1989; Gentner & Markman, 1997; Goswami, 1996, 2006), relatively little is known about the role of analogy in young children's acquisition of mathematical and scientific reasoning strategies. In the studies described herein, my colleagues and I explored how analogy plays a role as a learning mechanism in the acquisition and transfer of key scientific reasoning strategies: understanding determinacy and indeterminacy, generating hypothesis tests, and designing valid experiments.

Analogy proves to be a powerful tool for young children's acquisition of fundamental scientific processing strategies: Children as young as 5 and 6 years of age are capable of applying the strategy of distinguishing determinate from indeterminate evidence, 6- to 8-year-olds can learn and transfer the fundamental principle of testing a hypothesis, and 7- to 10-year-olds demonstrate the ability to map isomorphic problems and generalize CVS in designing valid experiments. Even the youngest children who participated in these studies demonstrated impressive abilities to acquire a given scientific strategy in the initial learning phase, recognized and appreciated the structural similarities between the analogous tasks, and implemented the general strategy beyond the original situation. Beyond the immediate context of these three studies, then, providing multiple analogous tasks that require the same basic strategy but share few superficial features seems likely to be a sensible and effective approach for those seeking to facilitate children's learning of scientific process strategies.

Developmental Differences in Learning Scientific Reasoning Strategies by Analogy

The studies discussed in this chapter provide evidence of consistent developmental differences in learning scientific reasoning strategies by analogy. The micro- and macroanalyses used in these studies shed light on how children at different ages change their process strategies with experience. Developmental differences are evident in the *rate* of strategy change: Younger children improved their performance more gradually because of their greater difficulties in perceiving the similarities among the tasks and in implementing the tasks' strategies across different domains; they did not significantly improve their performance until a later learning phase. In contrast, older children applied their learned strategies more readily when encountering isomorphic problems. Age differences related to the speed of strategy change were apparent in all three studies.

Developmental differences in learning were also evident in the *breadth* of strategy change, or the ability to generalize acquired strategies to other tasks and situations: Older children showed a fairly robust ability to generalize an acquired rule even after a long delay, whereas younger children experienced difficulty in generalizing the strategy as the gap between the learning situation and the new problems became more distant.

Older children's more robust learning and transfer are also evident in how they responded to various instructional methods. Compared with younger children, older children proved more responsive to experience and feedback in learning scientific reasoning strategies. On receiving explicit instruction, older children switched strategies more readily, and used more advanced strategies more effectively and consistently, whereas younger children were more likely to regress toward less sophisticated strategies. Older children were also more responsive than younger children to implicit feedback, which on its own was sufficient to elicit older children's emerging reasoning strategies. On the other hand, younger children's strategy use did not seem to benefit much from implicit feedback.

These patterns are consistent with developmental differences evident in children's learning and strategy change in various dimensions (Siegler, 1995,

1996). The developmental differences apparent in learning scientific process strategies by analogy also accord with earlier studies that revealed noticeable age differences in solving analogous insight problems. Younger children's learning tends to be more perceptually bound and more greatly influenced by the superficial features of problems than by their structural or causal properties (Chen, 1996; Chen, Yanowitz, & Daehler, 1995; Gentner & Markman, 1997). Furthermore, to draw the analogy between source and target problems, younger children rely more on explicit hints or aids that emphasize the relevance and usefulness of prior experience (Brown, Kane, & Echols, 1986; Chen, Sanchez, & Campbell, 1997; Crisafi & Brown, 1986; Holyoak, Junn, & Billman, 1984). With age, children become increasingly more effective in perceiving causal structures between isomorphic tasks, they become increasingly responsive to experience, and their strategy transfer becomes increasingly flexible and broad.

Educational Implications

Research on analogies in math and science education (e.g., Dagher, 1995; Newton & Newton, 1995; Ogborn & Martins, 1996; Richland, Holyoak, & Stigler, 2004) has focused almost exclusively on the pedagogical value of analogies when incorporated into classroom materials and in teachers' explanations with the aim of promoting conceptual change in students. The use of analogies in instruction, whether initiated by the text, the teacher, or the students themselves, has been shown to improve conceptual learning and problem solving in a variety of science contexts, including mathematics (Richland, Zur, & Holyoak, 2007), biology (Baker & Lawson, 2001), and physics (Chiu & Lin, 2005). Despite the widespread, perhaps even worldwide, use of analogies as an explanatory tool to introduce new concepts as seen across various disciplines (e.g., Pittman, 1999; Richland et al., 2007), analogy as an instructional tool for learning critical scientific process strategies has been much less explored.

Given the centrality of transfer in children's learning and its implications for education, the goal of facilitating children's application of acquired strategies to relevant situations has been pursued with new vigor. The three studies described herein focused on approaches that promote transfer by encouraging children to process the underlying structural features of tasks and to extract generalizable scientific reasoning strategies. Their findings demonstrate that analogy plays a central role in children's acquisition of such strategies, thus signaling effective approaches for early science education in the classroom, including explicit instruction, implicit feedback, and student-generated explanations.

DIRECT INSTRUCTION. Within educational settings, explicit instruction is often viewed as limited and less effective than other types of instruction because it does not require children's active processing; thus, knowledge acquired through explicit instruction is assumed to be of limited generalizability. In contrast to this widespread assumption, the present results indicate that direct instruction, combined with probes, can be highly effective and efficient in teaching children scientific reasoning skills. Providing explicit instruction in the original learning situation proved the most effective way to facilitate the transfer of scientific reasoning strategies across analogous tasks. Explicit instruction was also effective in fostering 4- and 5-year-olds' learning of the principles of determinacy and indeterminacy, in facilitating the acquisition and transfer of a hypothesis testing strategy, and in teaching elementary school students to design unconfounded experiments. The beneficial effects of direct instruction have also been demonstrated in young children's learning and transfer on other tasks (Klahr & Nigam, 2004; Rittle-Johnson, 2006; Toth, Klahr, & Chen, 2000). These findings are consistent with other studies that indicate that young children can overcome what appear to be stubborn misconceptions when they receive direct instruction and explicit feedback (Chen & Klahr, 1999; Klahr & Carver, 1988; Siegler, 1996; Siegler & Chen, 1998).

One reason for the power of explicit instruction lies in its ability to foster greater in-depth learning in the original context. The deeper the initial learning (e.g., Siegler, 2002, 2005), the more likely the subsequent transfer. Explicit instruction is a powerful tool for transfer because it helps children master the original tasks to a greater extent (e.g., Brown et al., 1986; Chletsos & De Lisi, 1991; Crowley & Siegler, 1999). This more robust initial learning seems to result in better retention, faster learning, and wider generalization on subsequent transfer tasks. The findings of the studies discussed in this chapter accord with other microgenetic studies on scientific reasoning skills (e.g., Kuhn et al., 1995; Schauble, 1996), arithmetic strategies (e.g., Siegler & Jenkins, 1989), and number conservation tasks (Siegler, 1995), which indicate that without direct instruction, children typically show only gradual improvement in the accuracy of their solutions and the quality of their explanations.

IMPLICIT FEEDBACK AND SELF-EXPLANATIONS. Direct instruction is not the only effective means of facilitating transfer: Children's strategy transfer also benefits from specific probing questions that encourage self-generated explanations (e.g., Rittle-Johnson, 2006; Siegler, 2002). Children's superior performance in transferring CVS in the no-training probe condition (Chen & Klahr, 1999) and the hypothesis testing strategy in the physical feedback-only condition (Chen et al., 2011) supports a growing body of studies demonstrating that the opportunity to generate self-explanations enhances children's learning (e.g., Chi, de Leeuw, Chiu, & LaVancher, 1994; Honomichl & Chen, 2006; Renkl, 2002; Rittle-Johnson, 2006; Siegler, 2002; Siegler & Chen, 1998). The enduring power of self-generated explanations in promoting remote transfer has not yet been well studied; the results of the three studies I have discussed in this chapter indicate that asking children to explain their own responses as part of the training experience does indeed have ongoing benefits in promoting long-term transfer.

Young children's learning of the scientific reasoning strategies also benefited from watching physical manipulations of the toy props as well as from implicit probing questions designed to direct children's attention to important problem features. In the example of overcoming the positive-capture strategy (Klahr & Chen, 2003), 5-year-olds learned from instruction, but their learning and transfer also improved as a result of their extended problem-solving experience, even in the absence of explicit instruction. In the case of learning CVS, children in the no-training probe condition (Chen & Klahr, 1999) experienced and benefited from guiding questions that prompted them to generate explanations about the design of their experiments and the conclusions they drew from them. The results indicate that even in the absence of explicit instruction, elementary school children can learn scientific reasoning strategies as a result of systematic questions designed to promote deeper understanding. In contrast, allowing a child to interact freely with experimental materials and devices without the benefit of guiding questions or other implicit feedback is insufficient for promoting discovery and transfer of scientific reasoning strategies.

Future Directions

The findings presented in this chapter indicate that analogy is a powerful tool for children's learning and transfer of domain-general scientific process strategies. These results are consistent with previous findings that signal the role of analogy in promoting learning and transfer in various domains and tasks, such as tool use, symbolic functioning, causal reasoning, memory strategies, mathematical reasoning, and theory of mind. Despite the broad and significant findings of these studies, however, numerous issues remain to be explored as researchers seek to understand more fully the connections between analogy and children's scientific reasoning strategies.

One direction for further research involves finer analyses of the cognitive components involved in children's learning and transfer of scientific process strategies. How do children encode these strategies in the original context? How do they access or retrieve the relevant information when encountering an analogous target problem? How do they map key elements between source and target tasks? How do they implement learned scientific process strategies to solve the novel tasks? And how do the findings about children's encoding, retrieving, mapping, and implementing of scientific reasoning principles accord with what we already know about these cognitive processes in other domains?

A second critical question worthy of further consideration is how various instructional approaches influence learning and transfer. Although both direct instruction and implicit feedback play a role in overcoming young children's misconceptions (e.g., Chen & Klahr, 1999; DeLoache, Miller, & Pierroutsaks, 1998; Gentner & Gentner, 1983; Klahr & Carver, 1988; Siegler, 1976, 1981; Siegler & Chen, 1998), a fruitful avenue for future research involves analyzing the precise roles that direct instruction, implicit feedback, and discovery learning play in the acquisition and transfer of scientific reasoning strategies. Direct instruction can be highly effective and efficient in teaching children scientific reasoning strategies inasmuch as it provides explicit feedback about children's correct and incorrect responses, systematic explanations of the scientific principles involved, and/or positive (correct) and negative (incorrect) illustrations of the principles. Similarly, children's strategy transfer also benefits from exploratory learning, especially when it is guided by probe questions, self-generated explanations, implicit feedback from children's own strategies, and/or manipulation of experimental materials in hands-on tasks. Future research will need to examine these elements systematically to pinpoint the precise effects associated with each instructional approach . Finally, one further avenue of research lies in exploring how the findings of these and future studies can be translated from laboratories to real world classroom settings, thereby making the vital link between empirical findings and classroom research on the one hand, and sound educational practice on the other.

References

Alibali, M. W. (1999). How children change their minds: Strategy change can be gradual or abrupt. *Developmental Psychology, 35,* 127–145. doi:10.1037/0012-1649.35.1.127

Baker, W. P., & Lawson, A. E. (2001). Complex instructional analogies and theoretical concept acquisition in college genetics. *Science Education, 85,* 665–683. doi:10.1002/sce.1031

Barnett, S. M., & Ceci, S. J. (2002). When and where do we apply what we learn? A taxonomy for far transfer. *Psychological Bulletin, 128,* 612–637. doi:10.1037/0033-2909.128.4.612

Bjorklund, D. F., Coyle, T. R., & Gaultney, J. F. (1992). Developmental differences in the acquisition and maintenance of an organizational strategy: Evidence for the utilization deficiency hypothesis. *Journal of Experimental Child Psychology, 54,* 434–448. doi:10.1016/0022-0965 (92)90029-6

Blöte, A. W., Resing, W. C. M., Mazer, P., & Van Noort, D. A. (1999). Young children's organizational strategies on a same-different task: A microgenetic study and a training study. *Journal of Experimental Child Psychology, 74,* 21–43. doi:10.1006/jecp.1999.2508

Bransford, J. D., Brown, A. L., & Cocking, R. R. (1999). *How people learn: Brain, mind, experience, and school.* Washington, DC: National Academy Press.

Brown, A. L. (1989). Analogical learning and transfer: What develops? In S. Vosniadou & A. Ortony (Eds.), *Similarity and analogical reasoning* (pp. 369–412). Cambridge, England: Cambridge University Press.

Brown, A. L., & Campione, J. C. (1981). Inducing flexible thinking: A problem of access. In M. Freidman, J. P. Das, & N. O'Connor (Eds.), *Intelligence and learning* (pp. 515–530). New York, NY: Plenum Press.

Brown, A. L., & Kane, M. J. (1988). Preschool children can learn to transfer: Learning to learn and learning from example. *Cognitive Psychology, 20,* 493–523. doi:10.1016/0010-0285(88)90014-X

Brown, A. L., Kane, M. J., & Echols, C. H. (1986). Young children's mental models determine analogical transfer across problems with a common goal structure. *Cognitive Development, 1,* 103–121. doi:10.1016/S0885-2014(86)80014-4

Bullock, M., & Ziegler, A. (1999). Scientific reasoning: Developmental and individual differences. In F. E. Weinert & W. Schneider (Eds.), *Individual development from 3 to 12: Findings from the Munich Longitudinal Study* (pp. 38–54). Munich, Germany: Max Planck Institute for Psychological Research.

Chen, Z. (1996). Children's analogical problem solving: Effects of superficial, structural, and procedural similarity. *Journal of Experimental Child Psychology, 62,* 410–431. doi:10.1006/jecp. 1996.0037

Chen, Z. (2007). Learning to map: Strategy discovery and strategy change in young children. *Developmental Psychology, 43,* 386–403. doi:10.1037/0012-1649.43.2.386

Chen, Z., & Klahr, D. (1999). All other things being equal: Acquisition of the control of variables strategy. *Child Development, 70,* 1098–1120.

Chen, Z., & Klahr, D. (2008). Remote transfer of problem-solving and scientific reasoning strategies in children. In R. Kail (Ed.), *Advances in child development and behavior* (Vol. 36, pp. 420–469). San Diego, CA: Academic Press.

Chen, Z., Mo, L., & Honomichl, R. (2004). Having the memory of an elephant: Long-term retrieval and the use of analogues in problem solving. *Journal of Experimental Psychology: General, 133,* 415–433. doi:10.1037/0096-3445.133.3.415

Chen, Z., Mo, L., Klahr, D., Tong, X., Qu, C., & Chen, H. (2011). *Learning to test hypotheses: Kindergartners and elementary school children's acquisition of scientific reasoning strategies.* Manuscript in preparation.

Chen, Z., Sanchez, R. P., & Campbell, T. (1997). From beyond to within their grasp: The rudiments of analogical problem solving in 10- and 13-month-olds. *Developmental Psychology, 33,* 790–801. doi:10.1037/0012-1649.33.5.790

Chen, Z., & Siegler, R. S. (2000). Across the great divide: Bridging the gap between understanding of toddlers' and older children's thinking. *Monographs of the Society for Research in Child Development, 65,* i–v, 1–96.

Chen, Z., Yanowitz, K. L., & Daehler, M. W. (1995). Constraints on accessing abstract source information: Instantiation of principles facilitates children's analogical transfer. *Journal of Educational Psychology, 87,* 445–454. doi:10.1037/0022-0663.87.3.445

Chi, M. T. H., de Leeuw, N., Chiu, M.-H., & LaVancher, C. (1994). Eliciting self-explanations improves understanding. *Cognitive Science, 18,* 439–477.

Chiu, M. H., & Lin, J. W. (2005). Promoting fourth graders' conceptual change of their understanding of electric current via multiple analogies. *Journal of Research in Science Teaching, 42,* 429–464. doi:10.1002/tea.20062

Chletsos, P. N., & De Lisi, R. (1991). A microgenetic study of proportional reasoning using balance scale problems. *Journal of Applied Developmental Psychology, 12,* 307–330. doi:10.1016/0193-3973(91)90003-M

Cognition and Technology Group at Vanderbilt. (1997). *The Jasper Project: Lessons in curriculum instruction, assessment, and professional development.* Mahwah, NJ: Erlbaum.

Coyle, T. R., & Bjorklund, D. F. (1997). Age differences in, and consequences of, multiple- and variable-strategy use on a multitrial sort-recall task. *Developmental Psychology, 33,* 372–380. doi:10.1037/0012-1649.33.2.372

Crisafi, M. A., & Brown, A. L. (1986). Analogical transfer in very young children: Combining two separately learned solutions to reach a goal. *Child Development, 57,* 953–968. doi:10.2307/1130371

Crowley, K., & Siegler, R. S. (1999). Explanation and generalization in young children's strategy learning. *Child Development, 70,* 304–316. doi:10.1111/1467-8624.00023

Dagher, Z. R. (1995). Analysis of analogies used by science teachers. *Journal of Research in Science Teaching, 32,* 259–270. doi:10.1002/tea.3660320306

DeLoache, J. S. (2004). Becoming symbol-minded. *Trends in Cognitive Sciences, 8,* 66–70. doi:10.1016/j.tics.2003.12.004

DeLoache, J. S., Miller, K. F., & Pierroutsaks, S. L. (1998). Reasoning and problem solving. In W. Damon (Series Ed.) & D. Kuhn & R. S. Siegler (Vol. Eds.), *Handbook of child psychology: Vol. 2. Cognition, perception, and language* (5th ed., pp. 801–850). New York, NY: Wiley.

Detterman, D. K. (1993). The case for prosecution: Transfer as an epiphenomenon. In D. K. Detterman & R. J. Sternberg (Eds.), *Transfer on trial: Intelligence, cognition, and instruction* (pp. 39–67) Norwood, NJ: Ablex.

Detterman, D. K., & Sternberg, R. J. (1993). *Transfer on trial: Intelligence, cognition, and instruction.* Norwood, NJ: Ablex.

Dunbar, K. (2001). The analogical paradox: Why analogy is so easy in naturalistic settings yet so difficult in the psychological laboratory. In D. Gentner & K. J. Holyoak (Eds.), *The analogical mind: Perspectives from cognitive science* (pp. 313–334). Cambridge, MA: MIT Press.

Fay, A. L., & Klahr, D. (1996). Knowing about guessing and guessing about knowing: Preschoolers' understanding of indeterminacy. *Child Development, 67,* 689–716. doi:10.2307/1131841

Flynn, E., O'Malley, C., & Wood, D. (2004). A longitudinal, microgenetic study of the emergence of false belief understanding and inhibition skills. *Developmental Science, 7,* 103–115. doi:10.1111/j.1467-7687.2004.00326.x

Gelman, R. (1969). Conservation acquisition: A problem of learning to attend to relevant attributes. *Journal of Experimental Child Psychology, 7,* 167–187. doi:10.1016/0022-0965(69)90041-1

Gentner, D. (1989). The mechanisms of analogical learning. In S. Vosniadou & A. Ortony (Eds.), *Similarity and analogical reasoning* (pp. 199–241). Cambridge, England: Cambridge University Press. doi:10.1017/CBO9780511529863.011

Gentner, D., & Gentner, D. (1983). Flowing waters or teeming crowds: Mental models of electricity. In D. Gentner & A. L. Stevens (Eds.), *Mental models* (pp. 199–241). Hillsdale, NJ: Lawrence Erlbaum Associates.

Gentner, D., & Markman, A. B. (1997). Structure-mapping in analogy and similarity. *American Psychologist, 52,* 45–56. doi:10.1037/0003-066X.52.1.45

Goldin-Meadow, S., & Alibali, M. W. (2002). Looking at the hands through time: A microgenetic perspective on learning and instruction. In N. Granott & J. Parziale (Eds.), *Microdevelopment: Transition processes in development and learning* (pp. 80–106). New York, NY: Cambridge University Press. doi:10.1017/CBO9780511489709.004

Goswami, U. (1995). Transitive relational mappings in three- and four-year-olds: The analogy of Goldilocks and the Three Bears. *Child Development, 66,* 877–892. doi:10.2307/1131956

Goswami, U. (1996). Analogical reasoning and cognitive development. In H. W. Reese (Ed.), *Advances in child development and behavior* (pp. 91–138). San Diego, CA: Academic Press.

Goswami, U. (Ed.). (2006). *Cognitive development: Critical concepts in psychology.* London, England: Routledge.

Halford, G. S. (1993). *Children's understanding: The development of mental models.* Hillsdale, NJ: Erlbaum.

Halpern, D. F. (1989). *Thought and knowledge: An introduction to critical thinking.* Hillsdale, NJ: Erlbaum.

Halpern, D. F. (1998). Teaching critical thinking for transfer across domains. *American Psychologist, 53,* 449–455. doi:10.1037/0003-066X.53.4.449

Holyoak, K. J., Junn, E. N., & Billman, D. O. (1984). Developmental analogical problem solving skills. *Child Development, 55,* 2042–2055. doi:10.2307/1129778

Holyoak, K. J., & Thagard, P. (1995). *Mental leaps: Analogy in creative thought.* Cambridge, MA: MIT Press.

Honomichl, R., & Chen, Z. (2006). Learning to align relations in young children: The effects of feedback and self-explanation. *Journal of Cognition and Development, 7,* 527–550.

Inhelder, B., & Piaget, J. (1958). *The growth of logical thinking from childhood to adolescence.* New York, NY: Basic Books. doi:10.1037/10034-000

Klahr, D. (2000). *Exploring science: The cognition and development of discovery processes.* Cambridge, MA: MIT Press.

Klahr, D., & Carver, S. M. (1988). Cognitive objectives in a LOGO debugging curriculum: Instruction, learning, and transfer. *Cognitive Psychology, 20,* 362–404. doi:10.1016/0010-0285(88)90004-7

Klahr, D., & Chen, Z. (2003). Overcoming the positive-capture strategy in young children: Learning about indeterminacy. *Child Development, 74,* 1275–1296. doi:10.1111/1467-8624.00607

Klahr, D., & Dunbar, K. (1988). Dual space search during scientific reasoning. *Cognitive Science, 12,* 1–48. doi:10.1207/s15516709cog1201_1

Klahr, D., & Nigam, M. (2004). The equivalence of learning paths in early science instruction: Effects of direct instruction and discovery learning. *Psychological Science, 15,* 661–667. doi:10.1111/j.0956-7976.2004.00737.x

Klayman, J., & Ha, Y. W. (1987). Confirmation, disconfirmation, and information in hypothesis testing. *Psychological Review, 94,* 211–228. doi:10.1037/0033-295X.94.2.211

Kuhn, D., Amsel, E., O'Loughlin, M. (1988). *The development of scientific thinking skills.* San Diego, CA: Academic Press.

Kuhn, D., Garcia-Mila, M., Zohar, A., & Andersen, C. (1995). Strategies of knowledge acquisition. *Monographs of the Society for Research in Child Development, 60*(4, Serial No. 245). doi:10.2307/1166059

Kuhn, D., Schauble, L., & Garcia-Mila, M. (1992). Cross-domain development of scientific reasoning. *Cognition and Instruction, 9,* 285–327. doi:10.1207/s1532690xci0904_1

Newton, D. P., & Newton, L. D. (1995). Using analogy to help young children understand. *Educational Studies, 21,* 379–393. doi:10.1080/0305569950210305

Ogborn, J., & Martins, I. (1996). Metaphorical understandings and scientific ideas. *International Journal of Science Education, 18,* 631–652. doi:10.1080/0950069960180601

Pittman, K. M. (1999). Student-generated analogies: Another way of knowing? *Journal of Research in Science Teaching, 36,* 1–22. doi:10.1002/(SICI)1098-2736(199901)36:1<1::AID-TEA2>3.0.CO;2-2

Renkl, A. (2002). Worked-out examples: Instructional explanations support learning by self-explanations. *Learning and Instruction, 12,* 529–556. doi:10.1016/S0959-4752(01)00030-5

Richland, L. E., Holyoak, K. J., & Stigler, J. W. (2004). Analogy use in eighth-grade mathematics classrooms. *Cognition and Instruction, 22,* 37–60. doi:10.1207/s1532690Xci2201_2

Richland, L. E., Zur, O., & Holyoak, K. J. (2007, May 25). Cognitive supports for analogies in the mathematics classroom. *Science, 316,* 1128–1129. doi:10.1126/science.1142103

Rittle-Johnson, B. (2006). Promoting transfer: Effects of self-explanation and direct instruction. *Child Development, 77,* 1–15. doi:10.1111/j.1467-8624.2006.00852.x

Ruffman, T., Perner, J., Olson, D. R., & Doherty, M. (1993). Reflecting on scientific thinking: Children's understanding of the hypothesis–evidence relation. *Child Development, 64,* 1617–1636. doi:10.2307/1131459

Schauble, L. (1990). Belief revision in children: The role of prior knowledge and strategies for generating evidence. *Journal of Experimental Child Psychology, 49,* 31–57. doi:10.1016/0022-0965(90)90048-D

Schauble, L. (1996). The development of scientific reasoning in knowledge-rich contexts. *Developmental Psychology, 32,* 102–119. doi:10.1037/0012-1649.32.1.102

Siegler, R. S. (1976). Three aspects of cognitive development. *Cognitive Psychology, 8,* 481–520. doi:10.1016/0010-0285(76)90016-5

Siegler, R. S. (1981). Developmental sequence within and between concepts. *Monographs of the Society for Research in Child Development, 46*(2, Serial No. 189).

Siegler, R. S. (1995). How does change occur: A microgenetic study of number conservation. *Cognitive Psychology, 28,* 225–273.

Siegler, R. S. (1996). *Emerging minds: The process of change in children's thinking.* New York, NY: Oxford University Press.

Siegler, R. S. (2002). Microgenetic studies of self-explanation. In N. Granott & J. Parziale (Eds.), *Microdevelopment: Transition processes in development and learning* (pp. 31–58). New York, NY: Cambridge University Press. doi:10.1017/CBO9780511489709.002

Siegler, R. S. (2005). Children's learning. *American Psychologist, 60,* 769–778. doi:10.1037/0003-066X.60.8.769

Siegler, R. S. (2006). Microgenetic analyses of learning. In W. Damon & R. M. Lerner (Series Eds.) & D. Kuhn & R. S. Siegler (Vol. Eds.), *Handbook of child psychology: Volume 2. Cognition, perception, and language* (6th ed., pp. 464–510). Hoboken, NJ: Wiley.

Siegler, R. S., & Chen, Z. (1998). Developmental differences in rule learning: A microgenetic analysis. *Cognitive Psychology, 36,* 273–310. doi:10.1006/cogp.1998.0686

Siegler, R. S., & Crowley, K. (1991). The microgenetic method: A direct means for studying cognitive development. *American Psychologist, 46,* 606–620. doi:10.1037/0003-066X.46.6.606

Siegler, R. S., & Jenkins, E. (1989). *How children discover new strategies.* Hillsdale, NJ: Erlbaum.

Siegler, R. S., & Opfer, J. E. (2003). The development of numerical estimation: Evidence for multiple representations of numerical quantity. *Psychological Science, 14,* 237–243. doi:10.1111/1467-9280.02438

Singley, M. K., & Anderson, J. R. (1989). *The transfer of cognitive skill.* Cambridge, MA: Harvard University Press.

Sodian, B., Zaitchik, D., & Carey, S. (1991). Young children's differentiation of hypothetical beliefs from evidence. *Child Development, 62,* 753–766. doi:10.2307/1131175

Toth, E., Klahr, D., & Chen, Z. (2000). Bridging research and practice: A research-based classroom intervention for teaching experimentation skills to elementary school children. *Cognition and Instruction, 18,* 423–459. doi:10.1207/S1532690XCI1804_1

Whitehead, A. N. (1929). *The function of reason.* Princeton, NJ: Princeton University Press.

3

Does Folk Science Develop?

Frank C. Keil

All of us are said to have a set of *folk sciences:* intuitive ways of understanding the world in areas such as biology, physical mechanics, and psychology. In addition, these folk sciences are thought to have deep and interesting similarities to the formal sciences. Both are usually described as having coherence and internal consistency, as well as specifying certain foundational or ontological kinds as the critical entities of concern (Carey, 1985; Slaughter & Gopnik, 1996). Folk and formal sciences also have important interrelations through the course of development and education. Thus, children come to appreciate some aspects of formal science as taught to them in the classroom in terms of both changing some of the misconceptions of their folk sciences and better appreciating methods and forms of reasoning used in the formal sciences.

In this chapter, my focus is on the ways in which naïve understandings of the world change in the elementary school years. How is the folk science of a 5-year-old, if there is one at all, different from that of a 10-year-old, or an adult? In what ways do aspects of the formal sciences come to exert influences on folk sciences in developed cultures? I argue that recent research on how we understand the mental representations of concepts and the nature of explanatory understanding also suggest new ways of thinking about what folk science is, how it develops, and how it is related to the more formal sciences. I also argue that without such a new view of what changes, it might seem that not much at all develops in the area of folk scientific understanding.

Traditionally, cognitive development, intuitive theories—and, by implication, the folk sciences—have often been conceived in ways that emphasized the child as an individual trying to make sense of the world on his own. The child is confronted either with natural phenomena or complex artifacts and then deciphers, as best he can, how things work. Cognitive scientists vary considerably in their views of how this process might work, with views ranging from constructivist and information-processing accounts of the child entertaining a series of ever-more-accurate explicit hypotheses to more behaviorist and dynamic systems views of a child acquiring information in a more associative manner than may occur without any explicit hypotheses at all. Some version of these views clearly has merit, because children do learn something about the world around them in terms of grasping its causal patterns; however, a problem with all these developmental accounts arises when one considers the adult end state. When construed as detailed mechanistic models of how the world works, folk science in the vast majority of adults seems to be an abysmal failure. If adults are asked to explain how a natural phenomenon (e.g., a heart pumping blood) or a device (e.g., a toilet flushing a substance) works, their explicit "working knowledge" may amount to little more than a few surface features and a very-high-level functional description that restates the phenomenon. We are surprisingly blind to our own ignorance as well, thinking we understand natural science phenomena and devices far better than we do (Keil, 2006; Lawson, 2006; Rozenblit & Keil, 2002). If such mechanistic models are all there is to folk science, then any account of what develops must be very modest. One doesn't need to posit much learning, regardless of the form, if the end state is an adult deeply mired in ignorance.

Perhaps I have exaggerated the end state a bit for most adults. Many of us have occupations, hobbies, or passions that can lead us to acquire deeper mechanistic understanding. An Olympic sailor really does know how every single piece of equipment on her boat works, such that she could probably take every component completely apart and reassemble it flawlessly. However, such islands of mechanistic expertise only serve to highlight how weak our folk sciences are in most respects. The Olympic sailor is likely to be just as ignorant about the operations of flush toilets and human hearts as her neighbor the accountant. It seems that detailed mechanistic knowledge happens on only rare, highly specialized occasions.

What, then, develops with respect to folk science? In the vast majority of areas, are we barely distinguishable from the young child, with only a few slender slivers of expertise in highly focused areas reflecting our jobs or our passions? Perhaps we know an additional mechanistic tidbit here and there, but nothing that would suggest substantial developmental accomplishments. If we are to construe folk science as the presence of explicit "how things work" diagrams in the head, we may be forced to such a conclusion. Perhaps there are extraordinary limits to how much children and adults can go beyond the core concepts that seem to be present in infancy (Carey & Spelke, 1996). In fact, a much richer array of cognitive abilities may develop during the late preschool and the elementary school years; we simply have to characterize them in different terms. An analysis reveals several classes of such abilities that involve major developmental advances in the ability to

- sense the causal density underlying various phenomena;
- see what sorts of causal relations are relevant and irrelevant to a phenomenon;
- extract coarse causal gists from much more complex patterns;
- distinguish some kinds of causal explanations (e.g., precedents) from other kinds (e.g., mechanisms);
- detect circularity in explanations;
- discover pathways to the most helpful experts;
- evaluate the credibility of speakers both in terms of their motivations, their abilities, and their past performance;
- consider where explanations or empirical investigations are likely to be most fallible; and
- know how to construct an ad hoc explanation on the fly using information that is on hand (even if the ability to retain such explanations is minimal).

If one considers all of these abilities to be part of folk science, then the developmental story is very rich indeed. Moreover, if one acknowledges that an enormous amount of what the child learns is second- or nth-hand through others, folk science can be construed as involving all the ways in which we learn to rely on information in other minds (Keil, Stein, Webb, Billings, & Rozenblit, 2008). In the next section, I briefly explore some of these to get a better sense of what develops.

Understanding the Limits of Scientific Methods

One of the pioneers in characterizing these alternative ways of thinking about what develops with respect to folk science is David Klahr. Klahr has repeatedly shown how children come to appreciate something about science as an enterprise in ways that may be largely orthogonal to having a deep mechanistic understanding. Consider, for example, his studies on the emerging understanding of experimental error (Masnick & Klahr, 2003). There is, in fact, a taxonomy of error types in scientific investigations that one must understand to be able to interpret experimental data appropriately. Building on prior work in the philosophy of science, Masnick and Klahr (2003) proposed one such taxonomy with three types of error that can occur during the following five stages of experimentation: of (a) design; (b) physical setup; (c) execution; (d) outcome measurement; and (e) analysis, with the following kinds of errors occurring at some of those stages: (a) design, (b) measurement, and (c) interpretation. Interpretation errors can occur in all stages, with the other error types occurring in one or two stages. In Masnick and Klahr's study, although second and fourth grade children were quite poor at designing unconfounded experiments to explore the properties of a ramp, they nonetheless had quite a good sense of different kinds of errors. Even the second graders were able to distinguish between the different kinds of error when they justified their actions or their conclusions. Errors of interpretation, however, were more difficult for them to understand. In terms of developmental change, the older children seemed to be much more aware of simultaneous errors as a possibility.

The general pattern seems to be one in which even quite young children have some sense of different kinds of error, but it can take several more years before they can simultaneously consider them and then design unconfounded experiments. A more sophisticated understanding of errors and how they interrelate also seems to be linked to increasing causal understanding of the system that one is exploring (Masnick & Klahr, 2003).

In another line of work on a different aspect of understanding the scientific process, Klahr and his colleagues have shown that, whereas 4-year-olds have a great deal of difficulty learning when evidence is indeterminate versus determinate, 5-year-olds are able to learn how to detect indeterminacy after several training trials and then continue to remember how to do so for several months thereafter (Klahr & Chen, 2003; see also Chapter 1, this volume). Younger children do not immediately sense when evidence is indeterminate; they need to be guided toward that inference, but in the early elementary school years they can learn to do so on one task and then show that understanding on analogous tasks.

Klahr (e.g., 2000) has also conducted monumental work on how children discover rules and principles in highly structured, local domains, a kind of knowledge acquisition that does reflect a form of detailed understanding. Just as learning chess or the rules of a complex video game can involve learning an intricate set of rules and procedures, so too can children come to master the rules of a local system, albeit with important limitations and predictable error patterns. When a domain is well structured with a clear set of explicit rules that form a codified set of principles, children can discover them. Their success here is intriguing in light of the great difficulties that everyone exhibits in folk science domains. Although young children can learn intricate sets of rules governing a system, they and even adults have vastly more difficulty naturally learning the principles governing the workings of everyday devices and natural phenomena.

These few examples hardly exhaust the body of work on children's emerging appreciation of the nature of the scientific enterprise. There is a surprisingly complex body of understanding to be mastered, all of which revolves around an increasing understanding of the limits of inquiry methods, both limits intrinsic to those methods and because of the cognitive limits of those engaging in the investigations. One also sees, however, that the young child does not start from scratch. Instead, a rich array of early emerging insights, sometimes present even in preschoolers, helps children get off the ground. This theme recurs in the other areas that I consider in the following sections. There may be some very basic ways that all of us, including young children, sense how understanding may be limited and how to remedy such limitations.

Sensing Causal Patterns Above and Beyond Those of Mechanism

As much as we might think we aspire to clockworks understanding,[1] we rarely succeed. The world of concrete mechanisms is decidedly unkind to our natural cognitive propensities. This is ironic given how often it is assumed that concrete forms of understanding are simpler, easier, and more developmentally primitive than abstract ones. Yet, there are alternative ways to track causal patterns that may be much more natural to human cognition. One of the simplest may be merely noting what kinds of properties are causally relevant to a domain. Colors, for example, tend to be more richly causally connected to natural kinds than they are to artifacts. The color of gold is closely linked to its atomic nature, and the color of many animals helps explain a range of phenomena, from mating habits to adaptations for habitats. In contrast, for most artifacts, color is often

---

[1]The term *clockworks understanding* is meant to indicate understanding of causal mechanisms in full detail, that is, in terms of all the causal interactions among all the parts of a system at a foundational level of explanation. For example, a clockworks understanding of a cylinder lock would entail knowing each separable part, its function, and how it interacts causally with all other parts, including hierarchical assemblies. A clockworks understanding of a kidney might occur at multiple levels, ranging from the biochemical to the physical/anatomical, but at any such level would consist of an exhaustive mechanistic account of all components (e.g., cells) and their interactions.

inconsequential. Color is not causally connected to our understandings of chairs, toilets, or helicopters. More generally, there are profiles of the causal relevancy of feature types (e.g., color, surface markings, shape) for various categories (e.g., animals, plants, natural substances, artifacts). Not only do children seem to "know" these profiles, but even some nonhuman primates can sense the differential relevance of color for food as opposed to, for example, tools (Santos, Hauser, & Spelke, 2002). Moreover, children as young as age 5 will use these differential profiles to evaluate explanations offered by others, judging that an alleged expert who emphasizes color, the precise number of parts, and surface markings in an explanation of a novel tool is less likely to know what he is talking about than another expert who emphasizes size, strength, and shape. When children hear experts making similar claims about novel animals or plants, however, they more likely to accept the experts' arguments (Keil, 2010).

Unlike clockworks understandings, which usually seem explicit in nature, children and adults can track causal patterns at other levels without always being consciously aware that they have done so. For example, many adults do not realize that they routinely describe the global purpose or function of objects (e.g., "A hammer is for x") but would not do so for natural kinds ("A tiger is for x"), even though they describe the functions of parts for both kinds ("A hammer's claws are for x," "A tiger's claws are for x"). Although it is true that young children will sometimes accept functional descriptions of entire natural kinds (Kelemen, 1999), they nonetheless are more discriminating in their naturalistic patterns of discovery, a behavior close to that explored so extensively by Klahr. For example, when preschoolers are taught to ask questions of a puppet about novel artifacts and animals, they are much more likely to ask what the artifact as a whole is for than they are for animals. In contrast, they ask roughly equally about the purposes of the parts of animals and artifacts (Greif, Kemler-Nelson, Keil, & Gutierrez, 2006). Although most adults are not consciously aware of knowing these distinctions, even preschoolers use them to guide their discovery process.

These kinds of abstract causal expectations are found in preverbal infants as well. It is now well established that preverbal infants have several expectations about inanimate physical objects, for example, that they cannot act on each other at a distance, that they persist when out of sight, and that solids cannot interpenetrate (Baillargeon, 2008; Spelke, Breinlinger, Macomber, & Jacobson, 1992). These expectations, however, might be said to involve concrete representations of objects and their interactions rather than more abstract representations. That view may not be correct given the ways in which infants have expectations about these principles holding for completely novel physical objects and situations; moreover, their reasoning is often described in very general and abstract terms, such as that physical objects will persist in time and space unless certain classes of interventions occur (Baillargeon, 2008). Other situations seem to require even more abstract causal understandings. Consider, for example, the pervasive pattern that intentional agents cause situations to go from disorder to order. When adults see a set of objects become transformed from a disordered collection into an array that is ordered along one or more dimensions (e.g., color, shape, size, kind), they will strongly infer that the change was caused by an intentional agent. By contrast, if an ordered array becomes disordered, adults envision a much wider range of agents, including both intentional agents and completely inanimate ones, such as when a bowling ball knocks over a neatly ordered set of pins.

Adults can become tongue-tied in their attempts to explain why only intentional agents can create order. Their intuition seems to revolve around the idea that agents must have some kind of idealized image in mind that guides their actions, or at least some kind of rule that they use to impose structure on an otherwise-unstructured set of objects. Even this is not strictly correct, because many quite simple organisms can create nonrandom structures, and even chemicals can form highly ordered crystal structures from amorphous liquids, but there is a clear bias in most contexts to expect intentional agents as the forces behind ordering events. These intuitions are also strong in young preschoolers, who are at near-ceiling levels of performance in linking intentional agents exclusively to a wide range of ordering events. These include many events they had never considered before, such as having a randomly arranged set of objects become reordered such that objects of one kind are always in a complementary spatial arrangement with objects of another kind, though even as the full set of complementary pairs is still arranged at random (Keil & Newman, 2008). Despite these extremely consistent and confident judgments, preschoolers are completely unable to explain their judgments. They just know that certain events could be attributed only to intentional agents.

The strength of these preschool intuitions, combined with a striking inability to explain them, suggests that such intuitions might be present in a nonverbal form even earlier. My colleagues and I therefore conducted a series of studies with preverbal infants to determine whether they looked longer at events in which inanimate agents created order than when they created disorder. Such a pattern was found in several distinct studies with infants under 1 year of age (Newman, Keil, Kuhlmeier, & Wynn, 2010). It is very difficult to characterize these infants' understanding in a manner other than a set of highly abstract principles about intentionality, agency, and randomness.

Children are able to use these ways of tracking high-level causal information to get a sense of how knowledge is clustered in the minds of others. Starting in the preschool years (Lutz & Keil, 2002), children are able to infer that phenomena sharing broad causal patterns, such as those governing physical mechanics versus biological functioning, are likely to be understood by the same expert. Thus, someone who has a detailed grasp of one phenomenon in biology is seen as more likely to have a deep grasp of another biological phenomenon than a person who has a deep grasp of one phenomenon in mechanics. This inference holds even if the two phenomena in biology are quite different, such as plant growth and human disease (Erickson, Keil, & Lockhart, 2010). By kindergarten, children can cluster experts in such large domains as physical mechanics, living kinds, social interactions, economics, and the like, and they do so by considering very broad and abstract causal patterns that are common to such domains (Keil et al., 2008). There are major developmental changes as well concerning the ability to avoid distraction by other forms of expertise (Danovitch & Keil, 2004; Keil et al., 2008), but at all ages children are able to use their sense of high-level causal patterns to make at least modest inferences about the division of cognitive labor in the culture around them.

In short, one way to address the apparent poverty of detailed mechanistic understandings is to recognize that a person who is clearly unable to provide virtually any details about the workings of biological systems, natural phenomena, or everyday devices, can be quite sophisticated in the ability to sense how broader causal patterns are linked to large domains such as intentional agents, living kinds, and tools. Moreover, such individuals can use their knowledge of these broader causal patterns to discern relevant sources of expertise. The presence of these forms of causal understanding in preschoolers, and even to some extent in infants, raises questions about what develops. To what extent do older children and adults go beyond these very early ways of tracking high-level causal patterns and area regularities? The full answer is not yet clear, but there are at least some dramatic patterns of change that suggest what develops and why.

Changing Patterns of Causal Understanding

Although children certainly show some increases in their causal understandings at the level of mechanism, I have suggested that progress in this area should not be the sole benchmark of emerging causal understanding. What, then, develops at levels other than clockworks understandings? One developmental change may involve more subtle refinements in understanding causal patterns at an intermediate level of generalization. Consider, for example, changes in thought about essences. A large body of evidence now supports the idea that children, toddlers, and perhaps even infants have essentialist biases in terms of how they interpret the behaviors and properties of other entities (e.g., Gelman, 2003; Newman & Keil, 2008). Children of all ages seem to assume that, for natural kinds at least, there are microstructural essences that are causally responsible for most phenomenal properties and behaviors of entities such as living kinds. This, then, is a form of highly abstract causal understanding.

Beneath that level of essentialist understanding, however, lie questions about how such a causal relationship is to be instantiated. For example, is the essence that results in surface properties evenly distributed throughout the substance of a natural kind, or does it have a central focus out of which causal arrows project to create surface features? It may seem obvious to adults that essences are homogeneously distributed, but this relation is not at all obvious to children, even those who are in the early years of elementary school. Thus, when children are asked to choose between causal patterns that have essential features evenly distributed throughout an organism versus patterns that have essences concentrated in just one location, younger children tend to choose focal locations in which the essence is localized in just one small region within the natural kind such that only that region is seen as causing surface properties. There is then a marked developmental shift to more distributed views that occurs in the later elementary school years (Newman & Keil, 2008). For artifacts, there is no shift, because children and adults alike tend to think that essences are localized to a particular part of the internal architecture. Thus, a particular local piece of machinery is thought to be the causal essence that distinguishes otherwise very similar artifacts, such as microwaves versus toaster ovens. For adults, of course, this is not true for similar natural kinds.

This developmental shift is not to a highly specific account of internal structure. Thus, fourth graders who strongly prefer the homogeneous view of essences still have almost no concrete idea of what the essences are. Almost no fourth graders referred to DNA or some other version of a genetic code (Newman & Keil, 2008). Their notion of a distributed essence was still largely unspecified in terms of its constituents. Nonetheless, they strongly felt that the essence could be found throughout the insides of an animal or plant. This understanding, then, represents a major developmental shift, and one that is in the direction of a more accurate account of real causal relations. Of course, the actual causal story of how microstructural biological insides cause surface properties is vastly more complicated and requires a grasp of the ontogenetic unfolding of biological structures and properties from a single fertilized egg, none of which most children or adults know. Thus, there is developmental change here, but all of it occurs at a level far above that of knowledge of specific biological components and their workings. It may well be that some of the more dramatic developmental changes in causal understanding occur at this intermediate level, below that of the highest causal gloss of a system but still far above the level of concrete, specific mechanisms.

The initial bias toward more focal causes may be related to a broader bias in terms of how children and adults alike interpret causal pathways. In particular, in several categorization tasks, people tended to favor the causes in a causal chain as opposed to the effects, even when both were equally well correlated with a set of entities; they also tended to favor the first causal element in a chain. This bias, known as the *causal status effect* (Ahn & Kim, 2000), has been demonstrated at many ages (Ahn, Gelman, Amsterlaw, Hohnstein, & Kalish, 2000; Meunier & Cordier, 2009). It may be that, all other things being equal, this bias causes a tendency to favor accounts in which there are focal single causes. It is not clear how children come to overrule this early bias, because they do not acquire a specific DNA mediated mechanism; but they do seem to first get the insight for nonliving natural kinds and then extend it to living kinds (Newman & Keil, 2008).

What might be some other ways in which causal understanding develops at this intermediate level between very broad causal biases, such as essentialism and specific concrete mechanisms? Some are likely to revolve around learning to apprehend such causal phenomena as negative and positive feedback loops, interactions instead of simple main effects, homeostasis, and symbiosis. In each case, children proceed from a position of ignorance or misconception to a closer approximation of the real causal pattern while nonetheless knowing almost nothing about the actual biological or physical instantiation of the process. These levels of causal understanding of the real world lie largely uncharted in developmental research, and yet they may be where some of the most dramatic changes occur.

Learning to Use Causal Information to
Guide Discovery and Exploration

In addition to learning more about midlevel causal patterns that provide some information about the functioning of entities, children also learn about other sorts of causal information that they can use to guide information-seeking behavior.

This knowledge is less about how things function at any level and more about general causal characteristics. For example, adults have strong intuitions of the domains that are governed by rich causal relations as opposed to those that have almost no intrinsic causal patterns. We all know that "dogs that hunt" is a much more causally rich category than "dogs with red collars." This knowledge in turn enables us to infer that there are likely to be expert resources on dogs that hunt but not on dogs with red collars, or that if we want to learn more about either topic there will be much more to learn about the category of dogs that hunt. It also tells us when we are likely to know all there is to know about a category as opposed to being novices in need of help. In short, some categories are merely categories because of one criterion that is common to all members. Others have members that cluster because of a rich network of causal relations, such as those behavioral, biological, and physical attributes that interact to make some kinds of dogs successful hunting dogs.

Despite the seemingly obvious contrast between these two kinds of categories, young children do not seem to grasp that one is much more causally dense than another. When kindergarteners are asked to judge which person would know more—one who knows all about dogs with red collars or one who knows all about dogs that hunt—they perform at chance levels. In contrast, fourth graders have the strong conviction that the person who knows all about dogs that hunt knows a great deal more (Keil, 2010). Across a wide variety of cases, young children have great difficulty distinguishing between categories that have a rich causal density and those that are causally empty and defined merely by a single criterion. By fourth grade, they are quite sophisticated.

However it seems that fourth graders have not developed a rich understanding of the functioning of members of these causally rich categories but rather have acquired the coarser sense that there is a complex web of causal relations underlying some categories and not others. Indeed, many of the fourth graders who strongly preferred some categories over others were often unable to provide any details at all about the nature of those causally dense relations (Keil, 2010). How, then, could such an understanding be of any use? One important benefit concerns heuristics that tell a child when a domain is worthy of future study or one for which they should keep track of experts whom they might want to access at a later date. Similarly, a sense of causal density might guide children's evaluations of the plausibility of alleged experts. Experts have knowledge about causal substance as opposed to more trivial knowledge. When we expand folk science by learning to use knowledge that exists in other minds, the ability to track causal density might be valuable even if it offers little direct insight into the nature of a category on its own. Kindergartners do not seem to be very able to use causal density to such an end, whereas fourth graders can do so with great potential effectiveness. It may be that future tasks will uncover some degree of this skill in younger children, but the studies conducted so far suggest that in those early ages it is likely to be fragile and not nearly as useful a guide to fruitful domains of information.

Many other kinds of causal information might be used in a similar manner to guide searches for more information, to know when to defer, and to evaluate alleged experts and alleged areas of expertise. For example, one can know whether information in an explanation seems to cohere as opposed to being a grab bag of largely unrelated statements. Thus, one should be more satisfied with explanations that show coherence, and seek information that increases coherence where possible. There are several ways to assess coherence that again can work at levels far above those of mechanism. For example, one can assess the likelihood that individual statements will be true given that others are true on the basis of a sense of conjoint probabilities of various event types (A. J. L. Harris & Hahn, 2009). Coherence can also be crudely assessed by the simple extent to which a set of statements tend to refer to each other without direct contradictions.

One can also know whether an explanation provides a concise gist as opposed to expanding on true but excessive detail for the task at hand. This sense can go above the level of mechanism in several ways. For example, there are structural clues to which ideas elaborate on others. Text passages that contain more ideas on which others elaborate are seen as creating better gists than those that contain more ideas that are themselves elaborations. Gists can be constructed in this way by automated systems that have no real grasp of conceptual content (Marcu, 2000), and it appears that similar heuristics are easily used by laypeople (Rottman & Keil, in press).

Another way to evaluate explanations involves knowing that lines of evidence in an explanation provide a stronger argument when they converge from several different angles as opposed to repeatedly coming from the same subdomain (a very old idea in the philosophy of science known as *consilience;* William Whewell, 1847). One can sense this pattern of convergence without grasping much detail (Kim & Keil, 2003; Kim, Yopchick, & de Kwaadsteniet, 2008), and it seems likely that children may acquire sensitivity to such information during middle childhood. For example, in related tasks that examined the use of sample diversity in inductive reasoning, there is marked improvement in the use of diversity during the elementary and middle school years (Heit & Hahn, 2001; Rhodes, Brickman, & Gelman, 2008).

Several current research projects exploring these and other facets of causal information that might guide searches for the best explanation. On the basis of preliminary findings, there seem to be marked developmental improvements in children's abilities to use all this information during the elementary school years. Some of the most important developmental changes may occur at this level of tracking causal patterns and using such patterns to seek and assess explanations.

Evaluating Explanations on Noncausal Grounds

I have argued that there are many levels of causal information in the world and that a tendency to focus on a level corresponding to clockworks mechanisms grossly underestimates the ways that both adults and children can use causal information to further their understanding. I have further argued that young children, well before the start of formal schooling, have a head start on this process by showing impressive sensitivities to causal patterns at these higher levels. At the same time, there are marked developmental changes during the elementary school years as children start to sense more finely grained causal patterns and then use those patterns in ways that involve seeking and evaluating knowledge, and knowing when they are and are not likely to need to defer to others. This account might seem to be the full story of folk science development, but there are several other aspects to what we would call folk science in all cultures that do not directly involve the apprehension of causal information at any level.

One facet concerns *circularity* in explanations. Although even adults can embrace circular arguments when the circles are large enough, a very small and explicit circle is easy for adults to discount. If one encounters an explanation of how brakes work that states that they work by reducing the speed of a device, one immediately realizes that no real explanation has been provided. The ability to see such circularities covers both causal circularities (e.g., the one just mentioned) as well as noncausal ones. For example, an explanation that a triangle has lines creating three vertices might be considered circular because it merely restates that it is a figure with three angles. It appears that the ability to see circularity in both causal and noncausal domains is a gradually emerging ability that may be crudely present in preschoolers in the right sorts of supporting contexts, but it becomes much more powerful during the elementary school years (Baum, Danovitch, & Keil, 2008; Sperber & Mercier, in press). In its most general terms, this ability seems to involve a sense of the actual circle of propositions regardless of the details of their content, because circularity can be stated over essentially blank propositions represented only by unelaborated and largely unfamiliar words (Brem 2003; Rips, 2002).

A different class of factors concerns a burgeoning literature on information about an informant's *competence* (P. L. Harris, 2007). Children use several forms of information to either discount or embrace what an informant tells them. If an informant has made factual mistakes in the past, even preschoolers are likely to discount any information that is provided after that point (Jaswal & Neely, 2006; Koenig & Harris, 2005; Vanderborght & Jaswal, 2009). If an informant is accepted by others whom the child trusts, the child is more likely to trust the informant—a kind of transitivity of the trust relationship. If an informant indicates hesitation, lack of confidence, or simply seems to be stupid, all those factors can cause the informant's testimony to be discounted. It is now clear that even preschoolers have intuitions along these lines (see preceding discussion), even as the skills become more robust during the school years.

A different dimension of trust in testimony concerns inferences about the motivations underlying another's testimony. When someone declares something that is blatantly self-serving, adults are usually quite likely to be skeptical about its truth. The candidate who declares that he is certainly the most qualified for a job is much less likely to be believed than the candidate who declares that another is the most qualified for a job (even if that is not a winning strategy). By the second grade, children clearly take into account such inferred motivations. It is interesting that younger children may not able to use this skill, and will sometimes actually think that statements supporting self-interest are more true (Mills & Keil, 2005, 2008), again indicating an important area of development in a broader characterization of folk science.

It might seem that the literature on children's trust is not the same as their having folk scientific knowledge, but a little reflection on the nature of formal science reveals that it would be odd if it were not also part of folk science. The formal sciences depend profoundly on trust and deference (Hardwig, 1991).

Even the supposed polymaths of earlier times, who are often envisioned as laboring as lone wolves, are well known for acknowledging how much of their formal science depended on others. Indeed, Newton felt a large debt to those scientists who preceded him. Although Newton is famous for laboring endless hours alone in an effort to understand many areas of physics and mathematics (Gleick, 2003), his interactions with others had profound influences on the growth of his ideas. In a 1676 letter to Robert Hooke, Newton explicitly acknowledged his debts when he wrote, "If I have seen further it is only by standing on the shoulders of giants" (quoted in Turnbull, 1959, p. 297). Elsewhere, Newton acknowledged the clear need for a division of cognitive labor, and in doing so cast doubt on the idea of true polymaths even in his time:

> To explain all nature is too difficult a task for any one man or even for any one age. 'Tis much better to do a little with certainty, & leave the rest for others that come after you, than to explain all things by conjecture without making sure of anything. (quoted in Westfall, 1980, p. 643)

Newton here seems to be capturing something quite basic about formal science: It is possible to have detailed highly specific knowledge in narrow slivers of expertise, but even in the early 1700s one could not hope to have comprehensive understandings across many domains. Formal scientists had to rely on slivers of expertise in other minds to support their own.

Perhaps folk sciences should be understood in different terms, as instances of the actions of solitary agents making sense of the world on their own. This conjecture, however, does not ring true. A little reflection reveals that the body of information that even a young child acquires through indirect means is enormous. For many preschoolers, most of the animals that they can recognize may have been learned through books or stories. The animal vocabularies of many North American children may be dominated by words for large African mammals, even when many of those children have never seen any of those animals directly, even in zoos. Witches, ghosts, and dinosaurs are all common concepts in preschoolers, even though we can be quite sure they have never encountered them firsthand.

It also does not seem to be the case that preschoolers are completely gullible sponges, indiscriminately absorbing any information that comes their way. To be sure, they can be fooled in ways that older children cannot, but they also seem to have some sense of the plausibility of explanations and can reject a wildly implausible explanation as well as an older child or an adult can (Shtulman & Carey, 2007). They see some claims as much sillier than others and will say so with confidence. Despite claims that children are ideal propagators of memes because of their complete gullibility (Dawkins, 1993), they are in fact quite able to doubt what some adults say, and they do so on reasonable grounds. In this way, they are able to titrate the value of information that they learn through others.

Thus, a large proportion of the information that children acquire about the world is learned not firsthand but through other sources, and from early on in the preschool years they understand that sources vary in quality. The ability to evaluate such sources is therefore not just a late-developing skill arising from formal instruction but instead a foundational part of the intrinsically social nature of knowledge acquisition. Whether it be learning a new word, how a device works, or about an invisible entity, children as young as preschool will focus more on information that conforms with positive evaluations of others.

This sense of the importance of sources of information may build on related abilities that appear in infancy. Consider, for example, differences in the extent to which infants rely on social referencing as a function of how much they trust and are familiar with adults who are indicating an emotional reaction to a situation or a stimulus (Corriveau, Meints, & Harris, 2009). They will titrate the perceived usefulness of another's emotional attitudes as a function of past experience with that person. They will also tend to trust others more when their attachment style to them is more secure.

Influences of Folk Science on Formal Science

In most cultures of the world today, folk science is no longer the only game in town. Young children in many cultures have heard of scientists, or other kinds of experts in science, technology, engineering, and math, even if they often hold narrow stereotypes of those experts (Newton & Newton, 1998). The question then arises as to how these emerging senses of formal science, and scientists, are linked to folk science. Do notions of formal science primarily trickle down to influence folk science, do ideas in folk science primarily invade formal sciences largely as misconceptions and misconstruals, or is there a more complex commerce in both directions? My sense is that the influence clearly runs in both directions and that the nature of these influences may be a major area of developmental change during the school years. In addition, we now may want to see the folk sciences as not simply clouding the formal sciences but as often providing cognitive tools that make the formal sciences more tractable and reliable.

Consider some ways in which folk science expertise might make a child's understanding of the formal sciences become more nuanced. Take, for example, the ability of elementary school children to consider an informant's self-interests in evaluating the message (Mills & Keil, 2005). Surprisingly, such factors are not always taken into account in the formal sciences. Indeed, it is only a relatively recent practice for newspaper reports of formal science research to describe the funding for that research and whether the research findings might benefit the funding agents. Even then, such practices tend to be regularly used at only the most prestigious national newspapers. Similarly, only recently have some scientific journals and universities started to ask for such information from formal scientists. Other subtle cues that children use to evaluate the credibility of sources may be similarly incorporated into the formal sciences, although such effects are not yet documented by experimental research.

Formal scientists may also benefit from children's skills at using coarse gists of causal relations to infer domains of knowledge and patterns of deference. Ask formal scientists how they know which experts to consult when buttressing their own activities, and they will almost always say that knowledge is intuitive and built from hunches and implicit heuristics. Given that even preschoolers use such heuristics to infer how knowledge clusters in other minds and how understanding of one phenomenon suggests understandings of other causally similar phenomena, it seems reasonable that the same heuristics are at work in formal scientists. For example, a cell biologist who is unsure about the physical constraints governing the sensitivity of electron microscopes has hunches about which colleagues to consult that are quite different from when that same biologist is unsure about the thermodynamics of a particular chemical reaction. Although that scientist may have only the most minimal knowledge of each of those other areas, she may have enough of a rough sense of the underlying causal terrains to know whom to consult.

In a similar way, formal science is deeply dependent on creating idealizations so that systems can be studied in a tractable manner, a skill that is widely used but that may arise from much more intuitive processes that begin in childhood. Scientists also make simplifying assumptions so as to prune a causal briar patch into something more elegant and cognitively manageable. They seem to do so in several ways. First, they tend to stick to one level of a reductionist hierarchy, not diving deeper to lower levels (Owens, 1989; Wilson & Keil, 1998). For example, some psychologists may try to envision how cognitive structures and processes are constrained by the biology of the nervous system, but they rarely if ever try to fully specify a mechanistic model of what is happening at the cellular level. Similarly, while attending to chemistry, the biologist also stops short of details that occupy chemists. Thus, few biologists ask how quantum bond angles are relevant to an aspect of cellular metabolism. Because we don't have a reliable way of specifying levels of reduction and whether there really are clearly objective levels that apply in the same way across all the subspecialties of such major areas as psychology, biology, chemistry, and physics, it is difficult to understand how scientists refrain from crossing levels. Somehow, scientists in practice draw these lines all the time to make their task more manageable, and they do so in a way that allows their science to advance.

A second kind of simplifying assumption is to make one's science "local" by ruling out those tendrils of causal influence that, although technically present, can be ignored for the purposes of the scientific task at hand. Without such simplifications, one runs the risk of having to consider the ways in which almost any event can potentially have a causal influence on any other that follows later—a scientific version of the "butterfly effect" problem (Hilborn, 2004). Elga (2007) considered this problem in detail and suggested that both scientists and laypeople see the world as localized nets of causal relations. Those nets form clumps and clusters that can be considered as stand-alone systems in which more remote influences are disregarded. When trying to understand the behavior of billiard balls on a table, we tend to consider just the forces at play between objects on the table, even though there are very small but real influences exerted by the moon; the people in the room; and countless other objects and events, such as sound waves. We may technically eliminate effects that would have to travel faster than the speed of light to have an influence (things outside what physicists call the *light cone;* Elga, 2007), but there is still a vast array of other real influences that are simply below some threshold in almost all matters of scientific inquiry.

Finally, scientists construct ideal systems that depart from reality in clearly fictitious but necessary ways to do the science. For a given task, physicists may ignore friction or air resistance. In another, biologists may disregard mutation rates on a genome. In still another, psychologists may not consider the time of day or time in a semester when conducting a study on reasoning. However, all these idealizations are exquisitely context sensitive and are adjusted on the fly in ways that are usually implicit but that can be central to the success of an experiment. For certain problems in mechanics, friction or air resistance is everything. Some questions in biology, including a number of formal computational models, rely critically on mutation rates. Finally, we all know how time of day or semester can wreak havoc with some kinds of cognitive tasks (Anderson & Revelle, 1994). Scientists effortlessly slip into idealizations, sometimes carefully specifying the idealized dimensions, at other times doing so in a largely implicit manner, but always in ways that can significantly depart from reality by making what can be enormous simplifications.

One analysis suggests three distinct kinds of idealizations: (a) those driven by a need for simplicity to make a problem tractable even if it distorts relations; (b) those in which only factors that make a causal difference for giving rise to the phenomenon are considered; and (c) those that acknowledge multiple idealizations for the same set of phenomena, all of which might be true but that can also be incompatible with each other (M. Weisberg, 2011). All three forms involve intricate cognitive decisions about how to construct a particular idealization. Moreover, although there are attempts to formalize some ways of constructing such idealizations (M. Weisberg, 2011), much of the process appears to occur at a more implicit level, a level that might also be at work in everyday folk science. Even in the heights of analytical science, the process through which scientists focus on certain causal processes and relations as most relevant is described as more of an art than an analytically driven procedure (Strevens, 2009).

It seems quite plausible that all of the processes that formal scientists use to simplify problems to make them cognitively tractable have their roots in the earliest forms of folk science in young children. Thus, with even more limited cognitive capacities, children must necessarily make gross simplifications in their attempts to understand complex systems. Scientists do not yet know what heuristics they use, but they might well show patterns that are later incorporated into the more formal sciences, such as tending to stay at one level of analysis, ignoring remote influences, and thinking in terms of idealizations even when they do not explicitly characterize them as such. One could even characterize some of their early attempts to induce oversimplified rules for systems as forms of idealizations (Klahr, 2000).

Influences of Formal Science on Folk Science

In the other direction, information in the formal sciences can trickle down to influence the folk sciences in several distinct ways. First, the formal sciences may provide more precise sources on which to ground deference. They can do this by providing labels or institutions as brands of expertise. They can also create stereotypes of scientists that, although misleading in many ways (Newton & Newton, 1998), may have some crude utility as indicators of more reliable sources of information. Similarly, stereotypes of laboratories, experiments, and research institutions may serve as rough guides to areas of expertise. The mere idea of such groups of specialized experts may prompt a search for cues to areas of expertise when one is in doubt.

The formal sciences may also introduce ideas that, although barely understood, can become seeds around which a new area of folk understanding can crystallize. Consider, for example, the concept of a *gene*. Most Western adults are very familiar with the term and may think they understand its meaning in some detail, even if they know little beyond the idea that something inside each of our body's cells has information that is responsible for traits. This idea, however, can quickly become a way of instantiating essentialism and of offering pat explanations for complex behaviors (the "gene for x" syndrome that is so prevalent in the press). This trickle-down effect may often cause serious distortions in laypeople's understanding, as well as in some scientists. Thus, the expected yields of the Human Genome Project (http://www.ornl.gov/sci/techresources/Human_Genome/home.shtml) were vastly higher than the actual yields to date (Goldstein, 2009). Laypeople and some scientists seemed to assume that there would be straightforward accounts of genetic influences on disease, such that certain alleles would be uncovered for various widespread diseases. Instead, there seems to be an extraordinary array of very rare variants that create disease, often in complex combinations, such that for the vast majority of common diseases, as well as for highly heritable traits (e.g., physical height), scientists have little idea of the genetic causes. "Genes" may have been a convenient conceptual hook on which to hang ideas about simple classes of general causes, but the ways that laypeople interpret them may also have resulted in several distortions, some of which may have originally come from formal scientists in their attempts to explain the benefits of the Human Genome Project.

Another downward influence of formal science on folk science is to describe a new technology around which new folk ideas can be organized. In some cases, however, the new technology is unwittingly interpreted in metaphorical terms that can cause serious distortions as well. Consider, for example, how the layperson typically understands neuroimaging data such as those generated by functional magnetic resonance imaging (fMRI). Partly because of some distortions introduced by the ways that scientists present information, the layperson often assumes that fMRI images of the brain with various areas "glowing" are analogous to a brain X-ray, when in fact such representations are only superficially similar and in reality reflect massive amounts of data processing and inference. People are unaware of the large inferential distance that separates initial signals received in an fMRI scanner and the final graphical representations. When they seize on the fMRI representations as photograph-like X-rays of the brain, they introduce other distortions of understanding (Roskies, 2008). In addition, they tend to weigh the information provided by neuroimaging data far more strongly than its real informational value would justify (McCabe & Castel, 2008; D. S. Weisberg, Keil, Goodstein, Rawson, & Gray, 2008).

These trickle-down effects describe ways in which formal science ideas can become distorted in folk science, even as they can also provide some new ways of understanding phenomena. There are, of course, many other influences of the folk sciences concerning ways to engage in inquiry and discovery. Older children do gradually learn subtle aspects of science as practice, such as causes of error, the need for decent sample sizes, and the importance of various controls. One poorly understood question concerns the extent to which the properties of the sciences as practices filter down to laypeople in ways that go beyond explicit instruction in the classroom. Does one learn to appreciate some of the methodological principles of the sciences by simply growing up in a culture and observing references to scientific studies in the media? There seems to be little evidence of such influences to date.

In short, there are many influences between the formal sciences and folk sciences that are not simple additions of formal knowledge onto the informal, or simple warnings about the fallibility of formal scientists arising from intuitions about the fallibility of folk scientists. Instead, the reciprocal effects are much more complex, both within the individual and within the mutual interactions in learning environment. Researchers are just beginning to understand how such influences among folk and formal sciences might work.

Conclusions and Future Directions

From one point of view, in which the folk sciences are described as mechanistic models of how the world works, the question of what develops seems quite mysterious because the end state is so minimal. Adults have almost no detailed understandings of how most everyday devices work, how living kinds function, or why natural phenomena occur as they do. This ignorance is often masked by illusions of explanatory competence that are easy to document in adults. If this is all there is to folk science, then development simply consists of just a few largely insignificant additions to the very coarse causal understandings we find in young children. From a different point of view that embraces a much broader notion of folk scientific competence, however, the developmental story is much more interesting.

This broader view includes an emerging understanding of discovery and induction processes, an area where the work of David Klahr has been so pioneering and pivotal. It also includes different ways of characterizing how individuals track causal structure and relations. There is a rich array of causal patterns at levels far above those of concrete mechanisms, and it is at these levels that young children are surprisingly adept in sensing patterns for such factors as causes of order, ways to ascribe function, and domains with rich versus shallow causal underpinnings. Children track all this information while being largely ignorant about mechanistic details. Development often seems to consist of moving down a bit in the levels at which information is tracked but still staying at levels above the mechanistic. Thus, elementary school children may shift in how they think essences are instantiated, but even the more mature form of such an understanding has none of the details of such elements as DNA. Children are then able to use all the ways they track causal patterns to evaluate both the quality of explanations and the credibility of alleged experts. They are also able to make inferences about likely areas of expertise and how to navigate the divisions of cognitive labor that are so intrinsic to all cultures. In all these respects, although even preschoolers show some evidence of these skills, there are dramatic increases in their effectiveness over the elementary and middle school years.

Folk science also develops in ways that do not involve causal information, such as techniques for evaluating the structures of explanations (e.g., circularity) and the ways in which the motives of informants and experts need to be considered in evaluating any information or explanations that they might provide. Here, too, there are major changes during the school years. The social infrastructure that supports and constrains scientific thought is complex and is an area where there is a great deal of growth during middle childhood.

All of these facets of folk science that go beyond simple mechanistic understanding also have an influence on the formal sciences. Many of the formal science practices, such as constructing gists, deferring to others, and making idealizations, are not taught and are not associated with explicit procedures. It seems very likely that formal scientists use those untaught intuitive skills that developed during early and middle childhood and that an understanding of how those aspects of folk science develop will greatly inform formal science as well. Finally, because of these subtle patterns, the ways that formal sciences influence the folk sciences are much more intricate and full of cycles of interactions than they are the simple replacing of misconceptions with correct ones or the grafting of details onto gaps in folk science.

The most provocative implication here is that we may learn a good deal more about how the formal sciences function by looking at all the ways that the folk sciences develop most dramatically, ways that involve causal patterns far above those of mechanism and that rely heavily on the social infrastructures in which folk sciences are embedded.

References

Ahn, W., Gelman, S. A., Amsterlaw, J. A., Hohenstein, J., & Kalish, C. W. (2000). Causal status effect in children's categorization. *Cognition, 76,* B35–B43. doi:10.1016/S0010-0277(00)00077-9

Ahn, W., & Kim, N. S. (2000). The causal status effect in categorization: An overview. In D. L. Medin (Ed.), *The psychology of learning and motivation: Vol. 40. Advances in research and theory* (pp. 23–66). San Diego, CA: Academic Press.

Anderson, K. J., & Revelle, W. (1994). Impulsivity and time of day: Is impulsivity related to the decay of arousal? *Journal of Personality and Social Psychology, 67,* 334–344. doi:10.1037/0022-3514.67.2.334

Baillargeon, R. (2008). Innate ideas revisited: For a principle of persistence in infants' physical reasoning. *Perspectives on Psychological Science, 3,* 2–13. doi:10.1111/j.1745-6916.2008.00056.x

Baum, L. A., Danovitch, J. H., & Keil, F. C. (2008). Children's sensitivity to circular explanations. *Journal of Experimental Child Psychology, 100,* 146–155. doi:10.1016/j.jecp.2007.10.007

Brem, S. K. (2003). Structure and pragmatics in informal argument: Circularity and question-begging. *Trends in Cognitive Sciences, 7,* 147–149. doi:10.1016/S1364-6613(03)00026-3

Carey, S. (1985). *Conceptual change in childhood.* Cambridge, MA: MIT Press.

Carey, S., & Spelke, E. (1996). Science and core knowledge. *Philosophy of Science, 63,* 515–533. doi:10.1086/289971

Corriveau, K. H., Meints, K., & Harris, P. L. (2009). Early tracking of informant accuracy and inaccuracy. *British Journal of Developmental Psychology, 27,* 331–342. doi:10.1348/026151008X310229

Danovitch, J. H., & Keil, F. C. (2004). Should you ask a fisherman or a biologist? Developmental shifts in ways of clustering knowledge. *Child Development, 75,* 918–931. doi:10.1111/j.1467-8624.2004.00714.x

Dawkins, R. (1993). Viruses of the mind. In B. Dahlbom (Ed.), *Dennett and his critics: Demystifying mind* (pp. 13–27). Oxford, England: Blackwell.

Elga, A. (2007). Isolation and folk physics. In H. Price & R. Corry (Eds.), *Causation, physics, and the constitution of reality: Russell's republic revisited* (pp. 106–119). New York, NY: Oxford University Press.

Erickson, J. E., Keil, F. C., & Lockhart, K. L. (2010). Sensing the coherence of biology in contrast to psychology: Young children's use of causal relations to distinguish two foundational domains. *Child Development, 81,* 390–409. doi:10.1111/j.1467-8624.2009.01402.x

Gelman, S. A. (2003). *The essential child: Origins of essentialism in everyday thought.* Oxford, England: Oxford University Press.

Gleick, J. (2003). *Isaac Newton.* New York, NY: Vintage Books.

Goldstein, D. B. (2009). Common genetic variation and human traits. *The New England Journal of Medicine, 360,* 1696–1698. doi:10.1056/NEJMp0806284

Greif, M. L., Kemler Nelson, D. G., Keil, F. C., & Gutierrez, F. (2006). What do children want to know about animals and artifacts? Domain-specific requests for information. *Psychological Science, 17,* 455–459.

Hardwig, J. (1991). The role of trust in knowledge. *The Journal of Philosophy, 88,* 693–708. doi:10.2307/2027007

Harris, A. J. L., & Hahn, U. (2009). Bayesian rationality in evaluating multiple testimonies: Incorporating the role of coherence. *Journal of Experimental Psychology: Learning, Memory, and Cognition, 35,* 1366–1373. doi:10.1037/a0016567

Harris, P. L. (2007). Trust. *Developmental Science, 10,* 135–138. doi:10.1111/j.1467-7687.2007.00575.x

Heit, E., & Hahn, U. (2001). Diversity-based reasoning in children. *Cognitive Psychology, 43,* 243–273. doi:10.1006/cogp.2001.0757

Hilborn, R. C. (2004). Seagulls, butterflies, and grasshoppers: A brief history of the butterfly effect in nonlinear dynamics. *American Journal of Physics, 72,* 425–427. doi:10.1119/1.1636492

Jaswal, V. K., & Neely, L. A. (2006). Adults don't always know best: Preschoolers use past reliability over age when learning new words. *Psychological Science, 17,* 757–758. doi:10.1111/j.1467-9280.2006.01778.x

Keil, F. C. (2006). Doubt, deference and deliberation. In T. Gendler & J. Hawthorne (Eds.), *Oxford studies in epistemology* (pp. 143–166). Oxford, England: Oxford University Press.

Keil, F. C. (2010). The feasibility of folk science. *Cognitive Science, 34,* 826–862. doi:10.1111/j.1551-6709.2010.01108.x

Keil, F. C., & Newman, G. (2008). Two tales of conceptual change: What changes and what remains the same. In S. Vosniadou (Ed.), *Handbook of research on conceptual change* (pp. 83–101). Mahwah, NJ: Erlbaum.

Keil, F. C., Stein, C., Webb, L., Billings, V. D., & Rozenblit, L. (2008). Discerning the division of cognitive labor: An emerging understanding of how knowledge is clustered in other minds. *Cognitive Science, 32,* 259–300. doi:10.1080/03640210701863339

Kelemen, D. (1999). Functions, goals and intentions: Children's teleological reasoning about objects. *Trends in Cognitive Sciences, 3,* 461–468. doi:10.1016/S1364-6613(99)01402-3

Kim, N. S., & Keil, F. C. (2003). From symptoms to causes: Diversity effects in diagnostic reasoning. *Memory & Cognition, 31,* 155–165. doi:10.3758/BF03196090

Kim, N. S., Yopchick, J. E., & de Kwaadsteniet, L. (2008). Causal diversity effects in information seeking. *Psychonomic Bulletin & Review, 15,* 81–88. doi:10.3758/PBR.15.1.81

Klahr, D. (2000). *Exploring science: The cognition and development of discovery processes.* Cambridge, MA: MIT Press.

Klahr, D. & Chen, Z. (2003). Overcoming the positive-capture strategy in young children: Learning about indeterminacy. *Child Development, 74,* 1256–1277.

Koenig, M. A., & Harris, P. L. (2005). Preschoolers mistrust ignorant and inaccurate speakers. *Child Development, 76,* 1261–1277. doi:10.1111/j.1467-8624.2005.00849.x

Lawson, R. (2006). The science of cycology: Failures to understand how everyday objects work. *Memory & Cognition, 34,* 1667–1675. doi:10.3758/BF03195929

Lutz, D. J., & Keil, F. C. (2002). Early understanding of the division of cognitive labor. *Child Development, 73,* 1073–1084. doi:10.1111/1467-8624.00458

Marcu, D. (2000). *The theory and practice of discourse parsing and summarization.* Cambridge, MA: MIT Press.

Masnick, A. M., & Klahr, D. (2003). Error matters: An initial exploration of elementary school children's understanding of experimental error. *Journal of Cognition and Development, 4,* 67–98. doi:10.1207/S15327647JCD4,1-03

McCabe, D. P., & Castel, A. D. (2008). Seeing is believing: The effect of brain images on judgments of scientific reasoning. *Cognition, 107,* 343–352. doi:10.1016/j.cognition.2007.07.017

Meunier, B., & Cordier, F. (2009). The role of feature type and causal status in 4- to 5-year-old children's biological categorizations. *Cognitive Development, 24,* 34–48. doi:10.1016/j.cogdev. 2008.05.003

Mills, C. M., & Keil, F. C. (2005). The development of cynicism. *Psychological Science, 16,* 385–390. doi:10.1111/j.0956-7976.2005.01545.x

Mills, C. M., & Keil, F. C. (2008). Children's developing notions of (im)partiality. *Cognition, 107,* 528–551. doi:10.1016/j.cognition.2007.11.003

Newman, G. E., & Keil, F. C. (2008). Where's the essence? Developmental shifts in children's beliefs about internal features. *Child Development, 79,* 1344–1356.

Newman, G. E., Keil, F. C., Kuhlmeier, V., & Wynn, K. (2010). Sensitivity to design: Early understandings of the link between agents and order. *Proceedings of the National Academy of Sciences of the United States of America, 107,* 17140–17145. doi:10.1073/pnas.0914056107

Newton, L., & Newton, D. (1998). Primary children's conceptions of science and the scientist: Is the impact of a national curriculum breaking down the stereotype? *International Journal of Science Education, 20,* 1137–1149. doi:10.1080/0950069980200909

Owens, D. (1989). Levels of explanation. *Mind, 98,* 59–79. doi:10.1093/mind/XCVIII.389.59

Rhodes, M., Brickman, D., & Gelman, S. A. (2008). Sample diversity and premise typicality in inductive reasoning: Evidence for developmental change. *Cognition, 108,* 543–556. doi:10.1016/ j.cognition.2008.03.002

Rips, L. J. (2002). Circular reasoning. *Cognitive Science, 26,* 767–795. doi:10.1207/s15516709 cog2606_3

Roskies, A. L. (2008). Neuroimaging and inferential distance. *Neuroethics, 1,* 19–30. doi:10.1007/ s12152-007-9003-3

Rottman, B. M., & Keil, F. C. (in press). What matters in scientific explanations: Effects of elaboration and content. *Cognition.*

Rozenblit, L., & Keil, F. C. (2002). The misunderstood limits of folk science: An illusion of explanatory depth. *Cognitive Science, 26,* 521–562. doi:10.1207/s15516709cog2605_1

Santos, L. R., Hauser, M. D., & Spelke, E. S. (2002). Domain-specific knowledge in human children and non-human primates: Artifact and food kinds. In M. Bekoff, C. Allen, & G. Burghardt (Eds.), *The cognitive animal* (pp. 205–216). Cambridge, MA: MIT Press.

Shtulman, A., & Carey, S. (2007). Improbable or impossible? How children reason about the possibility of extraordinary events. *Child Development, 78,* 1015–1032. doi:10.1111/j.1467-8624. 2007.01047.x

Slaughter, V., & Gopnik, A. (1996). Conceptual coherence in the child's theory of mind. *Child Development, 67,* 2967–2989.

Spelke, E. S., Breinlinger, K., Macomber, J., & Jacobson, K. (1992). Origins of knowledge. *Psychological Review, 99,* 605–632. doi:10.1037/0033-295X.99.4.605

Sperber, D., & Mercier, H. (in press). Reasoning as a social competence. In H. Landemore & J. Elster (Eds.), *Collective wisdom.* Cambridge, England: Cambridge University Press.

Strevens, M. (2009). *Depth: An account of scientific explanation.* Cambridge, MA: Harvard University Press.

Turnbull, H. W. (Ed.). (1959). *The correspondence of Isaac Newton.* Cambridge, England: Cambridge University Press.

Vanderborght, M., & Jaswal, V. K. (2009). Who knows best? Preschoolers sometimes prefer child informants over adult informants. *Infant and Child Development, 18,* 61–71. doi:10.1002/ icd.591

Weisberg, D. S., Keil, F. C., Goodstein, J., Rawson, E., & Gray, J. (2008). The seductive allure of neuroscience explanations. *Journal of Cognitive Neuroscience, 20,* 470–477.

Weisberg, M. (2011). *Three kinds of idealization.* Manuscript submitted for publication.

Westfall, R. S. (1980). *Never at rest: A biography of Isaac Newton.* New York: Cambridge University Press.

Whewell, W. (1847). *The philosophy of the inductive sciences.* London, England: Frank Cass.

Wilson, R. A., & Keil, F. C. (1998). The shadows and shallows of explanation. *Minds and Machines, 8,* 137–159. doi:10.1023/A:1008259020140

4

The Evolved Mind and Scientific Discovery

David C. Geary

Scientific discoveries are among humanity's greatest intellectual accomplishments (Murray, 2003) and are themselves the focus of historical and scientific enquiry (e.g., Klahr, 2000; Klahr & Simon, 1999; Simonton, 2009). Much has been learned about the individuals who make these discoveries and the motivational and cognitive mechanisms that underlie the discovery process. The puzzle of how the human mind evolved to enable scientific discovery in the first place remains to be completed, and the corresponding implications for teaching these discoveries, and the scientific method itself, to the evolved mind remain to be explored. In this chapter, I wander into Klahr and Dunbar's (1988) hypothesis space to generate ideas about how the cognitive mechanisms that are used during scientific problem solving evolved, and the implications for cultural evolution and the corresponding demands on children for learning about and understanding the gist of these discoveries in school (for broader discussions, see Geary, 2005, 2007, 2008). In so doing, I aim to offer a novel perspective that might be productively pursued by Klahr and others interested in better integrating the fields of cognitive development, scientific reasoning, and science education in order to enrich both theory and practice.

The size of the problem space involved in attempting to link human brain and cognitive evolution to the process of scientific discovery is substantial but can be trimmed by considering the selection pressures that drove the evolution of the hominid brain. I do this in the first section of this chapter and follow that with a discussion of the distinction between evolved biologically primary cognitive systems and the biologically secondary, culturally specific ones that are built from these. I use Darwin and Wallace's (1858) discovery of the principles of natural selection as a way to highlight the differences between scientific discovery of knowledge and children's development of folk knowledge of the same phenomena. This type of contrast provides a means of identifying specific conceptual impediments to children's learning of modern science and highlights how such discoveries change culture, as well as how different scientific explanations can be based on folk explanations of the same phenomena. In considering these differences in terms of how the mind has evolved to understand social, biological, and physical phenomena, and how we are asking children to understand the same phenomena based on historically recent discoveries of a handful of human beings, I highlight the complexity of the massive cultural intervention we call *schooling*.

Brain Evolution

Roughly 4 million years ago, our hominid ancestors, such as *Australopithecus afarensis,* had chimpanzee-size brains, or brains that were one third the size of modern human brains (Holloway, Broadfield, & Yuan, 2004; McHenry, 1994; Tobias, 1987). The change in absolute size is potentially misleading because australopithecines were smaller than modern humans and thus necessarily had a smaller brain. Nevertheless, when scaled to body size, the human brain remains about three times larger than that of our australopithecine ancestors. Scaled brain size is termed the *encephalization quotient* (EQ), with a value of 1 representing the average brain size among species in the same class (e.g., mammals), controlling for body size (Jerison, 1974). The EQ of an average mammal is therefore 1, and that of chimpanzees and australopithecines is 2. Humans have an EQ of approximately 6 (McHenry, 1994).

Changes in the architecture of the hominid brain accompanied the evolutionary increase in brain size in part because absolute increases in brain size result in correlated architectural changes. Doubling the size of a neocortical region, for instance, cannot be achieved by doubling the size of neurons. To maintain conduction properties (e.g., speed of transmission), dendrites that are doubled in length must be quadrupled in diameter (Kaas, 2000). The costs associated with proportional increases in the size of neurons may account for the most common pattern of larger cortical areas being associated with more neurons, although there are some neuronal size differences across cortical regions and species (Preuss, 2000). The point is that, with cortical expansion, each neuron must communicate with proportionally fewer other neurons. The result is an increased specialization of interconnected clusters of neurons, or, stated otherwise, the microarchitecture of expanded regions of neocortex necessarily becomes more modularized and specialized for processing more finely grained pieces of information (Changizi, 2003; Hofman, 2001; Kaas, 2000).

Evolutionary changes in brain organization are also evident in *endocasts,* that is, plaster casts of the inside of fossil crania (e.g., Holloway, 1973). Some endocasts provide an impression of the architecture of the outer surface of the neocortex, and these in turn suggest modest expansion of the frontal and parietal lobes and an increase in number of gyri and thus more neocortical surface area during hominid evolution (e.g., Holloway & de la Coste-Lareymondie, 1982; Holloway et al., 2004; Tobias, 1987). With the emergence of *Homo habilis* about 2.5 million years ago, Broca's area—which supports aspects of human language and gesture—appears to have expanded relative to australopithecines, and its architecture (pattern of sulcal and gyral folds) may have been similar to that of modern humans. The increase in the size of the parietal cortex is interesting as well (Holloway, 1996) because it is coincident with increasingly sophisticated tool use with and after the emergence of *H. habilis,* and because areas of the parietal cortex are engaged during tool use in modern humans (Johnson-Frey, 2003) and are involved in some components of controlled attention as related to working memory and mental imagery (Posner, 1994), as I elaborate below.

Comparative studies of brain anatomy across living primates, and especially in comparison with chimpanzees and other great apes, also inform our understanding of human brain evolution (e.g., Semendeferi, Armstrong, Schleicher, Zilles, & van Hoesen, 2001). Holloway (1968) estimated that the number of neurons in the human neocortex is only about 25% higher than in the chimpanzee neocortex, indicating that the expansion of hominid neocortical size was more strongly related to increases in the extent of neuronal interconnections (i.e., number of axons and size of dendrites) within and between brain regions than to an increase in number of neurons (see also Hofman, 2001). The size of the human frontal cortex is larger than that of great apes (Deacon, 1990) but only somewhat larger than expected on the basis of overall neocortex size (Semendeferi, 2001; Semendeferi & Damasio, 2000). Even so, the human prefrontal cortex has more neural connections with other brain regions and more gyrification, and thus more surface area, than that of great apes (Preuss, 2000; Rilling & Insel, 1999; Zilles, Armstrong, Moser, Schleicher, & Stephan, 1989). The combination allows for faster communication across adjacent regions that process similar forms of information, greater modularity and differentiation of functions within more specific areas of the prefrontal cortex, and greater integration of the prefrontal cortex with the rest of the brain (Deacon, 1990).

These anatomical changes do not fully inform us about function, but they do indicate that the hominid brain evolved into a more modularized but highly integrated organ. In comparison with the brains of our australopithecine ancestors, the human brain likely processes information in more finely grained detail, more quickly, with greater integration across neocortical regions, and with greater top-down regulation of information processing.

Selection Pressures

If we understand the selection pressures that drove the evolution of the hominid brain, then we can make inferences about the evolved functions of the anatomical changes just described. This inference is possible because the selection pressures inform us about the types of information that had to be processed to cope with survival or reproductive demands. Differences in the content of these pressures, as in the contrast between processing human faces versus the biological movement of hunted species, create advantages to modularized folk systems, as I discuss in more detail below; moreover, the fit between the information dynamics (e.g., rate of information change) of the proposed pressure and the dynamics and capacity of the cognitive system can be evaluated (see Geary, 2005). For instance, self-awareness is not necessary for coping with climatic pressures but is consistent with social ones. Similarly, the fast rate of information decay in the phonological buffer is more consistent with the need to cope with rapidly changing information, as in a discussion with another person, as contrasted with the slower rate of change in climatic conditions.

Scientists have proposed three classes of selection pressure as drivers of hominid brain evolution: (a) climatic, (b) ecological, and (c) social (Alexander,

1989; Ash & Gallup, 2007; Bailey & Geary, 2009; Kaplan, Hill, Lancaster, & Hurtado, 2000; Potts, 1998). Despite differences in the content of the proposed selection pressures, all of the models have a common core: the adaptive advantages of the ability to anticipate and mentally generate strategies to cope with anticipated future variation and change (for a review, see Geary, 2005). Climatic variation can result from long-term trends that affect populations that do not migrate (Potts, 1998) and from seasonal variation for hominid populations that migrated away from central Africa (Ash & Gallup, 2007; Kanazawa, 2008). Ecological models highlight the importance of hunting and other adaptations (e.g., tool use) that enable efficient extraction of biological resources from the many varied ecologies occupied by humans and our ancestors since *H. erectus* and on the complex learning required to master these skills (Kaplan et al., 2000). The basic idea is supported by findings that species with complex foraging or predatory demands have larger brain volumes and higher EQ values than related species with less complex foraging or predatory demands (e.g., Barton, 1996). Changes in tooth morphology and tool sophistication with the emergence of australopithecines, especially after *H. habilis,* are also consistent with coevolutionary change in hunting efficiency, diet, brain volume, and EQ (e.g., Aiello & Wheeler, 1995; Foley & Lahr, 1997).

Alexander's (1989) concept of ecological dominance merges ecological and social models of hominid brain evolution. The key idea is that hominids evolved adaptations that enabled increasingly efficient use of biological resources (e.g., hunting, cooking) and increasing control of physical ecologies (e.g., building shelters), resulting in a corresponding decrease in mortality risk and increase in population size. Expanding populations can result in rapidly decreasing ecological resources per capita, as originally argued by Malthus (1798), which creates the potential for runaway within-species competition (Alexander, 1989; Flinn, Geary, & Ward, 2005; Geary, 2005). The result was a turning point in our evolutionary history, a shift from primarily ecological selective pressures to primarily social ones. The shift in selection pressures is consistent with broad support for the *social brain hypothesis,* that is, the notion that social competition and cooperation were core selective forces contributing to hominid brain and cognitive evolution (e.g., Brothers, 1990; R. Dunbar, 1998, 2003; Humphrey, 1976). Social pressures result not only in advantages for fast identification and processing of social information (e.g., facial expressions) but also in more complex, dynamic, and less predictable social relationships.

Folk Modules and Mental Models

Information that is stable across generations, correlated with survival or reproductive outcomes, and partly heritable sets the stage for the evolution of brain and cognitive systems that quickly identify the corresponding information and result in adaptive (not optimal, but good enough) behavioral response. Simon (1956) termed these ecology–behavior links *bounded rationality,* Gigerenzer (e.g., Gigerenzer, Todd, & ABC Research Group, 1999) labeled them *fast and efficient heuristics,* R. Gelman (1990) referred to them as the *skeletal structure of evolved domains,* Geary and Huffman (2002) termed them *soft modularity,* and Timberlake (1994) described them as including the unconditioned stimulus–unconditioned response component of classical conditioning. The combination of advantages conferred to quickly identifying and responding to evolutionarily important information and the increased architectural modularity that accompanies evolutionary increases in brain size results in high potential for the evolution of modularized cognitive systems in the human mind (Pinker, 1997; Tooby & Cosmides, 1995).

One way to organize these modular systems is around the domains of folk psychology, folk biology, and folk physics, as represented in Figure 4.1. Highly specialized folk psychological modules are consistent with an evolutionary history of intense social selection pressures, and folk biological modules and the tool use component of folk physical modules (discussed later in this chapter) are consistent with intense ecological pressures. The combination supports Alexander's (1989) ecological dominance, social competition thesis (Flinn et al., 2005).

FOLK PSYCHOLOGY. Folk psychology is composed of the affective, cognitive, and behavioral systems that enable people to negotiate social interactions and relationships. People's social cognitions appear to be largely organized around the self, relationships and interactions with other people, and group-level relationships and interactions (Fiske & Taylor, 1991).

Self. *Self-awareness* is the ability to consciously represent the self as a social being, is integrally related to the ability to mentally time travel (Suddendorf & Corballis, 1997; Tulving, 2002), and may be unique to humans (Suddendorf & Busby, 2003). Self-awareness is also integral to the top-down generation of explicit representations of past and present states and the ability to create self-centered mental simulations of potential future states, as described in the Mental Models and Problem Solving section of this chapter.

A *self-schema* is a long-term memory network of information that links knowledge and beliefs about the self, including positive (accentuated) and negative (discounted) traits (e.g., warmth), episodic memories, and self-efficacy in various domains (Bandura, 1997; Fiske & Taylor, 1991; Markus, 1977).

Although the evidence is mixed, self-schemas can regulate goal-related behaviors, specifically, those in which one focuses effort, and whether one will persist in the face of failure (Sheeran & Orbell, 2000). Self-regulation results from a combination of implicit and explicit processes that influence social comparisons, self-efficacy, valuation of different forms of ability and interests, and the formation of social relationships (Drigotas, 2002). When evaluating the competencies of others, people focus on attributes that are central features of their self-schema and prefer relationships that provide feedback consistent with the schema. People value competencies at which they excel and discount those in which they are at a competitive disadvantage (Taylor, 1982). The combination may facilitate niche seeking and the development of niche-relevant competencies.

Individual. There are several types of universal human relationships (e.g., parent–child attachment, friendships) that are supported by the same suite of cognitive competencies (Bugental, 2000; Caporael, 1997). These include the

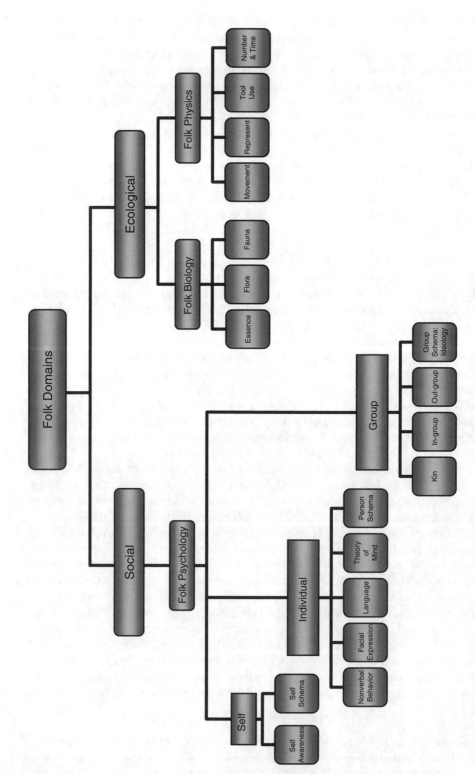

Figure 4.1. Proposed modular systems in the domains of folk psychology, folk biology, and folk physics.

ability to read nonverbal communication signals, facial expressions, language, and theory of mind (Adolphs, 1999; Brothers & Ring, 1992; Humphrey, 1976; Leslie, 1987; Pinker, 1994). *Theory of mind* represents the ability to make inferences about the intentions, beliefs, emotional states, and likely future behavior of other individuals, and it may be especially developed in humans (Baron-Cohen, 1995; Leslie, Friedman, & German, 2004). The functional individual-level system is also engaged during the dynamics of one-on-one social interactions, providing cues to the online feeling states and intentions of other people.

The integration of these modular systems with motivational and affective systems provides the basis for the development and maintenance of long-term relationships and results in *person schemas*. People develop these schemas for familiar people and people with whom they expect to have future social relationships (Fiske & Taylor, 1991). The person schema comprises a long-term memory network that includes representations of the other person's physical attributes, especially race, sex, and age, as well as memories for specific behavioral episodes and more abstract trait information. The latter varies across two continua: (a) sociability (warm to emotionally distant) and (b) competence (Schneider, 1973). The person schema will also include information about the person's theory of mind (Adolphs, 1999; Leslie, 1987). This schema would include memories and trait information about how the person typically makes inferences, responds to social cues, sets social and other goals, and so forth.

Group. A universal aspect of human behavior and cognition is the parsing of one's social world into groups. The most consistent of these groupings are in terms of kinship, ingroups and outgroups, and group schema; kin are almost always part of the ingroup. The group schema is an ideologically based social identification, as exemplified by nationality and religious affiliation. The corresponding selective pressure is the competitive advantage associated with large group size; that is, ideologies enable easy expansion of group size during group-level competition (Alexander, 1989).

In traditional societies, nuclear families are embedded in the context of a wider network of kin (Geary & Flinn, 2001). Individuals within these networks cooperate to facilitate competition with other kin groups over resource control and manipulation of reproductive relationships. As Alexander (1979) cogently argued, coalitional competition also occurs beyond the kin group, is related to social ideology, and is endemic throughout the world (Horowitz, 2001). As with kin groups, competition among ideology-based groups is over resource control.

FOLK BIOLOGY AND FOLK PHYSICS. People living in traditional societies use the local ecology to support their survival and reproductive needs. The associated activities are supported by, among other things, the folk biological and folk physical modules shown in Figure 4.1 (Geary, 2005; Geary & Huffman, 2002). The folk biological modules support the categorizing of flora and fauna in the local ecology, especially species used as food, medicines, or in social rituals (Berlin, Breedlove, & Raven, 1973; Malt, 1995; Medin & Atran, 2004). Folk biology also includes systems that support an understanding of the essence of these species (Atran, 1998), that is, heuristic-based decisions regarding the likely behavior of these species. In particular, its essence is knowledge about growth patterns and behavior that facilitates hunting and other activities involved in securing and using these species as resources (e.g., food). Physical modules are for guiding movement in three-dimensional physical space, mentally representing this space (e.g., demarcating the ingroup's territory), and using physical materials (e.g., stones, metals) for making tools (Pinker, 1997; Shepard, 1994). The associated abilities support a host of evolutionarily significant activities, such as hunting, foraging, and the use of tools as weapons. Finally, there is strong cross-species evidence for interrelated neural and cognitive systems that represent both number and time (Gallistel & Gelman, 1992; Meck & Church, 1983).

HEURISTICS AND ATTRIBUTIONAL BIASES. Gigerenzer et al.'s (1999) heuristics represent "rule of thumb" patterns of behavior that are evoked on the basis of the implicit (i.e., below conscious awareness) processing of key ecological or social cues. For humans, heuristics can also include explicit inferential and attributional biases that are integral features of folk knowledge. The attributional biases that favor members of the ingroup and derogate members of outgroups are well known (Stephan, 1985) and facilitate coalitional competition (Horowitz, 2001). Kahneman and Tversky's (1982) simulation heuristic involves use of the person schema to mentally simulate and make judgments about how the individual might react in one situation or another. The essence associated with folk biology allows people to make inferences (e.g., during the act of hunting) about the behavior of members of familiar species as well as about the likely behavior of less familiar but related species (Atran, 1998). Attributions about causality in the physical world also have been studied. Children and adults have, as an example, natural, naïve conceptions about motion and other physical phenomena (Clement, 1982).

MENTAL MODELS AND PROBLEM SOLVING. In *The Origin of Mind: Evolution of Brain, Cognition, and General Intelligence* (2005), I proposed that the core mechanism that enables people to anticipate and mentally generate strategies to cope with anticipated future variation and change is the *autonoetic mental model*. Such models are explicit attention-driven mental representations—supported by working memory—of situations that are centered on the self and one's relationship with other people or one's access to biological and physical resources. The representations often involve a form of mental time travel, specifically, mental simulations of past, present, or potential future states that can be cast as images, in language, or as episodic memories (i.e., memories of personal experiences; Paivio, 2007; Suddendorf & Corballis, 1997; Tulving, 2002). Following Alexander (1989), and integrating the work of Suddendorf and Corballis (1997), Tulving (2002), and Johnson-Laird (1983), I proposed that the ability to construct a self-centered explicit representation of past, present, and potential future states and the ability to engage in effortful reasoning and problem solving on the content of these representations are uniquely human and evolved as a result of the fluidity of social dynamics and social competition, following the evolutionarily earlier achievement of ecological dominance.

A key component of autonoetic mental models is the ability to create a mental representation of a desired or fantasized state and to compare this with a mental representation of one's current situation. The fantasized world is one in which the individual is able to organize and control social (e.g., social dynamics), biological (e.g., access to food), and physical (e.g., shelter) resources in ways that would have enhanced survival or reproductive prospects during human evolution. The mental simulation creates a problem space, including an initial state (one's current circumstances) and a goal state (the fantasized outcome). In *The Origin of Mind* (2005), I proposed that humans' ability to explicitly problem-solve in ways that reduced the difference between the initial and goal states evolved as a core feature of autonoetic mental models. The details are described in the book, but the gist is that the evolution of weak problem-solving methods such as means–ends analyses (Newell & Simon, 1972) was driven by the competitive advantage that results from the ability to inhibit evolved or learned heuristics and to then generate and mentally rehearse more novel social-competitive strategies and to mentally generate the strategies that support ecological dominance, for instance, constructing tools, planning hunts, and constructing shelters.

Despite humans' extraordinary ability to mentally simulate potential social or ecological conditions and problem-solve in the development of behavioral strategies to bring about the desired goal, people's reasoning about such conditions is influenced by many documented biases that often result in incorrect inferences or less-than-optimal solutions (e.g., Evans, 2002; Johnson-Laird & Byrne, 2002; Oaksford & Chater, 1998; Tversky & Kahneman, 1974). Evidence that some of these biases result from presenting the tasks in decontextualized or evolutionarily novel contexts is provided by the finding of a reduction in error rates when the same tasks are presented in evolutionarily contextualized (e.g., reciprocal exchange) contexts (Cosmides, 1989). In any event, there are individual differences in the ability to inhibit evolved or learned heuristics and prior knowledge and to generate abstract, decontextualized representations of the problem at hand. There may be even more individual variation in the ability to use formal logic (e.g., deduction based on a set of premises) to operate on these abstract representations (Stanovich, 1999). People who are able to do so can eliminate many reasoning biases and thereby produce more optimal solutions (Stanovich & West, 2000).

Even people who are capable of formal logical reasoning sometimes succumb to common biases (Stanovich & West, 2008). This occurs because use of formal logic requires the effortful suppression of heuristics and prior knowledge, and thus people tend to engage in formal problem solving only when necessary to achieve a specific goal. This tendency makes sense because evolved and learned heuristics are often effective for achieving day-to-day goals, and suppression of these to construct new strategies is necessary only when currently available ones are not effective; the latter situation in effect indicates some degree of novelty. Individual differences in the ability to suppress heuristics and prior knowledge or beliefs to engage in formal logical thinking is independently related to measures of general fluid intelligence, syllogistic reasoning, and cognitive flexibility, that is, openness to new ideas and alternative explanations of the same phenomenon (Stanovich & West, 2000; West, Toplak, & Stanovich, 2008). The important point for this discussion is that the ability to logically and critically evaluate evidence, as is necessary for learning and doing science, does not come easily to most people and, even for capable people, often requires conscious, explicit, and goal-directed effort.

Evolution of Childhood

As brain size has increased, the human developmental period has lengthened, with physical maturation increasing from about 10 to 13 years of age to the late teenage years or early 20s (Bogin, 1999). Given the risk of death before reproductive maturity, the benefits associated with a long developmental period must be substantial. To the extent that brain evolution was driven by the need to cope with social and ecological novelty and with dynamics that are not entirely stable and predictable across and within lifetimes, a key function of the long developmental period is to provide the opportunity for children to learn the nuances of the social, biological, and physical worlds in which they are embedded. It follows that many of the folk abilities (e.g., language) represented in Figure 4.1 should be open to experiential modification during the developmental period, and this is in fact the case (e.g., Kuhl et al., 1997; Pascalis et al., 2005; Paterson, Brown, Gsödl, Johnson, & Karmiloff-Smith, 1999). The mechanisms involved in the experience-driven adaptation of folk modular systems to variation in local conditions are, however, not well understood; specifically, the degree of inherent constraint and changes in developmental sensitivity to experiential modification remain to be fully established.

At a macro level, and following R. Gelman's (1990) lead, Geary and Huffman (2002) proposed that prenatal brain organization results in inherent neural and perceptual constraints that guide attention to and processing of stable forms of information (e.g., the general shape of the human face) in the folk domains shown in Figure 4.1. The result is biases in early postnatal attentional, affective, and information-processing capacities as well as biases in self-initiated behavioral engagement of the social, biological, and physical worlds (Bjorklund & Pellegrini, 2002; Scarr, 1992; Scarr & McCartney, 1983). The latter generate *evolutionarily expectant experiences,* that is, experiences that provide the social and ecological feedback needed to adjust modular architecture to variation in information patterns in these domains (Bouchard, Lykken, Tellegen, & McGue, 1996; Greenough, Black, & Wallace, 1987). These behavioral biases are expressed as common juvenile activities, such as social play and exploration of the ecology. These experience-expectant processes result in the modification of plastic features of folk modular systems, such that the individual is able to identify and respond to variation within these folk domains (e.g., discriminate one individual from another).

Primary and Secondary Learning

It appears that most of the adaptations of modular systems to local variation occur automatically and implicitly during children's natural activities. The result is that most daily interactions with other people and in the ecology occur with little need for conscious, explicit deliberation, in keeping with Simon (1956), Gigerenzer et al. (1999), and R. Gelman (1990). In theory, experiences that are not consistent with evolved or learned behavior–ecology links or heuristics will trigger engagement of mental models and explicit problem solving to cope with this inconsistency (Botvinick, Braver, Barch, Carter, & Cohen,

2001). In other words, situations or the behaviors of others that are out of the norm will trigger an attentional focus on the novel or inconsistent details and result in their representation in working memory, thus making them available for conscious, explicit problem solving. The engagement of these top-down systems may be the key to understanding how humans create evolutionarily novel cognitive abilities and many features of modern cultures; a discussion of the potential brain and cognitive mechanisms that are engaged in the creation of these evolutionarily novel abilities is beyond the scope of this chapter but is provided in Geary (2005).

The universal attentional, cognitive, and attributional biases that constitute folk domains are called *biologically primary* to distinguish them from the *biologically secondary* abilities that are culture specific and dependent on the engagement of explicit mechanisms for their emergence (Geary, 1995). Primary domains provide the foundation from which secondary ones can be built, and thus the boundary between them is necessarily fuzzy. A key point here is that the evolution of the attentional, working memory, and problem-solving competencies that support autonoetic mental models allows people to explicitly represent components of primary systems (e.g., phonetic sounds) in working memory and, through this, results in the potential to modify these systems from the top down to create or learn about evolutionarily novel knowledge or innovations (e.g., use of phonetic sounds in word decoding during the act of reading; see Geary, 2007).

Scientific Problem Solving

My thesis is that the evolved ability to generate autonoetic mental models and to engage in weak and formal problem solving on the content of these abstract representations is the foundation for the development of the biologically secondary scientific method and for all subsequent scientific discoveries (Geary, 2005, 2007). Even if social competition were the primary selection pressure that drove the evolution of the systems that support these models, people are predicted to also generate models related to folk biological and folk physical phenomena. This proposition follows from Alexander's (1989) sequence of ecological dominance followed by heightened social competition. The attainment of ecological dominance is predicted to have resulted from enhanced folk biological and enhanced aspects of folk physical (e.g., as related to tool use) modular competencies, as well as an interest in learning in these domains, and in devising novels ways of controlling biological (e.g., new weapons) and physical (e.g., better dams) resources.

Individual differences in one's interest in people (folk psychological motivation) and things (folk physical motivation) have in fact been demonstrated repeatedly over the past 5 decades (e.g., Goodenough, 1957; Roe & Klos, 1969). People's folk biological interests appear to represent another dimension, or are at least subsumed under a broader interest in living things, with subcategories of people and other living things. Another interest dimension that has emerged from the occupational literature is an abstract-to-concrete continuum (e.g., Campbell & Holland, 1972). The concrete pole reflects a focus on engagement in social endeavors or material economic activities (e.g., horticulture), whereas the abstract pole represents a focus on the symbolic representation and explanation of social and personal experience as well as natural phenomena (e.g., folk origin myths; Geary, 2007).

FOCUS OF SCIENTIFIC PROBLEM SOLVING. Newton's (1995) *Principia* provides an example of scientific reasoning focused on physical phenomena. He recognized that his understanding of these phenomena differed from that of other people, and he stated as much: "I do not define time, space, place and motion, as being well known to all. Only I must observe, that the vulgar conceive those quantities under no other notions but from the relation they bear to sensible objects" (Newton, 1995, p. 13).

Although Newton moved us beyond the "vulgar" intuitions of folk physics, he still relied on other aspects of folk physical systems to complete this work. His conceptualization of objects in motion and the gravitational and rectilinear (movement in a straight line) forces underlying the pattern of motion were based on his ability to explicitly use visuospatial systems to construct geometric representations of motion and then to apply Euclidean geometry and formal logic to mathematically prove the scientific accuracy of these representations. In short, Newton constructed explicit mental models of planetary motion and then used logic and mathematics to prove the patterns of motion were explained by gravitational attraction and rectilinear motion.

My proposal is that these explicit representations are possible because of the evolution of autonoetic mental models, but in this case the focus of the models was on a physical phenomenon rather than a social one, and the logical problem-solving operations on these representations was more exacting than is typically the case. Newton (1995) also tested his predicted patterns of planetary motion against empirical observations of this motion, illustrating an interaction between Klahr and Dunbar's (1988) hypothesis and experiment spaces. In all, people are predicted to be interested in understanding phenomena related to themselves and other people (folk psychology), the living world in general (folk biology), and the physical world, including how to use objects as tools (folk physics). For most of humanity, however, their explicit attributions about these phenomena are good enough for day-to-day life but often scientifically inaccurate, as Newton observed.

DISCOVERY OF NATURAL SELECTION. One can use Darwin and Wallace's (1858) discovery of the principles of natural selection as a more detailed example of complex, explicit, scientific problem solving in a knowledge-rich domain. As with all historical analyses, my discussion is necessarily speculative but illustrates the use of mental models and explicit problem solving to solve a scientific puzzle. Aspects of Darwin and Wallace's discovery process can be understood in terms of psychological studies of problem solving (Klahr & Dunbar, 1988; Klahr & Simon, 1999; Newell & Simon, 1972), specifically, a problem space, initial and goal states, relevant operators (rules that can transform the initial state into intermediate states), relevant knowledge, and schemata (a system of linked operators that can be used conjointly during problem solving).

It is clear from biographical studies and their own writings that Darwin and Wallace (1858) were explicitly interested in discovering the mechanisms responsible for the origin of new species or speciation (see Desmond & Moore, 1994; Raby, 2001). This investigation was an ill-structured problem in that the solution required knowledge that spanned many domains (e.g., the fossil and geological records), and the knowledge and operators needed to ultimately solve the problem were not known. As a result, it was not possible to solve this problem by means of inherent or previously learned heuristics.

Once the goal was defined, basic assumptions about the nature of the problem needed to be made. In the early 19th century and before this time, most naturalists, such as the paleontologist Owen (1860), assumed that the origin of species was driven by some form of divine intervention (Ospovat, 1981). This assumption was critical and ill-fated because it placed legal operators that involved natural causes (e.g., differential mortality), and thus the actual mechanisms of natural selection, outside of the problem space, which rendered the problem unsolvable. Darwin and Wallace (1858), in contrast, defined the problem space and operators in terms of natural, observable processes (Browne, 2002; Darwin, 1846; Desmond & Moore, 1994; Raby, 2001).

Some aspects of how Darwin and Wallace (1858) solved the problem of speciation are more certain than others, especially with respect to basic assumptions and some of the background knowledge that contributed to their discovery. The relevant knowledge was not Scripture but instead must have been based in part on folk biological systems, which were elaborated with extensive observations of nature and with academic learning, such as through the reading of Lyell's (1830) *Principles of Geology*. Malthus's (1798) observations and hypotheses also contributed greatly to Darwin and Wallace's goal-relevant knowledge and to the construction of associated legal operators, that is, the mechanisms that operated in nature, as shown in Exhibit 4.1. Darwin's understanding of these operators emerged slowly between 1838 and 1856–1857 (Ospovat, 1979, 1981).

Malthus's (1798) insightful monograph described a pattern of oscillating expansions and contractions of the size of human populations in preindustrial Europe and in other regions of the world. Expansion often continues beyond the carrying capacity of local resources, at which point the population crashes. The crashes represent a sharp increase in mortality, largely due to famine, epidemics, and conflicts with other people (e.g., wars) over control of land and other life-supporting resources. The spike in mortality reduces the population to a level below carrying capacity, that is, to a point at which there are once again excess resources, and thus another cycle of population expansion ensues. With respect to Malthus's description, Wallace noted the following in a letter written in 1887 and reprinted in Darwin's autobiography (F. Darwin, 1887/2000):

> This had strongly impressed me, and it suddenly flashed upon me that all animals are necessarily thus kept down—"the struggle for existence"—while variations, on which I was always thinking, must necessarily often be *beneficial,* and would then cause those varieties to increase while the injurious variations diminished. (pp. 200–201)

A few of the observations and inferences of Malthus (1798) and of Darwin and Wallace (1858) are recast as the legal problem-solving operators shown in

Exhibit 4.1.   Using Problem Solving to Discover Natural Selection

Legal Operators
Operator 1. For each reproductive cycle, the number of offspring produced is greater than the number of parents.
Operator 2. The probability of offspring survival varies with ecological conditions, such as resource availability (e.g., land, food):
A. When resources are plentiful, more offspring survive and populations expand.
B. When resources are scarce, more offspring die and populations contract.
Operator 3. Resource availability varies with population size:
A. Expansion gradually reduces quantity of resources available per individual.
B. Contraction gradually increases quantity of resources available per individual.
Operator 4. The probability of mortality or survival is not entirely random.
Operator 5. Some traits are correlated with the ability to extract resources from the ecology (or, e.g., avoid predation) and thus with the probability of mortality or survival.

Goal-Relevant Knowledge
Fact 1. Populations' numbers tend to be stable across generations.
Fact 2. Predation, disease, climate, and competition result in high mortality.
Fact 3. Individuals of the same species vary on most traits.
Fact 4. The fossil record suggests that species change gradually; some go extinct; and others emerge.
Fact 5. Variations of the same species and related species are found in the same or contiguous geographic regions.

Schemata: Natural Selection
Schemata 1. Same as Operator 1: Populations will expand, if unchecked.
Schemata 2. Schemata 1 is linked with Operators 2 and 3, coupling the oscillating pattern of population expansions and contractions to ecological conditions.
Schemata 3. Schemata 2 is linked to Operator 4, coupling population expansions and contractions with differential mortality and survival.
Schemata 4. Schemata 3 is linked to Operator 4, coupling differential mortality and survival to individual characteristics.
Schemata 5. Schemata 4 is linked with Operator 5, coupling individual characteristics that influence mortality and survival to ecological conditions.

Analogy: Artificial Selection
Feature 1. People selectively breed other species in order to exaggerate desired traits within a species (microevolution).
Feature 2. Selective breeding works because offspring are similar to parents on the selected trait.
Feature 3. Offspring must somehow (genes were not yet understood) inherit the selected trait.
Feature 4. Generations of selective breeding can lead to the emergence of different varieties of the same species (e.g., different breeds of dog) or the emergence of new species, such as domestic species from their wild ancestors (macroevolution).

the top section of Exhibit 4.1. The operators could easily be transformed into a computer simulation (Newell & Simon, 1972) or mathematical representation (MacArthur & Wilson, 1967) of the common oscillating pattern of population expansions and contractions described by Malthus for humans and later documented for other species (e.g., Witting, 2000). The operators represent the reproductive and survival-related mechanisms and dynamics that act in natural populations. In addition to reading Lyell (1830) and Malthus, Darwin (1846) and Wallace (1855) acquired goal-relevant knowledge through their extensive collecting and taxonomically organizing of species of many different kinds and through careful observation of these species in natural ecologies. In this respect, Darwin and Wallace accumulated experiences that would have expanded their folk biological knowledge in ways that occur for people living in traditional societies (e.g., Bailenson, Shum, Atran, Medin, & Coley, 2002), but with very different goals.

People in traditional societies—and throughout human evolution, no doubt—think about other species' behavior, where they reside, and their relation to their ecology for the goal of hunting or cultivating these species so they can be used as food and medicines (Atran, 1998). Consider this goal with respect to Facts 3, 4, and 5 in Exhibit 4.1. Individuals in traditional societies classify members of the same and related species together on the basis of similarities across individuals, not differences. These people are not, of course, aware of the geological record or the geographic distribution of species. In other words, Darwin and Wallace's (1858) folk biological knowledge was expanded beyond that found in traditional populations and applied to a very different type of problem. These expansions of folk biological knowledge are represented by Facts 3, 4 and 5 and placed constraints on how the problem of the origin of species was represented and, therefore, constraints on where in the problem space the legal operators could act.

The observation that population size tends to be stable across generations meant that the first operator in Exhibit 4.1—number of offspring produced is greater than the number of parents—could not act such that population size increased indefinitely. The observation thus constrained the problem space and created the subgoal of identifying additional operators that either halted reproductive activity when the population reached carrying capacity or reversed population expansions by some other mechanism. (It cannot be known exactly how Darwin and Wallace [1858] solved this subgoal, but a means–ends analysis is a possibility.) The subgoal is to identify the operators that maintain population size, given an initial state and operator (Operator 1) that resulted in a constantly increasing population size. The knowledge that was used to construct operators that reduced the distance between the initial state (increasing population size) and the end state (stable population size) of the subgoal included Fact 2, that is, predation, disease, climate, and competition result in high mortality. The pattern described by Malthus (1798) and appreciated by Darwin and Wallace—specifically, that the fluctuations in mortality rate varied with ecological conditions—contributed to the creation of Operator 2 and Operator 3. Coupling these operators creates Schemata 2 (see the third section of Exhibit 4.1), which solved the subgoal; population size is kept in check through high mortality.

The solving of this subgoal created the foundational schemata for natural selection. More precisely, when Schemata 2 is constrained by Fact 2 (predation, disease, climate, and competition result in high mortality), the result is a system that creates large numbers of individuals, most of whom perish before becoming parents. The next important constraint on the problem space arose from the observation that the probability of mortality or survival is not entirely random, creating a fourth legal operator (Malthus, 1798). Operator 4 is important because it links differential mortality or survival to population expansions and contractions, that is, Schemata 3. Schemata 4—mortality risk is correlated with characteristics of the individual—results when this operator is linked to Schemata 3. The fifth operator is crucial because it indicates that there must be mechanisms that operate such that beneficial variations increase in frequency and injurious variations decrease in frequency. The result is a recurrent pattern of population expansions and selective contractions, as described by Malthus (1798). With each contraction, the individuals with traits best suited to the change in conditions survive and reproduce in greater numbers than do individuals with injurious traits.

Analogical reasoning is another weak problem-solving method (Klahr & Simon, 1999) that contributed to Darwin's (1859) linking of Operator 5 to Schemata 4; specifically, the analogy provided by the breeding of domesticated species (see the bottom section of Exhibit 4.1). Domestic breeding highlighted how variability could be coupled with selection of favored traits to produce change within a species (microevolution) and to create new species (macroevolution). In the concluding chapter of *Origin of Species,* Darwin (1859) noted the importance of this analogy:

> Man does not actually produce variability . . . But man can and does select the variations given to him by nature, and thus accumulate them in any desired manner. He thus adapts animals and plants for his own benefit or pleasure. . . . It is certain that he can largely influence the character of a breed by selecting, in each successive generation, individual differences . . . This process of selection has been the great agency in the production of the most distinct and useful domestic breeds. . . . There is no obvious reason why the principles which have acted so efficiently under domestication should not have acted under nature. In the preservation of favoured individuals and races, during the constantly-recurrent Struggle for Existence, we see the most powerful and ever-acting means of selection. . . . More individuals are born than can possibly survive. A grain in the balance will determine which individual shall live and which shall die, which variety or species shall increase in number, and which shall decrease, or finally become extinct. (pp. 466–467)

In these closing statements, we see all of the legal operators (e.g., "More individuals are born than can possibly survive") and goal-relevant knowledge (e.g., breeders selectively breed other species on the basis of individual differences in preferred traits) pulled together to form a coherent framework of operators represented as Schemata 5. This organized system of legal operators defines the mechanisms and processes of natural selection and explains all of the facts in Exhibit 4.1 and many others. Once it was fully understood, Darwin used Schemata 5 in a heuristiclike manner, that is, it implicitly—and, of course, often—explicitly guided his subsequent thinking and experimental investigations of natural phenomena (Browne, 2002). During the formulation of his principles and their later application, Darwin often used mental visualization (e.g., with the tree-of-life diagrams) in combination with logic and verbal abstract principles (e.g., see Operator 1, Exhibit 4.1) to integrate the operators, knowledge, and schemata in constructing the principles of natural selection (Paivio, 2007).

Wallace did not believe that artificial selection provided a useful analogy for natural selection. He approached the final step through other forms of inductive reasoning and through deductive reasoning; Darwin used these processes as well but also relied on analogical reasoning. An illustration of how Wallace appeared to have explicitly reasoned about the problem is provided in an 1855 (p. 184) article titled "On the Law Which Has Regulated the Introduction of New Species." In this article, he proposed the following hypothesis: "Every species has come into existence coincident both in space and time with a pre-existing closely allied species" (p. 186). In other words, new species arise from extant species. Induction—formulating a general principle based on observable facts—played an important part in Wallace's formulation of this conclusion.

During his expeditions in the Amazon and throughout Malaysia, Wallace (1855) observed a pattern in the geographic distribution of species (Fact 5 in Exhibit 4.1), "closely allied species in rich groups being found geographically near each other, is most striking and important" (p. 189). He also described how the same pattern is evident in the fossil record. When this pattern was combined with deductions based on a number of premises and facts described in the article, Wallace concluded that related species (e.g., of butterflies) are found in the same geographic location because they all arose from a common ancestor that resided in this location. Wallace further concluded that the creation of new species from existing species "must be the necessary results of some great natural law" (p. 195). Wallace discovered the great natural law—natural selection—3 years later, when he linked Malthus's (1798) observations to the earlier noted favorable and unfavorable variations in traits (Darwin & Wallace, 1858).

There is little doubt that the discovery of natural selection also involved implicit processing and an implicit synthesis of relevant information, as suggested by Wallace's claim that "it suddenly flashed upon me" (F. Darwin, 1887/2000, p. 200). At the same time, biographers note that he had set the goal of understanding the mechanisms that resulted in the origin of species at least 13 years before this insight and had explicitly described and organized many critical aspects of natural selection 3 years before his final essay on natural selection (Raby, 2001; Wallace, 1855).

RELATION TO COGNITIVE EVOLUTION. In many ways, Darwin and Wallace's (1858) discovery was based on problem solving and other cognitive processes that are found in most members of our species, including visualization, use of weak problem-solving methods, and folk knowledge and interests. In other ways, they engaged in processes that are also found in our species but are a source of substantial individual differences in cognitive competence (Stanovich, 1999), including critical evaluation of induced abstract principles using formal logic and, for Darwin, experimentation to test his ideas. It is almost certain that their achievement was not the result of one single cognitive competence that is unique to scientific genius but instead a rare combination of competencies, experiences, and interests that were focused on achieving a specific goal (Murray, 2003). There are several points to be considered in this investigation of how Darwin and Wallace's discovery emerged from an interplay between folk interests and competencies, together with modification of these through the use of mental models and explicit, controlled problem solving.

The focus of Darwin and Wallace's (1858) interest was in the domain of folk biology and thus was not unusual. Their goal of understanding the origin of species was not unusual either, except it is more typically related to human origins. Origin myths appear to be a human universal that include supernatural (i.e., abstract) explanations of the how and why of personal experiences and of phenomena in the natural and biological world (Brown, 1991). In this sense, Darwin and Wallace's goal resulted from a mix of common folk biological and folk psychological interests and attributional biases. The mix of interests was part of the novelty of their goal, as was their explicit exclusion of supernatural processes—that is, inhibition of folk beliefs—from the problem space. Darwin (1871), of course, extended natural and sexual selection to humans, but Wallace's view was a combination of folk belief in the supernatural and natural selection; specifically, he argued that an intelligent designer guided the evolution of the human mind and morality (e.g., Wallace, 1869).

Their creation of the operators that eventually led to the discovery of natural selection was driven in part by evolutionarily novel information that contradicted beliefs about origins and stability of species (e.g., Lyell, 1830; Malthus, 1798). As I noted in *Mental Models and Problem Solving* (Geary, 2005), information or situations that are not readily explained or dealt with using evolved or learned heuristics are potential triggers for engagement of the explicit problem-solving system, and this was the case for both Darwin and Wallace. Their problem solving also required inhibition of common ways of thinking about other species (e.g., similarity among individuals of the same species) and explicit consideration of uncommon ways, specifically on the importance of within-species variation and cross-generational change. The latter highlights the critical importance of mental time travel. Although ancestor worship is common in traditional and other societies, indicating a human ability to think about time across generations, Darwin and Wallace (1858) extended this visualization to include the geological record, to visualize the relations among species across geological time, and to consider how species might change across generations, including future ones.

My points are that Darwin and Wallace's (1858) discovery emerged, in part, from a fusion of the folk biological interest in other species and the folk psychological interest in understanding our origins, as well as from the use of common problem-solving strategies, such as means–ends analysis and the use of analogy. The discovery itself, however, required, at least at times, suppression of folk biases and the effortful use of formal, logical reasoning to reconcile inconsistencies in folk beliefs with the implications of Lyell's (1830) and Malthus's (1798) work, among other sources, as well as visualization of the phylogenetic relations among species and of potential evolutionary change in species across time. Although it is only a hypothesis, I ask readers to consider that many of the latter processes were dependent on the evolution of the brain and cognitive mechanisms that support the use of autonoetic mental models for anticipating and developing strategies for coping with social and other ambiguous situations. I should note that self-awareness is obviously not an aspect of the discovery itself, but Darwin was keenly aware of the social and personal implications of his theory; also, mental models were likely used during our evolutionary history to anticipate and plan for ecological and climatic change, even if social competition was the primary selective pressure. In any case, the natural selection was and remains an evolutionarily novel way of understanding living things and their origins, including our own.

Secondary Learning

Newton's (1995) *Principia* and Darwin's (1859) *On the Origin of Species* are two of the most important books in the history of science because they introduced evolutionarily novel, but much more accurate, ways of understanding the physical and biological worlds. My brief description of Darwin and Wallace's (1858) extended, goal-directed, and painstaking discovery of natural selection underscores the nuances and complexity of the discovery process, as Klahr and colleagues have discussed (Klahr, 2000; Klahr & Simon, 1999), and highlights many of the difficulties children and adolescents are likely to have in their attempts to understand these principles as well as Newton's gravitational attraction and other biologically secondary concepts. I have discussed the implications for the cultural emergence of schools and for understanding children's motivation or lack thereof, in many cases, for learning these evolutionarily novel ways of understanding the world elsewhere (Geary, 2007, 2008). Now I want to illustrate how highlighting evolved biases in how humans think and learn and placing them in a modern cultural context help us gain a fuller appreciation of what we are asking of children in modern schools so that researchers can generate novel hypotheses about their associated learning in these evolutionarily novel but culturally important domains, including science.

Learning Natural Selection

Researchers will be in a better position to understand the relation between primary and secondary learning, and the potential impediments to the latter, if they understand the evolved function of primary folk knowledge, the ways in which people use this knowledge in natural settings, and the ways in which children naturally acquire this knowledge in the cultural context in which they are embedded. The assumption is that children's and adults' primary folk knowledge will be privileged in terms of how the corresponding information is organized in memory and how people use this information to make sense of their experiences, including those in school. The next step is to analyze how well these folk representations and attributional biases fit with the scientific understanding of the same phenomena. Areas in which implicit or explicit folk knowledge is consistent with scientific knowledge may be particularly useful for initial engagement of students in the topic or as entry points into instruction on complex topics (Geary, 1995). For instance, children's understanding that parents will produce offspring that look and behave like them may be a way to begin to introduce the biological understanding of genetic inheritance.

From this perspective, the more difficult task with secondary learning is predicted to emerge for concepts in which folk knowledge is inconsistent with our scientific understanding of the same phenomena. In Table 4.1, I use this approach to emphasize points of contrast between the scientific concept of natural selection and folk biological conceptions of the same or similar phenomena.

The first point of contrast is the goal of this knowledge. The goal for people in traditional societies is to use plants and animals for food and medicine. The knowledge is functional and embedded in people's day-to-day survival-related activities (e.g., Atran, 1998; McDade et al., 2007). Of course, the principles of natural selection also pertain to the domain of living things, but the secondary goal of understanding the mechanisms that drive cross-generational change within species and the origin of new ones is not a common folk biological goal (Medin & Atran, 2004). If anything, people's default assumption is supernatural origins, which, as noted earlier, will remove the actual mechanisms of natural selection from the problem space and thus make a deep conceptual understanding of these principles difficult to achieve. This constraint is to say nothing about how students' religious beliefs and existential concerns about the implications of evolution for themselves and humans in general (e.g., the inevitable extinction of our species) influence their openness to learning how evolution works (Poling & Evans, 2004; Schilders, Sloep, Peled, & Boersma, 2009). In any case, a related

Table 4.1 Differences in Key Features of Natural Selection and Folk Biology

Point of contrast	Folk biology	Natural selection
Goals	Use of plants and animals for food and medicines	Understand cross-generation change within species (microevolution) and the emergence of new species (macroevolution)
Variation and essence	All members of the species share an essence. The focus is on within-species similarity.	Heritable variation is the grist of evolutionary change.
Mechanism of selection	The essence can be passed from parent to offspring and changes based on needs of the species.	Nonrandom differences in mortality and reproductive success
Foci of change	The species' essence	Traits that influence survival or reproductive prospects
Relations among species	Kingdom, species, subspecies	All species are related.

Note. From *The Origin of Mind: Evolution of Brain, Cognition, and General Intelligence* (pp. 190–191), by D. C. Geary, 2005, Washington, DC: American Psychological Association. Copyright 2005 by the American Psychological Association.

point is that the goal of learning natural selection is embedded in a wider and evolutionarily novel belief system—modern science (Kuhn, 1989)—that, in and of itself, is not fully understood by most students (e.g., Bell, Lederman, & Abd-El-Khalick, 2000). Without an understanding of the goal of scientific theory and empirical research in general, students may not fully understand the importance of natural selection in the biological sciences and thus not fully understand the goal of learning about it (Scharmann & Harris, 1992).

The second point contrasts the folk biological conception of essence with the importance of within-species variation for natural selection to occur. Essentialism reflects an often-implicit assumption that "identity is vested in invisible qualities: that an entity is imbued with essence through and through; and that the essence is permanent, fixed, and cannot be removed" (S. A. Gelman, 2003, p. 322). Whether species' essence—that all tigers, for instance, have the same underlying qualities that make them behave in similar ways—derives specifically from evolved folk biological modules or from domain-general processes that are applied to all things that can be categorized is a point of debate (Atran, 1998; S. A. Gelman, 2003; Medin & Atran, 2004). Whatever their cognitive origin, children's nascent folk biological knowledge, traditional people's implicit inferences about individuals of the same species, and adults in modern cultures who do not understand evolution indicate the same bias: to think about species in terms of underlying qualities that make all members of the same species the same and to assume that variation from the prototypical representation of these species may in fact be harmful (Mayr, 2001; Shtulman, 2006; Shtulman & Schulz, 2008).

The bias to think of all members of the same species as being imbued with the same essence may make hunting these species easier (Atran, 1998), but such reasoning may be the core impediment to a deep conceptual understanding of natural selection (Mayr, 2001). This hindrance occurs because the concept of a species' essence runs counter to the fact that within-species variation is critical for natural selection to occur. One educational implication is clear: Children need to understand that individuals of the same species not only are similar to one another in important ways but also differ from one another. Some plants of any particular species will grow taller, with fewer leaves, whereas others will be shorter, with more leaves. Whether an understanding of variation should precede formal instruction on natural selection or whether an introduction to natural selection is needed to highlight the importance of variation is not known (Shtulman & Schulz, 2008).

The third and fourth points are also related to species' essence, but here the impediment relates to understanding the mechanisms and foci of natural selection, respectively. Shtulman (2006) found that more than 50% of the high school and college students attending Harvard University summer school had a transformational belief about evolutionary change, specifically, that the species' essence is the focus of the change and that all members of the species change in the same way across generations. This conception contrasts with actual mechanisms of change, that is, nonrandom individual differences in survival and reproduction, and with the foci of change, that is, individual traits or constellations of traits that influence survival and reproductive prospects. Accompanying the transformational conceptualization of evolutionary change is the incorrect belief that evolution is purposeful and leads to improvement in the species' essence (e.g., to better fit the ecology; Bishop & Anderson, 1990; Nehm & Reilly, 2007).

The fifth point concerns students' understanding of the depth of common ancestors and the evolutionary relations among seemingly very different species. Adults make judgments about the common ancestors of species on the basis of how similar they look to one another (Poling & Evans, 2004), which is consistent with the implicit taxonomies that are found when people in traditional societies categorize specimens of related species (e.g., of bird; Medin & Atran, 2004). The latter indicate that people's bias is to organize species at the kingdom level (e.g., plants vs. animals) and then at the genus (e.g., bluebirds) and species (e.g., Eastern and Western bluebirds) levels. This way of organizing the biological relations among species is, of course, much more restricted than Darwin's (1859) and Wallace's (1855) tree-of-life analogies, and it is a predicted impediment to believing the scientific relations among species that look different and the core evolutionary concept of a common ancestor.

My point is to highlight the added value of contrasting the relations between evolved folk biases and the evolutionarily novel knowledge we are asking children to learn in modern schools. In this example, one sees that the evolved goal of learning about the natural world is functional, whereas the goal of learning natural selection is not, or, stated otherwise, the latter goal is embedded in the broader epistemological framework of science that many students do not understand or appreciate; many students do not understand how or why natural selection is important within the broader context of using science to better understand the social, biological, and physical worlds, and thus they may not be motivated to consider it as an alternative to their folk beliefs. People's tendency to essentialize other species is related to the functional goal of using them for food and medicine but also results in beliefs and attributional biases (e.g., all tigers are the same) that conflict with the knowledge needed to understand how natural selection operates. These points of conflict are predicted to be core areas of students' confusion during the learning process and areas in which educational interventions may yield the greatest gains.

Conclusions and Future Directions

I have discussed the implications of an evolutionary perspective for academic learning in other places (Geary, 1995, 2002, 2007, 2008) and thus make only a few points in this final section. On a conceptual level, biologically secondary academic learning should be distinguished from biologically primary cognitive development, that is, the universal core of children's folk knowledge and how this knowledge emerges during the developmental period and in the contexts in which children are embedded. The latter would need to include studies of children's knowledge development in cultures that are similar to those in which the folk domains evolved. This approach is based on the assumption that the evolutionary expansion of the human developmental period may have occurred to enable experience-dependent adaption of folk systems to the local social, biological, and physical worlds, but these experiences are not always that same as those of children growing up in modern societies (Medin & Atran, 2004). Without these types of cross-cultural studies, it will be difficult to cleanly separate the core of folk knowledge from cultural influences and to fully understand how experiences in modern cultures influence the developmental expression of folk knowledge.

Readers may question whether we need to even consider evolved biases if there are strong cultural influences on the emergence of children's folk knowledge. The work of Atran, Medin, and others has demonstrated that despite experiential influences on the expression of folk biological knowledge, there appear to be identifiable and universal constraints on how this knowledge is organized and how it influences people's implicit and explicit understanding of the biological world (Atran, 1998; Medin & Atran, 2004; Shtulman, 2006). Legare and Gelman (2008) found that Sesotho-speaking (South African) children and adults who had been exposed to medical explanations about the transmission of the AIDS virus provided both medically accurate as well as folk bewitchment explanations for why a target individual contracted the virus. Both forms of explanation were simultaneously available to most of the participants, and whether one explanation was offered or the other varied with how the question about transmission was asked and with age. Young children and adults were more likely than adolescents to endorse a bewitchment explanation, suggesting "that the explicit information children receive in school regarding witchcraft (that it is not a cause of AIDS) has a temporary effect but not a lasting impact" (Legare & Gelman, 2008, p. 628).

Moreover, many of the Sesotho explanations implied the use of mental models to better understand the dynamics of disease transmission by incorporating both explanations; "The people that hated her paid the witches to put the virus in her path; jealousy and spells[;] people sent someone with AIDS to sleep with him" (Legare & Gelman, 2008, p. 635). Accurate medical knowledge did not replace folk beliefs, it only provided a potential alternative explanation that was sometimes used and sometimes not. These biases are not unique to folk biology or less educated people. Studies of college and other students in modern societies and in other folk domains have also revealed a consistent set of biases and a reluctance to replace these biases with explicitly provided scientific explanations for the same phenomena (e.g., K. Dunbar, Fugelsang, & Stein, 2007). If children had an evolved bias to imitate and learn cultural practices and explanations about social, biological, and physical phenomena without inherent prejudice about how this information is organized and understood, then children imbued in a scientifically literate society with many years of formal education should not show many of the folk biases described in the preceding section and elsewhere.

As I described in the Mental Models and Problem Solving section, active inhibition of folk explanations and use of formal logic may be necessary for the construction of evolutionarily novel, scientific explanations; however, moving beyond the constraints of folk knowledge and attributional biases that emerge from this knowledge requires effort and extended experience in the evolutionarily novel domain (Stanovich & West, 2000, 2008); otherwise, even scientific experts may revert to the presumed default folk biases. Furthermore, I argued that the evolved systems support the explicit generation of mental models and engagement of goal-directed problem solving are necessary, but not sufficient, for the discovery and creation of evolutionarily novel competencies and knowledge and that these systems are most likely to be engaged when evolved or learned heuristics do not provide a satisfactory explanation for the phenomena or situation under consideration. Darwin did not find supernatural explanations for the origin of species to be satisfactory because they were inconsistent with newly emerging biologically secondary discoveries (e.g., the geological record; Lyell, 1830) and with his own acute observations of nature (e.g., Darwin, 1846). Students may not be as motivated as Darwin or Newton to expend effort to engage these systems to inhibit folk explanations and to construct new ones, in particular when the folk explanations are good enough for their day-to-day understanding of the world.

References

Adolphs, R. (1999). Social cognition and the human brain. *Trends in Cognitive Sciences, 3,* 469–479. doi:10.1016/S1364-6613(99)01399-6

Aiello, L. C., & Wheeler, P. (1995). The expensive-tissue hypothesis: The brain and digestive system in human and primate evolution. *Current Anthropology, 36,* 199–221. doi:10.1086/204350

Alexander, R. D. (1979). *Darwinism and human affairs.* Seattle: University of Washington Press.

Alexander, R. D. (1989). Evolution of the human psyche. In P. Mellars & C. Stringer (Eds.), *The human revolution: Behavioural and biological perspectives on the origins of modern humans* (pp. 455–513). Princeton, NJ: Princeton University Press.

Ash, J., & Gallup, G. G., Jr. (2007). Paleoclimatic variation and brain expansion during human evolution. *Human Nature, 18,* 109–124. doi:10.1007/s12110-007-9015-z

Atran, S. (1998). Folk biology and the anthropology of science: Cognitive universals and cultural particulars. *Behavioral and Brain Sciences, 21,* 547–569. doi:10.1017/S0140525X98001277

Bailenson, J. N., Shum, M. S., Atran, S., Medin, D. L., & Coley, J. D. (2002). A bird's eye view: Biological categorization and reasoning within and across cultures. *Cognition, 84,* 1–53. doi:10.1016/S0010-0277(02)00011-2

Bailey, D. H., & Geary, D. C. (2009). Hominid brain evolution: Testing climatic, ecological, and social competition models. *Human Nature, 20,* 67–79. doi:10.1007/s12110-008-9054-0

Bandura, A. (1997). *Self-efficacy: The exercise of control.* San Francisco, CA: Freeman.

Baron-Cohen, S. (1995). *Mindblindness: An essay on autism and theory of mind.* Cambridge, MA: MIT Press/Bradford Books.

Barton, R. A. (1996). Neocortex size and behavioural ecology in primates. *Proceedings of the Royal Society of London: Biological Sciences, 263,* 173–177. doi:10.1098/rspb.1996.0028

Bell, R. L., Lederman, N. G., & Abd-El-Khalick, F. (2000). Developing and acting upon one's conception of the nature of science: A follow-up study. *Journal of Research in Science Teaching, 37,* 563–581. doi:10.1002/1098-2736(200008)37:6<563::AID-TEA4>3.0.CO;2-N

Berlin, B., Breedlove, D. E., & Raven, P. H. (1973). General principles of classification and nomenclature in folk biology. *American Anthropologist, 75,* 214–242. doi:10.1525/aa.1973.75.1.02a00140

Bishop, B. A., & Anderson, C. W. (1990). Student conceptions of natural selection and its role in evolution. *Journal of Research in Science Teaching, 27,* 415–427. doi:10.1002/tea.3660270503

Bjorklund, D. F., & Pellegrini, A. D. (2002). *The origins of human nature: Evolutionary developmental psychology.* Washington, DC: American Psychological Association. doi:10.1037/10425-000

Bogin, B. (1999). *Patterns of human growth* (2nd ed.). Cambridge, England: Cambridge University Press.

Botvinick, M. M., Braver, T. S., Barch, D. M., Carter, C. S., & Cohen, J. D. (2001). Conflict monitoring and cognitive control. *Psychological Review, 108,* 624–652. doi:10.1037/0033-295X.108.3.624

Bouchard, T. J., Jr., Lykken, D. T., Tellegen, A., & McGue, M. (1996). Genes, drives, environment, and experience. In C. P. Benbow & D. Lubinski (Eds.), *Intellectual talent: Psychometric and social issues* (pp. 5–43). Baltimore, MD: Johns Hopkins University Press.

Brothers, L. (1990). The social brain: A project for integrating primate behavior and neurophysiology in a new domain. *Concepts in Neuroscience, 1,* 27–51.

Brothers, L., & Ring, B. (1992). A neuroethological framework for the representation of minds. *Journal of Cognitive Neuroscience, 4,* 107–118. doi:10.1162/jocn.1992.4.2.107

Brown, D. E. (1991). *Human universals.* Philadelphia, PA: Temple University Press.

Browne, J. (2002). *Charles Darwin: The power of place.* New York, NY: Knopf.

Bugental, D. B. (2000). Acquisition of the algorithms of social life: A domain-based approach. *Psychological Bulletin, 126,* 187–219. doi:10.1037/0033-2909.126.2.187

Campbell, D. P., & Holland, J. L. (1972). A merger in vocational interest research: Applying Holland's theory to Strong's data. *Journal of Vocational Behavior, 2,* 353–376.

Caporael, L. R. (1997). The evolution of truly social cognition: The core configurations model. *Personality and Social Psychology Review, 1,* 276–298. doi:10.1207/s15327957pspr0104_1

Changizi, M. A. (2003). *The brain from 25,000 feet: High level explorations of brain complexity, perception and vagueness.* Dordrecht, The Netherlands: Kluwer Academic.

Clement, J. (1982). Students' preconceptions in introductory mechanics. *American Journal of Physics, 50,* 66–71. doi:10.1119/1.12989

Cosmides, L. (1989). The logic of social exchange: Has natural selection shaped how humans reason? Studies with the Wason selection task. *Cognition, 31,* 187–276. doi:10.1016/0010-0277 (89)90023-1

Darwin, C. (1846). *Journal of researches into the geology and natural history of the various countries visited by H. M. S. Beagle.* New York, NY: Harper & Brothers.

Darwin, C. (1859). *The origin of species by means of natural selection* (6th ed.). London, England: John Murray.

Darwin, C. (1871). *The descent of man, and selection in relation to sex.* London, England: John Murray.

Darwin, C., & Wallace, A. (1858). On the tendency of species to form varieties, and on the perpetuation of varieties and species by natural means of selection. *Journal of the Linnean Society of London. Zoology, 3,* 45–62.

Darwin, F. (Ed.). (2000). *The autobiography of Charles Darwin.* Amherst, NY: Prometheus Books. (Original work published 1887)

Deacon, T. W. (1990). Rethinking mammalian brain evolution. *American Zoologist, 30,* 629–705.

Desmond, A., & Moore, J. (1994). *Darwin: Life of a tormented evolutionist.* New York, NY: Norton.

Drigotas, S. M. (2002). The Michelangelo phenomenon and personal well-being. *Journal of Personality, 70,* 59–77. doi:10.1111/1467-6494.00178

Dunbar, K., Fugelsang, J., & Stein, C. (2007). Do naïve theories ever go away? In M. Lovett & P. Shah (Eds.), *Thinking with data: 33rd Carnegie Symposium on Cognition* (pp. 193–205). Mahwah, NJ: Erlbaum.

Dunbar, R. I. M. (1998). The social brain hypothesis. *Evolutionary Anthropology, 6,* 178–190. doi:10.1002/(SICI)1520-6505(1998)6:5<178::AID-EVAN5>3.0.CO;2-8

Dunbar, R. (2003, November 14). Evolution of the social brain. *Science, 302,* 1160–1161. doi:10.1126/science.1092116

Evans, J. S. (2002). Logic and human reasoning: An assessment of the deduction paradigm. *Psychological Bulletin, 128,* 978–996. doi:10.1037/0033-2909.128.6.978

Fiske, S. T., & Taylor, S. E. (1991). *Social cognition* (2nd ed.). New York, NY: McGraw-Hill.

Flinn, M. V., Geary, D. C., & Ward, C. V. (2005). Ecological dominance, social competition, and coalitionary arms races: Why humans evolved extraordinary intelligence. *Evolution and Human Behavior, 26,* 10–46. doi:10.1016/j.evolhumbehav.2004.08.005

Foley, R., & Lahr, M. M. (1997). Mode 3 technologies and the evolution of modern humans. *Cambridge Archaeological Journal, 7,* 3–36. doi:10.1017/S0959774300001451

Gallistel, C. R., & Gelman, R. (1992). Preverbal and verbal counting and computation. *Cognition, 44,* 43–74. doi:10.1016/0010-0277(92)90050-R

Geary, D. C. (1995). Reflections of evolution and culture in children's cognition: Implications for mathematical development and instruction. *American Psychologist, 50,* 24–37. doi:10.1037/ 0003-066X.50.1.24

Geary, D. C. (2002). Principles of evolutionary educational psychology. *Learning and Individual Differences, 12,* 317–345.

Geary, D. C. (2005). *The origin of mind: Evolution of brain, cognition, and general intelligence.* Washington, DC: American Psychological Association. doi:10.1037/10871-000

Geary, D. C. (2007). Educating the evolved mind: Conceptual foundations for an evolutionary educational psychology. In J. S. Carlson & J. R. Levin (Eds.), *Educating the evolved mind: Vol. 2. Psychological Perspectives on Contemporary Educational Issues* (pp. 1–99). Greenwich, CT: Information Age.

Geary, D. C. (2008). An evolutionarily informed education science. *Educational Psychologist, 43,* 179–195. doi:10.1080/00461520802392133

Geary, D. C., & Flinn, M. V. (2001). Evolution of human parental behavior and the human family. *Parenting: Science and Practice, 1,* 5–61. doi:10.1207/S15327922PAR011&2_2

Geary, D. C., & Huffman, K. J. (2002). Brain and cognitive evolution: Forms of modularity and functions of mind. *Psychological Bulletin, 128,* 667–698. doi:10.1037/0033-2909.128.5.667

Gelman, R. (1990). First principles organize attention to and learning about relevant data: Number and animate–inanimate distinction as examples. *Cognitive Science, 14,* 79–106. doi:10.1207/s15516709cog1401_5

Gelman, S. A. (2003). *The essential child: Origins of essentialism in everyday thought.* New York, NY: Oxford University Press.

Gigerenzer, G., Todd, P. M., & ABC Research Group (Eds.). (1999). *Simple heuristics that make us smart.* New York, NY: Oxford University Press.

Goodenough, E. W. (1957). Interest in persons as an aspect of sex differences in the early years. *Genetic Psychology Monographs, 55,* 287–323.

Greenough, W. T., Black, J. E., & Wallace, C. S. (1987). Experience and brain development. *Child Development, 58,* 539–559. doi:10.2307/1130197

Hofman, M. A. (2001). Brain evolution in hominids: Are we at the end of the road? In D. Falk & K. R. Gibson (Eds.), *Evolutionary anatomy of the primate cerebral cortex* (pp. 113–127). Cambridge, England: Cambridge University Press.

Holloway, R. L., Jr. (1968). The evolution of the primate brain: Some aspects of quantitative relations. *Brain Research, 7,* 121–172. doi:10.1016/0006-8993(68)90094-2

Holloway, R. L. (1973). Endocranial volumes of early African hominids, and the role of the brain in human mosaic evolution. *Journal of Human Evolution, 2,* 449–459. doi:10.1016/0047-2484(73)90123-1

Holloway, R. (1996). Evolution of the human brain. In A. Lock & C. R. Peters (Eds.), *Handbook of human symbolic evolution* (pp. 74–116). New York, NY: Oxford University Press.

Holloway, R. L., Broadfield, D. C., & Yuan, M. S. (2004). *The human fossil record: Vol. 3. Brain endocasts—The paleoneurological record.* Hoboken, NJ: Wiley.

Holloway, R. L., & de la Coste-Lareymondie, M. C. (1982). Brain endocast asymmetry in pongids and hominids: Some preliminary findings on the paleontology of cerebral dominance. *American Journal of Physical Anthropology, 58,* 101–110. doi:10.1002/ajpa.1330580111

Horowitz, D. L. (2001). *The deadly ethnic riot.* Berkeley: University of California Press.

Humphrey, N. K. (1976). The social function of intellect. In P. P. G. Bateson & R. A. Hinde (Eds.), *Growing points in ethology* (pp. 303–317). New York, NY: Cambridge University Press.

Jerison, H. J. (1974). *Evolution of the brain and intelligence.* New York, NY: Academic Press.

Johnson-Frey, S. H. (2003). What's so special about human tool use? *Neuron, 39,* 201–204. doi:10.1016/S0896-6273(03)00424-0

Johnson-Laird, P. N. (1983). *Mental models.* Cambridge, England: Cambridge University Press.

Johnson-Laird, P. N., & Byrne, R. M. J. (2002). Conditionals: A theory of meaning, pragmatics, and inference. *Psychological Review, 109,* 646–678. doi:10.1037/0033-295X.109.4.646

Kaas, J. H. (2000). Why is brain size so important: Design problems and solutions as neocortex gets bigger or smaller. *Brain and Mind, 1,* 7–23. doi:10.1023/A:1010028405318

Kahneman, D., & Tversky, A. (1982). The simulation heuristic. In D. Kahneman, P. Slovic, & A. Tversky (Eds.), *Judgment uncertainty: Heuristics and biases* (pp. 201–208). Cambridge, England: Cambridge University Press.

Kanazawa, S. (2008). Temperature and evolutionary novelty as forces behind the evolution of general intelligence. *Intelligence, 36,* 99–108. doi:10.1016/j.intell.2007.04.001

Kaplan, H., Hill, K., Lancaster, J., & Hurtado, A. M. (2000). A theory of human life history evolution: Diet, intelligence, and longevity. *Evolutionary Anthropology, 9,* 156–185. doi:10.1002/1520-6505(2000)9:4<156::AID-EVAN5>3.0.CO;2-7

Klahr, D. (2000). *Exploring science: The cognition and development of discovery processes.* Cambridge, MA: MIT Press.

Klahr, D., & Dunbar, K. (1988). Dual space search during scientific reasoning. *Cognitive Science, 12,* 1–48. doi:10.1207/s15516709cog1201_1

Klahr, D., & Simon, H. A. (1999). Studies of scientific discovery: Complementary approaches and convergent findings. *Psychological Bulletin, 125,* 524–543. doi:10.1037/0033-2909.125.5.524

Kuhl, P. K., Andruski, J. E., Chistovich, I. A., Chistovich, L. A., Kozhevnikova, E. V., Ryskina, V., . . . Lacerda, F. (1997, August 1). Cross-language analysis of phonetic units in language addressed to infants. *Science, 277,* 684–686. doi:10.1126/science.277.5326.684

Kuhn, D. (1989). Children and adults as intuitive scientists. *Psychological Review, 96,* 674–689. doi:10.1037/0033-295X.96.4.674

Legare, C. H., & Gelman, S. A. (2008). Bewitchment, biology, or both: The co-existence of natural and supernatural explanatory frameworks across development. *Cognitive Science, 32,* 607–642. doi:10.1080/03640210802066766

Leslie, A. M. (1987). Pretense and representation: The origins of "theory of mind." *Psychological Review, 94,* 412–426. doi:10.1037/0033-295X.94.4.412

Leslie, A. M., Friedman, O., & German, T. P. (2004). Core mechanisms in "theory of mind." *Trends in Cognitive Sciences, 8,* 528–533. doi:10.1016/j.tics.2004.10.001

Lyell, C. (1830). *Principles of geology: An attempt to explain the former changes of the earth's surface.* London, England: John Murray.

MacArthur, R. H., & Wilson, E. O. (1967). *The theory of island biogeography.* Princeton, NJ: Princeton University Press.

Malt, B. C. (1995). Category coherence in cross-cultural perspective. *Cognitive Psychology, 29,* 85–148. doi:10.1006/cogp.1995.1013

Malthus, T. R. (1798). *An essay on the principle of population as it affects the future improvement of society with remarks on the speculations of Mr. Godwin, M. Condorcet, and other writers.* London, England: Printed for J. Johnson, in St. Paul's churchyard.

Markus, H. (1977). Self-schemata and processing information about the self. *Journal of Personality and Social Psychology, 35,* 63–78. doi:10.1037/0022-3514.35.2.63

Mayr, E. (2001). *What evolution is.* New York, NY: Basic Books.

McDade, T. W., Reyes-García, V., Blackinton, P., Tanner, S., Huanca, T., & Leonard, W. R. (2007). Ethnobiological knowledge is associated with indices of child health in the Bolivian Amazon. *Proceedings of the National Academy of Sciences of the United States of America, 104,* 6134–6139. doi:10.1073/pnas.0609123104

McHenry, H. M. (1994). Tempo and mode in human evolution. *Proceedings of the National Academy of Sciences of the United States of America, 91,* 6780–6786. doi:10.1073/pnas.91.15.6780

Meck, W. H., & Church, R. M. (1983). A mode control model of counting and timing processes. *Journal of Experimental Psychology: Animal Behavior Processes, 9,* 320–334. doi:10.1037/0097-7403.9.3.320

Medin, D. L., & Atran, S. (2004). The native mind: Biological categorization and reasoning in development and across cultures. *Psychological Review, 111,* 960–983. doi:10.1037/0033-295X.111.4.960

Murray, C. (2003). *Human accomplishment: The pursuit of excellence in the arts and sciences, 800 B.C. to 1950.* New York, NY: HarperCollins.

Nehm, R. S., & Reilly, L. (2007). Biology majors' knowledge and misconceptions of natural selection. *Bioscience, 57,* 263–272. doi:10.1641/B570311

Newell, A., & Simon, H. A. (1972). *Human problem solving.* Englewood Cliffs, NJ: Prentice Hall.

Newton, I. (1995). *The principia* (A. Motte, Trans.). Amherst, NY: Prometheus Books. (Original work published 1687)

Oaksford, M., & Chater, N. (1998). *Rationality in an uncertain world: Essays on the cognitive science of human reasoning.* East Sussex, England: Psychology Press. doi:10.4324/9780203345955

Ospovat, D. (1979). Darwin after Malthus. *Journal of the History of Biology, 12,* 211–230.

Ospovat, D. (1981). *The development of Darwin's theory: Natural history, natural theology, and natural selection, 1838–1859.* Cambridge, England: Cambridge University Press.

Owen, R. (1860). Darwin on the origin of species. *Edinburgh Review, 3,* 487–532.

Paivio, A. (2007). *Mind and its evolution: A dual coding theoretical approach.* Mahwah, NJ: Erlbaum.

Pascalis, O., Scott, L. S., Shannon, R. W., Nicholson, E., Coleman, M., & Nelson, C. A. (2005). Plasticity of face processing in infancy. *Proceedings of the National Academy of Sciences of the United States of America, 102,* 5297–5300. doi:10.1073/pnas.0406627102

Paterson, S. J., Brown, J. H., Gsödl, M. K., Johnson, M. H., & Karmiloff-Smith, A. (1999, December 17). Cognitive modularity and genetic disorders. *Science, 286,* 2355–2358. doi:10.1126/science.286.5448.2355

Pinker, S. (1994). *The language instinct.* New York, NY: William Morrow.

Pinker, S. (1997). *How the mind works.* New York, NY: Norton.

Poling, D. A., & Evans, E. M. (2004). Religious belief, scientific expertise, and folk ecology. *Journal of Cognition and Culture, 4,* 485–524. doi:10.1163/1568537042484931

Posner, M. I. (1994). Attention: The mechanisms of consciousness. *Proceedings of the National Academy of Sciences of the United States of America, 91,* 7398–7403. doi:10.1073/pnas.91.16.7398

Potts, R. (1998). Variability selection in hominid evolution. *Evolutionary Anthropology, 7,* 81–96. doi:10.1002/(SICI)1520-6505(1998)7:3<81::AID-EVAN3>3.0.CO;2-A

Preuss, T. M. (2000). Taking the measure of diversity: Comparative alternatives to the model-animal paradigm in cortical neuroscience. *Brain, Behavior and Evolution, 55,* 287–299. doi:10.1159/000006664

Raby, P. (2001). *Alfred Russel Wallace: A life.* Princeton, NJ: Princeton University Press.

Rilling, J. K., & Insel, T. R. (1999). The primate neocortex in comparative perspective using magnetic resonance imaging. *Journal of Human Evolution, 37,* 191–223. doi:10.1006/jhev.1999.0313

Roe, A., & Klos, D. (1969). Occupational classification. *The Counseling Psychologist, 1,* 84–88. doi:10.1177/001100006900100324

Scarr, S. (1992). Developmental theories of the 1990s: Developmental and individual differences. *Child Development, 63,* 1–19. doi:10.2307/1130897

Scarr, S., & McCartney, K. (1983). How people make their own environments: A theory of genotype → environment effects. *Child Development, 54,* 424–435.

Scharmann, L. C., & Harris, W. M. (1992). Teaching evolution: Understanding and applying the nature of science. *Journal of Research in Science Teaching, 29,* 375–388. doi:10.1002/tea.3660290406

Schilders, M., Sloep, P., Peled, E., & Boersma, K. (2009). Worldviews and evolution in the biology classroom. *Education Research, 43,* 115–120.

Schneider, D. J. (1973). Implicit personality theory: A review. *Psychological Bulletin, 79,* 294–309. doi:10.1037/h0034496

Semendeferi, K. (2001). Advances in the study of hominoid brain evolution: Magnetic resonance imaging (MRI) and 3-D reconstruction. In D. Falk & K. R. Gibson (Eds.), *Evolutionary anatomy of the primate cerebral cortex* (pp. 257–289). Cambridge, England: Cambridge University Press.

Semendeferi, K., Armstrong, E., Schleicher, A., Zilles, K., & van Hoesen, G. W. (2001). Prefrontal cortex in humans and apes: A comparative study of area 10. *American Journal of Physical Anthropology, 114,* 224–241. doi:10.1002/1096-8644(200103)114:3<224::AID-AJPA1022>3.0.CO;2-I

Semendeferi, K., & Damasio, H. (2000). The brain and its main anatomical subdivisions in living hominoids using magnetic resonance imaging. *Journal of Human Evolution, 38,* 317–332. doi:10.1006/jhev.1999.0381

Sheeran, P., & Orbell, S. (2000). Self-schemas and the theory of planned behaviour. *European Journal of Social Psychology, 30,* 533–550. doi:10.1002/1099-0992(200007/08)30:4<533::AID-EJSP6>3.0.CO;2-F

Shepard, R. N. (1994). Perceptual–cognitive universals as reflections of the world. *Psychonomic Bulletin & Review, 1,* 2–28. doi:10.3758/BF03200759

Shtulman, A. (2006). Qualitative differences between naïve and scientific theories of evolution. *Cognitive Psychology, 52,* 170–194. doi:10.1016/j.cogpsych.2005.10.001

Shtulman, A., & Schulz, L. (2008). The relation between essentialist beliefs and evolutionary reasoning. *Cognitive Science, 32,* 1049–1062. doi:10.1080/03640210801897864

Simon, H. A. (1956). Rational choice and the structure of the environment. *Psychological Review, 63,* 129–138. doi:10.1037/h0042769

Simonton, D. K. (2009). Varieties of (scientific) creativity: A hierarchical model of domain-specific disposition, development, and achievement. *Perspectives on Psychological Science, 4,* 441–452. doi:10.1111/j.1745-6924.2009.01152.x

Stanovich, K. E. (1999). *Who is rational? Studies of individual differences in reasoning.* Mahwah, NJ: Erlbaum.

Stanovich, K. E., & West, R. F. (2000). Individual differences in reasoning: Implications for the rationality debate? *Behavioral and Brain Sciences, 23,* 645–665. doi:10.1017/S0140525X00003435

Stanovich, K. E., & West, R. F. (2008). On the relative independence of thinking biases and cognitive ability. *Journal of Personality and Social Psychology, 94,* 672–695. doi:10.1037/0022-3514.94.4.672

Stephan, W. G. (1985). Intergroup relations. In G. Lindzey & E. Aronson (Eds.), *Handbook of social psychology: Volume 2. Special fields and applications* (pp. 599–658). New York, NY: Random House.

Suddendorf, T., & Busby, J. (2003). Mental time travel in animals? *Trends in Cognitive Sciences, 7,* 391–396. doi:10.1016/S1364-6613(03)00187-6

Suddendorf, T., & Corballis, M. C. (1997). Mental time travel and the evolution of the human mind. *Genetic, Social, and General Psychology Monographs, 123,* 133–167.

Taylor, S. E. (1982). The availability bias in social perception and interaction. In D. Kahneman, P. Slovic, & A. Tversky (Eds.), *Judgment uncertainty: Heuristics and biases* (pp. 190–200). Cambridge, England: Cambridge University Press.

Timberlake, W. (1994). Behavior systems, associationism, and Pavlovian conditioning. *Psychonomic Bulletin & Review, 1,* 405–420. doi:10.3758/BF03210945

Tobias, P. V. (1987). The brain of *Homo habilis:* A new level of organization in cerebral evolution. *Journal of Human Evolution, 16,* 741–761. doi:10.1016/0047-2484(87)90022-4

Tooby, J., & Cosmides, L. (1995). Mapping the evolved functional organization of mind and brain. In M. S. Gazzaniga (Ed.), *The cognitive neurosciences* (pp. 1185–1197). Cambridge, MA: Bradford Books/MIT Press.

Tulving, E. (2002). Episodic memory: From mind to brain. *Annual Review of Psychology, 53,* 1–25. doi:10.1146/annurev.psych.53.100901.135114

Tversky, A., & Kahneman, D. (1974, September 27). Judgment under uncertainty: Heuristics and biases. *Science, 185,* 1124–1131. doi:10.1126/science.185.4157.1124

Wallace, A. R. (1855). On the law which has regulated the introduction of new species. *Annals & Magazine of Natural History, 16,* 184–196.

Wallace, A. R. (1869). Geological climate and origin of species. *London Quarterly Review, 126,* 187–205.

West, R. F., Toplak, M. E., & Stanovich, K. E. (2008). Heuristics and biases as measures of critical thinking: Associations with cognitive ability and thinking dispositions. *Journal of Educational Psychology, 100,* 930–941. doi:10.1037/a0012842

Witting, L. (2000). Population cycles caused by selection by density dependent competitive interactions. *Bulletin of Mathematical Biology, 62,* 1109–1136. doi:10.1006/bulm.2000.0200

Zilles, K., Armstrong, E., Moser, K. H., Schleicher, A., & Stephan, H. (1989). Gyrification in the cerebral cortex of primates. *Brain, Behavior and Evolution, 34,* 143–150. doi:10.1159/000116500

5

Educational Neuroscience: Applying the Klahrian Method to Science Education

Kevin Niall Dunbar

One of the most important foundational problems in the development of scientific theories has been the interplay between mechanistic and holistic accounts of scientific phenomena. For example, in the early 1870s, Jacques Loeb and Ernst Mach sought to formalize the disciplines of biology and physics (Pauly, 1987). Mach argued against theories concerning the existence of unobservable atoms, such as those proposed by Boltzmann (Pauly, 1987). Loeb and Mach felt that science should not become bogged down in debates reminiscent of the Middle Ages, when scholars argued over issues such as how many angels could dance on the head of a pin. Instead, they espoused the view that science should be based only on observable phenomena, control of variables, and clear experiments. At the time, biology was in the throes of instinct theory, in which over 1,000 instincts, such as the "air hunting instinct" or the "sleep instinct," were proposed as explanations for human behavior (McDougall, 1908). Both Mach and Loeb considered instinct theories highly subjective and circular (Pauly, 1987). They argued that science should provide mechanistic accounts of the world and eschew any theories that included unobservable, and often arbitrary, assumptions. This purely mechanistic approach reverberated through most scientific disciplines and fostered specific methods, theories, and assumptions that have left large footprints on science as it is known today.

More specifically, although Loeb and Mach's theories have been displaced, their methodological critiques had an enormous effect on biology, physics, psychology, and education. Several of Loeb's students became central figures in 20th-century psychology and biology (e.g., John Watson, the founder of behaviorism, and William Crozier, B. F. Skinner's advisor). Following Loeb, "Crozier fervently adhered to a program of studying the behavior of 'the animal as a whole' without appealing, as the psychologists did, to processes going on inside" (Vargas, 2005). Using Loeb's emphasis on mechanisms, Crozier also helped foster a generation of mechanistic biologists, notably Gregory Pincus.

This research was funded by the Spencer Foundation, the National Science and Engineering Research Council of Canada, the National Science Foundation, and grants from Dartmouth College and the University of Toronto.

Pincus, like Loeb, wished to establish control over phenomena and helped create the contraceptive pill. In bringing forth a mechanistic biology, Loeb spent much of his career at the Woods Hole Oceanographic Institution, which has been at the hub of the molecular biology revolution for the past half-century.

The mechanistic approach to science took hold of psychology and biology; however, a third place where mechanistic theories blossomed was in departments of education. In 1900, Edward Thorndike, one of the founders of educational psychology, met Loeb at Woods Hole and decided to pursue an experimental approach to education. Thorndike saw learning, in particular in educational settings, as the reinforcement of responses, and surmised that drill and practice were necessary for effective learning. Thus, from the 1920s until the late 1950s, learning theories based on mechanistic accounts of behavior were dominant approaches in both psychology and education.

During the 1950s, a battle raged between the mechanistic and the organismic approaches in all of these major fields. Biology was again a crucial battleground: The scene at the Department of Biology at Harvard was particularly acrimonious, where James Watson, the codiscoverer of the structure of DNA, frequently clashed with E. O. Wilson. Wilson emphasized organisms in their environment, whereas Watson reduced biology to its underlying molecular mechanisms. Wilson wrote a fascinating account of these "molecular wars" in his book *Naturalist* (1994):

> James Dewey Watson, the co-discoverer of the structure of DNA, served as one such adverse hero for me. When he was a young man, in the 1950s and 1960s, I found him the most unpleasant human being I had ever met. He came to Harvard as an assistant professor in 1956, also my first year at the same rank. At twenty-eight, he was only a year older. He arrived with a conviction that biology must be transformed into a science directed at molecules and cells and rewritten in the language of physics and chemistry. What had gone before, "traditional" biology—*my* biology—was infested by stamp collectors who lacked the wit to transform their subject into a modern science. He treated most of the other twenty-four members of the Department of Biology with a revolutionary's fervent disrespect. (pp. 218–219)

The landscape of psychology was on a similarly rocky path. Traditional American psychology was dominated by learning theory, which stood firmly in the mechanistic behaviorist tradition. Developmental psychology was no different. In his 1960 *Annual Review of Psychology* article on developmental psychology, Mussen stated that there "has been little evidence of progress toward systematic organization of the field" (p. 439). At that point in time, researchers dealt with specific aspects of development instead of the overall developmental process. Researchers in child development had been immersed in learning theory, which was an outgrowth of mechanistic behaviorism; however, the tide began to turn when Piaget's work (e.g., Piaget, 1936/1952) was translated into English. Piaget focused on both the logic of children's thinking and a qualitative understanding of the child's mind. His stage model of development was readily incorporated into developmental psychology.

At about the same time that Piaget's more holistic theories were infusing developmental psychology, the "cognitive revolution" was taking place in adult psychology. One branch of this movement was the information-processing approach, in particular that of Newell and Simon (e.g., 1972). Newell and Simon (1972) provided detailed models of cognitive processes and focused on specifying the precise mechanisms underlying complex cognitive situations. They replaced vague terms such as *encoding* and *retrieval* with computer models that clearly specified what these terms actually meant. Nowhere, however, was a precise mechanism more needed than in developmental psychology. Although Piaget had made an enormous contribution in focusing on qualitative changes across development, the mechanisms that led to these qualitative changes were unknown. (Miller [2002] provided an excellent discussion of the role information-processing approach to child development and its relation to other approaches to development.)

When David Klahr entered the field of child development, there were really only two approaches in use: (a) the mechanistic learning theory approach of researchers such as Kendler, and (b) the qualitative approach of Piaget. Many developmentalists attempted to quantify Piaget as a way of reconciling the two approaches (e.g., Laurendeau & Pinard, 1970). These researchers turned Piaget's qualitative observations into quantitative accounts of the ages at which children reach specific stages or whether certain substages in Piaget's theories really exist. The looming problem of specifying the underlying mechanisms of cognitive development was, however, left unanswered.

This problem was particularly acute for the concepts of *accommodation* and *assimilation*—the central mechanisms of change from one stage to another in Piaget's theory. Klahr sought to specify the precise mechanisms using computational models. One can think of Klahr's approach as the introduction of a language or formalism that allowed researchers to combine a mechanistic model with a rich qualitative understanding of central questions. Instead of seeing one approach as better than the other, Klahr has consistently brought the two seemingly opposite approaches together by specifying the precise computational mechanisms underlying development. This approach was central not only to his earlier work (Klahr & Wallace, 1976) and his work on scientific discovery (e.g., Klahr & Dunbar, 1988), but also to his more recent work on discovery learning versus direct instruction (e.g., Klahr & Nigam, 2004). This *Klahrian method* of taking complex issues and specifying the underlying mechanisms is one of the gifts that Klahr has given his students and colleagues.

In the fields of education and educational psychology, the battle between qualitative observations and quantitative accounts appeared to be unending, but beginning in the 1970s researchers sought to understand education not just by reducing it to one level but by combining different approaches into one (see, e.g., Dunbar & Blanchette, 2001, for earlier work on combining ecologically and mechanistically oriented approaches to science education). Most recently, my colleagues and I have argued that the many different approaches to education can come together in the new discipline of *educational neuroscience* (Dunbar & Fugelsang, 2005; Dunbar, Fugelsang, & Stein, 2007; Petitto, 2009; Petitto & Dunbar, 2004). The goal of our work is not to build bridges that could fall but instead, following the Klahrian method, to forge a new discipline that combines teaching practices, social factors, cognition, and brain functioning into one multifaceted discipline of educational neuroscience. Although we take a neuroscientific approach instead of a computational one, our goals are similar to Klahr's in that we seek to understand underlying mechanisms that are both theoretically significant and relevant to the resolution of important educational issues.

Combining Mechanistic and Situated Approaches to Understand Science Education

The Klahrian method involves three basic components: (a) qualitative research, (b) mechanistic qualitative research, and (c) a language for traversing between the mechanistic and the qualitative research. My colleagues and I began our educational neuroscience approach with naturalistic studies of scientists reasoning at laboratory meetings and found that the scientists devoted most of their time to proposing causal explanations for unexpected findings. In conducting this work, I first spent a year in three molecular biology laboratories and one immunology laboratory at a prestigious U.S. university. I used the weekly laboratory meeting as a source of data on scientific thinking, reasoning, and discourse. When my colleagues and I looked at the types of findings that the scientists made, we found that over half of the findings were unexpected and that these scientists had evolved a number of important strategies for dealing with such findings. One clear strategy that we observed was to reason causally about the findings: Scientists attempted to build causal models of their unexpected findings (Dunbar & Fugelsang, 2011). Many of the key unexpected findings were inconsistent with preexisting causal models. In subsequent qualitative research, we analyzed meetings in different laboratories at a prestigious Canadian university and at an Italian university. We obtained very similar findings at these institutions (Dunbar, 2011).

The next step in our use of the Klahrian method was to take the qualitative findings from the naturalistic research and investigate the mechanisms underlying the cognitive and the social mechanisms underlying these findings. We investigated these processes further using both neuroimaging (functional magnetic resonance imaging [fMRI], functional near-infrared spectroscopy [fNIRS], event-related potentials [ERPs], and magnetoencephalography) as well as behavioral analyses to study the neural underpinnings of specific mechanisms, such as causal and analogical reasoning. Our investigations of causal reasoning focused on discerning the neural mechanisms underlying confirmation bias. In Fugelsang and Dunbar's (2005) study, participants were asked to interpret data relative to plausible and implausible causal theories. The authors built a laboratory equivalent of the biology laboratories at which they had studied in which students obtained unexpected findings that were inconsistent with their preexisting theories. They investigated the brain activations when experimental outcomes were either expected or unexpected and where the underlying hypotheses being used were either plausible or implausible. Fugelsang and Dunbar found that evaluation of data that are consistent with a plausible causal theory recruited neural tissue in the caudate and parahippocampal gyrus. These data suggest that participants were attending to and encoding data that were consistent with their hypotheses. A different pattern of activation occurred, however, when participants were confronted with data that were inconsistent with their hypotheses: Data inconsistent with a plausible theory recruited neural tissue in the anterior cingulate, left prefrontal cortex, and precuneus (Fugelsang & Dunbar, 2005). This suggests that participants were treating the inconsistent data as errors and that the inconsistent data were not encoded.

My colleagues and I have proposed that these types of findings provide a neural instantiation of some of the mechanisms by which theory and data are integrated in the brain. We have also found other brain sites that participate in analogical reasoning when students are integrating theories (Green, Kraemer, Fugelsang, Gray, & Dunbar, 2010, in press). Thus, a number of different networks are activated when students and scientists reason about theory and data.

We have also used fMRI and ERPs to probe the ways that different contexts and expectations are involved in the recruitment of specific brain regions when reasoning about physical scenarios such as balls colliding and falling, which are almost universal scenarios in physics education (Fugelsang & Dunbar, 2009; Le, Neimier, & Dunbar, 2011; Roser, Fugelsang, Handy, Dunbar, & Gazzaniga, 2009). In one set of studies, participants were instructed to imagine that two objects were either billiard balls or positively charged particles. When the second object moved without being touched by the first object, students found the event implausible, yet when shown the same movie but told that these were two positively charged particles they found the events plausible (Fugelsang & Dunbar, 2009; Le et al., 2011). Even though the movies that the students observed were identical in both scenarios, the patterns of brain activation were very different in the different contexts. Regions in the right medial frontal gyrus were selectively recruited for plausible relative to implausible events when judging billiard balls, whereas regions in the left middle frontal gyrus were selectively recruited when judging positively charged particles. These findings support the hypothesis that people's understanding of causality is multidimensional and that contextual information changes the way that neural networks are recruited for the task (Fugelsang & Dunbar, 2009; Le et al., 2011). What is important for the present discussion is that neuroimaging research suggests that different contexts and instructions alter the recruitment of neural tissue instead of revealing one hard-wired function for each particular brain site.

In another set of tasks, the brains of physics and nonphysics students were imaged while they were viewing videos demonstrating either classical Newtonian physics, in which a large and a small ball fall at the same speed, or a non-Newtonian scenario, in which the larger ball drops faster than the small ball. When the nonphysics students saw the Newtonian movies (with two balls of different sizes falling at the same rate), their anterior cingulates showed increased activation, indicating that they regarded these events as strange or erroneous. Conversely, when the physics students saw the non-Newtonian movies (with the bigger ball falling faster than the smaller ball), their anterior cingulates showed increased activation (Dunbar et al., 2007). Thus, the physics students appeared to be regarding the non-Newtonian movie as erroneous, whereas the nonphysics students appeared to be regarding the Newtonian movie as erroneous. We have proposed that the selective recruitment of the anterior cingulate cortex, coupled with other task-related regions of interest, could be used as an index of conceptual understanding and the effects of education on the brain (Dunbar & Fugelsang, 2005; Naimi, Forster, & Dunbar, 2011).

In the next series of experiments, we turned to concepts discussed in most introductory chemistry courses: the molecular nature of matter (Nelson, Lizcano, Atkins, & Dunbar, 2007). Using fMRI, the brains of advanced chemistry and nonchemistry students were imaged while judging representations of molecules before and after a phase change (liquid to gas). In keeping with decades of educational research, the chemistry novices displayed a very different account of what happens when a liquid is heated from the chemistry experts. The novices stated that the water molecule breaks into oxygen or hydrogen molecules, whereas the experts stated that the spacing between the water molecules increase when there is a change of state. The imaging data revealed that chemistry experts showed relatively high levels of left inferior frontal activity on this task as compared with novices, whereas novices showed relatively high levels of inferior temporal and occipital activity as compared with experts. This pattern of results is consistent with chemistry novices treating the task as a form of perceptual classification, whereas chemistry experts treat the task as a form of semantic/conceptual classification. The results of this type of study suggest not that the advanced students have undergone a massive conceptual reorganization but simply that they have classified the information in a different way.

The results of the experiments summarized above suggest that a number of different neural mechanisms are involved in thinking about scientific concepts. First, when data are consistent with a preexisting concept, one sees indicators of learning, which allows learning to take place (Fugelsang & Dunbar, 2005). Second, when data are presented that are inconsistent with instantiated concepts, one sees specific brain structures activated, such as the anterior cingulate, that may prevent the recruitment of particular concepts necessary for learning. Most important, the results of these experiments suggest that even when students appear to be using scientific concepts appropriately, they may still have access to alternate explanations and may be inhibiting these alternative "old" constructs. Our finding that students activate inhibitory networks when they encounter data that are inconsistent with a plausible theory sheds new light on why it is so difficult for students to adopt alternate constructs: They may be encumbered by having to inhibit information that is inconsistent with their current representation. Our neuroimaging data on chemistry concepts indicate that many mechanisms are at work when students reason about concepts, such as the placing of concepts into different categories. The findings that fMRI can be used to distinguish between different uses of concepts, and that different patterns of activation are observed depending on the concept, suggest that conceptual change is neither as all-or-none nor as complete as suggested in the literature (see Naimi et al., 2011).

A key feature of the educational neuroscience approach is the use of the Klahrian method, that is, integrating multiple methods and conceptual frameworks. My colleagues and I have found this approach to be particularly useful when it comes to understanding the ways that scientists and students integrate different forms of knowledge. When we investigated scientists' discourse and reasoning in their own laboratories, for example, we found that scientists frequently used categorization, analogy, and unexpected findings together (Dunbar & Blanchette, 2001). Similarly, our fMRI work on analogical thinking has revealed that brain sites involved in categorization and in integrating information from different semantic domains are frequently activated together. In fact, a combination of neuroimaging and naturalistic data led us to propose the *microcategory account* of analogical reasoning (Green, Kraemer, Fugelsang, & Dunbar, 2008). This account emphasizes the role of categories in aligning terms for analogical mapping. Building on some of our earlier work (Dunbar & Blanchette, 2001), we used a semantic priming paradigm in which students judged whether an analogy was present in a set of items such as "*cat* is to *mouse* as *fish* is to *worm*" (Green et al., 2008). Students were asked to identify analogical relations, categorical relations, or conventionalized semantic relations in the four-word sets. After each four-word set was presented, a single target word appeared, and participants named this word aloud. Target words that referred to category relations in the preceding four-word sets were primed as strongly when participants identified analogies as when participants identified categories, suggesting that activation of category concepts plays an important role in analogical thinking. In addition, priming of category-referent words in the analogy and category tasks was significantly greater than priming of these words when participants identified conventionalized semantic relations. Because identical stimuli were used in all conditions, this finding indicates that it is the activation of category relations, distinct from any effect of basic semantic association, that led analogical reasoning to prime category-referent words. Thus, we found that aligning categories is an important component analogical reasoning. We have this sort of aligning of categories in our naturalistic studies of scientific thinking (Atkins, Velez, Goudy, & Dunbar, 2009; Dunbar & Blanchette, 2001).

In our most recent research using fMRI we have found that the amount of activation in the frontopolar cortex (also called the *rostrolateral prefrontal cortex,* or RLPFC) is directly related to the semantic relatedness of the terms of an analogy. The more distant the two components of analogy are, the greater the activation of the RLPFC (Bassok, Dunbar, & Holyoak, in press; Green et al., in press; Green, Fugelsang, Shamosh, Kraemer, & Dunbar, 2006). Furthermore, in our recent work on visitors' discourse patterns at a science museum, we have found that providing the visitors with analogs for scientific phenomena helps them coordinate the different information provided in an exhibit with their prior knowledge and expectations, thus leading to a more robust understanding of scientific phenomena (Atkins et al., 2009).

Using Analogy in Science Education

Although the above results point to some of the difficulties that students encounter when they are reasoning scientifically, or are engaged in scientific discourse, the work my colleagues and I have conducted on the educational neuroscience of analogy points to clear findings that foster conceptual change. Although many teachers and scientists have found that students do not effectively use analogies in learning new scientific concepts (e.g., Mestre, 2005), other research has been more successful with using analogy. In studying analogy generation both in our laboratories and in leading molecular biology laboratories and science museums, we have found that distant analogies are useful in helping communicate abstract conceptual thinking (Atkins et al., 2009; Dunbar & Blanchette, 2001). As I discussed in the previous section, analogies activate the RLPFC, which is involved in the integration of source and target information. Furthermore, we have found increased activation in the frontal poles and temporal lobes for distant analogies (Green et al., 2006, 2010, in press). In addition, recent work by Cho et al. (2010) showed that students must also engage in the inhibition of inappropriate analogs to successfully analogize. As mentioned above, my colleagues and I hypothesize that discarding or inhibiting prior concepts may be the area that presents the largest amount of difficulty for students in acquiring new scientific concepts. Much more needs to be learned in this area. We are currently investigating which brain regions are activated at which times during analogical reasoning for good and poor science students using near fNIRS. This new brain imaging technique measures both oxy and de-oxy hemoglobin levels in the brain and is less sensitive to movement artifacts than fMRI. Furthermore, the temporal resolution of fNIRS is much better than that of fMRI, and participants can talk while performing the tasks (Kovelman, Shalinsky, Berens, & Petitto, 2008). We have just started using this method and are already seeing that different types of analogies recruit different types of tissue depending on the task context (Forster & Dunbar, 2011). In addition, we are now using ERPs that are helping us disambiguate students' reactions to unusual causal events (Le et al., 2011; Roser et al., 2009).

Conclusions and Future Directions

What does educational neuroscience mean for science education? My colleagues and I propose that to achieve a robust and usable science of learning, it is important to move beyond the metaphor of building bridges between disciplines. Instead, our goal is to use multiple methods, theoretical stances, population groups, and cultures that build a mosaic of knowledge instead of the hegemony of one group over another. Our approach uses the Klahrian method of taking complex issues and specifying the underlying mechanisms. We feel that we are at the similar stage in our research to where Klahr was in the late 1960s and early 1970s: specifying underlying mechanisms of cognitive processes. We are using a neuroscience approach instead of a computational approach. The goals of our current work are similar to Klahr's: We seek to understand underlying mechanisms that are useful in real-world contexts and are relevant to important educational problems. To paraphrase Wilson's (1998) book *Consilience,* when this unified approach is used, important problems are solved, rather than brushed under the carpet in a flurry of revolution.

References

Atkins, L. J., Velez, L., Goudy, D., & Dunbar, K. N. (2009). The unintended effects of interactive objects and labels in the science museum. *Science Education, 93,* 161–184. doi:10.1002/sce.20291

Bassok, M., Dunbar, K. N., & Holyoak, K. J. (in press). Neural substrate of analogical reasoning and metaphor comprehension: Introduction to the special section. *Journal of Experimental Psychology: Learning, Memory, and Cognition.*

Cho, S., Moody, T. D., Fernandino, L., Mumford, J. A., Poldrack, R. A., . . . Holyoak, K. J. (2010). Common and dissociable prefrontal loci associated with component mechanisms of analogical reasoning. *Cerebral Cortex, 20,* 524–533.

Dunbar, K. (2011). *What is science? How we are all sometime scientists and scientists are often scientists.* Manuscript in preparation.

Dunbar, K. , & Blanchette, I. (2001). The *in vivo/in vitro* approach to cognition: The case of analogy. *Trends in Cognitive Sciences, 5,* 334–339. doi:10.1016/S1364-6613(00)01698-3

Dunbar, K. N., & Fugelsang, J. A. (2005). Causal thinking in science: How scientists and students interpret the unexpected. In M. E. Gorman, R. D. Tweney, D. Gooding, & A. Kincannon (Eds.), *Scientific and technical thinking* (pp. 57–79). Mahwah, NJ: Erlbaum.

Dunbar, K. N., & Fugelsang, J. A. (2011). *The educational neuroscience approach to science education.* Manuscript in preparation.

Dunbar, K. N., Fugelsang, J. A., & Stein, C. (2007). Do naïve theories ever go away? In M. Lovett & P. Shah (Eds.), *Thinking with data: 33rd Carnegie Symposium on Cognition* (pp. 193–206). Mahwah, NJ: Erlbaum.

Forster, E., & Dunbar, K. N. (2011, November). *Different types of analogy recruit different brain regions during analogy generation: A NIRS study.* Poster presented at the annual meeting of the Society for Neuroscience, Washington DC.

Fugelsang, J. A., & Dunbar, K. N. (2005). Brain-based mechanisms underlying complex causal thinking. *Neuropsychologia, 43,* 1204–1213. doi:10.1016/j.neuropsychologia.2004.10.012

Fugelsang, J. A., & Dunbar, K. N. (2009). Brain-based mechanisms underlying causal reasoning. In E. Kraft, B. Gulyas, & E. Poppel (Eds.), *Neural correlates of thinking* (pp. 269–279). Berlin, Germany: Springer-Verlag. doi:10.1007/978-3-540-68044-4_16

Green, A. E., Fugelsang, J. A., Shamosh, N., Kraemer, D., & Dunbar, K. N. (2006). Frontopolar cortex mediates abstract integration in analogy. *Brain Research, 1096,* 125–137. doi:10.1016/j.brainres.2006.04.024

Green, A. E., Kraemer, D. J. M., Fugelsang, J. A., & Dunbar, K. N. (2008). The microcategory account of analogy. *Cognition, 106,* 1004–1016. doi:10.1016/j.cognition.2007.03.015

Green, A. E., Kraemer, D. J. M., Fugelsang, J., Gray, J. R., & Dunbar, K. N. (2010). Connecting long distance: Semantic distance in analogical reasoning modulates frontopolar cortex activity. *Cerebral Cortex, 20,* 70–76. doi:10.1093/cercor/bhp081

Green, A. E., Kraemer, D. J. M., Fugelsang, J., Gray, J. R., & Dunbar, K. N. (in press). Mapping across semantic distance in creative analogical solution generation. *Journal of Experimental Psychology: Learning, Memory, and Cognition.*

Klahr, D., & Dunbar, K. (1988). Dual space search during scientific reasoning. *Cognitive Science, 12,* 1–48. doi:10.1207/s15516709cog1201_1

Klahr, D., & Nigam, M. (2004). The equivalence of learning paths in early science instruction: Effect of direct instruction and discovery learning. *Psychological Science, 15,* 661–667. doi:10.1111/j.0956-7976.2004.00737.x

Klahr, D., & Wallace, J. G. (1976). *Cognitive development: An information-processing view.* Hillsdale, NJ: Erlbaum.

Kovelman, I., Shalinsky, M. H., Berens, M. S., & Petitto, L. A. (2008). Shining new light on the brain's "bilingual signature": A functional near infrared spectroscopy investigation of semantic processing. *NeuroImage, 39,* 1457–1471. doi:10.1016/j.neuroimage.2007.10.017

Laurendeau, M., & Pinard, A. (1970). *The development of the concept of space in the child.* New York, NY: International Universities Press

Le, A., Neimier, M., & Dunbar, K. (2011). *Causal perception is not primary over causal cognition.* Manuscript in preparation.

McDougall, W. (1908). *An introduction to social psychology.* Boston, MA: Luce. doi:10.1037/12261-000

Mestre, J. P. (2005). *Transfer of learning: Research and perspectives.* Greenwich, CT: Information Age.

Miller, P. H. (2002). *Theories of developmental psychology* (4th ed.). New York, NY: W. H. Freeman.

Mussen, P. (1960). Developmental psychology. *Annual Reviews of Psychology, 11,* 439–478.

Naimi, A., Forster, E., & Dunbar, K. N. (2011). *Do non-physicists have naïve theories of physics? Brain imaging suggests not.* Manuscript in preparation.

Nelson, J. K., Lizcano, R. A., Atkins, L. J., & Dunbar, K. N. (2007, November). *Conceptual judgments of expert vs. novice chemistry students: An fMRI study.* Paper presented at the annual meeting of the Psychonomic Society, Long Beach, CA.

Newell, A., & Simon, H. A. (1972). *Human problem solving.* Englewood Cliffs, NJ: Prentice Hall.

Pauly, P. J. (1987). *Controlling life: Jacques Loeb and the engineering ideal in biology.* Cambridge, MA: Oxford University Press.

Petitto, L. A. (2009). New discoveries from the bilingual brain and mind across the lifespan: Implications for education. *Mind, Brain, and Education, 3,* 185–197.

Petitto, L. A. (in press). The educational neuroscience of language acquisition. *Mind, Brain, and Education.* doi:10.1111/j.1751-228X.2009.01069.x

Petitto, L. A., & Dunbar, K. N. (2004). New findings from educational neuroscience on bilingual brains, scientific brains, and the educated mind. In K. Fischer & T. Katzir (Eds.), *Building usable knowledge in mind, brain, & education.* Cambridge, England: Cambridge University Press. Retrieved from http://petitto.gallaudet.edu/~dunbarlab/pubpdfs/pettitodunbarIP.pdf

Piaget, J. (1952). *The origins of intelligence in children.* New York, NY: International University Press. (Original work published 1936) doi:10.1037/11494-000

Roser, M. E., Fugelsang, J. A., Handy, T. C., Dunbar, K. N., & Gazzaniga, M. S. (2009). Representations of physical plausibility revealed by event-related potentials. *NeuroReport, 20,* 1081–1086. doi:10.1097/WNR.0b013e32832e0c8d

Vargas, J. S. (2005). *A brief biography of B.F. Skinner.* Retrieved from http://www.bfskinner.org/BFSkinner/AboutSkinner.html

Wilson, E. O. (1994). The molecular wars. In *Naturalist* (pp. 218–237). Washington, DC: Island Press. Retrieved from https://www.msu.edu/course/lbs/333/fall/wilson.html

Wilson, E. O. (1998). *Consilience: The unity of knowledge.* New York, NY: Vintage Books.

6

Is Development Domain Specific or Domain General? A Third Alternative

Annette Karmiloff-Smith

The admirable work of David Klahr on complex reasoning processes and scientific discovery in children has led to important discoveries in educational research (Carver & Klahr, 2001; Klahr, 2005; Klahr & Li, 2005; Klahr & Nigam, 2004). My early research overlapped with Klahr's in the area of the complexities of scientific discovery in children but subsequently led to studies of much less complex processes in children with genetic disorders. In this chapter, I briefly examine domain-general theories, such as Klahr's, versus domain-specific theories, and offer a third alternative: a neuroconstructivist theory of domain-relevant biases that constrain the emerging specialization of brain structure and function throughout development. After indicating how this theory could account for brain plasticity and cognitive flexibility, I use several cases of atypical development to demonstrate the cascading developmental effects of initial genetic perturbations and the ways that tracing specific cognitive-level deficits back to deficits in more basic general processes help researchers better understand differing developmental trajectories across disorders. Grounded by that understanding of basic-level processes, researchers are now poised to study how children with neurodevelopmental disorders engage in more complex problem-solving tasks, such as those used in Klahr's developmental research. On the basis of my prior work, I hypothesize that differences in representational change may account for developmental progressions in typical versus atypical populations. In this way, the newly emerging field of educational neuroscience may well integrate earlier research on complex problem-solving strategies in older children with research on more basic-level processes in infants and toddlers in particularly productive ways.

Domain-General Approaches to Development

Developmental theorizing has frequently swung between domain-specific and domain-general approaches. The doyen of developmental psychology, Jean Piaget, was a prime example of the domain-general approach. He argued that three domain-general mechanisms—(a) assimilation, (b) accommodation, and (c) equilibration—underlie development across all domains, be they number, space, physical causality, social cognition, or language (Piaget, 1923/2001).

Several computational modeling approaches to child development are also domain general in nature. For example, Klahr used production system modeling (e.g., Klahr, Langley, & Neches, 1987) to account for children's problem solving across a wide variety of domains (see also Klahr, 1992, 1994, 1999, 2000, 2004; Klahr & Dunbar, 1989; Penner & Klahr, 1996).

Domain-Specific Approaches to Development

It was in the late 1970s and 1980s, mostly inspired by Fodor's (1983) modularity theory, that the domain-specific approach to human development came into full swing, in particular among nativist theorists (Spelke & Kinzler, 2007). Each cognitive domain was considered to embody specialized learning mechanisms that processed the proprietary inputs of only that particular domain. Thus, researchers argued that a theory-of-mind module (Leslie, 1992) involved a very different structure and processing from a syntactic module (Pinker, 1994; van der Lely, 2005) or a number module (Butterworth, 1999). Data supporting the domain-specific approach were drawn from findings from adult neuro-psychological patients (e.g., Duchaine & Nakayama, 2006) with specific cognitive deficits in an otherwise-unimpaired system (e.g., agrammatism, prosopagnosia) and from children with genetic disorders (e.g., Tager-Flusberg, Boshart, & Baron-Cohen, 1998; Temple, 1997; van der Lely, 2005) and seemingly equivalent domain-specific impairments (specific language impairment, developmental prosopagnosia).

Problems With the Domain-General and Domain-Specific Approaches

The domain-general approach obviously has difficulty in explaining uneven cognitive profiles, which are found in both typical and atypical development. A typically developing child may show very strong proficiency in, say, mathematics and be relatively weaker in reading. Other children may struggle with mathematics but be strong in language. Among populations developing atypically, a child with autism may show extremely good abilities in, for example, drawing but be incapable of stringing a few words together. An individual with Williams syndrome (WS) may display proficiencies in language but be unable to make simple addition calculations. At first blush, these uneven profiles are reminiscent of the dissociations invoked in studies of adult neuropsychological patients (but see Karmiloff-Smith, Scerif, & Ansari, 2003, for a discussion). So, in light of these uneven profiles, must one opt for the domain-specific approach to explain the starting state of the human mind/brain? The answer is not necessarily, because the domain-specific approach ignores the process of development whereby, instead of the starting point, domain specificity may be the outcome of a system that becomes specialized over developmental time as a result of processing different kinds of environmental inputs. Development really counts. Recall that even gene expression is not predetermined but a function of environmental experience over developmental time. Research on rodents eloquently illustrates this point, underlining the potential role of the environment in shaping patterns of gene expression (Kaffman & Meaney, 2007). Kaffman and Meaney (2007) studied brain development in rodent pups and demonstrated how differences in maternal behavior (e.g., amount of grooming) influence patterns of gene expression, which have lifelong effects on the animal's reactions to stress. Instead of thinking of gene expression as preprogrammed, they showed that differences in the amount of postnatal pup grooming and stroking change the amount and location of expression of certain genes involved in the body's responses to stress. These kinds of dynamic environment–gene relations may well be pervasive in mammalian brain development, including that of humans. In general, epigenesis is not deterministic under tight genetic control; instead, as Gottlieb (2007) stressed, epigenesis is probabilistic and seems to be under only very broad genetic control. Therefore, if the adult brain is highly specialized, it is likely the product of very complex gene–brain–cognition–behavior–environment dynamics, which give rise over developmental time to relatively domain-specific outcomes.

A Third Alternative: Domain-Relevant Starting States

It is within the neuroconstructivist account of development (Elman et al., 1996; Johnson, 2001; Karmiloff-Smith, 1992, 1998, 2006, 2007; Mareschal et al., 2007; Westermann, Karmiloff-Smith, & Thomas, 2010) that domain-relevant approaches have been proposed, in particular with respect to developmental disorders. The latter are deemed explicable at a very different level from the notion of intact/impaired domain-specific cognitive modules often invoked by nativists; instead, the neuroconstructivist approach argues that phenotypic outcomes are due to perturbations in far more basic processes early in development, such as a lack of or overexuberant pruning or differences in synaptogenesis, in dendritic growth, in the density and type of neurons, in firing thresholds, in poor signal-to-noise ratios, or in general in terms of atypical timing across developing systems (Karmiloff-Smith, Scerif, & Thomas, 2002). Rather than invoking a start state of innate, domain-specific modules handed down by evolution, the neuroconstructivist approach argues for increased plasticity for learning (Finlay, 2007), that is, for a limited number of domain-relevant biases, which become domain specific over developmental time by means of their competitive interaction with each other when attempting to process environmental inputs (Johnson, 2001; Karmiloff-Smith, 1998). Evolution is considered to be a trade-off between hyperspecialization together with a relative lack of flexibility, at one end of the species continuum, and maximum plasticity, together with some domain-relevant constraints, at the other end (Karmiloff-Smith, 1992, 2009; Quartz & Sejnowsky, 1997). In other words, from a neuroconstructivist viewpoint, the structure and function of adult brain specialization emerge developmentally during the ontogenetic process of gradual localization and specialization of function (i.e., progressive modularization; Elman et al., 1996; Johnson, 2001; Karmiloff-Smith, 1992, 1998). In this sense, it is probably the case that domain-specific outcomes are not even possible without the gradual process of development over time.

Brain Plasticity and Cognitive Flexibility

The sea slug, the ant, and the spider process complex information and output intricate behavioral patterns, yet, as Gleitman, Gleitman, and Shipley (1972) nicely put it, "the child knows something about language that the spider does not know about web-weaving." Indeed, many other species have complex special-purpose responses to the environment that humans do not possess in early childhood; however, humans ultimately develop an exceedingly rich, flexible cognitive system. What makes the human system flexible? An example of a surprising lack of flexibility from another species illustrates this point. The flight and parental behavior of one bird, the piping plover, are particularly interesting in this respect. If a predator comes too close to the plover's chicks or to a nest containing the plover's eggs, the adult bird will try to draw the intruder away by displaying a very complex flight pattern and pretending to have an injured wing. In this way, the adult bird pretends to be easy prey and lures the predator away, thus leaving the eggs or chicks unharmed. However, when the same adult bird has found a source of food and a predator nears, the plover does not make use of the same deceptive flight pattern at all. In other words, its exquisitely adapted flight for protecting its young is not generalizable to any other situation; there is a rigid mapping between a specific environmental situation and a complex innately specified action pattern. Human infants and children are not like this (Karmiloff-Smith, 1992): When they discover a solution to a problem, they try to generalize/adapt it to other situations and/or explore new strategies to solve the initial problem.

Many facts about early human brain and cognitive development point to a flexible, plastic, self-structuring system that is open to environmental influences. First, the cortex starts out highly interconnected in the very young infant (Huttenlocher & de Courten, 1987), and it is only very gradually, over time, with the strengthening of some connections and the pruning of others, that localization and specialization of brain function occur (Johnson, 2001). Second, there are changes to both white matter and gray matter across development (Giedd et al., 1999), with gray matter decreasing as intraregion connectivity is pruned and white matter increasing even through to adolescence as inter-regional connectivity increases. Thus, the dynamics of brain networks change over developmental time. Third, the thickness of fiber bundles in the corpus callosum between the two hemispheres is different in infancy compared with later development (Giedd et al., 1996), meaning that information flow between the two hemispheres changes over developmental time. Fourth, studies of the electrophysiology of the brain's processing of, for example, faces or speech, have revealed initial widespread activity across several regions of cortex in both hemispheres; it is only over developmental time that the electrophysiological activity becomes progressively fine-tuned to predominantly one hemisphere: the right hemisphere for faces, the left hemisphere for speech (de Haan, Humphreys, & Johnson, 2002; Johnson, 2001; Mills et al., 2000; Neville, Mills, & Bellugi, 1994). These developmental examples clearly indicate that brain structure and function are not static. Likewise, adult brain plasticity is well documented (Merzenich, 1995). Cortical networks are neither built in nor genetically determined, to be preserved or impaired in genetic disorders; instead, they are the emergent outcome of progressively changing processes, which dynamically interact with one another and with environmental input over developmental time, ultimately to give rise to the structured adult brain.

Neuroconstructivism maintains that the neonate cortex starts with some regional differentiation in terms of types of neuron, density of neurons, firing thresholds, and so on. These differences are not domain specific, aimed at the sole processing of proprietary inputs; neither do they amount to domain-general constraints. Instead, they are *domain relevant,* meaning that different parts of the brain have small structural differences, which happen to be more relevant to certain kinds of processing over others. Initially, however, brain activity is widespread in processing all types of input. It is the initial competition between regions that gradually settles which domain-relevant circuits become domain specific over time. That is why, for example, if a left hemispherectomy is carried out very early in development, brain circuits in the right hemisphere assume the functions that might have been predominant in the left hemisphere (Stiles, Bates, Thal, Trauner, & Reilly, 1998). Emergent specialization of function (e.g., for faces) might well be viewed as the fine-tuning of initially domain-relevant but coarsely-coded systems (e.g., for visual patterns), but this coding is initially for visual patterns in general, not for faces in particular. The face specialization is likely to emerge from the interaction between the environment (huge numbers of face stimuli over time) and the initial visual processing constraints, not from a prespecified, dedicated face-processing module, as some would argue (e.g., Duchaine & Nakayama, 2006).

For decades, the notion of plasticity tended to be reserved for the human system's response to damage. By contrast, it has become abundantly clear that development—whether typical or atypical—is characterized by plasticity for learning (Sur, Pallas, & Roe, 1990; Webster, Bachevalier, & Ungerleider, 1995), with the infant brain dynamically structuring itself over the course of ontogeny. Although some macrostructures, such as the overall six-layer structure of cortex, may well be under general genetic constraints, much of the microcircuitry of the cortex results from complex multilevel interactions over time. Human intelligence is not a *state*—a collection of static, built-in modules handed down by evolution; rather, human intelligence is a *process*—the emergent property of dynamic multidirectional interactions among genes, brain, cognition, behavior, and environment.

A Computational Model of Emergent Specialization

An eloquent illustration of emergent specialization can be found in a connectionist model of the dorsal and ventral streams. A small difference in activation levels (equivalent to a difference in neuronal firing thresholds) between two processing streams suffices, after competing to process identical inputs, to result in one stream eventually processing the location of objects and the other stream processing the features of objects (O'Reilly & McClelland, 1992). In other words, the "where" and "what" pathways in this model are not built in from the start, with one processing only spatial information and the other processing only featural information about objects. Both streams initially process all inputs, but an initial, tiny, domain-relevant difference in the speed of activation levels is sufficient to give rise to gradual, emergent specialization of the "where" and "what" pathways. Without this firing threshold difference, both streams would continue to process all inputs in a domain-general way. It is immediately clear, then, how a small deficit in, for example, the more rapidly activating stream could impair spatial processing because of its relevance to that domain. Systems are dynamic over developmental time (Thelen & Smith, 1994).

Mapping Genes to Phenotypes: The *FOXP2* Gene

A particularly telling example of domain relevance can be seen across studies of the *FOXP2* gene. Initially hailed as a "gene for language" (Pinker, 2001) and, even more specifically, "a gene for linguistic morphology" (Gopnik & Cragoa, 1991), it rapidly became clear that the gene contributed to something far more basic and general. The scientific history of the gene's discovery is instructive. Some members of a British family, known as the *KE family*, presented with serious speech and language deficits across generations, whereas other family members did not. The intergenerational deficits clearly suggested a genetic basis, and in 1998 a gene was identified—*FOXP2* on chromosome 7—that had two amino acid mutations in affected family members but not in unaffected ones (Fisher & Scharff, 2009; Fisher, Vargha-Khadem, Watkins, Monaco, & Pembrey, 1998). A comparison of human and chimpanzee *FOXP2*, whose lines separated some 4 to 6 million years ago, revealed no changes in the chimp *FOXP2*, whereas the human version of the gene had undergone small changes some 200,000 years ago. For some researchers (e.g., Mesoudi, Whiten, & Laland, 2006), the coincidence in timing was irresistible: In evolutionary terms, the human gene, whose mutation caused speech and language deficits in the KE family, had changed at just around the time that anthropologists had situated the onset of human language, also some 200,000 years ago. Was this the gene that explained why humans acquire language and chimpanzees do not?

Unfortunately for this ostensibly simple and attractive theory about human language, *FOXP2* is a highly conserved gene and is found in species as different as humans, apes, birds, rodents, and snakes. *FOXP2* is a *transcription factor*; that is, it is involved in switching on and off other genes. After the initial hype of calling *FOXP2* a "gene for language," *FOXP2* was subsequently studied in birds, mice, and chimpanzees. The first research questions concerned communication systems, remaining close to the notion that *FOXP2* makes a particular contribution to vocal communication. Research on birds that learn their song, such as zebra finches and canaries, showed that *FOXP2* is expressed significantly more during song learning than during subsequent song production (Bolhuis, Zijlstra, den Boer-Visser, & van der Zee, 2000; Haesler et al., 2004). A subsequent study of *FOXP2* expression in the mouse over developmental time showed that initially the gene was widely expressed in the brain, but its expression was then increasingly restricted to motor circuits, in particular the cerebellum (Lai, Gerrelli, Monaco, Fisher, & Copp, 2003). In the meantime, research on humans—specifically, the KE family—was beginning to reveal that deficits in affected family members were not confined to speech and language:

Impairments were also found in orofacial articulation (even for sequences of nonlinguistic tongue and facial movements), in fine motor control, and in the perception and production of simple rhythms (Vargha-Khadem, Watkins, Alcock, Fletcher, & Passingham, 1995). These various behaviors in humans, birds, and mice have something in common, which is not language: They all involve the skilled coordination and timing of rapid movement sequences. Therefore, *FOXP2* is highly unlikely to be a gene for language, but its mutation influences language because of cascading developmental effects of initial deficits in movement planning and timing on speech. Because timing and rapid movement sequence planning are most relevant to human speech, it is this domain that is the most obviously affected by the mutation; that is, the mutation is domain relevant to speech, but not domain specific to it. Focusing on this domain-relevant effect alters the questions that researchers should ask: not "What systems of oral communication are relatively similar in other species?" but "What behaviors in humans and other species require planning of the timing and coordination of rapid movement sequences?" Thus, in the human case, researchers might focus their efforts on studies of instrument playing or of learning a sign language in the visuo-manual mode, because both of these involve the skilled coordination and timing of rapid movement sequences. Researchers studying other species would examine not only vocal communication but also the range of behaviors outside communication in which rapid movement sequences and their intricate timing is particularly domain relevant.

Tracing Developmental Trajectories: Examples From Williams Syndrome

Cascading developmental effects of small initial perturbations are particularly relevant to our understanding of human disorders. In one developmental disorder, WS, the genetic mutations are present from conception and are due to a misalignment during meiosis of a section of one copy of chromosome 7 (Donnai & Karmiloff-Smith, 2000). A half-dosage of the deleted genes in WS that are normally expressed in the brain will be missing throughout cortical regions, so the effects of the gene dosage reduction are likely to be widespread, not specific to a single region of cortex or to a single purported module. The reduced expression of proteins, however, may affect different regions to greater or lesser degrees over developmental time, depending on how relevant their expression is to processing in that region.

If gradual specialization and localization of brain function are critical, then obviously empirical studies must trace development back to its infant beginnings (Karmiloff-Smith, 1998), building full developmental trajectories (Annaz, Karmiloff-Smith, & Thomas, 2008; Karmiloff-Smith, 1998; Karmiloff-Smith et al., 2004; Thomas et al., 2009). An example from human cognition— number—shows how a developmental approach can trace numerical abilities and deficits back to their origins in early infancy. A large body of experimental work has shown that older children and adults with WS have serious deficits in the numerical domain (Ansari & Karmiloff-Smith, 2002). Indeed, individuals with WS perform poorly on a vast number of numerical tasks, more poorly than matched individuals with Down syndrome (DS; Paterson, Girelli, Butterworth, & Karmiloff-Smith, 2006). In-depth studies of children with WS in the 5- to 12-year age range showed that although they could recite the count sequence fluently, they presented with serious problems in understanding cardinality (Ansari et al., 2003) and in making visual estimations of magnitude (Ansari, Donlan, & Karmiloff-Smith, 2007). In other words, when asked to get X marbles (with X varying from 1 to 9) from a bowl of marbles, they simply grabbed a handful, whereas the question "How many are there here?" generated an automatic procedure in which the individuals recited the count sequence, without realizing that the final one counted was in fact the cardinality of the set. In other words, they revealed that they did not know the purpose of their fluent counting.

To understand the roots of these deficits in children and adults, my colleagues and I have focused on infants and toddlers. An interesting pattern has emerged in which some initial infant abilities seemed "normal"—that is, like chronologically age–matched control infants—whereas other abilities were severely delayed. In a preferential looking task in which a series of pairs of objects were presented to infants until they got "bored," infants with WS, like healthy control infants, dishabituated when the number of objects changed to three. This was not the case for infants with DS, who performed more poorly than even mental age–matched control infants. In other words, infants and toddlers with WS successfully showed sensitivity to a change in small exact number (Paterson, Brown, Gsödl, Johnson, & Karmiloff-Smith, 1999; replicated in Van Herwegen, Ansari, Xu, & Karmiloff-Smith, 2008); however, when tested on large approximate number (groups of 16, 12, and eight dots with the comparison ratio of either 1:2 or 2:3), the infants and toddlers with WS failed to show discrimination (Van Herwegen et al., 2008). Research on large approximate number is currently underway with infants and toddlers with DS.

Given that later in childhood and adulthood, individuals with WS perform significantly worse on number tasks than those with DS, what do these opposite infancy results imply? They suggest that small, exact number discrimination may not be predictive of later numerical abilities and may merely reveal the tracking of a few objects in space instead of anything numerical. By contrast, large approximate number or magnitude discrimination does seem to be one of the early precursors to number development. So why do infants with WS fail the latter task? Again, a developmental trajectories perspective is critical. Brown et al. (2003) found that, early in development, infants with WS, but not those with DS, are very impaired on a double-step saccadic eye movement planning paradigm. They tested the hypothesis that compared with both chronological and mental age–matched typically developing infants and toddlers, and those with DS, infants and toddlers with WS displayed a deficit in using spatial representations to guide actions. The results showed that toddlers with WS were unable to combine extraretinal information with retinal information to the same extent as the other groups, and they displayed evidence of other deficits in saccade planning, suggesting a greater reliance on subcortical mechanisms than the other populations. The results also indicated that the visual exploration of the environment by toddlers with WS is less developed.

This early deficit in eye movement planning in WS could cascade over several domains (Karmiloff-Smith, 2009) and be one of the roots of those individuals' subsequent deficits in scanning large-magnitude displays, something on which my and my colleagues' preliminary results with infants and toddlers with DS show they accomplish with success. Thus, from an early deficit in the visual domain, together with problems in infancy with perceptual grouping (Farran, Brown, Cole, Houston-Price, & Karmiloff-Smith, 2007), emerges a deficit in the number domain in WS but not in some aspects of numerical processing in DS, in which visual acuity can be poor but the ability to plan eye movements and thus to scan the environment is good. In other words, tracing specific cognitive-level deficits in number back to infant deficits in more basic general processes helps one to construct differing cross-syndrome trajectories of development.

Representational Change

In the preceding sections, I have focused on the roots of developmental deficits in infants and toddlers, but what about subsequent development? In my previous work on typically developing children, I have argued that one salient aspect of human development was the ability to re-represent, in an explicit form, information that was initially embodied in procedural knowledge. I have termed this the *representational redescription hypothesis* (Karmiloff-Smith, 1979, 1984, 1990, 1992). Once representations are explicitly formed, they enable the system to become more flexible; that is, information can then be transported to other domains instead of remaining embedded in its initial procedural form. To explore this hypothesis, I have examined problem-solving abilities in children, not only in terms of success or failure but also with respect to the microdevelopmental details of change in their problem-solving strategies and in their mental representations of the task (Karmiloff-Smith, 1979, 1984, 1992; Karmiloff-Smith & Inhelder, 1974). A number of Klahr's classic, child-friendly problem-solving tasks (e.g., Klahr & Wallace, 1976) inspired the experiments used in my microdevelopmental research on typically developing children.

In my view, researchers now have sufficient knowledge of the basic cognitive architecture and abilities of individuals with WS and DS (and, of course, of a number of other developmental disorders). Thus, the time has come to focus research on the use of these individuals' abilities in problem-solving tasks, ones that are simple enough to engage participants with learning disabilities but also designed in such a way as to tap any representational changes that may or may not occur. Two examples of such tasks that are usable in studies of children with developmental disorders can be adapted from my own work on typically developing children (Karmiloff-Smith, 1984; Karmiloff-Smith & Inhelder, 1974). In one task, children are asked to balance a series of blocks on a narrow support. Some of the blocks are weighted at one end and thus do not balance at their geometric center. Most 5- and 9-year-olds successfully balance all the blocks, whereas 7-year-olds are not able to balance the weighted blocks, which they repeatedly try to balance at their geometric center despite negative feedback from numerous failures. Although this might be thought of as a U-shaped pattern of development in terms of success and failure, it is only U-shaped at the behavioral level. At the representational level, it shows a steady progression over developmental time, with 7-year-olds having developed a theory-in-action that all blocks balance at their geometric center. This makes them ignore counterexamples until their theory is consolidated. Thus, the success of 5- and 9-year-olds stems from different representations. In the youngest children, information about proprioceptive feedback is used for balance; in the oldest children, a simple theory involving the law of torque has developed from the counterexamples to the 7-year-olds' geometric-center theory (Karmiloff-Smith, 1984).

In a second experiment, I asked children to draw a closed railway circuit formed of eight straight and four rounded tracks (Karmiloff-Smith, 1979). Their drawings of the closed circuit were perfect. I then asked them to request each of the separate tracks so that this time they could build a circuit identical to the one they had drawn. Again they managed to build the closed circuit successfully. They were then asked to draw the circuit again. This time their drawing was not nearly as accurate as their initial drawing, because it now had exaggerated rounded corners. It was as if the task of representing each of the tracks separately and naming them ("a straight one," "a rounded one") changed the children's representation of the overall circuit, and this new representation was expressed in their second drawings (Karmiloff-Smith, 1979, 1984).

These are two rich examples from among many other ways of tapping representational change in typically developing children. Future research could focus on representational change in children with learning disabilities. Is a lack of representational change one of the fundamental problems in their development, with improvements due only to behavioral change? These are issues that may be fundamental to researchers' understanding of atypical development as well as to their ability to facilitate progress.

Conclusion

The research I have described in this chapter, and the future directions I have proposed, illustrate the value of integrating multiple perspectives that operate at the levels of basic processes and more complex problem solving. The genetic and neuroscientific evidence clarifies the domain-relevant biases that constrain the progressive specialization of basic processing, which underlies children's ability to form representations necessary for more complex problem solving. For example, by taking a neuroconstructivist approach to the precise understanding of a genetic disorder, WS, my colleagues and I have discovered that a core processing difficulty with eye movement planning was the basis for subsequent challenges with cardinality, an insight necessary for future investigations of these individuals' mathematical learning and problem solving. These studies will use a microdevelopmental approach, modeled so consistently by David Klahr throughout his productive career, to precisely specify children's developmental progression and the mechanisms underlying change.

References

Annaz, D., Karmiloff-Smith, A., & Thomas, M. C. (2008). The importance of tracing developmental trajectories for clinical child neuropsychology. In J. Reed & J. Warner-Rogers (Eds.), *Child neuropsychology: Concepts, theory and practice* (pp. 7–18). West Sussex, England: Wiley-Blackwell.

Ansari, D., Donlan, C., Thomas, M., Ewing, S., Peen, T., & Karmiloff-Smith, A. (2003). What makes counting count? Verbal and visuo-spatial contributions to typical and atypical number development. *Journal of Experimental Child Psychology, 85,* 50–62. doi:10.1016/S0022-0965(03)00026-2

Ansari, D., Donlan, C., & Karmiloff-Smith, A. (2007). Typical and atypical development of visual estimation abilities. *Cortex, 43,* 758–768. doi:10.1016/S0010-9452(08)70504-5

Ansari, D., & Karmiloff-Smith, A. (2002). Atypical trajectories of number development. *Trends in Cognitive Sciences, 6,* 511–516. doi:10.1016/S1364-6613(02)02040-5

Bolhuis, J. J., Zijlstra, G. G. O., den Boer-Visser, A. M., & van der Zee, E. A. (2000). Localized neuronal activation in the zebra finch brain is related to the strength of song learning. *Proceedings of the National Academy of Sciences of the United States of America, 97,* 2282–2285. doi:10.1073/pnas.030539097

Brown, J. H., Johnson, M. H., Paterson, S., Gilmore, R., Gsödl, M., Longhi, E., & Karmiloff-Smith, A. (2003). Spatial representation and attention in toddlers with Williams syndrome and Down syndrome. *Neuropsychologia, 41,* 1037–1046. doi:10.1016/S0028-3932(02)00299-3

Butterworth, B. (1999). *The mathematical brain.* London, England: Macmillan.

Carver, S. M., & Klahr, D. (Eds.). (2001). *Cognition and instruction: 25 years of progress.* Mahwah, NJ: Erlbaum.

de Haan, M., Humphreys, K., & Johnson, M. H. (2002). Developing a brain specialized for face processing: A converging methods approach. *Developmental Psychobiology, 40,* 200–212. doi:10.1002/dev.10027

Donnai, D., & Karmiloff-Smith, A. (2000). Williams syndrome: From genotype through to the cognitive phenotype. *American Journal of Medical Genetics, 97,* 164–171. doi:10.1002/1096-8628(200022)97:2<164::AID-AJMG8>3.0.CO;2-F

Duchaine, B. C., & Nakayama, K. (2006). Developmental prosopagnosia: A window to content-specific face processing. *Current Opinion in Neurobiology, 16,* 166–173. doi:10.1016/j.conb.2006.03.003

Elman, J., Bates, E., Johnson, M., Karmiloff-Smith, A., Parisi, D., & Plunkett, K. (1996). *Rethinking innateness: A connectionist perspective on development.* Cambridge, MA: MIT Press/Bradford Books.

Farran, E. K., Brown, J. H., Cole, V. L., Houston-Price, C., & Karmiloff-Smith, A. (2007). The development of perceptual grouping in infants with Williams syndrome. *European Journal of Developmental Science, 1,* 253–271.

Finlay, B. L. (2007). *E pluribus unum:* Too many unique human capacities and too many theories. In S. Gangestad & J. Simpson (Eds.), *The evolution of mind: Fundamental questions and controversies* (pp. 294–304). New York, NY: Guilford Press.

Fisher, S. E., & Scharff, C. (2009). FOXP2 as a molecular window into speech and language. *Trends in Genetics, 25,* 166–177. doi:10.1016/j.tig.2009.03.002

Fisher, S. E., Vargha-Khadem, F., Watkins, K. E., Monaco, A. P., & Pembrey, M. E. (1998). Localisation of a gene implicated in a severe speech and language disorder. *Nature Genetics, 18,* 168–170. doi:10.1038/ng0298-168

Fodor, J. (1983). *The modularity of mind.* Cambridge, MA: MIT Press.

Giedd, J. N., Blumenthal, J., Jeffries, N., Castellanos, F., Liu, H., Zijdenbos, A., . . . Rapoport, J. L. (1999). Brain development during childhood and adolescence: A longitudinal MRI study. *Nature Neuroscience, 2,* 861–863. doi:10.1038/13158

Giedd, J. N., Rumsey, J., Castellanos, F., Rajapakse, J., Kaysen, D., Vaituzis, A., . . . Rapoport, J. L. (1996). A quantitative MRI study of the corpus callosum in children and adolescents. Brain Research. *Developmental Brain Research, 91,* 274–280. doi:10.1016/0165-3806(95)00193-X

Gleitman, L. R., Gleitman, H., & Shipley, E. F. (1972). The emergence of the child as grammarian. *Cognition, 1,* 137–164. doi:10.1016/0010-0277(72)90016-9

Gopnik, M., & Cragoa, M. B. (1991). Familial aggregation of a developmental language disorder. *Cognition, 39,* 1–50. doi:10.1016/0010-0277(91)90058-C

Gottlieb, G. (2007). Probabilistic epigenesis. *Developmental Science, 10,* 1–11. doi:10.1111/j.1467-7687. 2007.00556.x

Haesler, S., Wada, K., Nshdejan, A., Morrisey, E. E., Lints, T., Jarvis, E. D., & Scharff, C. (2004). FOXP2 expression in avian vocal learners and non-learners. *Journal of Neuroscience, 24,* 3164–3175. doi:10.1523/JNEUROSCI.4369-03.2004

Huttenlocher, P. R., & de Courten, C. (1987). The development of synapses in striate cortex of man. *Human Neurobiology, 6,* 1–9.

Johnson, M. H. (2001). Functional brain development in humans. *Nature Reviews Neuroscience, 2,* 475–483. doi:10.1038/35081509

Kaffman, A., & Meaney, M. J. (2007). Neurodevelopmental sequelae of postnatal maternal care in rodents: Clinical and research implications of molecular insights. *Journal of Child Psychology and Psychiatry, and Allied Disciplines, 48,* 224–244. doi:10.1111/j.1469-7610.2007.01730.x

Karmiloff-Smith, A. (1979). Problem-solving processes in children's construction and representations of closed railway circuits. *Archives de Psychologie, 17,* 33–59.

Karmiloff-Smith, A. (1984). Children's problem solving. In M. E. Lamb, A. L. Brown, & B. Rogoff (Eds.), *Advances in developmental psychology* (Vol. 3, pp. 39–90). Hillsdale, NJ: Erlbaum.

Karmiloff-Smith, A. (1990). Constraints on representational change: Evidence from children's drawing. *Cognition, 34,* 57–83. doi:10.1016/0010-0277(90)90031-E

Karmiloff-Smith, A. (1992). *Beyond modularity: A developmental approach to cognitive science.* Cambridge, MA: MIT Press.

Karmiloff-Smith, A. (1998). Development itself is the key to understanding developmental disorders. *Trends in Cognitive Sciences, 2,* 389–398. doi:10.1016/S1364-6613(98)01230-3

Karmiloff-Smith, A. (2006). The tortuous route from genes to behaviour: A neuroconstructivist approach. *Cognitive, Affective, & Behavioral Neuroscience, 6,* 9–17. doi:10.3758/CABN.6.1.9

Karmiloff-Smith, A. (2007). Atypical epigenesis. *Developmental Science, 10,* 84–88. doi:10.1111/ j.1467-7687.2007.00568.x

Karmiloff-Smith, A. (2009). Nativism vs. neuroconstructivism: Rethinking developmental disorders. *Developmental Psychology, 45,* 56–63. doi:10.1037/a0014506

Karmiloff-Smith, A., & Inhelder, B. (1974). If you want to get ahead, get a theory. *Cognition, 3,* 195–212. doi:10.1016/0010-0277(74)90008-0

Karmiloff-Smith, A., Scerif, G., & Ansari, D. (2003). Double dissociations in developmental disorders? Theoretically misconceived, empirically dubious. *Cortex, 39,* 161–163. doi:10.1016/S0010-9452 (08)70091-1

Karmiloff-Smith, A., Scerif, G., & Thomas, M. S. C. (2002). Different approaches to relating genotype to phenotype in developmental disorders. *Developmental Psychobiology, 40,* 311–322. doi:10.1002/dev.10035

Karmiloff-Smith, A., Thomas, M., Annaz, D., Humphreys, K., Ewing, S., Brace, N., ... Campbell, R. (2004). Exploring the Williams syndrome face processing debate: The importance of building developmental trajectories. *Journal of Child Psychology and Psychiatry, and Allied Disciplines, 45,* 1258–1274. doi:10.1111/j.1469-7610.2004.00322.x

Klahr, D. (1992). Information processing approaches to cognitive development. In M. H. Bornstein & M. E. Lamb (Eds.), *Developmental psychology: An advanced textbook* (3rd ed., pp. 273–335). Hillsdale, NJ: Erlbaum.

Klahr, D. (1994). Children, adults, and machines as discovery systems. *Machine Learning, 14,* 313–320. doi:10.1007/BF00993981

Klahr, D. (1999). The conceptual habitat: In what kind of system can concepts develop? In E. K. Scholnick, K. Nelson, S. A. Gelman, & P. H. Miller (Eds.), *Conceptual development: Piaget's legacy* (pp. 131–161). Mahwah, NJ: Erlbaum.

Klahr, D. (2000). *Exploring science: The cognition and development of discovery processes.* Cambridge, MA: MIT Press.

Klahr, D. (2004). Commentary: New kids on the connectionist modeling block. *Developmental Science, 7,* 165–166. doi:10.1111/j.1467-7687.2004.00334.x

Klahr, D. (2005). Early science instruction: Addressing fundamental issues. *Psychological Science, 16,* 871–872. doi:10.1111/j.1467-9280.2005.01629.x

Klahr, D. & Dunbar, K., (1989). Developmental differences in scientific discovery processes. In D. Klahr & K. Kotovsky (Eds.), *Complex information processing: The impact of Herbert A. Simon* (pp. 109–143). Hillsdale, NJ: Erlbaum.

Klahr, D., Langley, P., & Neches, R. (Eds.). (1987). *Production system models of learning and development.* Cambridge, MA: MIT Press.

Klahr, D., & Li, J. (2005). Cognitive research and elementary science instruction: From the laboratory, to the classroom, and back. *Journal of Science Education and Technology, 14,* 217–238. doi:10.1007/s10956-005-4423-5

Klahr, D., & Nigam, M. (2004). The equivalence of learning paths in early science instruction: Effects of direct instruction and discovery learning. *Psychological Science, 15,* 661–667. doi:10.1111/j.0956-7976.2004.00737.x

Klahr, D., & Wallace, J. G. (1976). *Cognitive development: An information-processing view.* Hillsdale, NJ: Erlbaum.

Lai, C. S. L., Gerrelli, D., Monaco, A. P., Fisher, S. E., & Copp, A. J. (2003). *FOXP2* expression during brain development coincides with adult sites of pathology in a severe speech and language disorder. *Brain, 126,* 2455–2462. doi:10.1093/brain/awg247

Leslie, A. M. (1992). Pretence, autism, and the theory-of-mind module. *Current Directions in Psychological Science, 1,* 18–21. doi:10.1111/1467-8721.ep10767818

Mareschal, D., Johnson, M. H., Sirios, S., Spratling, M., Thomas, M., & Westermann, G. (2007). *Neuroconstructivism: Vol. I. How the brain constructs cognition.* Oxford, England: Oxford University Press.

Merzenich, M. M. (1995). Cortical plasticity: Shaped, distributed representations of learned behaviors. In B. Julesz & I. Kovacs (Eds.), *Maturational windows and cortical plasticity in human development: Is there a reason for an optimistic view?* Reading, MA: Addison-Wesley.

Mesoudi, A., Whiten, A., & Laland, K. N. (2006). Towards a unified science of cultural evolution. *Behavioral and Brain Sciences, 29,* 329–347. doi:10.1017/S0140525X06009083

Mills, D. L., Alvarez, T. D., St. George, M., Appelbaum, L. G., Bellugi, U., & Neville, H. (2000). Electrophysiological studies of face processing in Williams syndrome. *Journal of Cognitive Neuroscience, 12,* 47–64. doi:10.1162/089892900561977

Neville, H. J., Mills, D. L., & Bellugi, U. (1994). Effects of altered auditory sensitivity and age of language acquisition on the development of language-relevant neural systems: Preliminary studies of Williams syndrome. In S. Broman & J. Grafman (Eds.), *Atypical cognitive deficits in developmental disorders: Implications for brain function* (pp. 67–83). Hillsdale, NJ: Erlbaum.

O'Reilly, R. C., & McClelland, J. L. (1992). *The self-organization of spatially invariant representations* (Technical Report PDP.CNS.92.5). Pittsburgh, PA: Carnegie Mellon University.

Paterson, S. J., Brown, J. H., Gsödl, M. K., Johnson, M. H., & Karmiloff-Smith, A. (1999, December 17). Cognitive modularity and genetic disorders. *Science, 286,* 2355–2358. doi:10.1126/science.286.5448.2355

Paterson, S. J., Girelli, L., Butterworth, B., & Karmiloff-Smith, A. (2006). Are numerical impairments syndrome specific? Evidence from Williams syndrome and Down's syndrome. *Journal of Child Psychology and Psychiatry, and Allied Disciplines, 47,* 190–204. doi:10.1111/j.1469-7610.2005.01460.x

Penner, D. E., & Klahr, D. (1996). The interaction of domain-specific knowledge and domain-general discovery strategies: A study with sinking objects. *Child Development, 67,* 2709–2727. doi:10.2307/1131748

Piaget, J. (2001). *The language and thought of the child.* London, England: Routledge Classics. (Original work published 1923)

Pinker, S. (1994). *The language instinct: How the mind creates language.* New York, NY: Morrow.

Pinker, S. (2001). *How the mind works.* New York: Norton.

Quartz, S. R., & Sejnowski, T. (1997). The neural basis of cognitive development: A constructivist manifesto. *Behavioral and Brain Sciences, 20,* 537–556. doi:10.1017/S0140525X97001581

Spelke, E. S., & Kinzler, K. D. (2007). Core knowledge. *Developmental Science, 10,* 89–96. doi:10.1111/j.1467-7687.2007.00569.x

Stiles, J., Bates, E., Thal, D., Trauner, D., & Reilly, J. (1998). Linguistic, cognitive, and affective development in children with pre- and perinatal focal brain injury: A ten-year overview from the San Diego Longitudinal Project. In C. Rovee-Collier, L. Lipsit, & H. Hayne (Eds.), *Advances in infancy research* (pp. 131–163). Norwood, NJ: Ablex.

Sur, M., Pallas, S. L., & Roe, A. W. (1990). Crossmodal plasticity in cortical development: Differentiation and specification of sensory neocortex. *Trends in Neurosciences, 13,* 227–233. doi:10.1016/0166-2236(90)90165-7

Tager-Flusberg, H., Boshart, J., & Baron-Cohen, S. (1998). Reading the windows to the soul: Evidence of domain-specific sparing in Williams syndrome. *Journal of Cognitive Neuroscience, 10,* 631–639. doi:10.1162/089892998563031

Temple, C. M. (1997). Cognitive neuropsychology and its application to children. *Journal of Child Psychology and Psychiatry, and Allied Disciplines, 38,* 27–52. doi:10.1111/j.1469-7610.1997.tb01504.x

Thelen, E., & Smith, L. B. (1994). *A dynamic systems approach to the development of cognition and action.* Cambridge, MA: MIT Press.

Thomas, M. S. C., Annaz, D., Ansari, D., Serif, G., Jarrold, C., & Karmiloff-Smith, A. (2009). The use of developmental trajectories in studying developmental disorders. *Journal of Speech, Language, and Hearing Research, 52,* 336–358. doi:10.1044/1092-4388(2009/07-0144)

van der Lely, H. K. J. (2005). Domain-specific cognitive systems: Insight from grammatical specific language impairment. *Trends in Cognitive Sciences, 9,* 53–59. doi:10.1016/j.tics.2004.12.002

Van Herwegen, J., Ansari, D., Xu, F., & Karmiloff-Smith, A. (2008). Small and large number processing in infants and toddlers with Williams syndrome. *Developmental Science, 11,* 637–643. doi:10.1111/j.1467-7687.2008.00711.x

Vargha-Khadem, F., Watkins, K., Alcock, K., Fletcher, P., & Passingham. R. (1995). Praxic and nonverbal cognitive deficits in a large family with a genetically transmitted speech and language disorder. *Proceedings of the National Academy of Sciences of the United States of America, 92,* 930–933. doi:10.1073/pnas.92.3.930

Webster, M. J., Bachevalier, J., & Ungerleider, L. G. (1995). Development and plasticity of visual memory circuits. In B. Julesz & I. Kovacs (Eds.), *Maturational windows and adult cortical plasticity in human development: Is there reason for an optimistic view?* (pp. 73–86). Reading, MA: Addison-Wesley.

Westermann, G., Thomas, M., & Karmiloff-Smith, A. (2010). Neuroconstructivism. In U. Goswami (Ed.), *Wiley-Blackwell handbook of childhood cognitive development* (pp. 723–748). Oxford, England: Wiley-Blackwell.

7

Simulating Discovery and Education in a Soccer Science World

Jeff Shrager

Langley, Simon, Bradshaw, and Zytkow (1987) conceived of scientific discovery as a search through a space of possible models for those that explain what we observe about nature. Modern scientists are obviously conducting this search collaboratively, both within teams and across the wider scientific community. There are many interesting questions one could ask about the dynamics of science as a collaborative process. Of particular interest is the appearance over the past 15 years of self-publishing web technologies, such as forums and blogs. These technologies offer the enticing possibility of scientists publishing their own articles instead of having to wait for peer review. In the extreme, one can even imagine scientists putting their laboratory notebooks online. In previous work (Shrager, Billman, Convertino, Massar, & Pirolli 2009), my coworkers and I coined the term *Soccer Science* and argued that the always-on, uncensored, instantaneous, free, and ubiquitous nature of web publishing technology is (metaphorically) changing science from an (American) "football" model to a "soccer" model. *Football Science* is the science with which most people are familiar: Teams (usually laboratories, or sometimes larger collaborative groups) plan and experiment more or less independently; publish results through the long, narrow, quality-controlled publication cycle; and usually have the need or opportunity to reconsider their work versus that of other teams only at "breaks in the play"—that is, when a relevant article appears in a journal. The publication cycle dominates Football Science and enables the teams to engage in a somewhat leisurely read–plan–experiment–publish cycle. Shrager et al. (2009) contrasted this with the new world of *Soccer Science,* in which communication is continuous and interleaved with scientific work. In a Soccer Science world, instead of running many experiments and then pushing some results through a structured, peer-reviewed publishing cycle, researchers could self-publish their articles on the Web without peer review and could even publish unedited laboratory notebooks or raw data. In a Soccer Science world, one's work would have to be reconsidered on an almost literally continuous basis.

Just as soccer places a much greater cognitive load on each individual player than does football, and presumably leads to different strategies that involve greater satisficing, one would expect Soccer Scientists to experience a much greater planning load and to use strategies that satisfice much more extensively.

Soccer Science would make available a much larger flow of potentially relevant information much more rapidly. Shrager et al. (2009) hypothesized that the average quality of the information stream will drop, and high-quality information will be less clearly marked:

> In addition, the information will be less stable as quickly posted, preliminary information is more likely to be revised. These changes mean that identifying the high-quality information relevant to a particular researcher will be more difficult and so, other things being equal, will take more effort to find. In turn, scientists will either need to spend more time finding and filtering information and less time acting on it, or act based on less complete or reliable information. As the pace of information distribution in the community speeds up, this will push an individual researcher to act faster, for example, to avoid being scooped, which may in turn reduce an individual scientist's ability or willingness to review, reflect, or check, at the same time that external vetting is reduced. (p. 60)

The researchers also asked, "What cognitive and community-wide communication strategies will be most effective in a Soccer Science world?"

These questions are not mere academic exercises; they are upon us already. Even as I write this chapter, for example, the first volume of the newly minted *Journal of Participatory Medicine* (see http://www.jopm.org) has just come online with its inaugural October 2009 issue, featuring an essay wherein Richard W. Smith (2009), former editor of the *British Medical Journal*, discussed some of the problems of peer review and then encouraged the readership of the new journal to "join the revolution": "We don't yet have a clearly articulated alternative to peer review, but this is your chance to 'join the revolution' and together with the editors devise a better system for this journal" ("Open Questions," para. 1). Among the questions on which Smith asked readers to opine include one that, in essence, makes peer review irrelevant: "Should papers be put online as soon as submitted and reviewers and editors asked to place their comments online as completed?" ("Open Questions," para. 10). As we all know by now, as soon as something goes up on the web in any form, it is hard to distinguish from fact; a subsequent peer review would likely be a mere footnote. What effect would this have if it were done? Smith asked readers to venture their thoughts, "preferably based on evidence"; however, what sort of evidence can one have that might bear on a self-proclaimed revolution—in doing something that no one has tried before? Of course, there are the classic sources of evidence, including examples of other journals that have tried similar things, and studies that may bear indirectly on the matter. The goal of this chapter is to apply the technology of multiagent computational simulation to answer questions such as Smith's and broader questions regarding various models of scientific communication, education, social structures, and even individual scientific reasoning that scientists will confront in the fast-approaching Soccer Science world.

This chapter is based on a previous model (Shrager, 2010) that I used to explore the impact of varying levels of prepublication review on the efficiency of discovery across the biomedical community. Here, I extend that previous work in two ways. First, I describe how the model performs in parameter regimens that simulate a variety of kinds of scientific problem spaces. Second, motivated by the work of David Klahr, I add a developmental dynamic to the base model to examine how different levels of investment in science education might influence the efficiency of discovery by the scientific community.

Multiagent Simulations of Science

Multiagent computational simulations of complex sociocognitive systems have a long history in psychology, economics, and sociology (for reviews, see Lehtinen & Kuorikoski, 2007; Meyer, Lorscheid, & Troitzsch, 2009; and Ostrom, 1988). Ostrom (1988) referred to computer simulation as the "third symbol system" (the first being natural language and the second being mathematics) and argued that it should be viewed as "a medium through which theoretical propositions can be articulated and predictions can be generated" (p. 381). According to Ostrom, computational simulation enables researchers to study complex social behaviors that resist theoretical understanding using the first two symbol systems. Science, the process of discovery carried out by the community of scientists, is a highly complex sociocognitive system, and multiagent computer simulations may enable researchers to ask many interesting and important questions regarding the behavior of this system in many real and proposed settings. Given this potential, and the importance of science in every aspect of people's lives, it is surprising that there are so few examples of multiagent simulations in this domain; however, there are some.

In recent work, Payette (2009) defined *science* as a social process in which theory production and evaluation are distributed between agents who are, in the aggregate, implementing a search algorithm trying to maximize empirical adequacy. Payette developed a multiagent simulation model based on Hull's (1988) hypothesis that the scientific search algorithm is genetic, "where objects such as ideas, concepts, theories, etc., are produced, transmitted and selected in a Darwinian fashion" (Payette, 2009, para. 1). Scientists, according to Payette (following Hull), "propagate their ideas [and] acquire credit, i.e., the consideration of their peers, with whom they are both competing and collaborating" (para. 3). Payette pointed out the following:

> In a multi-agent model, agents are usually heterogeneous. They can be more or less creative, communicative, sociable, aggressive, generous, etc. These characteristics are expressed as real numbers and taken into account by the formal rules of behavior implemented by the agents. Agents are also situated in an environment where interactions are mostly local. (para. 4)

In Payette's model,

> This environment is a social network: Scientists interact with their students and their collaborators. They also write peer-reviewed articles that allow them to share their ideas with the whole community. These ideas are strings of information that can be formalized as vectors in a multidimensional space. When ideas are transmitted from one scientist to another, some bits of

information can be mutated, introducing noise in the transmission. Each idea is assigned some "empirical adequacy" value, using an arbitrary objective function. This function constitutes the problem space that the agents are working in. They do not have direct access to its values, but they can try to approximate them using "tests." Overall, we can measure the efficiency of the system by how close the subjective ratings given by the agents to their own ideas are to their "real," objective values. (para. 4)

Payette (2009) also made the following point:

The complexities of this model would make it analytically intractable, but simulation allow [sic] us to examine, one step after another, what happens in the system, and to see the effect that different parameters have on its efficiency at maximizing empirical adequacy. It is conceivable; for example, that too much interaction between scientists would lead the system to settle at a local optimum, while having small, close-knitted but independent communities would allow a more thorough exploration of the problem space. Different results here would suggest different norms as to how science should be socially organized. (para. 5)

In a similar, though less detailed model, Addis and Gooding (2008; see also Gooding & Addis, 2008) noted that "scientists inhabit a changing world of information-bearing experiments and social interactions, so the probability of a *particular* hypothesis being true must reflect both empirical information and the opinions of others" (p. 39). These researchers created a model based on a variant of Bayesian certainty updating that takes into account both observations and subjective opinions of other agents. They demonstrated that, under various parameter regimens, the simulated agents can home in on (or, under other regimens, diverge from) the "correct" theory.

Sun and Naveh (2004) noted that "most of the work in agent-based social simulation has assumed highly simplified agent models, with little attention being paid to the details of individual cognition. . . . Cognitive models that incorporate realistic tendencies, biases and capacities of individual cognitive agents can serve as a more realistic basis for understanding multi-agent interaction . . . . The mechanisms underlying individual cognition cannot be ignored in studying multi-agent interaction" (p. 1). Indeed, whereas Payette's (2009) model includes consideration of the career arc of the scientist from education through retirement, models ideas carried through publication, and credits relationships carried through the publication systems, his model of theories and of scientific decision making are both highly abstract.

The present model is somewhat more concrete than Payette's (2009) in these areas. Although it is still not a perfect representation of the way science works, readers will see that it can be used to make some relatively specific predictions. In the next section, I briefly review my model (Shrager, 2010) and describe how it has been parameterized for the experiments I discuss. I then document the experiments and results that I described earlier in this chapter regarding a variety of kinds of scientific problem spaces and how different levels of investment in science education may affect scientific progress.

Simulating Soccer Science: A Multiagent Model
of Biomedical Science

In modeling any system, one begins by identifying the players (agents) involved, describing the environment in which they operate, their decision algorithms, and the ways in which they interact. The players in my model include bioscientists, physicians, and patients (Shrager, 2010). Bioscientists represent the so-called drug hunters who search for treatments (i.e., drugs) from among the infinitude of molecules that could be effective drugs (most of which are not). They are guided in this search by many sorts of knowledge, including the results of the applied clinical work of physicians and the responses of patients' disease to proposed treatments; physicians must treat the patient before them by choosing from among the treatments offered by the bioscientists. Biomedicine is made especially complex by the fact that biology is not static; the diseases themselves evolve and may acquire resistance to the treatments being mustered against them. Thus, the disease could be said to be a player as well.

The environment in which biomedicine operates describes the space of treatments that is being searched and the way that disease responds to each treatment. In the model described herein, there is only one disease, which I think of as cancer. At the beginning of a given simulation run, the population is set to an initial level (usually 1,000), and no one is ill. (Being *ill* means having some level of the disease.) Each year, a fraction of the population is diagnosed with cancer (e.g., 0.01/year). When the disease is initially diagnosed in a given person, it is assigned a real-valued initial level (e.g., 0.1), and each year thereafter the disease "progresses" by being multiplied by a progression factor (e.g., 1.2). If the disease level reaches a particular threshold (usually 0.5) the person is said to "die" and is removed from the population. The simulations described herein are usually run for 100 simulated years, and multiple runs with the same parameters are usually undertaken, each with a different random seed. The reported results are usually the means and standard errors of the population remaining at the end of the simulation, over these multiple runs.

The present model explicitly represents the space of possible treatments that must be searched among for an effective treatment. There are three general sorts of spaces, distinguishable in terms of their rough topology, which I term (a) *black holes,* (b) *moonscapes,* and (c) *golf courses.* To envision these topologies, imagine that you have a sheet of rubber stretched horizontally, like the mat of a trampoline, and perfectly flat. Let the points on this sheet represent all plausible treatments. Now imagine that the sheet is not perfectly flat; for example, if one places rocks of various weights at various points on the surface, these will make indentations. Let the depth of any such indentation represent the effectiveness of the given treatment: the deeper the indentation, the more effective the treatment represented by that point. The goal of clinical medicine is to find a highly effective treatment; that is, one must search the sheet for a relatively deep indentation. This might seem a simple task, except there are two constraints: First, you must do it in the dark, so you are unable to see the sheet, only feel it; second, you can use the fingers of only one hand. This might seem an odd task, but it is not very far from what science must do in trying to find a good theory in a large space of possible theories while being unable to see where the good ones are, only being able to "feel for them" by way of experiment.

One can imagine many possible ways to find a deep indentation in the rubber sheet. One of these is as follows: Begin by touching the sheet at any random point with your index finger. This gives you a currently selected treatment, which I call the *index treatment*. Then, while holding your index finger on that (index) treatment, feel around with the other fingers of the same hand to see if you can find any spots that are deeper (i.e., that represent more effective treatments than the current one). If you find one that is deeper than the current one, move your index finger to this new index treatment. Then try again from there to find an even more effective treatment. Continue in this manner until you cannot touch any spots that are deeper (i.e., more effective) than the one you are currently indexing. When that happens, you declare victory, and the index treatment is the one that you report as the best that you can find.

This algorithm will have you "walking" your hand across the surface of the sheet, slowly seeking the deepest indentation that you can find by feeling in small, hand-sized increments. The standard term for this kind of algorithm is *hill climbing* (although in this case it might be better described as *hole descending*, but which way is labeled as more effective is obviously arbitrary). Again, this is not very far from a description of a significant part of the real drug discovery process: Drug hunters almost always begin with a drug that demonstrates some effectiveness and then modify it in small increments to try to improve its effectiveness, remove side effects, and so on. If drug hunters find a better drug, they switch to that one, and continue trying to improve on it until they cannot find a better one given the time and money constraints at hand. This is not very different from feeling around in a very large space in the dark.

Now, with our rubber sheet, hill-climbing method in mind, I can explain black holes, moonscapes, and golf courses. The black hole topology is analogous to having dropped a bowling ball someplace on the sheet, so that the whole thing is deformed into one giant funnel-shaped well. Hill climbing works extremely well in black hole spaces because no matter where you start, simply walking downhill will eventually get you to the deepest point (i.e., the single most effective treatment). Golf course topologies are quite different. Imagine that, instead of a bowling ball, you've set out many widely spaced marbles on the sheet so that most of the sheet remains flat except for a small number of shallow dents created by the marbles. Hill climbing will not work well on a golf course–shaped space because unless you get lucky and start near one of the marbles, you are mostly feeling around on a flat surface, will end up in a random walk, and will rarely improve at all beyond your starting level. To make progress on a golf course topology one needs rather strong hints regarding where to look, such as a map, or some better algorithm, such as stochastic search or genetic algorithms. Finally, moonscapes have a large number of overlapping "craters" representing local maxima—as though one had thrown many rocks of widely varying weight onto the sheet so that it is nowhere perfectly flat, but there are many indentations of widely varying depth. In this case, hill climbing will lead you to walk downhill from wherever you happen to start and end up in the bottom of the nearest crater, which is unlikely to be the deepest one.

This search gets you to a pretty good solution, but usually not to the one that is best globally.

It is interesting to ask which of these, or what combination, represents the spaces in various domains. In this chapter, I focus on the difference between black holes and golf courses. In reality, it is likely that treatment spaces are more like moonscapes, with many local maxima. However, locally (i.e., within a single crater), a moonscape is either a black hole or a golf course, and because in the sections that follow I generally deal with one disease and a small number of drugs, this approximation will suffice.

In the present model, the specifics of the space are described by the number of available drugs and their range of effectiveness. Ineffective drugs (i.e., ones that operate only by means of the placebo effect) have a treatment effectiveness of 1.0, and effective drugs have a treatment effectiveness of less than 1.0. After all the effective drugs are created, additional ineffective drugs are usually created with effectiveness values of 1.0, providing a set of distractors. In the present simulations, I use a uniform treatment effectiveness distribution model wherein the drug effect is uniformly distributed across a range of effectiveness centered on 1.0.

An example will make all of this clearer. Suppose that a patient (whom we shall assume is male) is diagnosed at an initial disease level of 0.1 and remains untreated for 3 years. In the 3rd year, he will have disease levels of 0.1 (initially); then 0.12 ($= 0.1 \times 1.2$); 0.144 ($= 0.12 \times 1.2$); and, finally, ~0.173. If he then begins treatment with a drug that has a treatment effectiveness of, say, 0.8, his next disease level will be $0.173 \times 1.2 \times 0.8 = 0.166$, then 0.159, and so on, and if he remains on this drug his disease level will never increase to the death threshold. Note that some drugs are worse than ineffective, having effectiveness values greater than 1.0; that is, they will make the disease worse (e.g., through side effects). Taking such drugs will shorten the patient's life.

Each year, each ill patient receives treatment according to a specific treatment model, which takes on one of these values:

- *Placebo.* All patients are treated with a drug that has an effectiveness of 1.0 (i.e., no effect: a placebo, although the placebo effects are not modeled).
- *Random.* The patient gets a random drug on the first visit, and then, if he has not measurably improved, he gets a new random drug on each presentation.
- *Best published treatment.* The patient initially gets the best drug that has been reported in the literature (as described below). On each visit, if he has not measurably improved, he is again treated with the best drug in the recent literature, which presumably will have changed since this patient's last visit. (*Recent* here is defined as within the past 100 publications—another parameter that can be explored later.)
- *No switch.* The patient initially receives either a random or the best published drug (in according with another parameter) and remains on this treatment regardless of what happens.
- *Hill climbing.* The patient gets an initial drug as in the no-switch condition, but if he has not measurably improved on the current

treatment it is changed on each visit to the next "most effective" treatment, if there is one.

The concept of having "measurably improved" is critical to this present model. Although the patient's level of disease is a single real value, similar to Payette's (2009) model, this value cannot be directly observed; instead, on a given visit to the doctor the disease level is measured with some error (e.g., with a standard deviation of 2.0). That the actual disease state is not directly observable, but can only be measured with some error, is critical to the way that the predictions are made about the present model.

As mentioned previously, agents interact in the present model through the literature, that is, via publication. Each time a patient visits the doctor, the patient or doctor (this distinction does not matter here) can "publish." The rules for publication are given by a publication regimen parameter, which may have one of the following two values (for more detail, see Shrager, 2010):

1. *Blog everything.* In this publication regimen, every time a person is treated, the treatment and differential disease states are pushed to the literature.
2. *Publish only after lengthy experience.* In this regimen, results are pushed to the literature only when the patient experiences a measurable improvement over a given number of years on the same drug. This number is called the *HMSDCALE* and is notated by "@." (A value of @1 is close to, but not quite the same as the blog-everything regimen because the latter will cause publication regardless of whether the patient's health improves.)

The following pseudo code summarizes the model as described so far:

- Each person in the community visits the doctor every year;
- if a person has already been diagnosed with a disease, the treatment regimen is executed;
- otherwise, stochastically diagnose this person as having cancer and initialize the treatment regimen for this person.

Treatment consists of the following:

- Record the person's current true disease state in his history.
- Update his true disease state according to the rate of natural progression of the disease.
- If the person reaches the death threshold, remove him from the simulation; otherwise, use the following procedure:
  - Multiply the person's true disease state by the treatment effectiveness.
  - Consider publishing according to the current publication regimen.
  - If the patient is not apparently improving (i.e., if his measured disease state is greater now than it was at the previous visit, i.e., year over year), change the person's treatment according to the current treatment regimen.

Basic Model Phenomena

There are many interesting parameter regimens of the present model that one could explore. I begin by describing some basic phenomena. Figure 7.1 depicts the basic model phenomena in terms of the total population of the community per year in a number of basic treatment regimens. Here, as with most simulation runs in this chapter, I have run 10 replications, each with a different random seed, to get a sense of the variance in the model's behavior.

As could be expected, the worst treatment regimen is to give every patient a placebo (P). The next worst are random treatments (the terms begin with an R). Recall that treatments change only when there is no measured year-over-year improvement in the patient's disease state. In practice, because there is measurement noise, treatments change rather regularly. All the hill-climbing regimens (which begin with Hc) perform much better than random treatment, and choosing the best published treatment first in hill climbing (represented by HcIbp) is superior to choosing a random treatment in hill climbing (HcIr). All of these results are, so far, predictable, but what about the no-switch (Ns) and

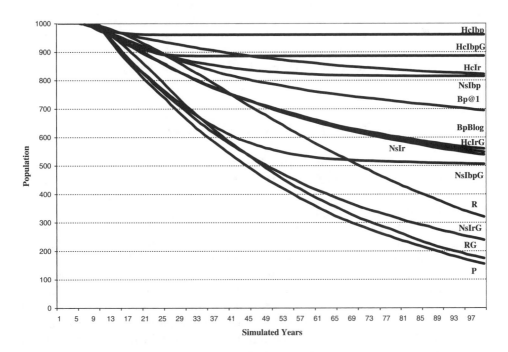

Figure 7.1. Basic results. Labels go with lines in order of the final population value, bottom to top, as follows: P = placebo; RG = random, golf course; NsIrG = no switch, initial (init) random, golf course; R = random; NsIbpG = no switch, init best published, golf course; NsIr = no switch, init random; HcIrG = hill climbing, init random, golf course; BpBlog = best published, blogging; Bp@1 = best published, publication requires one sequential improvement; NsIbp = no switch, init best published; HcIrG = hill climbing, init random; HcIbpG = hill climbing, init best published, golf course; HcIbp = hill climbing, init best published.

golf course (terms that end in G; e.g., HcIbpG) regimens? No-switch-and-initially-choosing-the-best-published-treatment (NsIbp) is worse than hill climbing in the same case (HcIbp), but not much worse than the same regimen in the golf course treatment effectiveness model (HcIbpG). The golf course model generally brings down the success rate significantly, for example, bringing a no-switch-initially-random-golf-course (NsIrG) treatment to a point that is even worse than random (on a non–golf-course treatment model), although still better than placebo. It is interesting that the no-switch-initially-best-published-golf-course (NsIbpG) treatment, the no-switch-random (NsIr) treatment, and the hill-climbing-random-golf-course (HcIrG) treatments are nearly identical, although their dynamics are very different: The dynamics of HcIrG and NsIr are nearly identical, whereas the dynamics of NsIbpG look more like the simpler hill-climbing models.

Many other interesting phenomena could be observed in these basic results, but these few suffice to demonstrate the basic phenomena of the model and explain that it works essentially as would be expected. Given this, we can move on to more interesting experiments.

In all of the above cases, publication is in the blog-everything mode, in which every usage is published, but note the entry in Figure 7.1 labeled Bp@1. This represents not blog-everything publication mode but instead the publish-only-after-lengthy-experience mode. I explored this parameter regime in detail in my earlier article (Shrager, 2010), and I briefly describe those results next. I then go on to describe new experiments regarding discovery and of birth and education.

(American) Football Versus Soccer Science

In my previous work (Shrager, 2010), I explored the publish-only-after-lengthy-experience mode across a range of HMSDCALE (i.e., @) values. HMSDCALE values near @1 are intended to model Soccer Science, for which there is a lower threshold of replicability required for publication. Higher values of HMSDCALE impose greater requirements for replication, eventually reaching a far-too-stringent requirement of demonstrating monotonic improvements over many years. In a more precise model—left for future work—one could model the actual statistically valid performance of the treatment; however, this would require elaboration of the model along a different (also interesting) dimension of the so-called n-of-1, or *personalized* treatment, up through randomized controlled clinical trials. In any part of that range, powerful statistics are hard to come by. At the n-of-1 end, each individual patient may be treated with a different drug, so that not only does the experiment have a within-subject design but also there is only one subject, and the same subject is in every cell. This is not impossible to analyze, just very weak statistically. At the opposite end of the range are the large-scale clinical trials. These are powerful statistically, but they gain this power at the cost of testing many subjects in a few balanced study arms. In my previous article (Shrager, 2010), I reported only results pertaining to the effects of publication on the treatment of individuals, under the assumption that the individuals (or their physicians) will use rapid communications technologies, such as blogging, under some rational, if not statistically valid, self-constraint, modeled here by the single HMSDCALE (@) parameter.

As expected, I observed that different levels of replicability requirement can accelerate or hinder scientific progress; too strict of a replication requirement (high @ values) prevents sharing of valid treatments, but too weak of a replication requirement (low @ values) "drowns good results in a sea of bad treatments" (Shrager, 2010, p. e10782). Moreover, I unexpectedly observed a nonlinear dip "between the point of too little review (@1–4) and the 'sweet spot' of five observed sequential improvements (@5)" (Shrager, 2010, p. e10782), although I did not offer an explanation for these unexpected nonlinearities.

These results demonstrate that the model succeeds both in obtaining predicted results and in uncovering interesting new results regarding the process of science as a collaborative project.

Discovery of New Treatments

In the preceding discussion, the set of available drugs was fixed at the beginning of a model run, and each patient (or, equivalently, each physician) was permitted to choose only from this fixed set. The model can, however, simulate a simple version of the discovery of new treatments as well. Recall that each treatment is linked to the next-best treatment (except, of course, for the best treatment). To model (simple) discovery, one does not include these links initially but adds them stochastically each year with some probability. Figure 7.2 depicts the model's performance under various values of discovery probability, comparing the case in which the best treatment is initially the best published one (left, checked, bars), versus a random initial treatment (right, diagonally striped, bars).

One can observe that lower probabilities of adding hill-climbing links leads, as would be expected, to poorer overall success but that this reaches a ceiling rather rapidly under the present parameter settings. Also as expected from the results discussed earlier in this chapter, the initial best published regimen is superior to the initial random one. This is, of course, not a very realistic biomedical search space, with mere dozens of possible treatments, as opposed to a huge (possibly infinite) set of real drug candidates. In future work, I intend to explore more realistic search spaces, but the basic phenomena are demonstrated even in this simple case.

Birth and Science Education

As described thus far, the model only loses population: Patients get sick and sometimes die, but no one is born. One can set up parameters, however, whereby people come into the population in addition to leaving it. Moreover, we are interested in modeling not just births but also the influence of discovery, and of science education, on the population. Two new parameters control these factors. First, a birth rate parameter gives the number of births per year per 1,000 living people. Second, we give a certain probability per year to a newly born person becoming a scientist. All the details of child development, career choice, science

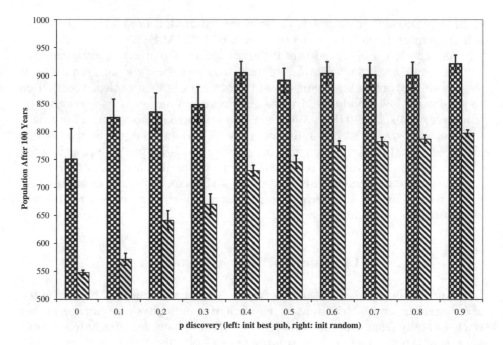

Figure 7.2. Discovery in hill-climbing mode. The probability (p) of adding a new drug each year increases left to right. All runs are hill climbing. Left (checked) bars represent the initial treatment selected based on the best published (best pub) result, right (diagonally striped) bars represent the initial (init) treatment chosen at random. Means and error bars represent 10 replicate runs with different random seeds.

education, and so forth, are rolled into this one parameter. In addition, in an extension of the discovery model discussed in the preceding section, new drugs are added to the set at a rate proportional to the fraction of scientists in the community and to the fraction of people with disease; specifically, one multiplies the rate of the discovery of hill-climbing links (as in the previously discussed results) by the fraction of people who have chosen to become scientists (controlled by the previously described parameter) and by the fraction of people living with disease. The intuition motivating this model is that the rate of discovery is presumptively based on both how many scientists there are and on the prevalence of disease, because (by hypothesis) scientists are interested in more common diseases (or perhaps the government funds research in this area more richly). As before, the newly added drugs are presumed to be better than anything that exists and are linked to the existing drugs via the hill-climbing links. (Drugs are never removed from the set, although they probably should be—future work!)

Figure 7.3 depicts the results of running with these parameters: The probability of newly born people becoming scientists (hereafter *pSci*) ranges from 0.0 to 1.0 by increments of 0.1; the most effective drug effectiveness (for the initial set of drugs) is 0.8; the number of initial drugs is three, the birth rate is five per 1,000 population per year, and the initial treatment is chosen

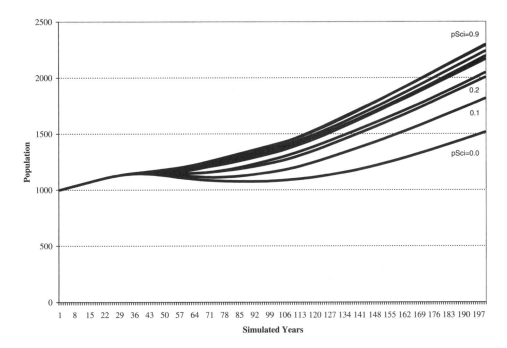

Figure 7.3. Birth, science education, and discovery combined. Plots are increasing values of the probability of newly born people becoming scientists (pSci; not all lines are labeled because of space limitations). Each curve is the mean of 50 replicate runs with different random seeds.

randomly. The figure depicts runs up to 200 years, and each curve is the mean of 50 runs.

As I had hoped, for some values of *pSci* one observes a nonmonotonic initial decline in the population, followed by a steady increase as cancer is eventually cured. Because in this modeling regimen all new drugs are by definition more effective than any existing ones, one will always eventually find a drug that reduces the disease state faster than it grows. Although there is nothing surprising about this result, it does demonstrate that the model can demonstrate nonlinear phenomena in predictable ways, and it speaks (in a not-too-surprising way) about the importance of science education.

Conclusions and Future Directions

Computer simulations have been used in biomedicine for at least 2 decades to model clinical trials (e.g., from Taylor & Bosch, 1990, through Buzoianu & Kadane, 2009), but a clinical trial, no matter how large and complex, is merely a single experiment in the vast space of experiments that the scientific community conducts in its search for true and useful understandings of nature. The goal of my efforts in multiagent modeling of science is to explore broader issues, such as the impact of open science and science education, as I have done in this chapter (and in Shrager, 2010). However, these models and results are barely a ripple on the surface of the sea of opportunities represented by multiagent simulation of science. This powerful scientific instrument enables researchers to investigate the ways in which complex social systems operate. Science is such a system, and scientists have just begun to use these powerful instruments to examine ourselves.

References

Addis, T. R., & Gooding, D. C. (2008). Simulation methods for an abductive system in science. *Foundations of Science, 13,* 37–52. doi:10.1007/s10699-007-9113-8

Buzoianu, M., & Kadane, J. B. (2009). Optimal Bayesian design for patient selection in a clinical study. *Biometrics, 65,* 953–961. doi:10.1111/j.1541-0420.2008.01156.x

Gooding, D. C., & Addis, T. R. (2008). Modelling experiments as mediating models. *Foundations of Science, 13,* 17–35. doi:10.1007/s10699-007-9114-7

Hull, D. (1988). A mechanism and its metaphysics: An evolutionary account of the social and conceptual development of science. *Biology and Philosophy, 3,* 123–155. doi:10.1007/BF00140989

Langley, P., Simon, H. A., Bradshaw, G. L., & Zytkow, J. M. (1987). *Scientific discovery: Computational explorations of the creative process.* Cambridge, MA: MIT Press.

Lehtinen, A., & Kuorikoski, J. (2007). Computing the perfect model: Why do economists shun simulation? *Philosophy of Science, 74,* 304–329. doi:10.1086/522359

Meyer, M., Lorscheid, L., & Troitzsch, K. G. (2009). The development of social simulation as reflected in the first ten years of *JASSS:* A citation and co-citation analysis. *Journal of Artificial Societies and Social Simulation, 12*(4). Retrieved from http://jasss.soc.surrey.ac.uk/12/4/12.html

Ostrom, T. M. (1988). Computer simulation: The third symbol system. *Journal of Experimental Social Psychology, 24,* 381–392. doi:10.1016/0022-1031(88)90027-3

Payette, N. (2009, October). *Simulating science: A multiagent model of scientific evolution.* Paper presented at the "Modeling Science: Understanding, Forecasting, and Communicating the Science System" conference, Amsterdam, The Netherlands. Retrieved from http://philosophie.ch/sopha2009//wp-content/uploads/322.pdf

Shrager, J. (2010). The promise and perils of pre-publication review: A multi-agent simulation of biomedical discovery under varying levels of review stringency. *PLoS ONE, 5,* e10782. doi:10.1371/journal.pone.0010782

Shrager, J., Billman, D., Convertino, G., Massar, J. P., & Pirolli, P. (2009). Soccer Science and the Bayes community: Exploring the cognitive implications of modern scientific communication. *Topics in Cognitive Science, 2,* 53–72. doi:10.1111/j.1756-8765.2009.01049.x

Smith, R. W. (2009). In search of an optimal peer review system. *Journal of Participatory Medicine, 1*(1), e13. Retrieved from http://www.jopm.org/opinion/2009/10/21/in-search-of-an-optimal-peer-review-system/

Sun, R., & Naveh, I. (2004). Simulating organizational decision-making using a cognitively realistic agent model. *Journal of Artificial Societies and Social Simulation, 7*(3). Retrieved from http://jasss.soc.surrey.ac.uk/7/3/5.html

Taylor, D. W., & Bosch, E. G. (1990). CTS: A clinical trials simulator. *Statistics in Medicine, 9,* 787–801. doi:10.1002/sim.4780090708

8

Moving Young "Scientists-in-Waiting" Onto Science Learning Pathways: Focus on Observation

Rochel Gelman and Kimberly Brenneman

> It is a capital mistake to theorize before one has data. Insensibly one begins to twist facts to suit theories instead of theories to suit fact.
> —Sir Arthur Conan Doyle, *A Scandal in Bohemia* (1891/1985)

The growing crescendo from schools, industry, government, and even the President of the United States presses academic researchers to provide ways to upgrade students' scientific literacies. This widespread push is motivated by the everyday demands we face in our increasingly technological society. We are confronted regularly with discussions of genetic engineering and its potential for reducing the risk of disease and improving the quality and quantity of food sources; statistical reports on the risks and benefits of pharmaceuticals; the need to interpret very, very large budget numbers and probabilistic statements about the outcome of economic policies or the interest charges on credit cards and bank accounts; and so on. No longer are these challenges for people with specialized training or education alone. More and more, they are simply skills that all citizens must have to evaluate the flow of information they encounter every day. Furthermore, jobs that require technical and scientific skills remain unfilled because of a lack of preparation of the workforce, and jobs that do not have such requirements are disappearing. For these reasons, identifying ways to improve scientific and technological literacy constitutes a critical research and educational agenda.

In this chapter, we join those who argue that it is a good idea to introduce young children to STEM (science, technology, engineering, and mathematics) topics and methods even during the preschool years (Bowman, Donovan, & Burns, 2001; Duschl, Schweingruber, & Shouse, 2006). First, there exists a cumulative research base with preschool-age, and even younger, children that documents their knowledge about causality; natural number arithmetic; and some of the principled ways in which animals, plants, and inert objects move and change over time (Bowman et al., 2001; Carey, 2009; Duschl et al., 2006;

The preparation of this chapter, as well as the reported results, was supported by National Science Foundation Grant EC-0529579. The opinions expressed herein are those of the authors only.

Gelman & Williams, 1998; Gopnik, Meltzoff, & Kuhl, 1999). Because these arenas of knowledge overlap with science domains, we and our colleagues expected that we could build from young children's competencies and create a program of appropriate learning options that would hold their attention and support them to build knowledge about science and its tools (Gelman, Brenneman, Macdonald, & Roman, 2009).

By choosing to work with children's relevant foundational knowledge, as well as their natural proclivities to explore and ask questions (Callanan & Oakes, 1992; Chouinard, 2007; Frazier, Gelman, & Wellman, 2009) and to try to make sense of the world around them (e.g., Schulz & Bonawitz, 2007), we have avoided a push-down curriculum made up of interesting facts that could not be explained in a way the children would understand. For example, we know of a program for kindergarteners that taught children that they would weigh less if they were on the moon. One of our (Rochel Gelman) friend's children was most eager to tell about this fact. When asked by an adult, "Would you weigh more when you come back to earth?" the child's immediate response was "Yes," but then she turned and said, "This doesn't make any sense," and left. Fortunately, she did not ask for an explanation, because the adult surely did not know the relevant physics. This paucity of knowledge was likely to have been the case for the child's kindergarten teacher as well; many adults have trouble understanding the physics involved in the account of this fact (McCloskey, 1983; McCloskey, Caramazza, & Green, 1980). Indeed, elementary and preschool teachers frequently report discomfort with their knowledge of science and their ability to incorporate it appropriately into the early education classroom (e.g., Greenfield et al., 2009). Basing our preschool science program on concepts that can be effectively explained to preschoolers has increased teachers' comfort level and feelings of competence with teaching science. After all, the program takes advantage of the reported competencies of their young charges.

Some Reminders

It is no longer assumed that young children learn whatever is in their environment, as if their minds were receptacles into which knowledge is poured. They, like all learners, often are active participants in their own learning. Second, it is a characteristic of human cognition that learners' attention is more likely to focus on inputs that can be related to already-existing knowledge and or beliefs. One's knowledge and beliefs influence how one interprets the environment. This is as true early in one's life as it is later. A poignant example comes from Vallone, Ross, and Lepper (1985), who showed a common news clip to groups of Israelis and Palestinians. Both groups contended that the report was biased against them. This is but one example of what is dubbed the *confirmation bias* in the social psychology literature. Failure to pose an alternative hypothesis and consider the evidence permeates our everyday lives.

A second example illustrates that the information that captures attention is related to what one already knows. Yoshida, Fernandez, and Stigler (1993) showed the same section of a videotaped math lesson to fourth graders in the United States and Japan and asked the students to describe it. The U.S. students tended to talk about nonmathematical items, including what the teacher was wearing, whereas Japanese students' comments focused on the mathematics in the lesson and revealed a deeper degree of understanding. The knowledge that they already possessed supported greater attention to mathematical information and further learning.

Details related to this particular example offer clues about the nature of environments that may support learning. To be sure, the differences between the two groups of students in Yoshida et al.'s (1993) study included a constellation of interrelated variables that reflect deep cultural differences, for example, the relative homogeneity of the Japanese students in a class. Still, some of these variables are worthy of attention in regard to any effort to teach mathematics. Japanese teachers of elementary school children know more mathematics, spend more time teaching a more organized mathematics lesson, and encourage their students to relate homework to lessons as well as successive lessons to each other (Stevenson & Stigler, 1992; Stigler & Hiebert, 1999). Put differently, Japanese students have more opportunities to assimilate material, to try to talk about it, and to consider alternative solutions. They also have teachers who know enough to nudge their pupils who make errors to consider another direction.

There are many other examples of how knowledge or the lack of knowledge influences what learners focus on in any potential learning situation (see Bransford, Brown, & Cocking, 1999). The foregoing particular result from Yoshida et al. (1993) is especially relevant for the discussion of possible STEM educational programs. From a pedagogical perspective, it illustrates the kinds of variables that have been identified as relevant for the design of teaching methods:

- Learners are more likely to attend to and assimilate inputs if these can be related to existing knowledge organizations.
- It helps to have the learners involved in the creation of and communication about possible solutions or answer paths.
- When the goal is to build understanding, as opposed to learning facts and algorithms, it takes a considerable amount of time on task.
- Learning about a domain is facilitated when knowledgeable individuals present different examples about the main or big ideas of the subject at hand. Put differently, when inputs are organized in terms of the principles that underlie the examples, the odds favor the acquisition of understanding even if the surface details of the exemplars vary (Richland, Zur, & Holyoak, 2007).
- Procedures and concepts are intricately linked (Gelman & Greeno, 1989; Lampert, 1986). When it comes to the topic of science, content and science practices naturally and necessarily go together (Duschl et al., 2006; Kuhn, 1962).

Science as a Domain

What does it mean to do, learn, or teach science? It does not mean to master or offer a list of facts and definitions of technical terms. Neither is it sufficient to merely teach about the experimental method. Engaging in science practices, such as observing or predicting, requires a focus on content. One needs something to observe and events to predict. Furthermore, the language that is relevant to the concepts in a given domain is closely related to the concepts therein, and the more one knows about a domain, the deeper the understanding of the language in that domain (Bransford et al., 1999; Carey, 2009). Different domains of knowledge build on different kinds of content from different sources. Likewise, the principles that organize domains vary. To illustrate, in the next few paragraphs we consider how the domain of history differs from that of science.

Historians reconstruct the past. They rely on written documents, artifacts, land arrangements, and art from a given time period, but they cannot be sure that they have all the relevant documentation from that time. In addition, there can be disputes as to what some documents record, especially when historians work in a language that has disappeared. The starting assumptions can have a profound effect on the resulting product. In point of fact, historians in different countries have, and still do, provide different accounts of the same period of time. The discovery of new documents from the past can have an enormous impact on what becomes accepted as knowledge of the past.

Scientists, in contrast, are concerned with explaining the natural world. Topics include the objects on, in, and surrounding the earth; the states and changes of these objects; the energy conditions that influence matter; the organization and function of biological matter; the nature of inert entities; laws of motion; and how entities interact with their ecological niches, as well as many other topics. Experiments and their related procedures provide the relevant data for explanations. Notebooks (or computer files) are used to keep track of theoretical motivations, design concerns, observed data and their organization, the results of various conditions, and further hypotheses and ideas for new explorations. Different branches of science focus on particular topics, but all assume that the to-be-found laws are universal and organized in coherent ways and that the findings and generalizations flow from the use of experimental and modeling methods. When students learn science, all of these factors come into play, and all are incorporated into the educational programs that have been developed to study and foster science learning in real-world settings. Regardless of the specific branch of science, there is a fundamental commitment to the role of observations as the source of data, be it to obtain initial evidence about a phenomenon or to test a theory. New observations that are reliable and open to inspection by others can drive major shifts in what are taken as the basic facts to explain through theory.

On Scientific Observations

To do science today is to ask about the natural phenomena in the world and do so in a systematic way, using the methodological, physical, and even mathematical tools of the discipline. In turn, the tools build on fundamental commitments to gather repeatable, observable data. This recognition of the central role of observation is relatively new in our history. "The man who first taught that observations are essential and supreme in science was Galileo Galilei" (Cropper, 2001, p. 3). The history of science also details the important role of instruments that enhanced observational powers, including the microscope, barometer, thermometer, computer, scale, ruler, graduated cylinder, clock, telescope, and other items. So too are there history lessons about the role of the observer's background knowledge and access to tools that make observable what cannot be seen by the naked eye.

Galileo (1564–1642) provided an early example of the interaction among one's observations, hypotheses, and prior knowledge. He was trained in the art of drawing, an advantage when he used his telescope to record his observations of the surface of the moon. Galileo knew that the shading of light and its reflections could be due to depths and shapes, from which he correctly concluded that there were mountains and craters on the moon. His other observations of the sun and Jupiter contributed to his move to endorse Copernicus' proposal that the earth rotated around the sun. Doing so landed him in very serious trouble with the Roman Catholic Church, which held that the earth was the center of the universe and, therefore, that the sun rotated around the earth. The Church's view that the sun and the moon were perfectly smooth also clashed with Galileo's observations to the contrary (Cropper, 2001).

The critical idea that Galileo gave us is that our senses provide information about the world. Another critical idea is that one cannot count on gaining all relevant observations from the surfaces of an object. Often it is necessary to make a prediction about the insides and then proceed to investigate. The work of Vesalius (1514–1546), an anatomist, provides a lovely example of this theme.

Apparently, it never occurred to anyone before Vesalius to do a thorough dissection of a human body in conjunction with a very careful set of observations (Cropper, 2001). So strong was the authority of the ancient writers that surgeons and physicians were taught what Galen (130–200) claimed were the facts of anatomy for 1,500 years after his death. The results of the Vesalius dissection and its documentation made it clear that Galen was wrong in many ways. For example, Galen's description of human anatomy had the arteries in the left ventricle of the heart carrying the purest blood to the brain and lungs and the veins in the right ventricle carrying blood to the stomach and liver. He also concluded that there are two bones in the human jaw. In fact, Vesalius correctly determined that there is but one jawbone (Cropper, 2001). William Harvey (1578–1657) also helped establish the importance of direct observation with his detailed and experimental observations that established knowledge about the circulation of blood.

In astronomy, Tycho Brahe (1546–1601) became known for the care and precision of his observations of planetary motion, as did his famous assistant, Johannes Kepler (1571–1630), who realized that the correct mathematical description of planetary motion about the sun was that it was elliptical and that planets swept out equal areas in equal amounts of time (Cropper, 2001). Francis Bacon (1561–1626) also emphasized the importance of systematic observation in the acquisition of evidence-based knowledge, and by the middle of the 17th century the importance of observations was widely accepted by the leading scientists of the day (Cropper, 2001).

In the 21st century, many of the accepted observational tools have become extremely expensive. Physicists depend on accelerators; astronomers require better and better telescopes and cameras; doctors and neuroscientists have become wedded to ultrasound, functional magnetic resonance imaging machines; and the list goes on and on. A public that has a better understanding of the scientific view of observations and devices that enable their collection of data would be better able to engage in cost–benefit analyses.

As discussed above, the observational tools of science serve investigators who collect information about the world, its contents, and surrounds. These tools are used to extend observational power and gather information that is be relevant to a hypothesis, a prediction, or an experiment about the nature of the world. In addition to physical science tools, there are methodological tools that depend on observation. These include recording and dating one's observations in a way that others can read, predicting and checking, measuring, reporting, comparing and contrasting, designing and interpreting experiments, and others. In our work, we have found that these science tools can be introduced to young learners in a way that extends their natural proclivities and puts them on constructive learning pathways for school science.

On Building Up in a Preschool Science "Curriculum"

When it comes to the topic of early science knowledge and reasoning, we and other researchers have demonstrated that preschool children can learn quite a bit about some areas of science and arithmetic, without the kind of formal instruction that occurs in schools. They do so pretty much on the fly as they interact with their environment and knowledgeable others. The domains include arithmetic with a range of natural numbers, physical and social causality, the nature of the inanimate–animate distinction, and some knowledge about chemical and physical features of materials (Bowman et al., 2001; Carey, 2009; Duschl et al., 2006; Gelman & Williams, 1998).

Young children have natural habits of mind that stand them in good stead as "scientists-in-waiting." Even as they are just learning language, they select objects and events in the world—initially by pointing, and then with language—and seek to share their observations and/or to gather more information about these phenomena through referential pointing and shared gaze (Tomasello, 1995). They ask questions about things in the world and how they work or fail to work. Chouinard's (2007) analyses of four children's transcripts in the Child Language Data Exchange System database (see http://childes.psy.cmu.edu/) uncovered the fact that information-seeking questions occurred at the amazing rate of 76 per hour. Keep in mind that some children were not even 2 years old, an age at which they do not have much productive syntax. This calls to mind one of our sons crawling up the stairs in the house asking "What's this?" The reply—a stair—did not suffice. He asked the same question over and over and over again, day after day. Then one day he stopped asking the question. This sort of thing happens repeatedly: Children use questions as they seek not just to label the world but also to explain what they have observed and the patterns they have noticed (Callanan & Oakes, 1992; Chouinard, 2007; Frazier et al., 2009).

Children often play with the same objects over and over again and eventually know a great deal about their properties, such as whether they will float, balance, or roll smoothly. In their now-classic paper, Karmiloff-Smith and Inhelder (1974) reported on young children's persistent efforts to balance blocks. One of the blocks had a piece of lead, offset from the center. Children got to the point where they placed all of the blocks at their midpoint and labeled the off-center block as "no good." They set it aside but finally made a new effort to balance all of the blocks. Again, the trick block presented a problem. With repeated trials, the "no good" block attracted attention, a development that led to success. The block was moved back and forth across another block until it did balance. This set in motion a new theory of balance that explained their observations and placements of all of the blocks. Together, children's competence and knowledge about some of the content of science domains and their tendencies to observe and explain can be used in the development of coherent science curriculum for preschool. It takes more than these to be a scientist, though. Like David Klahr, we are skeptical about the idea that children will always, on their own, learn to formulate questions, use the experimental method, and generate explanations that consider the laws of science and the logic of scientific inquiry. Indeed, we doubt that many adults do this in their daily lives. In a sense, then, it is not just young children who are scientists-in-waiting—so too is a large majority of the U.S. population. We join other researchers in this volume in efforts to develop instructional materials that will move more children from child to scientist, in an effort to support a more scientifically literate citizenry.

Preschool Pathways to Science

Many of the physical and methodological tools of science can be reasonably introduced to even very young learners. For more than a decade, we have worked to develop the Preschool Pathways to Science (PrePS) program, which leverages children's natural curiosity, spontaneous exploration, and explanation-seeking activities (e.g., Callanan & Oakes, 1992; Chouinard, 2007; Jirout, 2009; Karmiloff-Smith & Inhelder, 1974/5; Schulz & Bonawitz, 2007) about some science concepts to create a program to support preschool science learning. Given changes in views of the preschool mind from descriptions of its deficits to a focus on its competence, we believed the time was ripe to develop an educational program that built on science-relevant conceptual competencies and habits of mind identified by cognitive developmental science. The idea was to move children onto relevant learning paths for the science they would encounter in elementary school but to do so in a way that was deeply rooted in cognitive science. In taking on this challenge, we joined Klahr and others who have attempted to bring together education and cognitive science as "beacons of mutual illumination" (Klahr, Chen, & Toth, 2001).

The content areas chosen for exploration in the PrePS program come from children's own interests and, critically, from competencies that preschoolers already have in science-relevant domains. The conceptual content is explored fully over time instead of moving rapidly from one idea to another. Children might study various aspects of *change* or *form and function* for months. This feature of the program reflects research showing that multiple opportunities to work with, think about, experiment with, and communicate about similar conceptual content in multiple, varied ways maximize the probability that students will attend to at least some of the offered lessons in the manner intended by the teachers. It also reflects an aspect of the constructivist mind; it is easier to learn more about something one already knows a bit about (Bransford et al., 1999).

In the PrePS approach to science education, content matters, and so too does the way content is presented; however, teaching children content without having them engage in science practices makes science seem like a list of facts and subtly reinforces the idea that science is something that *other* people do and think about (Gelman et al., 2009). Our goal with PrePS is to encourage all children to move from being scientists-in-waiting to becoming scientific thinkers by allowing them to wonder, explore, and investigate big conceptual ideas using the same science practices used by older scientists. Together, the conceptual–language side and the practice–tool side form a coherent approach to how science is characterized and implemented.

Children in the PrePS program are encouraged to think, talk, and work scientifically as a way to develop understanding. These practices are interdependent. Students who are observing, predicting, and checking are also learning the vocabulary words to describe these actions. In our work with preschoolers, we focus on five key science practices used to describe ways of thinking and doing science:

- observe, predict, and check;
- compare, contrast, and experiment;
- relate vocabulary, discourse, and language;
- count, measure, and other mathematics; and
- record and document.

Each practice is thought of as a group of related skills. Of course, in the end, all of the skills can be related to one other.

Building Observation Skills

In the following paragraphs, we focus in particular on efforts to develop children's understanding of observation. Given its fundamental role in science and in many other science practices, we introduce observation early in the program, use it repeatedly, and expand its use throughout the school year. Children come to think differently about an item that they are observing instead of just glancing at (Gelman & Brenneman, 2004).

For many years, we have introduced 3- to 5-year-old children to the idea of observation using an apple. During group time, the teacher provides an apple for each child, or passes around one apple. She or he introduces the term *observation* and explains that making an observation is noticing something about the apple: how it looks, feels, smells, sounds, or even tastes. (Children are told that tasting will come later.) Then the teacher asks children to share something that they notice about the apple as the fruit is passed. Children's observations (e.g., "It looks red," "It smells sweet," "It's cold") are written down by the teacher, aide, or another adult. In these early experiences, children's participation is more important than accuracy. For example, if a child says, "The apple smells juicy," the teacher does not correct that statement and instead probes meaning by asking, for example, "It smells juicy? What does juice smell like?"

In the next, related learning experience, children are introduced to the idea of *prediction* and are encouraged to make predictions about what they would observe inside an apple. Children's ideas are written down so that these can be referenced as the apple is cut to check children's predictions. Again, children make observations of the inside of the apple (e.g., "It's wet," "It's white and a little bit green," "There are five seeds!"). Checking their predictions provides more evidence of the critical role that observation plays in scientific exploration.

Watching a video of a class observing an apple for the first time is striking because the children attend so carefully to the task. Over the years, adults who have watched this activity have remarked that the children acted as if they had never seen an apple before. They had *seen* apples before, of course, but they had not *observed* them. The introduction of a new science term and practice transformed a familiar apple into an object for scientific exploration and allowed students to consider this common, everyday object in a new, more focused, way (Gelman & Brenneman, 2004).

In subsequent activities, we progress to making observations about other, less familiar items, and as we do so we very intentionally begin to have children link the observations they make to their senses, or the sources of the information that they are gathering. For example, one activity involves a coconut, which is a great item for illustrating that one can make many different observations about the same object or event. Children describe the coconut and practice linking each of their observations to a particular sense as the source of the information: brown, hairy like a lion, round, has circles on the end (eyes); rough, hairy (skin); juice inside (ears); smells like dirt, smells yucky (nose); heavy (muscles). In a recent visit to a classroom, children begged to eat the coconut to make observations about its taste and texture. Their reviews were uniformly negative. The coconut was "not good" and tasted "yucky," but we remain impressed by their curiosity and spirit of exploration.

These introductory activities lay a foundation for a more in-depth exploration of observation and senses. Adapted from the work of our colleagues Christine Massey and Zipora Roth with K–1 learners, the activities go beyond matching body parts (e.g., eyes and ears) with functions (e.g., seeing and hearing). This knowledge is important, but some might view it as an endpoint for preschoolers. Our studies suggest that young children are capable of learning more, and this "more" forms a critical foundation for later science thinking skills. In a series of classroom learning experiences, children explore the unique capabilities and limits of each sense and link each sense to the kinds of information it gathers. Activities involve solving a problem, such as identifying matches or finding "which one of these things is not like the others," and each situation is set up by the teacher so that a particular sense is the best tool to solve the problem (Massey & Roth, 2004). In this way, the unique powers of each sense are highlighted.

To illustrate, one activity features a unique function of vision. Whereas shape and texture information often can be discovered through other senses, it is only through vision that we get information about color. Children are shown crayons and cube blocks on a tray, each in an array of colors. Students are presented with an opaque fabric pouch, told that the object inside matches one item on the tray, and asked to determine, without looking, whether the item is a crayon or a block. Children can succeed by feeling the item through the fabric. When asked to describe how they know that it is, for example, a crayon, children discuss attributes such as its length, skinniness, and pointy end. With the shape of the item established, we ask children to tell us its color. No amount of feeling will allow children to know for sure, although most children are happy to guess. Whereas all children agree on the item's shape, guesses about color vary considerably, which provides a potent illustration both of differing degrees of certainty when weighing evidence and of the special role of vision in determining color.

The complete activity series provides children with chances to reflect on the sources of their knowledge so that they begin to understand not just *that* they know something, but *how* they know it (Massey & Roth, 2004). Taking time to reflect on each sense and the information one can gain by using it supports metacognitive development and early awareness of knowledge (in general, and science knowledge specifically) as something that is constructed on the basis of experience. As they reflect on sources of evidence, they also are asked to explain the evidence they used to draw a conclusion, judge the adequacy of the evidence they have gathered, and determine whether more evidence is needed. Most children say that they need to see inside the pouch to know for sure what the color of the hidden item is. These developing insights are foundations for further learning about science as a way of knowing, and of coordinating and interpreting evidence (Duschl et al., 2006).

Results from the "Using Senses as Tools for Observation" unit in the PrePS program with preschoolers have been encouraging. For children in a university preschool, postunit performance on tasks that required them to determine which sense could be used to solve a discrimination problem ("Can a particular sense be used to tell which of two items is sweet, green, has a scent, etc.?") was comparable to performance in a sample of kindergarteners in urban schools (Massey & Roth, 1997). Both of the age groups represented achieved high overall scores of 84% (pre-K, university site) and 85% (kindergarten, inner city site), which encouraged us to work in schools that serve families of lower socioeconomic status.

When we pilot-tested the unit with these students, many of whom were learning both English and Spanish, we began with pretests to gauge baseline levels of understanding. The preassessments revealed that most children were unable to identify the function of many of their senses. They had difficulty completing sentences such as "With our eyes we_____" and assessing the truth of statements such as "Do we taste with our ears?" A teacher in one classroom worked with us to provide a series of learning experiences about senses, and another classroom (by design) served as the comparison. After these lessons, children in the intervention classroom were more likely (79% of learners vs. 27%) to perform well when matching senses with their functions than were children who had not participated.

The results from this admittedly small sample are bolstered by recent pre- and postintervention data from a larger sample. Among a diverse (mostly dual-language learner) sample of 4-year-olds ($N = 47$, mean age at pretest = 54.3 months, range: 48–60), 15 children were able to answer more than half of the questions about the basic functions of their senses at both the pre- and posttest, which occurred approximately 3 months apart. Fourteen children could not do this at either time. Eighteen children moved from not passing to passing. No child moved in the opposite direction. As a group, children's posttest scores were reliably greater than their pretest scores, $t(46) = -7.01, p < .001$, one-tailed.

Among the 15 learners who were already further along the learning pathway than their peers (i.e., who already showed some understanding of the basic functions of their senses), we expected to find evidence of growth in their understandings of the unique capabilities of each sense. This prediction follows from the assumption that learning is more likely to occur if one already knows something about the input. The second portion of our assessment required children to apply their knowledge to a series of problem-solving situations. Children who passed the questions about the basic functions of their senses (getting eight or more correct out of 15) were introduced to a set of six unisense robots. Each robot had just one sensory capacity, marked with a familiar icon, such as an eye or an ear (Massey & Roth, 1997; see also O'Neill & Chong, 2001). Children were told about each robot's capability and then were asked a series of questions to be sure that they understand what each unisense robot can do. For example, after being introduced to the ear robot, children are asked whether it can hear (yes), whether it can see (no), and whether it can tell heaviness (no). They were asked three questions for each of the six robots (including one for muscles). Children rarely had any difficulty with these questions.

Once it had been established that children understood the robots, children completed a series of six trials. In each, the child was presented with a pair of similar items that differ on a critical dimension (e.g., two identical-looking candies with different flavors, two squares of paper of different colors). The task on each trial was to say whether a particular sense robot, all by itself, could make the discrimination between the two items (e.g., "Can the ear robot tell which one of these papers is green?"). Although overall scores were only about 68% correct at posttest, a t test comparing pre- and posttest scores showed a reliable increase in children's responding, $t(13) = -1.81, p < .05$, one-tailed.[1] We suspect that if these children had received more learning opportunities with individual feedback that the improvement would have been greater (Gelman, 1969).

Explorations of senses and observation also lend themselves to the introduction and use of certain science tools. Magnifiers work with our sense of vision to allow us to observe objects and details that are too small to see well without magnification. Balance scales can be introduced as tools that help us tell which of two things is heavier. This is especially useful when we cannot discriminate just by using our muscles, because the felt weights of the items are not

---

[1]Complete data sets are available for 14 children. One child was inadvertently tested on the robots even though he achieved a score of only 7 on the pretest screener, and his data are included. Two children who passed the screener did not complete the robot tasks.

very different. Both of these science tools are often found in preschool classrooms, in the science or discovery areas; however, observations of preschool science areas confirm that children do not often visit these compared with the time they spend in the art, dramatic play, and block areas (Tu, 2006). Furthermore, when children do interact with science tools, they do not necessarily use them in the intended manner. This situation is a specific instance of a larger truth: Learners do not always interpret learning inputs or materials as intended (Gelman, 1994). Even a small amount of adult guidance can make the difference between magnifiers and balance scales being used as science tools or props to simulate cooking and stirring in dramatic play. For example, when balance scales are introduced to children as tools for observing and comparing weights of objects, children are more likely to spend time in the science area and to learn how to interpret the movement of the scale, compared with children who do not have this introduction (Nayfeld, Brenneman, & Gelman, in press).

Science journals are another tool that we incorporate into preschool science investigations. Documenting is a key feature of the well-regarded Reggio Emilia approach to early education (see http://www.reggioalliance.org/), and this evidence of the educational benefits of incorporating drawing into children's activities inspired our use of science journals with preschoolers. After children explore a new object or participate in an experiment, we ask them to record their observations in a science journal. As a science tool, journals provide a motivation for details, because these will be incorporated into a drawing and description (Brenneman & Louro, 2008). Children have a specific goal to record what they have noticed about, for example, the inside of a small cactus, seeds that have sprouted, or balls rolling down ramps of different heights. Adults can support children's attention to key features, and enhance the representational power of their journal entries, by constraining the task in certain ways. Focused observation prompts from adults can be useful for encouraging more realistic recordings of information (Vlach & Carver, 2008). Incorporating contrast also encourages young children to draw more realistically (e.g., Davis & Bentley, 1984). For example, when we ask children to represent the results of a growth experiment by drawing both a healthy plant and an unhealthy plant, drawings are more likely to include relevant features, such as color, stem shape (droopy or straight), leaf size, and number of leaves, because these contrasts are relevant to plants' health (Brenneman & Louro, 2008).

The use of science journals can help children solidify their understandings because they provide a chance for learners to think again about a science experience as they record what they see and know. Deeper, more durable learning occurs when hands-on learning experiences are enhanced with opportunities to apply new knowledge to a related problem, to make a graph, or to create a journal entry (see also Massey, 2004). Journal entries also provide teachers with insight into students' observations and understandings. The drawings that children create provide a window into their ideas about the most important or relevant features of an object or situation (Doris, 1991; White & Gunstone, 1992). Although their drawing skill can limit the features children can represent clearly, our habit of asking them what they would like to write on their drawing provides an opportunity for them to describe their observations and drawings (Brenneman & Louro, 2008; Gelman et al., 2009). As teachers listen and probe, they have the opportunity to assess what children have learned from their science explorations and to determine what might have been misunderstood.

Conclusions and Future Directions

We have found that young children's inquisitiveness fits well with a program that teaches them to make systematic observations about questions of interest, using the tools and practices of science. Through encouragement in the use of these tools, processes, and their technical names across a variety of content lessons, children acquire science terms as they practice using the skills and tools to which those terms refer. It is clearly possible to encourage young scientists-in-waiting to start to become scientists. As an illustration, consider the nature of the conversation we had recently when we returned to a classroom we had been in a month earlier. At that time, we had engaged children in discussions and experiments about the function of blubber for animals that live in cold environments (Gelman et al., 2009). Many children approached us to ask whether we remembered the blubber. We responded by asking questions about what the children themselves remembered about the experimental procedure, about the question we were exploring, and about the results that we had found. Children did a remarkable job, using vocabulary words such as *blubber, test,* and *experiment.* They were able to describe the method (use one bag filled with blubber/vegetable shortening and one that is not and place them into snow) and the results (we found out that blubber keeps our hands warmer). When asked how she knew the answer to a particular question, one girl responded, in a matter-of-fact tone, "I'm a scientist," a phrase we had not used with her.

This example illustrates that the children remembered the key vocabulary, goals, and conditions of the experiment. The conversation was also extremely animated and full of positive affect. This is quite typical of most of the children this age with whom we have worked. They pay attention, listen, and participate in lessons that occur during group time—even if these go on for 20 minutes. Many children and/or their parents tell us that the school activities led to at-home discussions about what the children had done during the school day, taking science out of the classroom and into the rest of their lives (Gelman & Brenneman, 2004). The inclusion of opportunities to do classroom science builds on children's natural proclivities, extends these to incorporate the practices and tools of science, and—we hope—helps ensure that science continues to be an enjoyable and positive experience that is considered an integral part of everyday experience. By providing repeated opportunities to engage productively with both the content and processes of science, educators foster the promise in each young scientist-in-waiting, providing critical support as he or she grows from child to scientist.

References

Bowman, B. T., Donovan, M. S., & Burns, M. S. (2001). *Eager to learn: Educating our preschoolers.* Washington, DC: The National Academies Press.

Bransford, J., Brown, A., & Cocking, R. (1999). *How people learn: Brain, mind, experience, and school.* Washington, DC: The National Academies Press.

Brenneman, K., & Louro, I. F. (2008). Science journals in the preschool classroom. *Early Childhood Education Journal, 36,* 113–119. doi:10.1007/s10643-008-0258-z

Callanan, M. A., & Oakes, L. M. (1992). Preschoolers' questions and parents' explanations: Causal thinking in everyday activity. *Cognitive Development, 7,* 213–233.

Carey, S. (2009). *The origin of concepts.* New York, NY: Oxford University Press.

Chouinard, M. M. (2007). Children's questions: A mechanism for cognitive development. *Monographs of the Society for Research in Child Development, 72,* 1–112.

Cropper, W. H. (2001). *Great physicists: The life and times of leading physicists from Galileo to Hawking.* Oxford, England: Oxford University Press.

Davis, A. M., & Bentley, M. (1984). Young children's interpretation of the task demands in a simple experimental situation: An example from drawing. *Educational Psychology, 4,* 249–254. doi:10.1080/0144341840040305

Doris, E. (1991). *Doing what scientists do: Children learn to investigate their world.* Portsmouth, NH: Heinemann.

Doyle, A. C. (1985). A scandal in Bohemia. In *Sherlock Holmes: The complete illustrated short stories.* London, England: Chancellor Press. (Original work published 1891)

Duschl, R. A., Schweingruber, H. A., & Shouse, A. W. (2006). *Taking science to school: Learning and teaching science in grades K–8.* Washington, DC: The National Academies Press.

Frazier, B. N., Gelman, S. A., & Wellman, H. M. (2009). Preschoolers' search for explanatory information within adult–child conversation. *Child Development, 80,* 1592–1611. doi:10.1111/j.1467-8624.2009.01356.x

Gelman, R. (1969). Conservation acquisition: A problem of learning to attend to relevant attributes. *Journal of Experimental Child Psychology, 7,* 167–187.

Gelman, R. (1994). Constructivism and supporting environments. In D. Tirosh (Ed.), *Implicit and explicit knowledge: An educational approach* (Vol. 6, pp. 55–82). New York, NY: Ablex.

Gelman, R., & Brenneman, K. (2004). Relevant pathways for preschool science learning. *Early Childhood Quarterly Review, 19,* 150–158.

Gelman, R., Brenneman, K., Macdonald, G., & Roman, M. (2009). *Preschool pathways to science (PrePS): Facilitating scientific ways of thinking, talking, doing, and understanding.* Baltimore, MD: Brookes.

Gelman, R., & Greeno, J. G. (1989). On the nature of competence: Principles for understanding in a domain. In L. B. Resnick (Ed.), *Knowing and learning: Essays in honor of Robert Glaser* (pp. 125–186). Hillsdale, NJ: Erlbaum.

Gelman, R., & Williams, E. (1998). Enabling constraints for cognitive development and learning: Domain specificity and epigenesis. In D. Kuhn & R. Siegler (Eds.), *Handbook of child psychology (5th ed.): Vol. 2. Cognition, perception and language* (pp. 575–630). New York, NY: Wiley.

Greenfield, D., Jirout, J., Dominguez, X., Greenberg, A., Maier, M., & Fuccillo, J. (2009). Science in the preschool classroom: A programmatic research agenda to improve science readiness. *Early Education and Development, 20,* 238–264. doi:10.1080/10409280802595441

Gopnik, A., Meltzoff, A. N., & Kuhl, P. K. (1999). *The scientist in the crib: What early learning tells us about the mind.* New York, NY: HarperCollins.

Jirout, J. (2009, October). *Curious curiosities: A study of children's scientific curiosity and exploration.* Paper presented at "From Child to Scientist: Mechanisms of Learning and Development— A *Festschrift* in Honor of the Scientific and Educational Contributions of David Klahr," Pittsburgh, PA.

Karmiloff-Smith, A. & Inhelder, B. (1974). If you want to get ahead, get a theory. *Cognition, 3,* 195–212.

Klahr, D., Chen, Z., & Toth, E. (2001). Cognitive development and science education: Ships that pass in the night or beacons of mutual illumination? In S. Carver & D. Klahr (Eds.), *Cognition and instruction: 25 years of progress* (pp. 75–120). Mahwah, NJ: Erlbaum.

Kuhn, T. S. (1962). *The structure of scientific revolutions.* Chicago, IL: University of Chicago Press.

Lampert, M. (1986). Knowing, doing, and teaching multiplication. *Cognition and Instruction, 3,* 305–342. doi:10.1207/s1532690xci0304_1

Massey, C. (2004, November). *Learning about light and shadows: Designing instruction for conceptual change with young learners.* Invited presentation given at the meeting of the National Academy of Sciences Committee on Science Learning in Grades K–8, Washington, DC.

Massey, C., & Roth, Z. (1997, April). *Feeling colors and seeing tastes: Kindergarteners' learning about sensory modalities and knowledge acquisition.* Paper presented at the biennial meeting of the Society for Research in Child Development, Washington, DC.

Massey, C., & Roth, Z. (2004). *Science for developing minds series: A science curriculum for kindergarten and first grade.* . Philadelphia, PA: Edventures.

McCloskey, M. (1983). Naive theories of motion. In D. Gentner & A. L. Stevens (Eds.), *Mental models* (pp. 299–324). Hillsdale, NJ: Erlbaum.

McCloskey, M., Caramazza, A. & Green, B. (1980, December 5). Curvilinear motion in the absence of external forces: Naive beliefs about the motion of objects. *Science, 210,* 1139–1141. doi:10.1126/science.210.4474.1139

Nayfeld, I., Brenneman, K., & Gelman, R. (in press). Science in the classroom: Finding a balance between autonomous exploration and teacher-led instruction in preschool settings. *Early Education and Development.*

O'Neill, D. K., & Chong, S. C. F. (2001). Preschool children's difficulty understanding the types of information obtained through the five senses. *Child Development, 72,* 803–815. doi:10.1111/1467-8624.00316

Richland, L. E., Zur, O., & Holyoak, K. J. (2007, May 25). Cognitive supports for analogies in the mathematics classroom. *Science, 316,* 1128–1129. doi:10.1126/science.1142103

Schulz, L. E., & Bonawitz, E. B. (2007). Serious fun: Preschoolers engage in more exploratory play when evidence is confounded. *Developmental Psychology, 43,* 1045–1050. doi:10.1037/0012-1649.43.4.1045

Stevenson, H., & Stigler, J. M. (1992). *The learning gap.* New York, NY: Summit Books.

Stigler, J. M., & Hiebert, J. (1999). *The teaching gap: Best ideas from the world's teachers for education in the classroom.* New York, NY: Free Press.

Tomasello, M. (1995). Joint attention as social cognition. In C. Moore & C. Dunham, (Eds.), *Joint attention: Its origins and development* (pp. 103–130). Mahwah, NJ: Erlbaum.

Tu, T. (2006). Preschool science environment: What is available in a preschool classroom? *Early Childhood Education Journal, 33,* 245–251. doi:10.1007/s10643-005-0049-8

Vallone, R. P., Ross, L., & Lepper, M. R. (1985). The hostile media phenomenon: Biased perception and perceptions of media bias in coverage of the Beirut massacre. *Journal of Personality and Social Psychology, 49,* 577–585.

Vlach, H. A., & Carver, S. M. (2008). The effects of observation coaching on children's graphic representations. *Early Childhood Research & Practice, 10*(1). Retrieved from http://ecrp.uiuc.edu/v10n1/vlach.html

White, R., & Gunstone, R. (1992). *Probing understanding.* London, England: Falmer Press.

Yoshida, M., Fernandez, C., & Stigler, J. M. (1993). Japanese and American students' differential memory for teachers' statements during a mathematics lesson. *Journal of Educational Psychology, 85,* 610–617. doi:10.1037/0022-0663.85.4.610

9

Supporting Inquiry About the Foundations of Evolutionary Thinking in the Elementary Grades

Richard Lehrer and Leona Schauble

In this chapter, we address the following question: What is foundational for science learning? Moreover, we intend the term *foundational* to carry two different meanings. First, there is the overarching question of goals, that is, what science education should be organized to achieve. Second, we mean foundational for further learning and development. What are the developmental underpinnings of the knowledge, reasoning, and forms of activity that we value in science education, and how is it possible to build systematically on them across the years of a child's education—or, for that matter, beyond? This, of course, is territory that David Klahr has long been exploring, and we have been fortunate to encounter him at many a trail and signpost on this journey.

It is the focus on foundations, in both senses, that leads to our interest in organizing instruction around disciplinary dispositions, or ways of knowing that are core to and characteristic of the different subjects or fields of study. Cultivating disciplined ways of knowing not only involves helping students learn about the products of the discipline (in this case, science "content knowledge") but also entails learning about the ways that scientific knowledge gets made, revised, and, sometimes, abandoned (Lehrer, 2009). These ways are highly variable, not only between but also within scientific fields, and finding an appropriate way of characterizing scientific thinking has been a matter of ongoing debate in the field (Lehrer & Schauble, 2006). Scientific work can be observational, comparative, experimental, or theoretical; it can be conducted in physics laboratory experiments or in biological field studies. Nevertheless, we argue that the core work of science is oriented toward constructing, revising, applying, and defending models of the natural world (Giere, 1988; Hesse, 1962). Modeling has been described as the signature of research in the sciences (Nersessian, 2008), although it is not prominent in school science. To the extent that models appear at all in school, they are usually used as illustrative devices for explaining concepts instead of as scientific theory-building tools and practices (Windschitl & Thompson, 2006).

This chapter is based on research supported by the National Science Foundation under Grant 0628253. Any opinions, findings, and conclusions or recommendations expressed in the chapter are those of the authors and do not necessarily reflect the views of the National Science Foundation.

This sense of modeling is best acquired by beginning, at one's own level, to participate in the practice of modeling. We use the word *practice* deliberately, to distinguish it from mere activity. *Practice* implies that one is engaged with the epistemic culture of modeling—the goals, problems, representations, and forms of argument valued by the discipline (Knorr-Cetina, 1999). Therefore, with participating teachers, we immerse students in modeling approaches to science from kindergarten onward. Early in the process, we decided against the path of simply giving students scientific models and asking them to interpret or apply them. Instead, we hope to encourage students to engage in what Hestenes (1992) called the *modeling game,* that is, using and inventing all manner of ways for representing the natural world as a means of pursuing questions about it. Of course, we are not anticipating that students would never consider conventional models and methods, only that they achieve a firm grounding in the nature of the phenomena and some consideration of potential models before they entertain conventional solutions. Our research program involves working closely with teachers as they reorganize science and mathematics instruction around this enterprise. We then longitudinally study the forms of student learning that emerge under instruction concentrated on the development of the disciplinary disposition of modeling.

In this chapter, we demonstrate how we work closely with teachers to develop inquiry sequences that simultaneously build students' repertoire of models for broad use across investigations, their understanding of change and variability in increasingly complex ecologies, and the sophistication of their judgments regarding the quality of evidence and explanations. We further suggest that developing such disciplinary dispositions requires extended engagement in learning communities that both need and value such scientific practices.

Two Aspects of Modeling

There are two aspects of modeling that modulate its difficulty for young students. The first has to do with the status of the model as a kind of *analogy,* that is, one in which objects and relations in the model represent objects and relations in the natural world. The second has to do less with structure and more with creating *material conditions* for the conduct of inquiry. Both are related in that observations are always materially and theoretically laden.

Analogies

Analogies vary in the nature of the mappings between the base and target systems (Gentner & Toupin, 1986). The analogies easiest to grasp are those that preserve literal similarity between the representing and represented worlds. Our term for these models is *physical microcosms,* and they seem to help the youngest students negotiate the leap into practices of representation. A physical microcosm can literally be a part of a natural system; we call these *remnants.* For example, Figure 9.1 shows a block of ice cut from a pond that elementary school children were studying throughout the year. The layers of ice and detritus

Figure 9.1.   Layers of ice and detritus from the retention pond in winter.

were studied in an attempt to resolve questions about whether the pond froze from the top down or the bottom up and to consider the implications of the two alternatives for the animals that overwinter there.

A physical model can also be a copy or a partial copy in a different scale, such as a globe or a model of a cell. In one of our participating sites, students have constructed an experimental rain garden, with plots in which the amount of moisture and kind of soil substrate are systematically varied. The rain garden is a model system that supports investigation into plant life and environments: a place of study meant to support more general conclusions about the variety of ways that plants and environments interact. The representational overhead of a physical microcosm like this is relatively low; that is, it does not require a lot of deciphering for students to hold in mind what is meant to symbolize what. The literal resemblance of physical microcosms has its dangers as well, however; deliberate selection of the elements is required because it can be a matter of confusion for students to grasp which elements of the natural world are being represented by the model system. That is because physical microcosms exemplify and do not merely re-create (Goodman, 1976)—an aspect that can be challenging for youngsters, who tend to resist "leaving out" any elements of the original phenomena being represented. For example, some of our students studying decomposition have designed compost columns as microcosms for closely tracking processes of decay. Considering how to design the columns invariably leads to debates about what should be included and excluded (e.g., first graders considered whether bits of Styrofoam, which they observed in the playground, needed to be included) and about the representational status of different elements of the columns (e.g., fifth graders wondered whether shredded paper could signify twigs). Although physical microcosms provide an entrée to modeling, they are not merely tools for children, because designing and sustaining these systems is often a foundation for inquiry in the sciences (Nersessian, 2008; Nersessian, Kurz-Milcke, Newsletter, & Davies, 2003).

Scientists do not just observe the world; they also inscribe it, usually in ways that enhance aspects that they consider theoretically important (Latour, 1990, 1999). Accordingly, we frequently ask students to invent multiple forms of inscription, with different forms to highlight different aspects of the phenomenon. This focus on children's invented representations is another interest that we share with David Klahr (e.g., Triona & Klahr, 2007); for example, students might make several drawings of a plant throughout its life cycle to illustrate timing in the appearance of features such as leaves, buds, and seed pods. These drawings may be accompanied by measurements of the heights of individual plants, which are then reinscribed as differences or as coordinate graphs to depict change over time. A graph of plant growth does not include all the features that are emphasized in the drawings, but it shows something that cannot be seen simply by watching the plants over time, namely, that growth has a characteristic shape. Moreover, when children plot the growth of all their plants on the same coordinate and consider how to draw a line to represent the growth of all the plants together, the shape of the curve can serve as a form of generalization, representing the growth of an entire collection of plants (see Figure 9.2, Panel b). In addition to graphs, other representational forms include maps, drawings (often with enhancing features, e.g., magnification of detail, or "zoom-ins," to show things that cannot be seen because they are hidden by other objects), diagrams, data tables, mathematical functions—an almost boundless set of inventions and conventions.

The representations that we call *syntactic* are particularly difficult for children to comprehend. We call them *syntactic* because they do not preserve any resemblance to the entity being represented; instead, they map only the structure from one context to the other. For example, third graders constructed a microcosm of variation in stream substrate in a wading pool in their classroom. They observed crayfish movement and recorded crayfish location during particular periods of observation. They used spinners partitioned to represent different kinds of stream substrate to investigate whether crayfish prefer to hide in specific kinds of substrates or whether their presence in one area or another is due merely to chance. Thinking of a spinning device as having anything to do with substrate choice entailed a considerable mental leap, however, because spinners resemble neither a crayfish nor the crayfish's behavior in any evident way. Although youngsters sometimes struggle to master representational systems that do not resemble their referents, grasping this form of representation is an important step for them because most scientific models and representations do not preserve resemblance.

Although representational forms vary in their complexity, we do not mean to convey that students leave behind the easier ones, such as drawings, once they encounter those, such as syntactic representations, that are more challenging. Instead, scientists at all levels of expertise use all kinds of representations, often juxtaposing representational systems, each of which

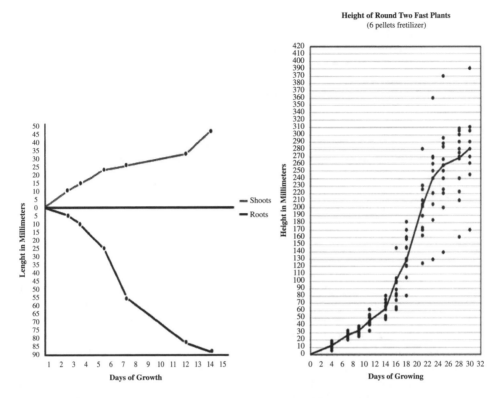

Figure 9.2. Different uses of the same inscriptional form. From *Symbolizing and Communicating in Mathematics Classrooms: Perspectives on Discourse, Tools, and Instructional Design* (p. 351), by P. Cobb, E. Yackel, and K. McClain, 2000, Hillside, NJ: Lawrence Erlbaum. Copyright 2000 by Taylor & Francis Group. Reprinted with permission.

amplifies and reduces different aspects of the natural system, a quality that Latour (1999) termed *circulating reference*. What interests us is how these representational forms come to be regarded as talking to one another as students increasingly make sense of them and, concurrently, of the situations that they represent. For example, a class of second graders reasoned flexibly about multiple representations of plant growth: drawings, pressed plant silhouettes, graphs of various kinds, and cylinders constructed to capture changes in the plants' canopies over time. Each representation highlighted different aspects of the plants' growth, and the students' fluency with the *collection* of representations, in particular, their ability to predict how changes in one representation reflected in changes in another, lent a layered and nuanced quality to their understanding of growth. Their initial understandings were predominantly growth as scaling—similarity—but the ensemble of representational forms supported conceptions of growth that featured changing rates, accompanied by morphological changes, depicted by an *S* curve on the graph (Lehrer, Schauble, Carpenter, & Penner, 2000).

In sum, regardless of the form of analogy, models are distinguished from other systems of representation by their epistemic status as analogs symbolizing selected components and relations of a natural system. Models, then, are particular forms of argument, whereby claims are framed by models and competing claims are framed by alternative models (Lehrer & Schauble, 2010). For physical microcosms, contest about what is being exemplified ranges from the literal—parts of the physical systems that merit inclusion—to the adequacy and status of representational and syntactic descriptions of the microcosm's operation. For representational and syntactic analogs, children are also positioned to consider which aspects of natural systems are worth representing, but they must further consider how these systems of representation describe relations in ways that support claims about a natural system, ranging from claims of existence (e.g., "This is the species I see") to mechanisms.

Materiality

Beyond its structure, a second aspect of modeling is its materiality; that is, modeling entails a struggle with the physical world to arrange the conditions for seeing. Rarely do school students get much chance to participate in the critical phase of developing materials, comparisons, observational schemes, experiments, and/or instruments. For pragmatic reasons, educators tend to avoid these difficulties by specifying the question to be pursued and then providing step-by-step instructions for carrying out the "investigation." Even in most university courses, limitations of time, materials, and laboratory space, coupled with a concern that students might fail to "discover" the intended relationship or finding, restrict students to recipelike laboratories with fixed questions and known "right" answers. Although such cookbook investigations certainly stem from understandable motivations, the scripting fundamentally distorts the inquiry process. Constructing situations, machines, and materials to investigate the world is a defining element of scientific practice. Pickering (1995), a contemporary philosopher of science, referred to these activities as achieving a "mechanic grip" on the world, a phrase that evokes the struggle that ensues when scientists try to wrestle the natural world into a position in which they can effectively study it.

When we invite students to enter the modeling game, we ask them to participate in generating scientifically fruitful questions; to wrestle with ways of arranging the conditions for seeing; to consider how to measure and the qualities of measures; to develop and deploy an increasingly powerful representational repertoire; and especially, to learn a much broader range of mathematics than children typically encounter. Arithmetic alone does not suffice to support a modeling agenda, so our teachers and children are also learning about measurement, chance, and geometry and space as ways of describing the natural world. All of this is accomplished within a bounded and structured subject matter, so that students' developing knowledge and their developing reasoning bootstrap each other.

Along with the commitment to modeling as a way of generating knowledge comes a commitment to a particular perspective on the science content that is taught. Leading with modeling is not feasible in a curricular context in which students are required to skip superficially over a broad number of unrelated topics, so an important implication is the need for sustained study within a bounded domain of knowledge. For many years, educators have been arguing for more focus and less coverage in science education, but the field has been unable to make principled choices about what we can afford to do without. Moreover, in part because of the proliferation of topics in the typical science curriculum, scholars have not delivered a strong base of research about the development of student knowledge in specific areas of science that could inform choices about most effective sequencing; instead, scope and sequence typically are guided not by research about student learning but by simple decomposition of disciplinary knowledge (as if learning were simply the gradual acquisition of parts of what experts know).

Improving this situation is a long-term agenda for the field. We regard improving science instruction as requiring repeated iterations of the following cycle:

- obtaining a consensus on the identification of central conceptual themes in science that are theoretically important, are broad in scope, and provide ready entry points appropriate for children of varying expertise yet are sufficient challenge for those who are more knowledgeable;
- assembling existing research and experience to specify initial conjectures about how the long-term development of student knowledge develops within the target domain (these conjectures are articulated so they can be empirically tested);
- designing and implementing instruction that both tests and builds on these conjectures about development; and
- revising both the conjectures and the instruction over time, on the basis of student learning data collected as the instruction is conducted.

If content is to build effectively on children's conceptual resources, it may need to be sequenced in ways radically different from the ones tried in the past. Of the ideas that have been considered very difficult to learn, some are well within reach of young children, if one plans for the time to build toward them in a systematic fashion. Similarly, some ideas that have been regarded as self-evident really are not, given the ways children tend to misunderstand or misuse them. There is no way to know that a proposed sequence is workable until it has been empirically tested, often over a number of replications. Because we work with students in grades K through 6, empirical testing means following students over a number of years, assessing the forms of learning that occur, and using those findings to further retune the instructional sequence and our conjectures about learning.

We are currently pursuing this general strategy to investigate the potential of modeling approaches to the life sciences in the elementary and middle school grades; more specifically, we are seeking to learn about the kinds of knowledge and thinking that can provide a generative foundation to prepare elementary and middle school students to understand the theory of evolution when they encounter it later in high school. Evolution is an integrative theory in biology

(Mayr, 1991), but decades of research suggest that students find it notoriously difficult to understand. Perhaps one of the reasons it is difficult (along with many other difficult ideas in science) is that educators do not begin to address its complexities early enough and fail to unpack them over time in a way that is ambitious but realistic with respect to students' cognitive resources. Instead, once students are enrolled in high school biology, instructors unload a set of highly complex and concentrated ideas into a few pages of a biology text and worry little, if at all, about how students can grasp their entailments. Assessments, too, tend to target students' capability to repeat declarative knowledge, and they fail to tap students' propensity to use knowledge to generate or evaluate explanations, arguments, or implications. What kinds of knowledge, experiences, and habits of mind would need to be established, starting long before high school, if students were to be better prepared to grapple with and understand a counterintuitive theory such as evolution?

We are currently conducting this research in two contrasting contexts, with public school teachers and their students from grades K through 6 in two states. The first, Site A, includes a bilingual elementary school recently opened to serve a growing population of Mexican immigrants in a district near a medium-sized city in the upper Midwest and the middle school where these same students later attend Grades 6 through 8. We consider Site A to be relatively high capacity with respect to its teaching expertise, community support, and teachers' histories of working together to understand student learning. Both of us have worked in that district for the past 15 years, although we no longer live nearby. Site B includes a paired elementary and middle school located on the same block in a different medium-sized city in the middle South. These schools are surrounded by one of the oldest housing projects in the United States. They are in a relatively low-capacity district that is on its state's watch list for repeatedly failing to meet No Child Left Behind benchmarks. In this district there is less financial and political support for public schools, higher proportions of students who are poor members of racial/ethnic minority groups, and a tradition of top-down governance and decision making that discourages teacher initiative in regard to what gets taught and how. Both sites serve students who might be described as at risk, but the sites differ sharply in their policies and the resources that they devote to student learning and teacher improvement. In the next section, we illuminate our approach to student learning.

Identifying Central Conceptual Structures and Conjecturing About Their Development

Because science is created in an epistemic culture (Knorr-Cetina, 1999), we first identify the epistemic forms of the particular scientific discipline, especially how its practitioners generate knowledge. Because we are not practitioners, we rely on first-hand accounts of colleagues in the discipline, social studies of science, and historic accounts. To approach the nature of foundations of evolution, we rely on conversations with biologists (entomologists, ecologists, and botanists), especially those with interests and clear commitments to education;[1] historical accounts of the development of evolutionary theory, especially the work of Darwin, Gould, and Mayr; our reading of contemporary science and learning research; and our 15 years of prior work in modeling approaches to biology. Collectively, we arrived at three interrelated themes that seem to be critical seeds of evolutionary reasoning: (a) variability, (b) change, and (c) ecology.

VARIABILITY. The first theme, variability, follows from the key role played by variability in evolution. Without variability, evolution cannot occur. Because evolution acts on populations, not individuals, the mathematics of distribution is an important conceptual tool for thinking about populations. Moreover, models of evolution distinguish between *directed* and *random* processes that produce distributions. For example, genetic recombination and mutations are random processes that produce distributions of characters within a species, whereas selection represents a directed process.

Children (adults, too!) tend to think of species as being constituted by a kind of essence that makes them what they are, so they are inclined to pay more attention to similarities than to differences (Evans, 2000, 2001; Samarapungavan & Weirs, 1997; Shtulman, 2006). It is not, however, all that difficult to get children to notice and describe differences within and between species. This is a good starting point for thinking about variability. On the other hand, learning to think systematically—and, eventually, mathematically— about difference (i.e., learning to conceive of differences as structured by distribution) is a longer term agenda. In our instruction, we typically start with simple descriptions of difference based on counts and measures (e.g., "How *much* taller is your plant than mine?"). By the fifth and sixth grades, students are in a position to reason about qualities of distributions of organisms, including ideas of typicality and spread of selected attributes (Lehrer & Schauble, 2004). In Table 9.1, we summarize some of the milestones of learning about variability that we conjecture are important transitions in student reasoning (major benchmarks are summarized in the far left column, and greater detail is provided in the second column). The first level (VAR1) is a description of the typical baseline of student thinking that we observe among young or inexperienced students. Each of the remaining levels (VAR2–5) represents what we consider a major shift in students' ways of conceiving variability. The general description of each major level (in the second column of the table) is further detailed by sublevel descriptions (in the third column). In turn, these milestones are expressed as learning performances (in the final column of the table) to exemplify the forms of behavior that we would consider as indicating a particular level of reasoning.

CHANGE. Evolution typically involves change at different levels of scale. To make the space of change more amenable to children, we focus on three levels: (a) organismic, (b) population, and (c) system. Population change serves

---

[1] We thank Robert Bohanan, Kefyn Catley, Dick Holland, John Jungck, and Paul Williams for their generous contributions.

Table 9.1. Benchmarks of Understanding of Variability (VAR)

VAR1	Difference described: Describe qualitative differences in a collection.	VAR1a	Observe/describe/inscribe qualitative differences in a collection.
			• "Some of the leaves in this maple tree are smaller and others are larger."
			• "Even though these are all soldier fly larvae, some are a lot longer than others."
			• "Some of the Fast Plant seeds sprouted on Day 2, some sprouted on Day 3, and some didn't sprout at all."
			• "We saw fruit fly larvae in some of the compost columns but not in others."
VAR2	Difference measured: Develop or appropriate a measure and apply to a collection.	VAR2a	Develop/appropriate a measure of an attribute and order the collection on the measure.
			• "We measured the widths of all 63 plants and arranged them from least to greatest."
			• "We measured dissolved oxygen in each of the jars and figured out which jars had the most, and which the least, [dissolved oxygen]."
			• "Two Fast Plant seeds sprouted on Day 3, eight Fast Plant seeds sprouted on Day 4, and the other 10 seeds that we planted did not sprout."
			• "Four plants had true leaves on Day 8, and 5 plants had true leaves on Day 9, and one that sprouted died before it had true leaves."
			• "Eight of the 10 compost bottles that we set up had fruit fly larvae in them."
			• "Two of the bottles had at least 30 fruit fly adults in them, and six that had fruit flies had fewer than 10 fruit fly adults."

VAR3	Distribution: Structure a collection of measures as a distribution.		
VAR3a	Display measures of an attribute in a way that makes aggregate properties of the collection visible.		• "We graphed the number of hairs that plants had on Day 14."

• "We had 100 Fast Plants that produced true leaves. Ten of these had leaves without hairs, 40 had up to 10 hairs, 25 plants had 11–20 hairs, 10 plants had 21–30 hairs, seven plants had 31–40 hairs, four plants had 41–50 hairs, two plants had 51–60 hairs, and one plant had 61–70 hairs. One plant had true leaves, but died before we counted hairs."

VAR3b	Use statistics that describe qualities of the distribution, such as central tendency or spread.

• "The first fruit fly adults hatched 3 days before the last fruit fly adult, so the range was 4 days. Eighty percent of the adults hatched on the second day of the hatching period."

VAR3c	Relate statistics describing distribution to biological events or processes.

• "In our first generation of plants, the mid-50% of the data was from 25–50 hairs per plant. But when we bred the hairiest plants to other hairy plants, we got a generation in which the mid-50 was from 40–62 hairs per plant. We are pretty sure the plants are getting hairier."

(continued on next page)

Table 9.1. Benchmarks of Understanding of Variability (VAR) *(Continued)*

VAR4	Model distribution: Develop a model that accounts for the distribution observed.	VAR4a	Develop model of process accounting for distribution.	• "Each Fast Plant started its growth at a little bit of a different time. All of them started out at 0 mm, which is why all of the heights are stacked up on the left side of the graph early in the growth cycle. But as the plants began to grow, we began to see a bell-shaped curve, showing that most of the plants had a similar height, although a few were shorter and a few were taller than average. So, when I built my model, I used a spinner to show the chance of starting the growth spurt earlier or later."
		VAR4b	Evaluate model results.	• "When I ran the model with different starting times for growth, the heights that we modeled had the same bell shape as the heights that we found in our data. But there was more spread in our data than the model predicted."
		VAR4c	Propose model revision in light of model evaluation.	• "I changed the model to get more spread in the distribution of plant heights by adding another component—the plants did not all follow the same rate of change, again, just by chance."
VAR5	Model competition: Develop competing models for the same distribution of observed values.	VAR5a	Compare competing models of observed distribution.	• "In my first model, plant heights varied from generation to generation, but all the variability was just by chance. In the second model, I included the effects of differences in light."
		VAR5b	Develop and apply criteria for assessing relative fit and validity of competing models.	• "I think the model is good if it captures the central tendency in the data. I don't care as much about whether it shows the extremes that we sometimes got." • "I think that it is important for the model to produce the extreme values because those matter when we think about change over long periods of time."

as a fulcrum in the sense that change at this level represents accumulated change at an organismic level, and the time course of change at the population level is often determined by systemic change, such as seasonal variation or some disruption, such as drought, fire, or the introduction of a new species. Change is difficult to conceive because, by definition, it does not hold still while it is being studied; therefore, it is necessary to find ways to fix, or hold steady, states of the objects and events under investigation. That is one reason we emphasize drawings, diagrams, data, and mathematization. The youngest students in our research begin by describing change in the form of organisms (e.g., change from a larva to an adult insect) or in features of environments (e.g., seasonal shifts). Drawings are a helpful first start because they focus children's attention on what is there to be seen. Over time, children acquire a broader tool kit of ways for depicting change, including measurement, especially rates, to describe phenomena such as the growth of a plant or changes in speed of a stream flow. Describing change in populations usually means describing changes in distributions, by coordinating spread and center and linking these ideas with an understanding of chance. (Ideas of distribution need to be incorporated with conceptions of chance when one thinks about sampling.) To date, we have only begun to explore the system level, via a few investigations using computational modeling systems such as StarLogo (see http://education.mit.edu/projects/starlogo-tng). Table 9.2 illustrates some of the landmarks of organismic change, again exemplified by learning performances. Because we have been studying students' reasoning about change for a number of years, this benchmark map is more finely differentiated than that for variability. Therefore, for purposes of illustration, here we are only including Levels 4 through 8. These are the levels that describe most of the shifts in thinking about change that we observe in our elementary grade students.

ECOLOGY. *Ecology* describes a system of relationships that governs the relative abundance and distribution of organisms. Accordingly, evolutionary processes of natural selection and mutation are constrained and defined by ecologies, which are often organized at multiple levels and scales. School approaches to evolution often treat ecology as separate from evolution and do not provide students with the means of uncovering the network of relations that describes an ecology.

Our conjectures about landmarks in reasoning about ecologies are displayed in Table 9.3 (once again, we have included only the first five levels, for illustrative purposes). We believe that initial steps toward conceiving of ecologies are modest: Children readily associate organisms with particular locations and can come to see places as providing resources. This is, however, a very limited understanding of interaction. Differentiation of place represents a step toward a more nuanced view. An environment that is initially defined by a student's ability to see or walk around a place eventually becomes differentiated into a number of different micro-environments: The side of a rock that faces the current is now regarded as different from the downstream side because different organisms meet their needs there. The edge of the pond provides resources to cattails and similar plants that are not available elsewhere.

Table 9.2. Benchmarks of Understanding Change (CHG) in Individual (IND) Organisms

CHG IND 4	Representational redescription of change: Develop resemblance-based representations of change of particular attributes that support indirect comparison.	CHG IND 4a	Index change in one or more attributes at two or more points in time, but via verbal/textual description or by representations intended as copies.	• Colored drawings that depict changes in the color of a rotting banana across several weeks of observation. • Use of shading or cross-hatching to depict changes in texture.
		CHG IND 4b	Qualitatively compare one or more copy-type representations of the same continuous attribute made at different points in time.	• Strings cut to different lengths represent changes in the length of roots of a hyacinth bulb that grows in a transparent container. Student notes that the strings are getting "longer and longer."
		CHG IND 4c	Coordinate two or more representations of change described at levels CHG IND 4a or b.	• Child annotates strips that represent changes in the height of his plant with small pictures, copied from his journal, that represent appearance of the first leaf, first bud, and first open flower.
CHG IND 5	Measures and counts: Describe change based on count or difference of one or more measured attributes.	CHG IND 5a	Characterize changes in one or more attributes as changes in counts or measures.	• "My plant had only three true leaves last week, but this week it has seven."
		CHG IND 5b	Characterize a measure (including units) on the basis of the selected attribute.	• Use millimeters to record heights of a plant on different days. • Use a timeline to show emergence of life cycle changes.
		CHG IND 5c	Interpret change as difference between two measurements.	• "My Fast Plant grew 22 mm." • "It took 5 days before I saw the first true leaf."

CHG IND 5d	Compare net change in more than one individual and justify reasoning.	• "Jenna's plant grew 9 mm more than mine did."
CHG IND 5e	Coordinate descriptions of change in counts or measures on two or more organisms or within attributes of the same organism.	• Compare change in height of different species of flowering bulbs. • Compare timing of life cycle events of two or more different insects.
CHG IND 6	Rate: Describe change as rate or changing rate.	
CHG IND 6a	Coordinate time elapsed with counts or measures of change, but without expressing the relationship as a rate.	• "My plant grew 3 mm between Days 5 and 7, and then it grew 7 mm between Days 8 and 11."
CHG IND 6b	Determine the rate of change by dividing the difference between two measurements of one attribute by the difference in time.	• "My plant grew 12 mm in 3 days, so it grew 4 mm per day."
CHG IND 6c	Interpret graph/table of rate of change.	• Student reads graph as showing that her plant grew 6 mm per week during the first week but 9 mm per week during the second week. Student concludes that rates of growth differ at different points in the plant's life cycle.
CHG IND 6d	Compare rates of change across more than one organism and justify reasoning.	• Student appeals to graph to claim that one plant grew faster than another "overall," but goes on to explain that there were periods during growth when the first plant was growing faster.
CHG IND 6e	Coordinate rate description with a qualitative inscription.	• Coordinate rate graph with pressed plant display.

(continued on next page)

Table 9.2. Benchmarks of Understanding Change (CHG) in Individual (IND) Organisms (*Continued*)

CHG IND 7	Derived or composite measure: Invent derived or composite measures and use the measures to describe change.	CHG IND 7a	Develop categories that depend on representational correspondence to measure change over time.	Use colored paint chips to measure changes in a plant's color over time.
		CHG IND 7b	Develop categories in measures that do not rely on representational correspondence and use them to measure change.	• Invent a bushiness index to measure elodea growth. • Invent a toothpick test to measure changes in the density of algae.
		CHG IND 7c	Invent a composite measure that combines other measures and use it to measure change.	• A measure of changes in "jar health" that combines total dissolved oxygen, bushiness of elodea, and number of living animals
		CHG IND 7d	Invent a composite measure that combines and relatively weights other measures with respect to their perceived importance in the change being studied.	• "Dissolved oxygen contributes more to the composite measure of 'jar health' than does the number of living animals, so I will give it twice as much weight in my index for measuring changes in jar health."
CHG IND 8	Multivariate: Coordinate change in one measured variable with change in a measure second measured variable.	CHG IND 8a	Notice/describe differing patterns of change.	• Use a table to conclude that dissolved oxygen in a jar changes cyclically while bushiness of elodea always changes positively—first quickly, and then more slowly.
		CHG IND 8b	Determine ratio of change in first to change in second measure relative to time.	• Use tables of measures of head "height" and body height to explore the hypothesis that there is a direct relationship between changes in head size and body height as people grow from toddler to adolescent.

Table 9.3. Benchmarks of Understanding Ecology (ECO)

ECO 1	Analogy to humans: Initial criteria for life are based on overt resemblance to familiar organisms, especially people. Initial criteria for habitat are based on analogy to home.	ECO 1a	Pose question: Is it alive? Where does it live?	• May judge some nonliving things as alive because they move on their own or otherwise seem to have qualities that children associate with life ("The moon is alive because it follows me").
		ECO 1b	Judge humans and mammals as living.	• May exclude plants (because they do not seem to move), insects, and unfamiliar mammals from the category of "living." • May anthropomorphize animals ("The chipmunks are scared of us because they don't know us; that's why they run away.").
		ECO 1c	Consider places where living organisms are seen as their homes.	• For example, spiders live in webs, birds in nests, squirrels in trees. • May not understand that some animals (e.g., snails) have portable shelters.
ECO 2	Associate organisms to place: On the basis of direct observation, associate organisms to physical spaces. that are described with respect to general location (e.g., ground, air, pond, forest, lawn).	ECO 2a	Pose questions: Who lives here? Where do they live?	• Rely on repeatable or shareable observations that establish links between habitat and organism. • Where in our pond do the crayfish hang out? • What lives in the stream?
		ECO 2b	Make gross differentiations of space where organisms live.	• Make gross differentiations in kinds of places "under/on the ground, in trees, in the water," etc. • "Fruit flies cluster around vegetables and fruits." • "Isopods are found near rotting wood."

(continued on next page)

Table 9.3. Benchmarks of Understanding Ecology (ECO) (Continued)

	ECO 2c	Describe features and/or behaviors of biotic and abiotic components of places.	• Drawings or physical models of organisms that differentiate characters: for example, a drawing that differentiates head, thorax, and abdomen of insects. • Counts of attributes: Number of stripes on an isopod, number of segments in a larval stage, number of instars for an insect. • Catalog organism's behavioral repertoire: "Isopods can walk, run, and curl up." • Describe features of abiotic components: Compare texture, moisture, color of two samples of soil.
	ECO 2d	Notice relative frequencies of organisms in one or more places.	• "There are lots of ants on the playground but almost none closer to the school." • "All the tadpoles in the pond were clustered near that one rock."
	ECO 2e	Expand criteria for life to include ability to move on its own, eating, and/or evidence of growth. (This extends the category of "living" to plants, reptiles, familiar insects, etc.)	• "The mold in our compost columns seems to be growing—I think it's alive!" • "Even though the trees have no leaves in the winter, we will see buds in the spring. I don't think they actually die in the winter; I think they are resting."
ECO 3	Organism's needs: Relate organism to habitat via organism's needs and ways of satisfying those needs. The relationship is perceived to be unidirectional: The habitat satisfies needs.	ECO 3a	Pose questions about needs of the organism.	• What does the organism need to live? • How does the organism go about satisfying its needs?
		ECO 3b	Differentiate a space as affording opportunities for providing resources to meet the needs of one or more organisms.	• Differentiate components of a physical space, such as shoreline versus shallow versus deep water of a pond, and describe the availability of light in each place.

ECO 3c	Describe the advantage of macroscopic attributes that allow the organism to use the resources in a habitat. For example, these attributes might include an observable behavior or a morphological structure.	• "The exoskeleton of the beetle protects it from harm." • "When the isopod curls up, it is less visible to predators." • "Moving helps the organism find food or escape." • "In water some organisms can walk and swim. Some of them are surface-breathers and others can breathe in deeper parts of the pond."
ECO 3d	Develop diagnostic macroscopic attributes for identification or comparison.	• "You can learn a lot more about an insect by looking at its mouthparts than by paying attention to its color." • "Fly larvae do not have legs. They have little hairs to sense. But beetle larvae have three pairs of legs."
ECO 3e	Notice that place or time may be associated with the presence or absence of particular organisms. (N.B.: This expands sense of place to include a potential temporal dimension.)	• "There were a lot of soldier fly larvae in the compost in September, but a lot fewer in January." • "Different parts of the compost pile have different organisms living there." • "Some decomposers live in the leaf litter, others under rocks, and some underground." • "We see a lot more insect life at the pond in the afternoon than in the morning."
ECO 4a	Pose questions about how particular qualities of environment affect survival.	• "How much sun does this plant need to flower?" • "Will limiting the food supply change the timing of the cabbage white butterfly's life cycle? Will it affect the number of larvae who make it to the adult stage?" • "What is the water temperature needed to support life in this fish pond?" • "Which parts of a pond's or river's bottom might crayfish prefer?"
ECO 4	Survival of organism: Consider how particular qualities of physical space, climate, and time potentially affect survival of organisms or assemblages of organisms.	

(continued on next page)

Table 9.3. Benchmarks of Understanding Ecology (ECO) (*Continued*)

ECO 4b	Develop hypotheses about mechanisms by which abiotic qualities of the habitat (e.g., light, moisture) affect resources required for survival.	• "This stream flows pretty swiftly, so it may have enough dissolved oxygen to support trout." • "This side of the hill is on the north, and the way it slopes means that there is very little sunlight. That may be why we are finding fewer saplings on this side of the hill than on the top." • "We made a pond with four different types of substrate. The crayfish seem to stay in the substrate with the larger rocks. Texture seems more important to them than color. I think they use the rocks to hide from predators."
ECO 4c	Differentiate a large-scale space by recourse to mathematical description (e.g., polar or rectangular coordinates) and/or change over time.	• "This two-dimensional map of the pond will help us find out if cattails are always missing in areas where the current is strong. We will monitor this area over here at location 5F on the map over the spring, summer, winter, and fall to see if we ever observe cattails growing there."
ECO 4d	Consider how attributes of an organism better suit that organism to use the resources available in one location when contrasted to those of another.	• "A bess beetle has strong, crushing mouth parts, so it can break down the material in a decomposing log, but insects with sucking mouth parts can't eat the wood."

Code	Description	Examples
ECO 4e	Explain what attributes that vary together in a habitat imply for survival of an organism or assemblages of organisms.	• "Our evidence shows areas of the stream that flow quickly are cooler than those that pool. They might also be the areas where water will bring down lots of insects for fish to catch." • "Isopods live in the leaf litter because it is moist, which makes it possible for them to breathe; it is dark, which makes them less visible to predators; and because they eat decomposing material."
ECO 5	Environment–organism interactions: Characterize interactions among organisms and environments.	
ECO 5a	Pose questions.	• "How does the organism interact with the environment and with other organisms?"
ECO 5b	Represent roles and interactions in trophic systems.	• "How do algae and fungi work together in lichen?" • "Since we don't see any aquatic plants in the Little Harpeth River, where is the organic carbon that fuels the system coming from?" • "What do fungi do, and how do they help other organisms survive?"
ECO 5c	Describe, measure, and model important ecosystem components that are not directly visible, such as nutrients and microbes, and climate.	• "Why does dissolved oxygen in our aquaria decrease when the amount of algae increases? Isn't algae a photosynthesizer that produces oxygen?" • "What is the role of bacteria in the Little Harpeth River system?"

The cattails, in turn, host a diverse range of insects, with differences in the resources provided above and below the waterline. This early differentiation of place seems to co-occur with children's increasing fascination with a particular organism. We have repeatedly observed students "adopting" an organism, such as algae, damselfly larvae, or clams, and becoming the class expert on this particular organism. Seeing the place where it lives from that organism's perspective seems to help instigate the differentiation of place that we have described.

Another major shift in ecological thinking occurs as children shift from regarding organisms as actors, and the environment as merely a passive stage or resource basin, toward understanding that relationships between organisms and environment are complex and bidirectional. For example, earthworms are found in soil, but they also affect the qualities of the soil; soldier fly and beetle larvae both live in and affect the nature of compost. The transformations wrought by these insects set the stage for other organisms, a phenomenon known as *succession*.

COORDINATING VARIABILITY, CHANGE, AND ECOLOGY. Children's early essentialist ideas tend to be coupled with a focus on intentionality as an explanatory principle for the current morphology of living things, a kind of thinking that some have called *teleological reasoning* (Gelman, Coley, & Gottfried, 1994). This reasoning may lead students to conclude that change within a species can be achieved by an organism within its lifetime (perhaps deliberately, as the organism adapts to novel environmental conditions) and then passed down to its offspring. This Lamarckian form of theorizing may be students' way of assimilating the instruction to their prior beliefs about species. As Evans (2001) pointed out, "The crux of the problem seems to be that natural selection requires students to accept strongly counterintuitive notions concerning random change and variation at the level of a population" (p. 219). It is this kind of population thinking, with associated ideas about random change and shifting distributions, that we propose to address by means of modeling approaches.

Moreover, evolution is challenging to understand because one must coordinate relations among several central concepts, such as natural selection and mutation, and must orchestrate these relations into larger systems, especially ecologies (e.g., natural selection and mutation operate in ecological systems, not as independent events on single organisms). Perhaps what is most problematic is that students typically encounter these central concepts as declarative knowledge in textbooks, supplemented with occasional examples, instead of as modeling practices, yet scientists rely on specific models of natural selection. The construct of natural selection is in the details of the model, not in the generalities of the concept (see Giere, 1988, concerning the relationship between models and scientific principles). Natural selection becomes a plausible generalization through its instantiation as a model in vastly different circumstances. Instead of beginning with the generalization at high school, then, our approach is to begin by immersing young students in circumstances in which modeling and representation provide explanatory power for addressing questions of interest.

Designing Instruction and Investigating Student Learning

Having explained how we generate initial conjectures about ideas worth teaching and prospective trajectories of development, we turn now to the design of instruction and coordinated investigation of student learning. We work closely with teachers and domain experts to design instruction, orienting teachers toward the progression of learning that is made explicit by our conjectured trajectories about the forms of learning that we hope to sustain. (This collaboration is a long-term effort because teachers' initial orientation toward the subject matter is usually governed by the topical- or module-oriented view characteristic of school science. Additional details about our work with teachers are reported in Lehrer & Schauble, 2000, 2005.)

Instruction begins with student investigations of ecologies and focuses on change and variability within ecological frameworks. Hence, students have the opportunity to think about the implications of change and variability for the functioning of an ecological system. Ecologies, by their nature, are local, so we work with teachers and content experts to design investigations that will be fruitful in particular locales. In one setting, the ecology is a part of the school's yard that has been allowed to grow wild, whereas in another setting students investigate the ecology of a local river or pond. The design of instruction is guided by several generative principles, although not every form of instruction exemplifies all of them.

Learning in Depth

First, students have the opportunity to learn in depth, through repeated investigation of the same ecology. This sustained focus positions students to develop knowledge about how a particular natural system functions, instead of confining themselves to the initial random walks that often accompany investigation of new conceptual terrain. Initial investigations are often not fruitful for either children or practicing scientists, but these failures can be productive (Kapur, 2008) as students (and scientists) develop basic familiarity with potentially important components of the natural system and with tools that can be used to investigate it.

Posing Questions

Students at all ages are encouraged to pose questions that can be addressed by means of investigation. Our goal is to seek revisions and generation of new questions by students over time. These revisions are assisted by teachers, who are continually orienting the discussion toward ideas that are most scientifically fruitful and asking students to articulate and reflect on their own criteria for what counts as an "interesting" question and as convincing evidence. Figure 9.3 displays the questions about a local pond that were posed by members of a third-grade class before their first visit there. As is typical in the first round of students' questions, some are not apt to make contact with important concepts; however, others (e.g., those that focus on animals' strategies for surviving in the

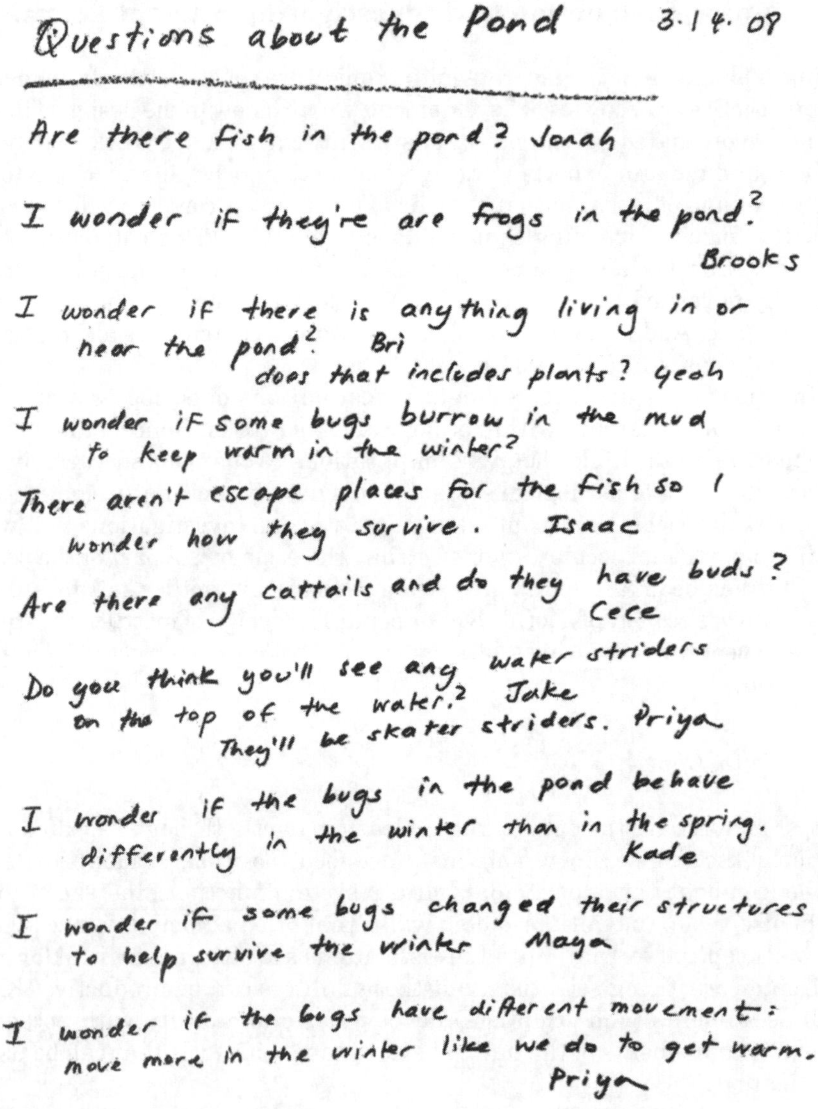

Questions about the Pond   3.14.09

Are there fish in the pond? Jonah

I wonder if they're are frogs in the pond?[2]
                                    Brooks

I wonder if there is anything living in or
near the pond?[2]   Bri
          does that includes plants? yeah

I wonder if some bugs burrow in the mud
    to keep warm in the winter?

There aren't escape places for the fish so I
wonder how they survive.   Isaac

Are there any cattails and do they have buds?
                              Cece

Do you think you'll see any water striders
on the top of the water?[2] Jake
        They'll be skater striders. Priya

I wonder if the bugs in the pond behave
  differently in the winter than in the spring.
                              Kade

I wonder if some bugs changed their structures
  to help survive the winter Maya

I wonder if the bugs have different movement:
move more in the winter like we do to get warm.
                              Priya

Figure 9.3.   Third graders' initial questions about the pond.

pond over the winter) suggest opportunities for investigation that are connected
to important ecological ideas.

Comparative Study

Third, we consider it important that students have the opportunity to learn by
contrasting cases. This method of comparison is prevalent in biological studies but
is generally underemphasized in science education, which is overly preoccupied
with experiment (Petrosino, Lehrer, & Schauble, 2003; Rudolph & Stewart, 1998).

Students compare a pond in one locale with a pond in another, a pond with a stream, soils from the prairie with those from a forest, or the variability of one characteristic of an organism (i.e., height of plants) with that of another characteristic (e.g., number of seeds produced per plant). Comparisons such as these often prompt new questions and, when feasible, new investigations, including experiments.

Getting a Grip

Fourth, students are involved in arranging the conditions of investigation, in "getting a grip," that is, participating in the development of means to answer their inquiries. In investigations of aquatic ecologies, students in the fifth and sixth grades designed physical microcosms—aquatic ecologies in a jar— to investigate questions such as the effects of pH on plant growth. Harnessing the jar systems to inquiry was difficult, but the difficulties provided occasions for further learning (Lehrer, Schauble, & Lucas, 2008). Figure 9.4 displays a physical microcosm constructed by third-grade students who were attempting to resolve a question about why crayfish (a water crustacean) were found in some portions, but not others, of a pond they were investigating. One conjecture

Figure 9.4. Third-grade students study crayfish preferences for different types of pond substrate.

was that the crayfish preferred certain kinds of substrate, in particular, those in which the color or the texture made it more difficult for them to be seen by predators. Children and their teacher brought this question into the classroom for more intense study. They partitioned a wading pool into four equal sections and arranged a different kind of substrate (including no substrate at all) in each of the quadrants. Then they filled the pool with water and added crayfish. On eight occasions, each child observed the number of crayfish in each of the four sections. They pooled these observations by placing small stickers (representing each observation) onto a partitioned, circular piece of paper. As the observations accumulated, the preferences of the crayfish became clear. Several competing explanations were suggested. One was that the crayfish preferred substrate that was similar to their own color, that would camouflage and thus protect them from predation. Another was that the rocks formed shelters that allowed the crayfish to effectively shield themselves from observation by predators but that any rock color would do. The critical test was proposed by a first grader: Place halves of broken green flowerpots in the area of the pool that the crayfish least preferred. If crayfish prefer shelter and not color, then that is the region they should occupy. That region was subsequently overrun by the crayfish.

Inventing Measures and Representations

We position students to invent measures and inscriptions and to coordinate these measures and representations as means for answering questions. These aspects of scientific practice are often underemphasized in school science.

When they invent measures, scientists often reconsider qualities of natural systems. During a comparison of the life forms found in different plots in the "wild" portion of their schoolyard, third graders conjectured that some of the differences observed were due to moisture. The classroom teacher chose this moment to ask students how the moisture of different plots could be compared. One student proposed a measure that came to be known as the "paper towel measure." *Moist,* she asserted, means the amount of water left on the hands after washing, if one uses the school's permitted allotment of three presses on the paper towel dispenser to dry one's hands. (We can attest that each press results in a very small amount of paper towel.) The class then developed other indicators of *wet* and *dry*.

Measures, in their turn, often result in refinement of questions. During an investigation of aquatic ecology, a group's underspecified question about the effects of fish on the aquatic system ("What is the effect of the fish?") was transformed into a question that was amenable to empirical investigation once children had been introduced to ways of measuring water chemistries. In this case, the question evolved into "What is the effect of the fish on levels of dissolved oxygen?" (Lehrer et al., 2008).

Inventing representations involves students in thinking about the functions and uses of inscription and in closer examination of the natural systems they are seeking to depict. It is important that children come to understand that inscribing does not mean copying but always involves reduction (selection) and amplification (Latour, 1999). For example, Figure 9.5 shows how a first grader's

Figure 9.5.   A first grader's drawing depicts parts of a plant.

drawing of a plant in the school prairie displays what is otherwise hidden from view. The top panel is a photo of the plant, and the bottom panel depicts her inscription. In her drawing, the root system is amplified. She has also tried to create a close-up of the plant's leaf. At the same time, the drawing shows reduction; not all the plants' leaves are shown in the drawing, which also omits the appearance of the soil surface.

Amplification and reduction guide what others see. During a study of compost in a school's backyard, fifth-grade students investigated whether the types of organisms living in the compost were changing over time. This is a difficult question to answer, however, because it involves identifying the larval forms of insects, and many larvae look similar. At first, the general consensus was that the larval forms were "worms" and all were the same kind of animal. One of these forms is displayed in the photo in Figure 9.6. Closer inspection by

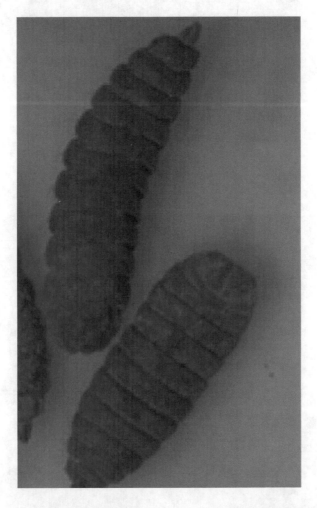

Figure 9.6.   Are all these animals "worms"? Are they all the same species?

(continued on next page)

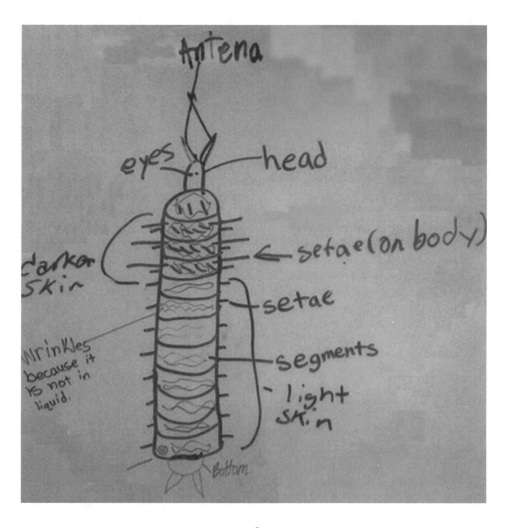

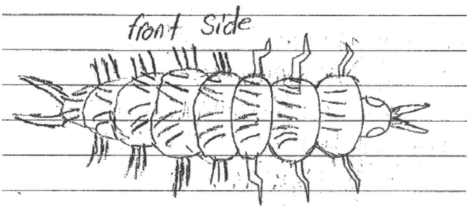

Figure 9.6.   *(continued).*

a fifth-grade student suggested that, in fact, not all "worms" were alike. His drawings made visible features that had escaped the notice of his classmates and teachers but not that of a visiting ecologist. The drawings exposed the diagnostic characters of the organisms that made differentiation possible. The teacher asked this student what other kinds of organisms might have segments. This form of noticing is important for making inferences about relatedness of different organisms; the student's journal entry is displayed in Figure 9.7.

Inscriptions also support projection of concepts. For example, the left panel of Figure 9.2 illustrates a comparison of root and shoot growth that was pursued in a third-grade class. This mathematical form was first developed to describe change in shoot growth (plant height) of individual plants and was later redeployed or projected into investigation of the growth of the roots, also for individual plants. The right panel of Figure 9.2 illustrates another projection of this mathematical form, but this time to a collection of plants. This use involved an adjustment of the form to consider methods for finding typical heights amid variability. Students considered different ways of drawing a line to summarize "how all our plants grew together." A debate that was provoked involved the idea of a summary line and whether a plant height not actually achieved by any individual plant could be used to represent the collective on a particular day of measure. This question is rather sophisticated, although it is unlikely to arise

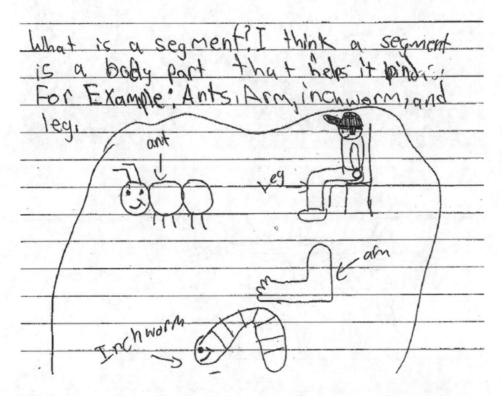

Figure 9.7. A fifth grader's reflections about the animals that have segmented body parts.

if students are simply taught to compute measures of center. How can an event that never occurred be considered typical?

Inscriptions are often fruitfully commingled, as suggested by our previous discussion of Latour's (1999) ideas about circulating reference. For example, a map can be notated with color shading and labels to depict areas where real estate has values within a similar range. Combining inscriptions in this way is characteristic of disciplinary practices, and we seek to nurture its embryonic forms. For example, Figure 9.8 partially displays a representation of a core sample from soil taken for a first-grade comparative study of a local prairie, wetland, and forest. (The core sampler was operated by high school buddies who were taking a course in ecology.) This sample from the prairie has been glued as a remnant onto a paper strip, and children have written about what they noticed. The complete representation is 5 feet long and communicates a rather impressive record of the soil core, which was obtained by drilling 5 feet into the prairie. (Note that the length of the core, once removed from the ground, was no longer evident to the children who were watching its removal; however, its length reappeared dramatically in the remnant representation.) The remnant representations from each of the three locations were juxtaposed on the wall of the classroom to provoke conversation about differences in the soils and the consequences for organisms living in the prairie, forest, and wetland. The children carefully studied the root systems of plants that were dug from these locations. They further pursued relationships between soil type and root structures by comparing plants with different root structures (carrots vs. radishes) that were grown in root chambers with different kinds of soil (sand vs. clay). For the first graders involved, the representation in Figure 9.8 serves as both an important reminder of what they did that day in the field with their high school buddies and a record of the qualities of the soil (its color, texture, even changes in its temperature) that were enhanced in the representation but less visible outdoors in the field.

Figure 9.8.   The first foot of soil from the prairie.

Collective Participation

A sixth principle of the instruction is that students participate collectively, in a manner that makes the social side of scientific practice visible. The educational design should plan for situations that provide value added from the collective—forms of data sharing that allow better resolution of a question and/or spur new forms of investigation—and dialogue that encourages student dispositions to sustain investigation.

Although forms of collective participation typically vary across classes and, within a classroom, from year to year, we have been particularly interested in a form, called a *research meeting,* developed by a fifth- and sixth-grade teacher, Deb Lucas. Research meetings are intended to capture both the structure and function of an activity common in many science laboratories. Students are accountable for describing their question, explaining what they have learned so far (including evidence to back claims), sharing any difficulties encountered, and appealing for help from the larger student group. Listeners are also accountable; they must make suggestions and reflect about what they have learned from the presentation. They are also expected to raise questions if there are parts of the presentation that they do not understand. At the start, simply asking listeners to restate the assertions or evidence offered by presenters is one way of initiating students into the expectation that they need to both listen to and communicate with other students, not just the teacher.

The disposition to conduct inquiry is fostered by engaging students in the esthetics of inquiry. For example, students collectively consider qualities of "interesting questions" and "convincing evidence." Figure 9.9 displays the product of classroom conversation about the qualities of good research questions that occurred in one sixth-grade room. This photo shows the state of the poster at the end of a school year and, as the differences in writing suggest, by this point it had been revised multiple times as students identified new criteria that they wanted to add. Often, students' initial concerns are with questions that can be pursued with the materials at hand (are doable) and that are not easily answered with a simple "yes" or "no." Dispositions to inquire are evident in criteria such as "Good questions are questions you are eager to answer" and questions that you make "your own." As the investigation continued, students began to understand how collective understandings can contribute to individual investigation, as expressed by the reference in Figure 9.9 to questions on which other students can "piggyback." As the school year proceeded, students increasingly evaluated individual investigations for their potential to contribute to the understanding of the entire group.

Similar classroom conversations are directed toward the aesthetics of evidence. Students' initial criteria emphasized that evidence was believable if it came from trustworthy sources or direct experience ("I know it's true because I experienced—saw, heard, smelled, tasted, touched—it and recorded my observations"). These are, indeed, sensible grounds and ones that we anticipated. Less expected was the emergence later in the year of criteria that tied evidence to forms of data representation and culminated in the statement that evidence deserves to be valued to the extent that it is germane to the research question being investigated, not simply a tour of whatever the investigator noticed.

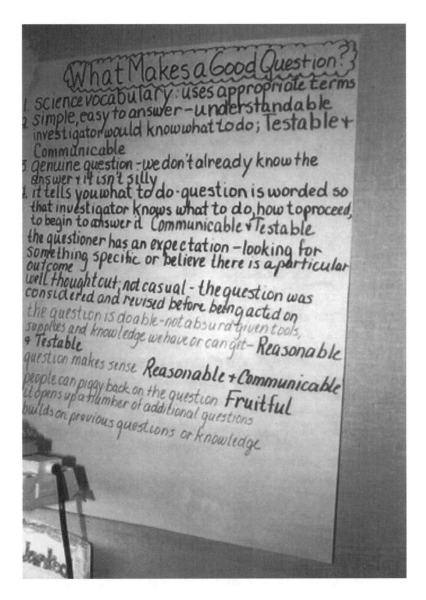

Figure 9.9. Sixth graders' criteria for qualities of a good research question.

Conclusions and Future Directions

The teachers and we plan together for sequences of investigations of this kind, beginning with those that require simple tools and little content knowledge. As occurs with practicing scientists, outcomes of initial investigations provoke new questions and, over time, new investigations that are increasingly challenging, both biologically and mathematically. Our goal is that, across years of this work, students develop a repertoire of inscriptions (graphs, tables, diagrams) and models (difference, rates, and logistic curves to describe the growth of organisms or populations; distributional change; chance models of choice) that were for-mulated to address current investigations but will continue to have extended utility beyond them. In addition, we expect students to build coherent and structured knowledge about specific parts of the biological world that were identified by researchers and teachers for their potential to make concepts and principles of broad scope visible and accessible to students. By the time they reach high school and encounter the formal study of evolution, these students will have received repeated opportunities to investigate change and variability in local ecologies; to struggle with challenges of method and measure; and to structure, interrogate, and draw conclusions from data. Moreover, students will have repeatedly considered and revised their criteria for what serves as an interesting biological question and for the qualities of evidence that are convincing in defense of an explanation. We suspect that disciplinary dispositions are forged only over extended periods and perhaps only when people are continually in contexts where those forms of thinking and reasoning are needed and valued.

We consider these questions about disciplinary dispositions to be intrinsically developmental, although their study requires divergence in some ways from the kinds of study that are more typical in the field. By now, readers have no doubt noticed that the questions we raise in this chapter closely parallel those that David Klahr has also been pursuing for at least as long as we have known him: Is scientific thinking similar to or different from everyday thinking? Can children be said to reason scientifically, or is this a form of thinking exclusive to adults, or even professional scientists? Do children base their reasoning on evidence, or do they just insist on repeating their prior beliefs? Can they grasp important ideas about how to design investigations? How and why do they invent representations for solving problems and communicating with others? What ideas do they hold about variability, error, and uncertainty? As we catalog our mutual interests, the degree of overlap seems astonishing. It has been personally informative for us—and, we think, a sign of health within the field—that we continue to identify complementary ways of tackling similar problems.

References

Evans, E. M. (2000). The emergence of beliefs about the origins of species in school-age children. *Merrill–Palmer Quarterly, 46,* 19–52.

Evans, E. M. (2001). Cognitive and contextual factors in the emergence of diverse belief system: Creation versus evolution. *Cognitive Psychology, 42,* 217–266. doi:10.1006/cogp.2001.0749

Gelman, S. A., Coley, J. D., & Gottfried, G. M. (1994). Essentialist beliefs in children: The acquisition of concepts and theories. In L. A. Hirschfield & S. A. Gelman (Eds.), *Mapping the mind: Domain specificity in cognition and culture* (pp. 341–366). New York, NY: New York University Press. doi:10.1017/CBO9780511752902.014

Gentner, D., & Toupin, C. (1986). Systematicity and surface similarity in the development of anal-ogy. *Cognitive Science, 10,* 277–300. doi:10.1207/s15516709cog1003_2

Giere, R. N. (1988). *Explaining science: A cognitive approach.* Chicago, IL: University of Chicago Press.

Goodman, N. (1976). *Languages of art.* Indianapolis, IN: Hackett.

Hesse, M. B. (1962). *Forces and fields: The concept of action at a distance in the history of physics.* Mineola, NY: Dover.

Hestenes, D. (1992). Modeling games in the Newtonian world. *American Journal of Physics, 60,* 732–748. doi:10.1119/1.17080

Kapur, M. (2008). Productive failure. *Cognition and Instruction, 26,* 379–424. doi:10.1080/07370000 802212669

Knorr-Cetina, K. D. (1999). *Epistemic cultures: How the sciences make knowledge.* Cambridge, MA: Harvard University Press.

Latour, B. (1990). Drawing things together. In M. Lynch & S. Woolgar (Eds.), *Representation in scientific practice* (pp. 19–68). Cambridge, MA: MIT Press.

Latour, B. (1999). *Pandora's hope: Essays on the reality of science studies.* Cambridge, MA: Harvard University Press.

Lehrer, R. (2009). Designing to develop disciplinary dispositions: Modeling natural systems. *American Psychologist, 64,* 759–771.

Lehrer, R., & Schauble, L. (2000). Modeling in mathematics and science. In R. Glaser (Ed.), *Advances in instructional psychology* (Vol. 5, pp. 101–159). Mahwah, NJ: Erlbaum.

Lehrer, R., & Schauble, L. (2004). Modeling natural variation through distribution. *American Educational Research Journal, 4,* 635–679. doi:10.3102/00028312041003635

Lehrer, R., & Schauble, L. (2005). Developing modeling and argument in elementary grades. In T. A. Romberg, T. P. Carpenter, & F. Dremock (Eds.), *Understanding mathematics and science matters* (pp. 29–54). Mahwah, NJ: Erlbaum.

Lehrer, R., & Schauble, L. (2006). Scientific thinking and science literacy. In W. Damon, R. Lerner, K. Ann Renninger, & I. E. Sigel (Eds.), *Handbook of child psychology (6th ed.): Vol. 4. Child psychology in practice* (pp. 153–196). Hoboken, NJ: Wiley.

Lehrer, R., & Schauble, L. (2010). What kind of explanation is a model? In M. K. Stein (Ed.), *Instructional explanations in the disciplines* (pp. 9–22). New York, NY: Springer. doi:10.1007/978-1-4419-0594-9_2

Lehrer, R., Schauble, L., Carpenter, S., & Penner, D. (2000). Designing classrooms that support inquiry. In J. Minstrell & E. V. Zee (Eds.), *Inquiring into inquiry learning and teaching in science* (pp. 80–99). Washington, DC: American Association for the Advancement of Science.

Lehrer, R., Schauble, L., & Lucas, D. (2008). Supporting development of the epistemology of inquiry. *Cognitive Development, 23,* 512–529. doi:10.1016/j.cogdev.2008.09.001

Mayr, E. (1991). *One long argument: Charles Darwin and the genesis of modern evolutionary thought.* Cambridge, MA: Harvard University Press.

Nersessian, N. J. (2008). Creating scientific concepts. Cambridge, MA: Cambridge University Press.

Nersessian, N. J., Kurz-Milcke, K., Newsletter, W. C., & Davies, J. (2003). Research laboratories as evolving distributed cognitive systems. In R. Alterman & D. Kirsh (Eds.), *Proceedings of the Twenty-fifth Annual Conference of the Cognitive Science Society* (pp. 857–862). Mahwah, NJ: Erlbaum.

Petrosino, A., Lehrer, R., & Schauble, L. (2003). Structuring error and experimental variation as distribution in the fourth grade. *Mathematical Thinking and Learning, 5,* 131–156. doi:10.1207/S15327833MTL0502&3_02

Pickering, A. (1995). *The mangle of practice: Time, agency, and science.* Chicago, IL: University of Chicago Press.

Rudolph, J., & Stewart, J. (1998). On the historical discord and its implications for education. *Journal of Research in Science Teaching, 35,* 1069–1089. doi:10.1002/(SICI)1098-2736(199812) 35:10<1069::AID-TEA2>3.0.CO;2-A

Samarapungavan, A., & Weirs, R. W. (1997). Children's thoughts on the origin of species: A study of explanatory coherence. *Cognitive Science, 21,* 147–177. doi:10.1207/s15516709cog2102_2

Shtulman, A. (2006). Qualitative differences between naïve and scientific theories of evolution. *Cognitive Psychology, 52,* 170–194. doi:10.1016/j.cogpsych.2005.10.001

Triona, L., & Klahr, D. (2007). A new framework for understanding how young children create external representations for puzzles and problems. In E. Teubal, J. Dockrell, & L. Tolchinsky (Eds.), *Notational knowledge: Developmental and historical perspectives* (pp. 159–178). Rotterdam, The Netherlands: Sense.

Windschitl, M., & Thompson, J. (2006). Transcending simple forms of school science investigation: Can pre-service instruction foster teachers' understandings of model-based inquiry? *American Educational Research Journal, 43,* 783–835. doi:10.3102/00028312043004783

10

Engineering in and for Science Education

Christian D. Schunn, Eli M. Silk, Xornam S. Apedoe

In various policy circles involving state governors, the U.S. Congress, or industry leaders in high-tech fields interested in education, there has been considerable excitement recently about increasing exposure to and performance in STEM: Science, Technology, Engineering, and Mathematics (National Academy of Engineering, 2007). A very serious problem underlies this excitement. Most large companies depend primarily on new product lines to generate their profits, and the United States has tied its self-identity to high-tech innovation. At the same time, many countries in Europe and Asia have considerably increased their capacities for technological innovation, with some U.S. firms now offshoring the design work as well as manufacturing. Currently, approximately 90% of the world's engineers live in Asia, and a large, continually increasing proportion of the PhD-level engineers in the United States grew up in Asia. In other words, both the economy and self-identity of the United States are at risk.

How did we get here? Salient in everyone's mind is the regular poor showing U.S. children have in international assessments of proficiency in mathematics and science, such as the Third International Mathematics and Science Study (TIMSS; see http://ustimss.msu.edu/info.html) and the Program for International Student Assessment (PISA; see http://nces.ed.gov/surveys/pisa/). TIMSS has been conducted in mathematics and science every 4 years since 1995 with fourth- and eighth-grade students (and occasionally with 12th graders) in approximately 40 to 50 countries depending on the grade level and year. There has been some growth in mathematics performance but no growth in science performance in the United States over that period. Overall, U.S. children demonstrate above-average performance in mathematics at fourth and eighth grades, but they are not in the top five countries (which consist primarily of Asian countries). In science, U.S. students are above average at both grades but are slipping in relative performance from fourth grade (eighth spot) to eighth grade (11th spot). To see how that trend across grades continues, one must look to PISA. Since 2000, PISA has been administered approximately every 3 years to 15-year-olds in approximately 50 countries. (Whereas TIMSS focuses on particular grade levels, PISA focuses on particular ages.) In both mathematics literacy and science literacy, U.S. students scored below average for all countries and below most developed countries. In sum, in terms of mathematics and science performance, U.S. children begin high, but not at the top, and they slowly slide in performance, finishing well below many other developed countries.

Urgent calls for improving U.S. performance in science and mathematics are not a new phenomenon; similar calls to action were made in the 1960s and 1980s (National Research Council, 2007, 2009). However, what is new is the broader focus on STEM as a whole, now including technology (the artificial world) and engineering (the way people design it) in the call to action. It is not just about being smart but about producing adults who are fluent and can innovate with technology. Other important factors are career interest and college degree enrollments. Although undergraduate enrollments overall in the United States have greatly increased in the past 25 years, enrollments in STEM fields have not grown, and in some disciplines have actually decreased in absolute numbers (National Academy of Engineering, 2007). Overall, U.S. students are simply not that interested in science and engineering careers (National Research Council, 2007, 2009). Thus, U.S. policymakers need to improve the K–12 setting such that more children are able and willing to pursue careers in high-tech fields.

Of the STEM disciplines, engineering is the most poorly positioned in K–12 instruction to obtain more curriculum time. Current reform efforts in the United States tend to be focused on mathematics. Performance in mathematics, in addition to English language arts, is commonly the primary measure used in the current high-stakes accountability system to evaluate overall district and school performance. Even though other subjects may be tested, they are not given nearly as much weight—and the gains over the past decade by the United States in mathematics but not science are consistent with this testing focus on mathematics over science. Only one state has a clear focus on engineering in its accountability system, and very few children in the United States are exposed to engineering at the K–12 level (National Research Council, 2009). For science or technology, one could argue that more effective instruction could produce better outcomes; however, the same argument cannot be made for engineering because it is simply absent from the curricula of most schools. Including engineering within technology education also is a very limited solution, because many students do not take any technology education classes and because a very large proportion of technology education teachers are poorly prepared to teach the science and mathematics that engineering methods require (National Research Council, 2009).

It is logical, therefore, that in the short and medium term, engineering can see significant gains across the board at the K–12 level only if engineering instruction is included within science or mathematics instructional time. That integration can happen only if there is synergy between engineering instruction and science or mathematics instruction; in the given policy context, we cannot trade increases in engineering for decreases in mathematics or science.

In this chapter, we explore this potential synergy. What is the relationship between science and engineering, especially with respect to instructional outcomes? We focus on the case of science–engineering synergy because science instruction is likely more open to revision than mathematics instruction and because more data exist on that pairing. In the first half of the chapter, we provide a conceptual analysis of the overlap between science and engineering. In the second half, we consider empirical data on the value of applying science processes in engineering design tasks and the value of engineering design tasks for building scientific knowledge and thinking skills.

Conceptual Analysis

There are many areas of overlap between science and engineering, although there are distinct differences as well. In the following sections, we address these similarities and differences.

Science and Engineering: Competing Epistemologies

At the top level of description as epistemologies, science and engineering are competing rather than similar. Science has an analytic goal: the explanation of natural phenomena. The analysis goal brings with it a reduction or narrowing, with different sciences focusing on different components of larger issues. For example, economists, political scientists, sociologists, social psychologists, and cognitive psychologists interested in educational reform will not only bring different methodologies to the shared broader issue but also will be attacking variables and phenomena that have little overlap across disciplines (with, e.g., economists examining dollars spent on various choices, political scientists examining interconnections between policies and voter interest, social psychologists examining the effects of teacher–student interactions on student self-images, and cognitive psychologists examining the relationship between cognitive demands of instructional activities on student learning). Similarly, biologists, chemists, and earth scientists interested in the broader issue of global warming investigate different variables and phenomena that have little overlap across disciplines.

In contrast, engineering has a synthetic goal: the creation of artifacts that meet particular needs. The synthetic goal involves integrating a broad amount of knowledge from diverse areas to solve a specific problem. For example, a curriculum development team would need to consider economic, political, social, and cognitive components in order to build an effective curriculum. Similarly, a strategy for burying carbon in genetically engineered rapid-growth tree farms would have to consider the chemistry of photosynthesis, the biology of tree growth patterns, and the interactive effects on the surrounding micro- and mesoecosystems, to name just a few factors.

To meet these different overarching goals, professionals in the fields of science and engineering have evolved different research cycles. In both scientific discovery and engineering design, it is understood that the overall process is more complex, iterative, and interactive than simple, linear, or cyclical flow diagrams suggest (Klahr & Dunbar, 1988), but nonetheless there are distinct steps that occur in a typical order. Figure 10.1 shows components that are commonly mentioned in descriptions of science (Panel A) and engineering (Panel B).

At this top-level description of component processes, engineering design seems quite distinct from scientific discovery. The goals and major processes

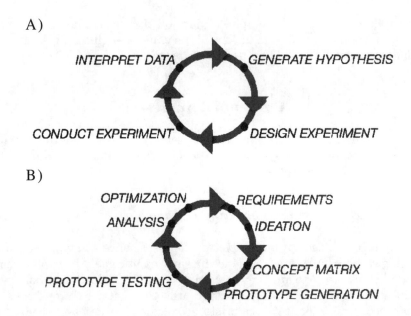

Figure 10.1.   Typical processes included in descriptions.

differ. Furthermore, it is not just a matter of different terms for the same processes. Consider the two points of maximum semantic overlap: (a) ideation/ generate hypothesis and (b) prototype testing/conduct experiment. Other than the fact that both are creativity tasks, generating ideas for possible solutions to an engineering problem and generating hypotheses to explain a natural phenomenon are different in many ways. Engineering solutions are relatively concrete, and hypotheses are relatively abstract. Engineering solutions must manage very diverse constraints, whereas hypotheses can be very narrow, derived from one subdiscipline. Similarly, testing a prototype and conducting a scientific experiment involve different processes. Both can involve precise conditions and measurement tools; however, a scientific experiment aims to generate patterns between variables, whereas prototype testing examines whether a particular solution meets required specifications.[1] In addition, parts of the engineering process are less aligned with the primary science processes, such as requirements documents, concept decision matrices, and optimization. Overall, examination of just the top-level epistemologies suggests that the potential synergy between engineering and science is minimal.

Overlap of the Process, Not of the People

One related red herring is the overlap between engineering design and science within individuals, which has some tricky twists that need to be unpacked.

---

[1]Prototype testing can involve a systematic range of testing conditions to make sure the prototype works under a variety of conditions; however, the goal of this testing is not to find the pattern across the tests but more of a binary pass–fail overall or the determination of a "breaking" point.

Donald Stokes (1997) wrote a very influential book, *Pasteur's Quadrant,* in which he argued that there can be important synergies between basic and applied research within some individuals. Some individuals (e.g., Niels Bohr) have only the understanding goal associated with basic research; they do not care at all about applications (as in engineering). Other individuals (e.g., Thomas Edison) have only the building goal associated with applied research; they do not care at all about implications for understanding the natural world. There are also very influential individuals who had both basic and applied research goals that were interrelated and both highly influential, however. For example, Louis Pasteur is credited with inventing pasteurization and contributing important experimental data to the development of the germ theory of disease (as well as other scientific contributions in biology and chemistry). Stokes argued, rather convincingly, that Pasteur's applied research directly led to important basic research; that is, Pasteur had both engineering and scientific goals, at different points in time, but with synergy between the goals.

How does Pasteur's Quadrant relate to the overlap between engineering and science? Is engineering a means of knowledge creation as well as a way of building objects using knowledge, or is it just the case that engineering can lead to new questions that science answers, and sometimes the same people who raise the question also answer it? Consider an example of some individuals who excel at two different tasks. Do those data, per se, make the tasks themselves overlapping? Suppose some world-class French horn players were also world class checkers players. That would not imply that checkers and French horn playing involve the same skills. In the case of Pasteur, there seems to be substance to the synergy, in that the work on the applied problem led to data that were scientifically important. But does overlap of individuals with synergy of outcomes imply overlap in processes? A person can be a Presbyterian and a business owner. Attending a particular church can provide useful business contacts, but that does not mean that religious worship and business are the same process.

The distinction between science and engineering within individuals has been complicated by actions of the Nobel Prize committee. Consider the 2009 Nobel Prize in physics. Two of the prizewinners were Willard Boyle and George Smith for the invention of an imaging semiconductor circuit: the CCD sensor. The invention is itself an act of engineering design, not an act of science. The invention certainly involved physics and likely influenced later work in physics, but the award was given for the engineering of the invention itself. Assuming that the Nobel Prize committee is not confusing engineering with science, one might consider their choice to be evidence of a deeper synergy between science and engineering than has been previously considered.

Computational Parallels Between Science and Engineering

Another way of exploring overlap of processes is to investigate computational considerations, because cognitive scientists often define process overlap by means of computational overlap, either at the level of the main function being computed or in the algorithms doing the computing (Anderson, 1990; Marr, 1982).

Figure 10.2 illustrates that both scientific discovery and engineering design have a sequence of divergent and convergent search processes. In science, there is a task of finding a hypothesis that might account for the data. Here, a broad computational search, in which many different options are considered, must be undertaken (Cheng, 1990; Langley, Simon, Bradshaw, & Zytkow, 1987). In engineering, there is the task of generating ideas for possible solutions to the design problem (Campbell, Cagan, & Kotovsky, 2003). Again, the search space is potentially quite large. In both cases, the human problem-solver uses heuristics to make the search process more efficient (Klahr, Fay, & Dunbar, 1993). In particular, analogy has been named as a particular process that can guide the finding of new ideas in scientific discovery (Dunbar, 1997) and engineering design (Christensen & Schunn, 2007; Tseng, Moss, Cagan, & Kotovsky, 2008). Interestingly, studies of engineering and science idea generation processes describe a common computational problem, namely, one of getting stuck on an early idea. In the case of science, this is called a *confirmation bias* (Tweney, Doherty, & Mynatt, 1982); in the case of engineering, it is called *design fixation* (Jansson & Smith, 1991).

There are also important parallels within the convergent process of both fields. In science, the problem solver must choose among available hypotheses, selecting the best one. In engineering, the problem solver must choose among available design ideas, selecting the best one. This selection process can be done empirically, through experimentation/prototype testing (Schauble, Klopfer, & Raghavan, 1991), or it can be done conceptually, in science through error minimization by applying different theories (in formulas or models) to data, and in engineering through analysis and optimization of computational models of the to-be-designed object. Overall, at the computational level there appears to be much overlap between scientific discovery and engineering design, but consideration at other levels may help to refine the boundaries and further hone the potential synergies between the two.

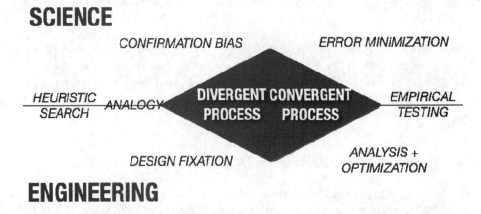

Figure 10.2.   Parallels between the computational processes and process problems in scientific discovery and engineering design.

Subgoals and the Yin–Yang of Science and Engineering

Another way of expressing the overlap between science and engineering is in terms of reversible nested subgoal–supergoal relationships. From the perspective of engineering design, scientific discovery can be thought of as a subgoal. As part of the process of designing a solution, the designer may have to analyze data, explain observed prototype failures, and develop models—analysis, explanation, and modeling are very recognizable components of science. From the perspective of scientific discovery, however, engineering design can also be thought of as a subgoal of science. While trying to make a discovery, the scientist might *design* a hypothesis, *design* an experiment, and/or *design* an instrument (Apedoe & Ford, 2010). Each of these scientific design tasks can be quite complex, and some scientists specialize in those elements. For example, consider the distinction between *theorists* and *experimentalists* in many fields (Klahr & Dunbar, 1988) and the complex undertaking of modern instrument design in the natural sciences. The mutual subgoal–supergoal relationship suggests that scientific discovery and engineering design, even when kept largely distinct, may have the potential to motivate each other and support one another.

Conceptual Analysis Summary

Scientific discovery and engineering design have fundamentally different goals with conceptually distinct epistemologies, yet there are underlying computational similarities with interesting overlaps in search heuristics. Furthermore, there are multiple subgoal–supergoal relationships between design and science, and this relationship may be a major source of synergy within individuals who excel at both engineering design/applied science and basic science. Some empirical work must be done to examine the obtained synergies between science and design, however. Pioneering work by Klahr and Carver (1988) suggests that transfer can be observed in complex processes that have logical overlap, but failures to find transfer are a commonly cited challenge to research on learning (Bransford & Schwartz, 2001).

Empirical Analyses of the Science–Engineering Overlap

In this section, we summarize three studies that we conducted to examine the empirical overlap between science and engineering in terms of strategies underlying successful problem solving and in terms of learning gains in science knowledge and process skill achieved by completing engineering tasks.

Study 1: Strategies Underlying Successful Engineering Design in Students

Tschirgi's (1980) seminal work suggests that children do not consistently use basic science strategies, such as "vary one thing at a time" (VOTAT) when engaged in design tasks in which the outcomes of a test have clear desirable or undesirable outcomes (e.g., whether a good cake is produced or not). Follow-up work by Schauble et al. (1991) systematically manipulated within the same physical space whether students were given engineering goals (make a fast boat) or scientific goals (find out what makes boats go fast or slow). They found that students given the engineering goal explored less of the space and made more inferences about causality than students given the science goal. However, these projects used settings that were science centric in that there were pairs of conditions for each "test." Engineering design tests tend not to be done that way, but instead as isolated endeavors, which may further reduce the systematicity of search under engineering goals or reframe the search in new ways. Furthermore, Tschirgi did not examine the relationships among student strategies in design, design success, and student learning.

To examine these issues, Apedoe and Schunn (2009) conducted a study using the "earthquake task" (see Figure 10.3). Students were given 54 wood blocks and asked to design the tallest structure that will withstand 20 seconds of a simulated earthquake on a table that shakes in two dimensions (left to right and back and forth). They worked with 59 teams of three to five high school students each. These students had previously worked together on a multiweek engineering design task in their science classrooms, and thus they were familiar with each other in another design context. The teams were given 20 minutes to create the tallest stable structure. They could test as many designs as they wanted, and there was a prize offered for the team with the tallest stable structure. The students were videotaped, and the authors coded

Figure 10.3.   Earthquake test example student design.

the strategies that they used from the video. They also administered a posttest that individually asked students to describe design principles regarding what made for more successful designs.

What strategies are most useful in this task? Students used a range of different strategies. We focus here on two particular strategies: (a) VOTAT and (b) adaptive growth. The VOTAT strategy is the one classically associated with scientific reasoning. In theory, by varying only one feature from one trial to the next, students are better positioned to learn what factors matter because they avoid confounds in the experimental data, although it is worth noting that a definition of what constitutes a primitive feature, like in real science, is complex. *Adaptive growth* is a common design-oriented strategy found in this task: When the given design fails, make the next one the same height or smaller; when the given design succeeds, make the next one taller. The adaptive growth strategy may seem very specific to this particular task, but parallel design strategies have been found in experimental design (Schunn & Anderson, 1999; Schunn & Klahr, 2000).

In Table 10.1, we present the relative use of these two strategies by the high-performing teams (who achieved a mean success of 26 stable levels) and the low-performing teams (who achieved a mean success of only four stable levels). Overall, VOTAT was used much less often than adaptive growth by both high- and low-performing teams; however, the height of the highest successful structures did correlate with use of the adaptive growth strategy ($r = .33$), whereas high- and low-performing groups did not differ in relative use of VOTAT (Apedoe & Schunn, 2009). The low-performing teams also used a range of other strategies, but no one strategy from this list was associated with poor performance. Thus, Apedoe and Schunn's (2009) study provided a simple confirmation that design seems to evoke different strategies from designers and that these design-oriented strategies are more closely associated with design success than classic scientific reasoning strategies.

One way of characterizing Table 10.1 is that it helps one examine the fit of science and design strategies for success in design. This characterization then raises the corresponding science goal question: To what extent do these strategies support learning about factors that matter? In Table 10.2, we present such an analysis (Apedoe & Schunn, 2009). In this task, students discovered a number of design principles that influence the stability of tall structures. Across the top of the table are four design principles that were significantly related to relative strategy use. The cells of the table are the point-biserial correlations between strategy use by the team and whether the students reported each of

Table 10.1   Relative Use of the Vary-One-Thing-at-a-Time (VOTAT) and Adaptive Growth Strategies by High- and Low-Performing Teams in Apedoe and Schunn's (2009) Study

Strategy	High-performing teams (26 levels)	Low-performing teams (four levels)
VOTAT	24% of trials	19% of trials
Adaptive growth	74% of trials	48% of trials

Table 10.2 Point-Biserial Correlations Between Relative Degree of Strategy Use and Endorsement of Design Principles From Apedoe and Schunn's (2009) Study

Strategy	Pyramid/triangle	Compact	Wide base	Narrow top
VOTAT	.55*	.60*	−.05	.09
Adaptive growth	.03	.00	.55*	.38*

Note. VOTAT = vary one thing at a time.
*$p < .05$.

these principles. It is interesting to note that both VOTAT and the adaptive growth strategy were positively associated with what students learned from the design task but that the two strategies resulted in different knowledge. Thought of another way, the design strategies significantly influenced search through the design space, and thus it is not surprising that different kinds of knowledge emerged. Future research is needed to unpack whether this effect stems from emphasizing knowledge (what is clearly deducible) versus performance (what is semantically crucial) per se or whether it comes from taller structures highlighting different design features. It is also interesting to note that the pyramid/triangle principle associated with the VOTAT strategy is perhaps a more holistic perspective on the more componential principles associated with the adaptive growth strategy.

Study 2: Design-Based Science Learning and Science Content Gains

A number of researchers have explored the use of design to produce gains in scientific content. One approach is simply a motivational boost: Introduce some application-of-science tasks, such as engineering design tasks, to increase motivational levels in students, but the method of knowledge acquisition remains fundamentally one of science (Hulleman & Harackiewicz, 2009). Another approach is to use engineering design as the method of knowledge acquisition (Hmelo, Holton, & Kolodner, 2000; Kolodner et al., 2003; Mehalik, Doppelt, & Schunn, 2008; Puntambekar & Kolodner, 2005; Roth, 2001; Sadler, Coyle, & Schwartz, 2000).

Here we describe one study (Mehalik et al., 2008) implemented in a range of public urban schools that used measures very typical of traditional knowledge assessments in classrooms and on high-stakes tests. If engineering is to go to scale inside science classrooms, it must work under those conditions and produce science knowledge gains that will be evident on relevant test scores.

Mehalik et al. (2008) examined pre–post learning on basic science content knowledge (electricity concepts, e.g., voltage, current, and resistance and their changes in various configurations of series and parallel circuits). Two different curricular units were contrasted: (a) the experimental group used a design-based science learning unit called the *alarm systems unit,* and (b) the control group used a hands-on *scripted-inquiry unit* that is widely used in the United States to teach this content.

The scripted-inquiry unit taught the concepts through a series of investigations in which students posed a question, conducted some experiments with simple materials (a circuit board, batteries, wires, resistors, bulbs, and a multimeter) and were guided to find certain key relationships through worksheets. The curriculum also contained formative and summative assessment items to be used throughout. The school district in question had been using this unit already for many years, and the unit was taught over a 4-month period. Although the unit covered a wide range of electricity/electronic topics, we focused on the basic voltage, current, and resistance topics covered during the first 4 to 6 weeks.

The alarm systems unit involved a design project spanning 4 to 6 weeks of instructional time that was used to replace the first 4 to 6 weeks of the scripted-inquiry curriculum. The overarching activity was one long design task: to create a prototype of an alarm system (in groups of three or four students) to meet some need in the students' own lives. At the top level, the unit had three main phases: (a) problem definition, (b) prototyping, and (c) communication (see Figure 10.4), roughly following an authentic engineering design process, which kept students in the primary role of engineers throughout the 6 weeks. The materials space of the alarm systems unit was basically the same as the one in the scripted-inquiry unit, with some minor change in the particular batteries and addition of a few more variations on indicators and detectors to allow for more variations across student teams (see Figure 10.5 for example materials used in a student prototype).

There are three key features of the alarm systems unit with respect to its relationship to science learning. First, the bulk of the science content learning happens during the prototyping phase, which occupies about 50% of the total time. As is commonly the case in project-based learning, students spent a fair amount of time on other tasks beyond simple content learning. Thus, if this kind of approach is to compete favorably with more traditional approaches, it

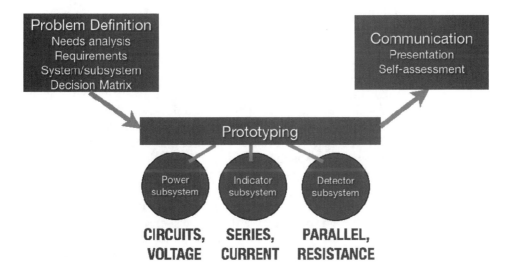

Figure 10.4. The overall storyline of the alarm systems unit.

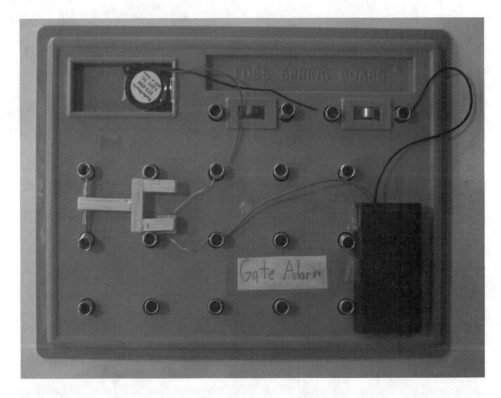

Figure 10.5. Example materials in a student-designed alarm system. This example includes a buzzer in the upper left (indicator subsystem), an on-switch in the upper right, the "gate" switch in the lower left (detector subsystem), and a battery pack in the lower right (power subsystem).

needs to be especially powerful during the prototyping phase. Of course, it is worth noting that inquiry approaches to science instruction also have significant overhead costs in time.

The second key feature with respect to science learning is the decomposition of the larger prototyping task into sequential design of subsystems. Engineers typically think of artifacts as a system with subsystems, and commonly taught approaches to engineering design emphasize a decomposition of the larger design task into subsystem design (Otto & Wood, 2001; Ulrich & Eppinger, 2008). Thus, this decomposition of the larger design task into subsystems was authentic to engineering design, but it also has important advantages with respect to science learning because it organizes student learning to attend to particular science concepts along the way. In the alarm systems unit, the students work on three subsystems: (a) power, (b) indicator, and (c) detector (see Figure 10.4). Each of these three subsystems is necessary to a functioning alarm, regardless of which kind of alarm the students are building (e.g., touch-down alarm, locker alarm, or a pill-reminder alarm). Also, each of these three subsystems involves particular science concepts that must be learned in order to create well-functioning subsystems. For example, the detector subsystem requires that students master the concepts of resistance and parallel circuits. Thus, the subsystems ensure that students must encounter all the critical science concepts and roughly organize the order of this science learning such that teachers can guide the process and the whole class can build a shared understanding.

The third key feature is what happens during the prototyping of each of the subsystems. Here is where the students learn the science. How does the proto-typing process produce this knowledge? Left to their own devices, students can often be relatively unsystematic, succeeding in neither design nor science learning. The alarm systems unit did provide some structure to this learning, asking students to be reflective designers: carefully documenting each design, explaining the goals of the design, making predictions for outcomes, describing the outcomes, and developing a plan for next steps. Indeed, here is where the supergoal–subgoal relationship of engineering and science come into play. As the students became stuck in achieving engineering goals, they would ask questions about how things work in the fashion of science, analyzing patterns in available data. Of course, the students would rarely conduct systematic experiments as they would in the scripted-inquiry class; however, as Schauble et al.'s (1991) study showed, knowledge might nonetheless be obtained from such design-based experimentation strategies.

Mehalik et al.'s (2008) study was implemented in 26 eighth-grade science classrooms in a large urban district, with 10 teachers and almost 600 students in the experimental condition and five teachers and slightly over 450 students in the control condition. The schools involved in each of the conditions were closely matched on student demographics and performance variables (e.g., mathematics and reading scores on high-stakes tests).

Both groups took short, paper-based, multiple-choice pre- and posttests that focused on basic understanding of electricity concepts that were the primary focus of the scripted-inquiry instruction. On these tests, experimental condition students showed over twice the pre–post gains as the control condition students, with a large effect size ($d = 0.89$). This result was especially surprising given that the students in the control condition nominally spent more time on science learning than the students in the experimental condition. One teacher chose to split her own sections and used the embedded assessments found in the scripted-inquiry curriculum as the measure of learning. Even on this measure, which is tightly aligned with the scripted-inquiry curriculum, students in the experimental condition heavily outperformed students in the control condition.

The results of Mehalik et al.'s (2008) first study provide some explanation for how students in the experimental condition were able to make some gains in science knowledge: Design strategies can produce knowledge. There remains, however, the mystery of why students in the experimental condition learned significantly more science with noticeably less time spent on science learning. We believe that student motivation levels were likely very important. Many of the teachers reported that student motivation levels were much higher with the design unit than in their previous years of instruction with the scripted-inquiry unit. From this study alone, we do not know whether design versus science was the key to increasing motivation or whether other differences between the units—for example, salient features with respect to student motivation levels might be tight scripting versus more open-ended tasks, or a sequence of smaller tasks versus one larger task—might have been key. Hulleman and Harackiewicz (2009) suggested that the opportunity to think about practical applications of knowledge per se has large motivational benefits in science classrooms.

Study 3: Design-Based Science Learning and Science Process Gains

The results from Schauble et al.'s (1991) and Mehalik et al.'s (2008) studies, as well as results from other laboratories in which design has been used to teach science content, suggest that science content knowledge can be acquired through design processes. Which content is acquired likely depends on the strategies used by the designer and the part of the conceptual space exposed by those strategies in the given design space. What about science process skills, though? Students are expected to also learn the processes of science, especially the skills related to what kinds of evidence provides ambiguous versus unambiguous support for a given conclusion. Given the different fundamental epistemologies and overall procedures of practice in engineering and science, one might worry about whether students will make any progress in science reasoning skills from design experiences, or perhaps, even worse, show decrements due to mismatched practices. True negative transfer is not usually obtained (Singley & Anderson, 1989), but that may depend on whether the children clearly view the situations of science and engineering as different. If engineering methods are taught in science classrooms *and* engineering methods clash with science methods, then negative transfer might occur.

A few studies of students engaged in design tasks have suggested that their reasoning often does not look very science-like (Roth, 2001; Schauble et al., 1991); however, those studies did not provide much scaffolding to guide good engineering practices; we would not expect students to demonstrate solid reasoning processes when conducting a science task if they have been provided little instruction on good scientific practices (Kuhn, 1989, 1991). Thus, our question becomes: With instruction in good engineering practices, does the experience with an engineering task provide gains or losses in scientific reasoning skills? A study of the Learning By Design curriculum provided some evidence of improvements of scientific reasoning skills (Kolodner, Gray, & Fasse, 2003); however, that study was conducted in upper and middle-income settings, and the measures were not typical pencil-and-paper assessments that drive district decision making. It is important to show how the impact will scale more broadly across settings and on measures that are more typically used.

Silk, Schunn, and Strand-Cary (2009) conducted a follow-up study using the alarm systems unit again, but this time focusing on process gains. They used a pencil-and-paper multiple-choice test based on previously validated measures of scientific reasoning (Lawson, 1987) and from items released from the TIMMS. On the basis of their more detailed analysis of science and engineering practices having supergoal–subgoal relationships, the authors did not expect to find such negative transfer and, in fact, expected to find positive transfer.

Silk, Schunn, and Strand-Cary's (2009) primary method was to simply look at pre–post gains on this measure in students implementing the alarm systems unit; however, to provide some context for any observed gains, they also compared pre–post gains observed in another study using two other science curricula: (a) a new inquiry-based curriculum that was previously shown to outperform other inquiry curricula on gains in reasoning skills, and (b) a textbook-based curriculum. Because one does not expect to see much reasoning gain from a textbook approach, the authors actually collected pretest data at the end of sixth grade and posttest data at the end of eighth grade for the students in the textbook condition, whereas the design and inquiry groups had the pretest in the middle of eighth grade and the posttest at the end of eighth grade.

In Figure 10.6, we present the mean performance in each group. Most important for the question at hand is that one can see pre–post gains in scientific reasoning scores in the design group, instead of no effect or even reduced scores. This figure also presents a few other interesting results. First, the students in the design group were very close to chance performance on the pretest. Seventy-three percent of the students were members of traditionally underserved racial/ethnic minority groups, and 82% were of low socioeconomic status, and, for a variety of reasons, both of these factors are frequently predictive of science test scores. However, these students had also experienced 7½ years of hands-on science in this district. In only a few months of experience with the design unit, they appear to have made more progress on scientific reasoning than in the previous 7 or so years of science instruction.

A second interesting feature of the data in Figure 10.6 is that the gains in the design group are similar to the gains in the inquiry group and larger than the gains observed in the textbook group, even though the textbook group experienced 2 years of instruction. It is worth noting that students in the inquiry group were from a more affluent setting, and this likely explains the higher

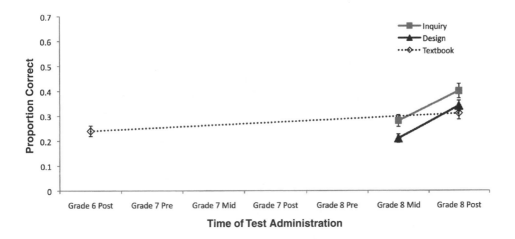

Figure 10.6. Mean scientific reasoning performance pre- and posttest in each of the three groups in Silk, Schunn, and Strand-Cary's (2009) study.

pretest scores, but it also makes the equivalence in gains between this inquiry condition and the design group all the more impressive.

Conclusions and Future Directions

In this chapter, we have presented a detailed analysis of science and engineering to suggest that they have important differences in overall goals and storyline, as well as important similarities in underlying processes. Furthermore, we presented data to show that engineering design activities can produce scientific content knowledge and gains in scientific reasoning skills.

How can these analyses and results be reconciled? On the basis of similarities in underlying processes, and on Klahr and Carver's (1988) seminal work showing that programming experiences led to general debugging skills that could be applied to nonprogramming tasks with similar debugging processes, we expected to find gains in learning that will transfer. Thus, if engineering involves some pattern explanation tasks as subgoals, then students engaged in engineering activities should make progress on those skills and show evidence of such progress on measures of the logic of pattern explaining (i.e., measures of scientific reasoning) and measures of particular pattern explanations (i.e., measures of science content knowledge). Indeed, as shown in Figure 10.7, we and our colleagues have often organized our design-based learning materials around a combined design–science learning cycle (Apedoe, Reynolds, Ellefson, & Schunn, 2008; Ellefson, Brinker, Vernacchio, & Schunn, 2008). As students

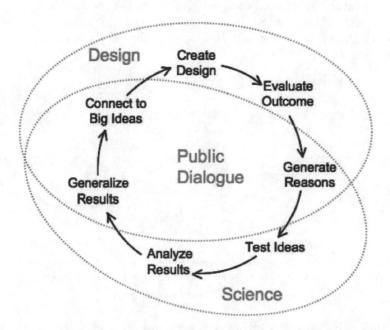

Figure 10.7.   The design–science learning cycle that connects design and science activities.

work on the design of each subsystem, they need to engage in scientific reasoning activities to develop a better understanding of the science that supports that subsystem design. In sum, we make explicit the distinctions between the epistemologies and skills of scientific discovery versus engineering design, but we actively encourage their connections.

The differences in goals and storylines can, however, also produce differences in learning outcomes. We have found that design involves different strategies that can change which scientific content knowledge is acquired. Furthermore, we have seen that many students, especially students who have traditionally showed poor performance in science classrooms, found the design activities more interesting and motivating, and these motivational benefits could themselves produce secondary gains in science content and skills.

Now, returning to the issue of STEM: Can we hope for real gains in science, technology, engineering, and math in the current educational context? From our experiences, we do have some optimism for the possibility of gains in engineering via science classrooms because of the apparent positive results for science from such inclusion. How such synergies will develop for technology and math remain to be seen, but in our recent work we have attempted to make explicit some of those connections (Silk, Higashi, Shoop, & Schunn, 2010; Silk, Schunn, & Shoop, 2009). At the same time, we are working on the development of more design-based learning units in a range of disciplines at the high school level that try to simultaneously make progress in the learning of science, engineering, and technology concepts (Apedoe et al., 2008; Ellefson et al., 2008).

References

Anderson, J. R. (1990). *The adaptive character of thought.* Hillsdale, NJ: Erlbaum.

Apedoe, X. S., & Ford, M. (2010). The empirical attitude, material practice, and design activities. *Science & Education, 19,* 165–186. doi:10.1007/s11191-009-9185-7

Apedoe, X. S., Reynolds, B., Ellefson, M. R., & Schunn, C. D. (2008). Bringing engineering design into high school science classrooms: The heating/cooling unit. *Journal of Science Education and Technology, 17,* 454–465. doi:10.1007/s10956-008-9114-6

Apedoe, X. S., & Schunn, C. D. (2009, April). *Understanding how students solve novel design challenges.* Paper presented at the Annual International Conference of the National Association for Research in Science Teaching, Garden Grove, CA.

Bransford, J. D., & Schwartz, D. L. (2001). Rethinking transfer: A simple proposal with multiple implications. *Review of Research in Education, 24,* 61–100.

Campbell, M., Cagan, J., & Kotovsky, K. (2003). The A-design approach to managing automated design synthesis. *Research in Engineering Design, 14,* 12–14.

Cheng, P. C.-H. (1990). *Modeling scientific discovery.* Milton Keynes, England: Open University Press.

Christensen, B. T., & Schunn, C. D. (2007). The relationship of analogical distance to analogical function and pre-inventive structure: The case of engineering design. *Memory & Cognition, 35,* 29–38. doi:10.3758/BF03195939

Dunbar, K. (1997). How scientists think: On-line creativity and conceptual change in science. In T. B. Ward & S. M. Smith (Eds.), *Creative thought: An investigation of conceptual structures and processes* (pp. 461–493). Washington, DC: American Psychological Association. doi:10.1037/10227-017

Ellefson, M. R., Brinker, R. A., Vernacchio, V. J., & Schunn, C. D. (2008). Design-based learning for biology. *Biochemistry and Molecular Biology Education, 36,* 292–298. doi:10.1002/bmb.20203

Hmelo, C. E., Holton, D. L., & Kolodner, J. L. (2000). Designing to learn about complex systems. *Journal of the Learning Sciences, 9,* 247–298. doi:10.1207/S15327809JLS0903_2

Hulleman, C. S., & Harackiewicz, J. M. (2009, December 4). Promoting interest and performance in high school science classes. *Science, 326,* 1410–1412. doi:10.1126/science.1177067

Jansson, D., & Smith, S. (1991). Design fixation. *Design Studies, 12,* 3–11. doi:10.1016/0142-694X(91)90003-F

Klahr, D., & Carver, S. M. (1988). Cognitive objectives in a LOGO debugging curriculum: Instruction, learning, and transfer. *Cognitive Psychology, 20,* 362–404. doi:10.1016/0010-0285 (88)90004-7

Klahr, D., & Dunbar, K. (1988). Dual space search during scientific reasoning. *Cognitive Science, 12,* 1–48. doi:10.1207/s15516709cog1201_1

Klahr, D., Fay, A. L., & Dunbar, K. (1993). Heuristics for scientific experimentation: A developmental study. *Cognitive Psychology, 25,* 111–146. doi:10.1006/cogp.1993.1003

Kolodner, J. L., Camp, P. J., Crismond, D., Fasse, B., Gray, J., Holbrook, J., . . . Ryan, M. (2003). Problem-based learning meets case-based reasoning in the middle-school science classroom: Putting learning by design into practice. *Journal of the Learning Sciences, 12,* 495–547. doi:10.1207/S15327809JLS1204_2

Kolodner, J. L., Gray, J. T., & Fasse, B. B. (2003). Promoting transfer through case-based reasoning: Rituals and practices in learning by design classrooms. *Cognitive Science Quarterly, 3,* 183–232.

Kuhn, D. (1989). Children and adults as intuitive scientists. *Psychological Review, 96,* 674–689. doi:10.1037/0033-295X.96.4.674

Kuhn, D. (1991). *The skills of argument.* Cambridge, England: Cambridge University Press. doi:10.1017/CBO9780511571350

Langley, P., Simon, H. A., Bradshaw, G. L., & Zytkow, J. M. (1987). *Scientific discovery: Computational explorations in the creative process.* Cambridge, MA: MIT Press.

Lawson, A. E. (1987). *Classroom Test of Scientific Reasoning: Revised paper and pencil version.* Tempe: Arizona State University Press.

Marr, D. (1982). *Vision: A computational investigation into the human representation and processing of visual information.* New York, NY: Holt.

Mehalik, M. M., Doppelt, Y., & Schunn, C. D. (2008). Middle-school science through design-based learning versus scripted inquiry: Better overall science concept learning and equity gap reduction. *Journal of Engineering Education, 97,* 71–85.

National Academy of Engineering. (2007). *Rising above the gathering storm: Energizing and employing America for a brighter economic future.* Washington, DC: The National Academies Press.

National Research Council. (2007). *Taking science to school: Learning and teaching science in grades K–8.* Washington, DC: The National Academies Press.

National Research Council. (2009). *Understanding and improving K–12 engineering education in the United States.* Washington, DC: The National Academies Press.

Otto, K. N., & Wood, K. L. (2001). *Product design.* Upper Saddle River, NJ: Prentice Hall.

Puntambekar, S., & Kolodner, J. L. (2005). Toward implementing distributed scaffolding: Helping students learn science from design. *Journal of Research in Science Teaching, 42,* 185–217. doi:10.1002/tea.20048

Roth, W.-M. (2001). Learning science through technological design. *Journal of Research in Science Teaching, 38,* 768–790. doi:10.1002/tea.1031

Sadler, P. M., Coyle, H. P., & Schwartz, M. (2000). Engineering competitions in the middle school classroom: Key elements in developing effective design challenges. *Journal of the Learning Sciences, 9,* 299–327. doi:10.1207/S15327809JLS0903_3

Schauble, L., Klopfer, L. E., & Raghavan, K. (1991). Students' transition from an engineering model to a science model of experimentation. *Journal of Research in Science Teaching, 28,* 859–882. doi:10.1002/tea.3660280910

Schunn, C. D., & Anderson, J. R. (1999). The generality/specificity of expertise in scientific reasoning. *Cognitive Science, 23,* 337–370. doi:10.1207/s15516709cog2303_3

Schunn, C. D., & Klahr, D. (2000). Discovery processes in a more complex task. In D. Klahr (Ed.), *Exploring science: The cognition and development of discovery processes* (pp. 161–199). Cambridge, MA: MIT Press.

Silk, E. M., Higashi, R., Shoop, R., & Schunn, C. D. (2010). Designing technology activities that teach mathematics. *Technology Teacher, 69*(4), 21–27.

Silk, E. M., Schunn, C. D., & Shoop, R. (2009). Synchronized robot dancing: Motivating efficiency and meaning in problem solving with robotic. *Robot Magazine, 17,* 42–45.

Silk, E. M., Schunn, C. D., & Strand-Cary, M. (2009). The impact of an engineering design curriculum on science reasoning in an urban setting. *Journal of Science Education and Technology, 18,* 209–223. doi:10.1007/s10956-009-9144-8

Singley, M. K., & Anderson, J. R. (1989). *The transfer of cognitive skill.* Cambridge, MA: Harvard University Press.

Stokes, D. E. (1997). *Pasteur's Quadrant: Basic science and technological innovation.* Washington, DC: Brookings Institution Press.

Tschirgi, J. E. (1980). Sensible reasoning: A hypothesis about hypotheses. *Child Development, 51,* 1–10. doi:10.2307/1129583

Tseng, I., Moss, J., Cagan, J., & Kotovsky, K. (2008). The role of timing and analogical similarity in the stimulation of idea generation in design. *Design Studies, 29,* 203–221. doi:10.1016/j.destud.2008.01.003

Tweney, R. D., Doherty, M. E., & Mynatt, C. R. (1982). Rationality and disconfirmation: Further evidence. *Social Studies of Science, 12,* 435–441. doi:10.1177/030631282012003004

Ulrich, K. T., & Eppinger, S. D. (2008). *Product design and development* (4th ed.). New York, NY: McGraw-Hill.

11

To Teach or Not to Teach Through Inquiry

Erin Marie Furtak, Richard J. Shavelson,
Jonathan T. Shemwell, and Maria Figueroa

Ever since *inquiry* was advanced by science education reformers as an instructional method (Brandwein, 1962; Rutherford, 1964; Schwab, 1962), the efficacy of this approach for helping students learn has been questioned. At the same time, accepted definitions of what constitutes inquiry teaching have been slow to develop. *Scientific inquiry* was defined in the *National Science Education Standards* (National Research Council [NRC], 1996) as "the diverse ways in which scientists study the natural world and propose explanations based on the evidence derived from their work" (p. 2). Scientific inquiry teaching, then, is a way of teaching and learning in which students are engaged in these thinking processes and activities of scientists. In a later addendum, the NRC further parsed their definition of inquiry into Essential Features, Fundamental Understandings, and Fundamental Abilities (NRC, 2001b).

Although meta-analyses and syntheses have suggested that inquiry teaching and learning have a small-to-moderate effect on student learning compared with that of traditional or "direct" lecture and textbook-based instruction (Bredderman, 1983; Furtak, Seidel, Iverson, & Briggs, 2009; Lott, 1983; Minner, Levy, & Century, 2010; Schroeder, Scott, Tolson, Huang, & Lee, 2007; Shavelson & Towne, 2002; Shymansky, Hedges, & Woodworth, 1990; Weinstein, Boulanger, & Walberg, 1982; Wise & Okey, 1983), researchers have for decades openly questioned inquiry and its associated constructivist instructional approaches (e.g., Kirschner, Sweller, & Clark, 2006; Mayer, 2004; Shulman & Keislar, 1966; Tobias & Duffy, 2009).

Just as education policy documents began to emphasize a focus on teaching science through a process of inquiry, the politics of what should and should not count as evidence for research on educational interventions was heating up. The NRC's report *Scientific Research in Education* set forth—although clearly not for the first time—that causal inferences were only possible in education with certain types of designs, one of which, when implemented properly, was termed the "gold standard" or the controlled, randomized experiment (Schneider, Carnoy, Kilpartick, Schmidt, & Shavelson, 2007; Shavelson & Towne, 2002). This report was released into a political climate obsessed with accountability after the recent passage of the No Child Left Behind (NCLB) Act of 2001 (2002) and the Math and Science Initiatives (U.S. Department of Education, 2004), which jointly emphasized high-quality research in science education to "provide schools with scientific evidence of the effectiveness of interventions in mathematics and science by supporting systematic research on the effectiveness of educational interventions" (U.S. Department of Education, 2006, p. 19).

Thus, when David Klahr and Milena Nigam (2004) published their paper, "The Equivalence of Learning Paths in Early Science Instruction," it was into a charged climate in which policymakers were eager to seize on strong evidence derived from an experimental study that supported direct instruction. In a study of 112 third- and fourth-grade children, Klahr and Nigam found

> not only that many more children learned from direct instruction than from discovery learning, but also that when asked to make broader, richer scientific judgments, the many children who learned about experimental design from direct instruction performed as well as those few children who discovered the method on their own. These results challenge predictions derived from the presumed superiority of discovery approaches in teaching young children basic procedures for early scientific investigations. (p. 661)

Such strong claims about the success of direct instruction immediately caught the attention of political and educational communities and reignited the philosophical debate over behavioral, empiricist assumptions about learning and the cognitive, rationalist view (Begley, 2004; Case, 1996; Cavanagh, 2004; Tobias & Duffy, 2009).

However, the previous excerpt is taken from the abstract of Klahr and Nigam's (2004) paper. As we show, a close reading of the Methods section reveals that the condition Klahr and Nigam labeled *discovery learning* still featured the instructor providing goals to the students, and the condition labeled *direct instruction* was a version of guided inquiry teaching (Furtak, 2004). Unfortunately, the labels given to these conditions were seized on by the media and those falling in the empiricist camp interested in making a case against inquiry-based teaching (Begley, 2004; Cavanagh, 2004).

The ensuing controversy raged in *Education Week,* scholarly journals, and education conferences. We contend that one of the recurring aspects of that controversy—the issue of whether to teach through inquiry—is perhaps not the most constructive question to address. Rather, we argue that a more nuanced view of inquiry-based teaching, as expressed in Hmelo-Silver, Duncan, & Chinn (2007) and in Klahr's subsequent "post-direct instruction" publications (Klahr, 2009; Klahr & Li, 2005), is necessary to help us determine the approaches that are more or less appropriate to help students learn.

This chapter unpacks Klahr and Nigam's (2004) *Psychological Science* article with a particular focus on the ways in which the authors defined the two conditions contrasted in their study. We then explore the different terms Klahr and Nigam used in that paper, focusing on the controversy sparked by the use of those definitions in light of the outcome of their experiment. Then, we revisit some of the publications that were released after Klahr and Nigam's paper to describe the debate it sparked. Finally, we set forth our own argument for a more nuanced definition of inquiry and discuss the importance of definitions in the politically loaded arena of inquiry-based teaching.

Reform-Based Jargon

The concept of *discovery learning* was often discussed in the early inquiry-based teaching and learning literature. Discovery learning is based on the principle that students will develop more thorough, transferable, and interconnected knowledge if they are allowed to explore phenomena for themselves. In discovery activities, learners formulate what they are learning using their own language derived from experience (Kendler, 1966). Historically, discovery learning consisted of a hands-off teaching style on the part of the teacher, leaving students to construct understanding on their own. It is interesting that even in the years in which inquiry-based teaching was gaining steam, discovery learning was shown to have predictably inconsistent and most often ineffective influences on students' learning (Shulman & Keislar, 1966), and educators began describing inquiry-based teaching as featuring guidance on the part of the teacher.

The term *hands-on* is associated with, if not synonymous with, discovery teaching. It is the more commonly used term among practitioners and curriculum developers, focusing on the importance of students manipulating materials as they learn. Hands-on mathematics instruction was famously skewered in Cohen's (1990) "The Case of Mrs. Oublier," the elementary school teacher who prioritized student handling of instructional materials over their meaningful cognitive engagement with the important ideas to be learned. Flick (1993) described hands-on science as having two meanings; in one sense, hands-on refers to an overarching philosophy of reform-oriented instruction, and in the other, hands-on science refers to a type of activity in which students actively manipulate materials for themselves. Klahr, Triona, and Williams (2007) further described hands-on interventions as being either physical or virtual.

Direct instruction refers to an instructional approach originally developed by Englemann in the 1960s. According to Rosenshine (2006), the term has five overlapping uses: teacher-led instruction without regard to quality, instructional procedures used by effective teachers, instructional procedures to teach cognitive strategies, instructional procedures in the Direct Instruction Systems in Arithmetic and Reading programs, and instruction in which teaching is portrayed negatively. Taking the latter, Kirschner (2009) colorfully described direct instruction as belonging to one side of the animated debate over educational reforms that falsely cast traditional teaching as "classical, sage-on-the-stage, expository and didactic approaches of universal truths" (p. 144). Klahr and Nigam's (2004) work, although admittedly far removed from Englemann's original work, seems more closely aligned with Rosenshine's third use of direct instruction as an approach intended to teach cognitive strategies.

Rather than focusing on the differences among these diffusely defined terms, it may be more useful to think about scientific inquiry as lying on one side of a continuum of different methods of teaching science. The continuum is bordered on one end by traditional, direct instruction in which students are told what answers they are expected to learn by their teacher. At the other end of the continuum, students are left to their own devices to learn, an approximation of discovery learning. In the past, the completely open-ended classroom situations we call *discovery learning* have been associated with inquiry-based teaching; however, we argue that even the most open-ended classroom environments that

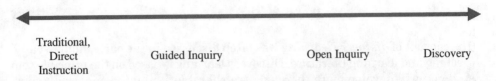

Traditional,
Direct   Guided Inquiry   Open Inquiry   Discovery
Instruction

Figure 11.1. Continuum representing forms of science instruction.

could be considered inquiry-based occur in the context of scientific ways of knowing. Thus, we distinguish open inquiry from discovery learning because the former takes place in the context of scientific ways of knowing, but activities are still student directed (problems, methods, and answers left open to students; Shulman & Tamir, 1973). Thus, reform-oriented science instruction often takes place somewhere in between the extremes, where students are guided, through a process of scientific investigation, to particular answers that are known to the teacher. This version is called *guided inquiry teaching*. Although guided inquiry and open inquiry are shown occupying the center of this continuum, they may float in either direction of the continuum depending on the level of structure provided in a given investigation (see Figure 11.1).

Although Klahr and Nigam's choice in 2004 of the term *discovery learning* to describe one of their conditions is consistent with early descriptions of this approach, their condition falls at the far end of our continuum, and the students' poor learning gains align with other results from the science education community that have discredited discovery learning over the past 40-plus years. Their choice of direct instruction to describe their treatment condition is where the controversy began. Their direct instruction is actually very much consistent with descriptions of guided scientific inquiry teaching. Thus, the problem arose when readers of Klahr and Nigam's research equated the discovery approach with inquiry-based teaching and learning when their direct instruction condition was in fact a better approximation of this teaching method. The consequences, as we describe next, were played out in various public arenas of educational policy and research.

What's the Matter With Direct Instruction? Klahr and Nigam's (2004) Paper

The control-of-variables strategy (CVS) is an approach that helps students develop unconfounded experiments in which one variable is tested at a time. Klahr has previously argued (Klahr, 2000; Klahr & Simon, 1999) that acquisition of a CVS strategy is an essential step in the development of scientific reasoning skills. Chen and Klahr (1999), the first in a series of CVS studies, involved three training conditions along the direct instruction to discovery learning continuum. These conditions were combinations of the CVS training with or without probe questions for each contrast explored in the lesson. Results of the study indicated that students in the three treatment conditions (CVS training with probe, no CVS training with probe, and no CVS training without probe) experienced learning gains along a continuum, with students in the CVS training with probe condition learning the most, and students in the no training/no probe condition learning the least.

In response to this paper, which established that students in the most direct condition learned more, Chinn and Malhotra (2001) argued that CVS does not prepare students with skills that could be transferred to authentic inquiry contexts. Thus, Klahr and Nigam's (2004) experiment was designed as a direct response to what Klahr called *epistemological critique* and replicated Chen and Klahr (1999) with a simpler treatment contrast and a transfer task, which took the form of evaluating CVS for science fair posters.

Klahr and Nigam's (2004) *Psychological Science* article contrasted two kinds of experimental lessons designed to teach students the CVS. The study engaged 112 randomly assigned third- and fourth-grade students to two experimental conditions involving the CVS strategy. Both conditions began with an exploratory phase in which students investigated a ball-and-ramp apparatus, with a focus on how changing different parts of the apparatus (e.g., placement of the ball, height of the ramp) affected the ultimate distance the ball rolled when released. At this point, students participated in an initial assessment of their ability to design four kinds of experiments. Then, students in the control condition—labeled the *discovery learning* condition—were allowed to continue to explore the apparatus with no direct guidance or feedback beyond the statement of an objective for the experiment. The treatment condition—labeled *direct instruction*—involved the teacher providing goals, materials, examples, and explicit explanations on how to control variables. Students discussed with the teacher the experiments they observed to develop the skills being taught. The assessment phase began immediately following instruction. Students in both conditions were again asked to design four kinds of experiments. Then, about a week later, students engaged in the transfer task in which they evaluated science fair posters made by sixth-grade students at another school.

Results clearly indicated a positive, significant impact of the direct-instruction CVS treatment over the discovery-learning control. CVS scores for students in the direct-instruction condition increased dramatically from exploration to assessment phase, and although student performance in the discovery condition increased as well, the difference was much smaller. In addition, students in the direct instruction condition performed significantly better on the transfer task, in which they created science fair posters. These results led Klahr and Nigam (2004) to conclude the following at the end of their paper:

> These results suggest the need to reexamine the long-standing claim that the limitations of direct instruction, as well as the advantage of discovery methods, will invariably manifest themselves in tasks requiring broad transfer to authentic contexts . . . such results could provide evidence-based guidance to teachers for achieving a balanced portfolio of instructional approaches to early science instruction. (p. 666)

Given what Klahr and Nigam (2004) described to be the nature of the two experimental conditions, this was a well-founded conclusion. However, as a reticent Klahr reflected in a later publication (Klahr & Li, 2005), he had vastly underestimated the way in which his results could "be used to support or attack specific aspects of science education practice and policy" (p. 233). Klahr did not just get caught in the crossfire in the ongoing "science wars"—his results were to be used as ammunition in this battle.

Ensuing Controversy in *Education Week*

The first author had just finished reading a prepublication copy of Klahr and Nigam's (2004) paper when she came across a November 10, 2004, edition of *Education Week* highlighting Klahr and Nigam's findings. In an article titled "NCLB Could Alter Science Teaching" (Cavanagh, 2004), the coming science assessment mandated by NCLB legislation was cited as a reason for science teachers to reconsider their commitment to hands-on instruction, described in the article as filling test tubes with yeast and combining vinegar and baking soda to make volcanoes. In this article, Klahr and Nigam's paper was presented as evidence against a hands-on approach to teaching. After describing the results of Klahr and Nigam's study, the article went on to explain the following:

> While descriptions of direct instruction vary widely, it is often defined as a model that promotes highly structured lessons, in which teachers present material to students in an explicit way, rather than having them attempt to arrive at conclusions on their own through in-class experimentation. . . . Direct instruction tends to contrast with discovery learning, a model that generally asks students to acquire knowledge through laboratory work, experiments, and periodic guidance from teachers. Supporters of discovery learning (sometimes linked with a model called "inquiry-based learning") say the approach encourages students to develop a broad understanding of scientific concepts, which they are likely to retain over time. (Cavanagh, 2004, p. 12)

In contrast to our suggested interpretation of Klahr and Nigam's conditions in the introduction, the *Education Week* article placed discovery learning and inquiry-based learning into the same category, rather than viewing the direct-instruction condition as more consistent with inquiry-based learning.

The first author wrote the following letter to *Education Week* arguing that the article misstated the conditions of Klahr and Nigam's study and should not have claimed that the results of that study suggest that a direct-instruction approach might be a likely outcome of NCLB (Furtak, 2004):

> I was discouraged to see the terms "hands-on," "discovery," and "inquiry" used almost interchangeably in your front-page article, "NCLB Could Alter Science Teaching." The three approaches to science teaching actually have subtly different meanings that imply different levels of teacher involvement.
>
> While hands-on learning is a somewhat generic term that applies to any instance in which students are manipulating materials, discovery learning consists of hands-off teaching methods—those that allow students to develop their own meaning through experience. In contrast, inquiry teaching is highly dependent on involvement by the teacher, as students

generate research questions from theory, develop research methods, collect and interpret evidence, and develop scientific explanations. Cornell University's Barbara A. Crawford places inquiry teaching at the opposite end of a continuum of teacher involvement from discovery, stating that this form of teaching requires more intervention than discovery teaching.

The nuances between hands-on, discovery, and inquiry teaching are relevant when they are contrasted, as a whole, with direct instruction. David Klahr and Milena Nigam carefully define their study as addressing the difference between discovery learning and direct instruction. The discovery condition provided, as their study states, "no teacher intervention beyond the suggestion of a learning objective: no guiding questions and no feedback about the quality of the child's suggestion of materials, explorations, or self-assessments." It is perhaps no wonder that such students did not learn as effectively as those who were taught using direct instruction. Few in the educational community continue to make the argument that discovery learning, in the absence of specific goals and feedback, will lead to student learning; in fact, quite the opposite has been shown.

While the federal No Child Left Behind Act will likely have an impact on how science is taught in schools, I object to the suggestion that, on the basis of one study, inquiry teaching might be lumped together with discovery learning as a potential argument for the advantages of direct instruction, especially when other studies have indicated the effectiveness of inquiry and discovery teaching. A discussion of best practices in science teaching would perhaps be a more constructive approach to anticipating the achievement pressures that will arrive with No Child Left Behind-mandated testing in science. (p. 41)

The same issue of *Education Week* featured a letter by Alfie Kohn and Sharon Janulaw (2004) of the California Science Teachers Association, who succinctly stated the following:

> It's important . . . to understand the limits of this study, which was conducted with only about 100 3rd and 4th graders and, more important, used a "discovery" condition that really isn't representative of the sort of teaching recommended by most experts. It would be a mistake to assume that any deficiencies of a model unique to this experiment, or any effects with this particular age group, can be generalized to all inquiry-based approaches or to all students. (p. 41)

Two weeks later, *Education Week* published Klahr's (2005) response to these two letters. He first rebutted Kohn and Janulaw's criticism of his sample size, referring to his statement at the end of the original article that more research needed to be performed. He also argued that his conditions were indeed representative of what happened in everyday science classrooms:

> Is it really so different? Our discovery condition presented the experimental apparatus to the children. It presented them with a goal, "see if you can set up the ramps to see if the height of the ramp makes a difference," and then students were free to explore, in a hands-on fashion, various kinds of arrangements, run the experiments, observe the results, and finally, under teacher suggestion, move on to another goal, such as "see if you can set up the ramps

> to see if the surface of the ramp makes a difference in how far the ball rolls." I would venture that this is not so far from what passes for discovery learning in many elementary school classrooms. (Klahr, 2005, p. 36)

Klahr went on to emphasize that the purpose of the study was not to contrast the effectiveness of the conditions, but to explore their impact on students' ability to perform a "far-transfer task."

In response to the first author's letter, Klahr (2005) wrote that she referred to the descriptions of the conditions as they were described in

> the original journal article, rather than on the way it was summarized in *Education Week*, and she reiterates our argument for the need for our field to make more precise use of terminology before moving on to policy decisions. Indeed, it is surprising that science educators so often abandon one of the foundations of science—the operational definition—when they engage in heated debates about discovery, inquiry, hands-on, and the rest. No science can advance without clear, unambiguous, operationally defined procedures. Neither can education science.
>
> Finally, as a "bench scientist" who decided only in the past dozen years or so to venture out of the psychology lab into the messy and challenging world of educational research, I must say that I tremble when reporters call. Even with repeated iterations on exactly what my studies do and don't suggest, I am often surprised to see the context in which they are presented (as in the provocative headline for the article that generated this exchange). (Klahr, 2005, p. 36)

Unfortunately, the misuse of Klahr and Nigam's results was not limited to *Education Week*'s mainstream audience but also occurred in the *Monitor on Psychology* (Adelson, 2004) and the *Wall Street Journal* (Begley, 2004). In an example of wider impact, Kirschner et al. (2006) summarized Klahr and Nigam's study in their subtly titled 2006 publication, "Why Minimal Guidance During Instruction Does Not Work: An Analysis of the Failure of Constructivist, Discovery, Problem-Based, Experiential, and Inquiry-Based Teaching." They wrote the following:

> Klahr & Nigam (2004), in a very important study, not only tested whether science learners learned more via a discovery versus direct instruction route but also, once learning had occurred, whether the quality of learning differed. Specifically, they tested whether those who had learned through discovery were better able to transfer their learning to new contexts. The findings were unambiguous. Direct instruction involving considerable guidance, including examples, resulted in vastly more learning than discovery. Those relatively few students who learned via discovery showed no signs of superior quality of learning. (pp. 79–80)

By taking the descriptions of the discovery and direct-instruction conditions at face value, and, therefore, as evidence in support of their thesis, Kirschner et al. made the same mistake as *Education Week*.

Although they did not directly reinterpret Klahr and Nigam's conditions, Hmelo-Silver et al. (2007) published a strong rebuttal to Kirschner et al. (2006) a year later, making a powerful argument for the importance of guidance in inquiry-based learning approaches, arguing that these approaches were improperly labeled *minimally guided instruction.*

Why So Much Attention?

We suggest two possible reasons for the attention received by Klahr and Nigam's (2004) paper: the design of the study itself and the political context into which it was released. With respect to study design, very few gold-standard experimental studies of inquiry-based teaching have been conducted in the past 10 years, as revealed by recent syntheses and meta-analyses (Furtak et al., 2009; Minner et al., 2010; Schroeder et al., 2007). This shortage, combined with the U.S. government's interest in this type of study, meant that when a researcher of Klahr's stature released the results of an experimental investigation into discovery learning and direct instruction, the study generated a great deal of attention. With respect to political context, the findings of this study fit within the political and value debate about the appropriate theory of learning and teaching that should underlie science education. This debate is reminiscent of the usually false dualisms that have plagued educational ideas for the past 100 years and more, as exhibited in the works of John Dewey (e.g., 1938). One position holds that science is a set of facts to be clearly and effectively communicated to students. The other position holds that students can only construct knowledge for themselves and only under their own volition. A tendency to side with one position or another, and therefore set up the philosophies as competing, probably accounts for the notoriety of the Klahr and Nigam findings. The fact that neither position adequately describes what effective teaching and learning is about, and that Klahr and Nigam provided good evidence that this is the case, was lost in the heat of the debate.

What Kirschner et al. (2006) appeared to have missed is that mainstream science education had moved past the question of minimal guidance and had developed multiple metaphors for the ways in which inquiry-based instruction is guided or scaffolded by the teacher. Indeed, Shulman and Keislar (1966) had already published a critical appraisal of this version of discovery learning 40 years before Kirschner et al. Science educators and science education researchers now discuss guided inquiry, model-based inquiry, problem/project-based instruction, and other approaches that more explicitly describe the vital role of the teacher in providing instructional scaffolds and in helping students to construct meaning from their inquiry-based experiences.

Defining Inquiry

Klahr's (2005) criticism of science education reform in his letter to *Education Week* was well-founded. Despite decades of focus on inquiry-based reforms, the field has yet to converge on a singular, operational definition of inquiry-based teaching. The very term *inquiry* itself can be ascribed multiple meanings, which is in part a source of confusion about what the term means. The term *inquiry* has been alternately used to describe (a) scientific ways of knowing, that is, the work that scientists do; (b) a way for students to learn science; (c) an instructional approach; and (d) curriculum materials. Furthermore, when talking about inquiry, individuals often confound what we will call here the *cognitive* aspects of inquiry and the extent to which student activities in inquiry are guided by the student or by the teacher. In this section, we briefly detail both aspects of inquiry.

Cognitive Aspects of Inquiry

Duschl (2003) suggested a framework for inquiry that is based on research and scholarly findings in cognitive and social psychology, history and philosophy of science, and educational research. Duschl intended these three domains as a description of the context of assessment of inquiry; however, these domains can also serve as a framework for defining important characteristics of inquiry-based science teaching and learning. The three domains include conceptual structures and cognitive processes that are used during scientific reasoning; epistemic frameworks used when scientific knowledge is developed and evaluated; and social processes and forums, which shape how knowledge is communicated, represented, argued, and debated. Where school science is concerned, Duschl's epistemic domain can be further subdivided into the (a) ways in which students generate knowledge and develop understanding of the nature of science (Chinn & Malhotra, 2002; Flick & Lederman, 2004; Schwab, 1962; Windschitl, 2004) and (b) methods or "heuristics of discovery" (Bruner, 1961, p. 30)—that is, asking scientifically oriented questions, designing experiments, executing procedures, and data representations (NRC, 2000; Schwab, 1962).

However, these cognitive dimensions of inquiry seem to be less at issue than guidance in the controversy over Klahr and Nigam's (2004) paper, in which the goals for the activity were held constant between the two conditions contrasted. Rather, students in the direct-instruction condition received instruction about good and bad experiments, supplemented with probing questions, whereas students in the discovery-learning condition received neither of these (Strand-Cary & Klahr, 2008).

Guidance Dimensions of Inquiry

Bruner (1960) referred to the process of guiding student learning as *scaffolding*, or "a way that assures that only those parts of the task within the child's reach are left unresolved, and knowing what elements of a solution the child will recognize though he cannot yet perform them" (p. xiv). Teachers orchestrate a zone of proximal development by scaffolding—helping students solve scientific problems that lie beyond what they would be able to achieve alone through careful guidance (Vygotsky, 1978). Therefore, the strategies a teacher uses to lead a discussion during scientific inquiry teaching, for example, create a halo of social learning around the student (Lave & Wenger, 1991).

Schwab (1962) provided an early description of the amount of guidance or direction provided to students in three levels. The simplest involves the teacher or curriculum posing problems and providing methods for addressing the problem, leading to the student discovering a result that was not previously known. A second level involves a more structured problem with methods and answers left open, and a third level leaves the problem, methods, and answers completely to students. Shulman and Tamir (1973) added a fourth level of description, in which the problem and method are provided to students and the answer that students reach is already determined.

The NRC's *Inquiry and the National Science Education Standards* defined a continuum of directedness across the Essential Features of inquiry, varying across the extent of learner self-direction and direction from the teacher or materials (NRC, 2000, p. 29). The continuum is shown in Table 11.1.

The NRC addendum explains that teachers should use the more guided side of the continuum (right side) when learning is focused on particular science concepts, whereas open inquiry (left side) is better suited to helping students to develop scientific reasoning skills (NRC, 2001b). Although the addendum emphasizes the importance of both open and guided scientific inquiry teaching, it does not seem to suggest that a range of direction might coexist within the span of one investigation or, for that matter, in the span of one discussion. That is, at different phases, student activity might fall on one end or another or switch back and forth. It does, however, pose the following question:

> How does a teacher decide how much guidance to provide in an inquiry? In making this decision, a key element is the intended learning outcomes. Whether the teacher wants students to learn a particular science concept, acquire certain inquiry abilities, or develop understandings about scientific inquiry (or some combination) influences the nature of the inquiry. (NRC, 2000, p. 30)

Although the addendum follows this statement with examples of different investigations, these examples are predicated on the assumption that, given the type of learning outcome, the guidance will be either teacher directed or student directed, but not both.

Revisiting Klahr and Nigam

Given these dimensions of inquiry, we are better equipped to return to Klahr and Nigam's (2004) study to explore how the labels given to the conditions—and the way those conditions were interpreted—were fodder for the ongoing controversy in science education.

We argue that the controversy surrounding Klahr and Nigam's (2004) article can be traced to the different interpretations of guidance in the conditions as labeled, as the conditions map onto descriptions of guided inquiry in the science education literature and as they were interpreted by advocates of direct instruction. We represent these differences in Figure 11.2, as plotted against the continuum of science instruction presented in Figure 11.1.

Klahr and Nigam (2004), as we have already discussed, labeled their conditions *direct instruction* and *discovery learning*. However, given our examination of reform science education jargon, the conditions actually represented a more

Table 11.1. Essential Features of Classroom Inquiry and Their Variations

Essential feature	Variations			
1. Learner engages in scientifically oriented questions	Learner poses a question	Learner selects among questions, poses new questions	Learner sharpens or clarifies question provided by teacher, materials, or other source	Learner engages in question provided by teacher, materials, or other source
2. Learner gives priority to evidence in responding to questions	Learner determines what constitutes evidence and collects it	Learner directed to collect certain data	Learner given data and asked to analyze	Learner given data and told how to analyze
3. Learner formulates explanations from evidence	Learner formulates explanation after summarizing evidence	Learner guided in process of formulating explanations from evidence	Learner given possible ways to use evidence and formulate explanation	Learner provided with evidence
4. Learner connects explanations to scientific knowledge	Learner independently examines other resources and forms the links to explanations	Learner directed toward areas and sources of scientific knowledge	Learner given possible connections	
5. Learner communicates and justifies explanations	Learner forms reasonable and logical argument to communicate explanations	Learner coached in development of communication	Learner provided broad guidelines to sharpen communication	Learner given steps and procedures for communication

More ——————— Amount of learner self-direction ——————— Less

Less ——————— Amount of direction from teacher or material ——————— More

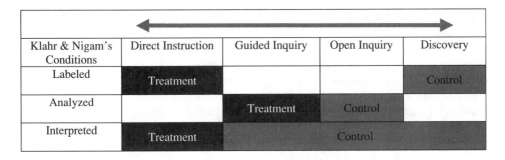

	Direct Instruction	Guided Inquiry	Open Inquiry	Discovery
Klahr & Nigam's Conditions	Direct Instruction	Guided Inquiry	Open Inquiry	Discovery
Labeled	Treatment			Control
Analyzed		Treatment	Control	
Interpreted	Treatment	Control		

Figure 11.2. Klahr and Nigam's (2004) conditions as labeled, analyzed, and interpreted.

nuanced comparison, rather than a comparison of extremes. Students in both conditions participated in an initial exploration and assessment phase in which students were first introduced to the ball-and-ramp apparatus and "worked with the apparatus . . . they were asked to make comparisons to determine how different variables affected the distance that balls rolled after leaving the downhill ramp" (pp. 662–663). Then, their baseline competence was assessed by asking them to construct four experiments—two to test the effect of steepness and two to test the effect of run length on how far the ball rolled.

Next came implementation of the two conditions. Students in the treatment condition

> observed as the experimenter designed several additional experiments—some confounded, some unconfounded—to determine the effects of steepness and run length. For each experiment, the instructor asked the children whether or not they thought the design would allow them to "tell for sure" whether a variable had an effect on the outcome. Then the instructor explained why each of the unconfounded experiments uniquely identified the factor that affected the outcome, and why each confounded experiment did not. (Klahr & Nigam, 2004, p. 663)

In contrast, students in the control condition

> continued to design their own experiments, focused on the same two variables that the direct-instruction children were focusing on, but without any instruction on CVS or any feedback from the experimenter. (p. 663)

In our analysis of these descriptions, students in both conditions were engaged in some aspects of inquiry-based instruction, with varying amounts of focus on experimental design, control of variables, and evaluation of evidence into explanations. In the condition labeled *direct instruction,* students observed several more experiments—some confounded, some unconfounded—and were asked to explain for each experiment whether it would be possible to "tell for sure" whether a variable had an effect on the run length of the ball. They then received feedback from their instructor based on their responses, an intervention essential to helping students derive meaning in inquiry-based contexts (Atkin & Coffey, 2003; NRC, 2001). Furthermore, having had the opportunity to view a sample of videotapes of the instructional sequences from this study, we saw that in the discovery conditions, students were able to "mess about" with materials a la Hawkins (1974) and received some guidance from the graduate student supervising the session. In contrast, the direct-instruction condition featured a dialogue between the student and instructor, with the facilitator helping the student to set up and use the apparatus as well as talk about what was happening. Thus, the treatment condition could more properly be labeled *guided inquiry*.

Klahr and Nigam (2004) made a point to explain that their treatment and control conditions did not contrast "active" and "passive" learning, and that students in both conditions engaged in the design of experiments and manipulation of the ball and ramp. Instead,

> the main distinction is that in direct instruction, the instructor provided good and bad examples of CVS, explained what the differences were between them, and told the students how and why CVS worked, whereas in the discovery condition, there were no examples and no explanations, even though there was an equivalent amount of design and manipulation of materials. (p. 663)

Furthermore, Klahr (2009) later stated that students in both conditions received guidance on how to perform the activity. Given the emphasis in the first phase of the lesson on experimental approaches, we argue that even the control group activities were embedded in the content of inquiry, with a focus on testing and design. Thus, this condition represented elements of both open inquiry—in which students design their own experiments on the basis of prior observations and data—and discovery learning.

These differences in labeling probably would have gone undetected if they had not been picked up and used as ammunition by advocates of direct instruction. However, the debate was again a difference in interpretation of the conditions. Although Klahr and Nigam used the term *inquiry* in their paper only once, to describe prior critiques of the CVS strategy, advocates of direct instruction took Klahr and Nigam's label of their treatment at face value and then lumped all variations of inquiry and discovery into the same category. In this view, Klahr and Nigam's paper provided strong evidence for their argument for a return to traditional instruction. Ironically, in the first sentence of their paper condemning "minimal guidance," Kirschner et al. (2006) foreshadowed the "evidence for the superiority of guided instruction" that they would present in their paper (p. 75)—while missing the nuance that Klahr and Nigam's paper was actually itself presenting a compelling argument for the role of guidance in inquiry-based teaching.

In later publications, Klahr was regretful about his choice of terms to label the conditions in the study. Arguing that his findings applied only to the most extreme forms of discovery learning, he acknowledged that the direct-instruction condition could have been more appropriately labeled *guided discovery* (Klahr & Li, 2005). In fact, he was surprised that, although the Chen and Klahr (1999) paper established the effectiveness of the guided CVS condition, it was the 2004 paper, which used more of the educational jargon terms, that caught the attention of the science wars (D. Klahr, personal communication, 2009). Klahr found that the most unanticipated aspect of portrayals of his research in the popular media has been the power of labels:

> In hindsight, we may have muddied the interpretation of our findings by incorporating popular terminology like "direct instruction" and "discovery learning" into articles and public presentations . . . Only when we tuned in to the recent political debate in California about the permissible amounts of "hands-on science" vs. "direct instruction" did we become fully aware of how easy it is for someone to pick up our terminology, and imbue it with whatever meaning suits their purpose. (Klahr & Li, p. 235)

Klahr used this experience to prod the educational community to come to a consensus on operational definitions for the reform-based terms that continue to muddy educational reform efforts. He also expressed his own reticence in choosing educational labels to describe his own research. One of his later studies found that students in discovery conditions with both physical and virtual hands-on activities had learning gains (Klahr et al., 2007). This study also presented a matrix in which contrasts between multiple types of science instruction, including domain specific and domain general, hands-on and hands-off, and discovery and direct instruction were more carefully defined. In addition, Klahr (2009) also noted his chagrin in admitting that, at the same time he was arguing for unambiguous definitions to describe educational reforms, he himself used conventional—and controversial—terminology to describe his own study.

Closing Thoughts

In closing, we return to the title of this chapter, "To Teach or Not to Teach Through Inquiry." Is the question generated by the controversy in which Klahr and Nigam found themselves: whether or not we should teach through inquiry or how we should define inquiry? We agree with Klahr's assertion that the fuzzy boundaries surrounding the multiple jargon terms involved in this paper—*discovery, hands-on, inquiry, constructivist, direct instruction, traditional teaching*—do little to help the field advance toward a better understanding of "what works" in terms of global instructional approaches. However, we are not naïve enough to expect the field to easily sit down and come to an operational definition anytime soon; such an effort raises inevitable questions about purposes, participants, and interpretations of research results.

Despite the controversy that Klahr and Nigam's (2004) study may have stirred, their study was on the right track. Aside from the labels they may have improperly applied to their conditions, they were precise about what was being varied and controlled in their study, and they provided in-depth descriptions of each intervention in their article. Furthermore, once the controversy erupted, Klahr was a model of transparency in showing videotapes of the conditions to other researchers, and he engaged in active discussion of the teaching and learning interactions that had occurred in both conditions. Ultimately, he admitted that he did not know what he was getting into when he made the decision to use educational reform jargon to describe experimental conditions in his CVS study. This experience causes us to reflect that we researchers should be very explicit in describing treatments and very careful about labeling them.

In closing, we suggest that even commonly accepted labels and instructional jargon for science education reforms will not get us all the way toward a more complete understanding of how students learn. After all, the ways in which any instructional condition is implemented will clearly vary on the basis of individual teachers' interpretations of curriculum materials and the context in which the conditions are being taught. We might come to a more sophisticated understanding of Klahr and Nigam's (2004) study by exploring the involvement of specific instructional strategies in the treatment and control groups. For example, given recent meta-analyses of the impact of feedback on student learning and performance (Black & Wiliam, 1998; Hattie & Timperley, 2007; Kluger & DeNisi, 1996), it is perhaps no wonder that students working in a condition in which they received no feedback on what they were or were not doing properly performed below students who did receive feedback. Our attention may be more constructively focused on detailed analyses of teaching–learning interactions rather than global teaching approaches (Seidel & Shavelson, 2007) as we struggle toward consensus in the politically charged arena that is educational reform.

References

Adelson, R. (2004). Instruction versus exploration in science learning. *Monitor on Psychology, 35*(6), 34–36.

Atkin, J. M., & Coffey, J. (Eds.). (2003). *Everyday assessment in the science classroom.* Arlington, VA: NSTA Press. doi:10.2505/9781935155706

Begley, S. (2004, December 10). The best ways to make schoolchildren learn? We just don't know. *The Wall Street Journal,* p. B1.

Black, P., & Wiliam, D. (1998). Assessment and classroom learning. *Assessment in Education: Principles, Policy & Practice, 5,* 7–74. doi:10.1080/0969595980050102

Brandwein, P. F. (1962). *Elements in a strategy for teaching science in the elementary school: The Burton lecture.* New York, NY: Harcourt, Brace, & World.

Bredderman, T. (1983). Effects of activity-based elementary science on student outcomes: A quantitative synthesis. *Review of Educational Research, 53,* 499–518.

Bruner, J. (1960). *The process of education.* Cambridge, MA: Harvard University Press.

Bruner, J. (1961). The act of discovery. *Harvard Educational Review, 31,* 21–32.

Case, R. O. B. P. (1996). Changing views of knowledge and their impact on educational research and practice. In D. R. Olson & N. Torrance (Eds.), *Handbook of education and human development: New models of learning, teaching, and schooling* (pp. 75–99). Oxford, England: Blackwell.

Cavanagh, S. (2004). NCLB could alter science teaching. *Education Week, 24*(11), 1, 12–13.

Chen, Z., & Klahr, D. (1999). All other things being equal: Children's acquisition of the control of variables strategy. *Child Development, 70,* 1098–1120.

Chinn, C. A., & Malhotra, B. A. (2001). Epistemologically authentic scientific reasoning. In K. Crowley, C. D. Schunn, & T. Okada (Eds.), *Designing for science: Implications from everyday, classroom, and professional settings* (pp. 351–392). Mahwah, NJ: Erlbaum.

Chinn, C. A., & Malhotra, B. A. (2002). Epistemologically authentic inquiry in schools: A theoretical framework for evaluating inquiry tasks. *Science Education, 86,* 175–218. doi:10.1002/sce.10001

Cohen, D. K. (1990). A revolution in one classroom: The case of Mrs. Oublier. *Educational Evaluation and Policy Analysis, 12,* 311–329.

Dewey, J. (1938). *Experience and education.* New York, NY: Touchstone.

Duschl, R. A. (2003). Assessment of inquiry. In J. M. Atkin & J. Coffey (Eds.), *Everyday assessment in the science classroom* (pp. 41–59). Arlington, VA: NSTA Press.

Flick, L. B. (1993). The meanings of hands-on science. *Journal of Science Teacher Education, 4,* 1–8. doi:10.1007/BF02628851

Flick, L. B., & Lederman, N. G. (Eds.). (2004). *Scientific inquiry and nature of science: Implications teaching, learning, and teacher education.* Dordrecht, the Netherlands: Kluwer Academic.

Furtak, E. M. (2004, December 1). Standardized science: Mandatory testing's impact on teaching and learning [Letter to the editor]. *Education Week,* p. 41.

Furtak, E. M., Seidel, T., Iverson, H., & Briggs, D. C. (2009, August). *Recent experimental studies of inquiry-based teaching: A meta-analysis and review.* Paper presented at the 13th biennial conference of the European Association for Research in Learning and Instruction, Amsterdam, the Netherlands.

Hattie, J., & Timperley, H. (2007). The power of feedback. *Review of Educational Research, 77,* 81–112. doi:10.3102/003465430298487

Hawkins, D. (1974). Messing about in science. In D. Hawkins (Ed.), *The informed vision: Essays on learning and human nature* (pp. 65–75). New York, NY: Agathon Press.

Hmelo-Silver, C. E., Duncan, R. G., & Chinn, C. A. (2007). Scaffolding and achievement in problem-based and inquiry learning: A response to Kirschner, Sweller, and Clark (2006). *Educational Psychologist, 42,* 99–107. doi:10.1080/00461520701263368

Kendler, H. H. (1966). Reflections on the conference. In L. S. Shulman & E. R. Keislar (Eds.), *Learning by discovery: A critical appraisal* (pp. 171–176). Chicago, IL: Rand McNally.

Kirschner, P. A. (2009). Epistemology or pedagogy, that is the question. In S. Tobias & T. M. Duffy (Eds.), *Constructivist instruction: Success or failure?* (pp. 144–157). New York, NY: Routledge.

Kirschner, P. A., Sweller, J., & Clark, R. E. (2006). Why minimal guidance during instruction does not work: An analysis of the failure of constructivist, discovery, problem-based, experiential, and inquiry-based teaching. *Educational Psychologist, 41,* 75–86. doi:10.1207/s15326985ep4102_1

Klahr, D. (2000). *Exploring science: The cognition and development of discovery processes.* Cambridge, MA: MIT Press.

Klahr, D. (2005, January 5). Terms of debate: A science study's author responds to critics. *Education Week,* p. 36.

Klahr, D. (2009). "To every thing there is a season, and a time to every purpose under the heavens": What about direct instruction? In S. Tobias & T. M. Duffy (Eds.), *Constructivist instruction: Success or failure?* (pp. 291–310). New York, NY: Routledge.

Klahr, D., & Li, J. (2005). Cognitive research and elementary science instruction: From the laboratory, to the classroom, and back. *Journal of Science Education and Technology, 14,* 217–238. doi:10.1007/s10956-005-4423-5

Klahr, D., & Nigam, M. (2004). The equivalence of learning paths in early science instruction: Effects of direct instruction and discovery learning. *Psychological Science, 15,* 661–667. doi:10.1111/j.0956-7976.2004.00737.x

Klahr, D., & Simon, H. A. (1999). Studies of scientific discovery: Complementary approaches and convergent findings. *Psychological Bulletin, 125,* 524–543.

Klahr, D., Triona, L. M., & Williams, C. (2007). Hands on what? The relative effectiveness of physical versus virtual materials in an engineering design project by middle school children. *Journal of Research in Science Teaching, 44,* 183–203. doi:10.1002/tea.20152

Kluger, A. N., & DeNisi, A. (1996). The effects of feedback interventions on performance: A historical review, a meta-analysis, and a preliminary feedback intervention theory. *Psychological Bulletin, 119,* 254–284. doi:10.1037/0033-2909.119.2.254

Kohn, A., & Janulaw, S. (2004, December 1). Standardized science: Mandatory testing's impact on teaching and learning [Letter to the editor]. *Education Week,* p. 41.

Lave, J., & Wenger, E. (1991). *Situated learning: Legitimate peripheral participation.* Cambridge, England: University of Cambridge Press.

Lott, G. W. (1983). The effect of inquiry teaching and advance organizers upon student outcomes in science education. *Journal of Research in Science Teaching, 20,* 437–451. doi:10.1002/tea.3660200507

Mayer, R. E. (2004). Should there be a three-strikes rule against pure discovery learning? The case for guided methods of instruction. *American Psychologist, 59,* 14–19. doi:10.1037/0003-066X.59.1.14

Minner, D., Levy, A., & Century, J. (2010). Inquiry-based science instruction—what is it and does it matter? Results from a research synthesis years 1984 to 2002. *Journal of Research in Science Teaching, 47,* 474–496.

National Research Council. (1996). *National science education standards.* Washington, DC: National Academies Press.

National Research Council. (2000). *Inquiry and the national science education standards.* Washington, DC: National Academies Press.

National Research Council. (2001). *Classroom assessment and the national science education standards.* Washington, DC: National Academies Press.

No Child Left Behind Act of 2001, Pub. L. No. 107-110, § 115, Stat.1425 (2002).

Rosenshine, B. (2006). *Five meanings of direct instruction.* Lincoln, IL: Center on Innovation & Improvement.

Rutherford, F. J. (1964). The role of inquiry in science teaching. *Journal of Research in Science Teaching, 2,* 80–84. doi:10.1002/tea.3660020204

Schneider, B., Carnoy, M., Kilpartick, J., Schmidt, W. H., & Shavelson, R. J. (2007). *Estimating causal effects: Using experimental and observational designs.* Washington, DC: American Educational Research Association.

Schroeder, C. M., Scott, T. P., Tolson, H., Huang, T.-Y., & Lee, Y.-H. (2007). A meta-analysis of national research: Effects of teaching strategies on student achievement in science in the United States. *Journal of Research in Science Teaching, 44,* 1436–1460. doi:10.1002/tea.20212

Schwab, J. J. (1962). *The teaching of science as enquiry.* Cambridge, MA: Harvard University Press.

Seidel, T., & Shavelson, R. J. (2007). Teaching effectiveness research in the past decade: The role of theory and research design in disentangling meta-analysis results. *Review of Educational Research, 77,* 454–499. doi:10.3102/0034654307310317

Shavelson, R. J., & Towne, L. (Eds.). (2002). Committee on Scientific Principles for Education Research, Center for Education, Division on Behavioral and Social Sciences and Education, National Research Council. *Scientific research in education.* Washington, DC: National Academies Press.

Shulman, L. S., & Keislar, E. R. (Eds.). (1966). *Learning by discovery: A critical appraisal.* Chicago, IL: Rand McNally.

Shulman, L. S., & Tamir, P. (1973). Research on teaching in the natural sciences. In R. M. W. Travers (Ed.), *Second handbook of research on teaching* (pp. 1098–1148). Chicago, IL: Rand McNally.

Shymansky, J. A., Hedges, L. V., & Woodworth, G. (1990). A reassessment of the effects of inquiry-based science curricula of the 60's on student performance. *Journal of Research in Science Teaching, 27,* 127–144. doi:10.1002/tea.3660270205

Strand-Cary, M., & Klahr, D. (2008). Developing elementary science skills: Instructional effectiveness and path independence. *Cognitive Development, 23,* 488–511. doi:10.1016/j.cogdev.2008.09.005

Tobias, S., & Duffy, T. M. (2009). *Constructivist instruction: Success or failure?* New York, NY: Routledge.

U.S. Department of Education. (2004). *The facts about . . . science achievement.* Retrieved from http://www.ed.gov/nclb/methods/science/science.html?exp=1

U.S. Department of Education. (2006). *Mathematics and science initiative concept paper.* [Electronic version]. Retrieved from http://www.ed.gov/rschstat/research/progs/mathscience/concept_paper.pdf

Vygotsky, L. S. (1978). *Mind in society: The development of higher psychological processes.* Cambridge, MA: Harvard University Press.

Weinstein, T., Boulanger, F. D., & Walberg, H. J. (1982). Science curriculum effects in high school: A quantitative synthesis. *Journal of Research in Science Teaching, 19,* 511–522. doi:10.1002/tea.3660190610

Windschitl, M. (2004). Folk theories of "inquiry": How preservice teachers reproduce the discourse and practices of an atheoretical scientific method. *Journal of Research in Science Teaching, 41,* 481–512. doi:10.1002/tea.20010

Wise, K. C., & Okey, J. R. (1983). A meta-analysis of the effects of various science teaching strategies on achievement. *Journal of Research in Science Teaching, 20,* 419–435. doi:10.1002/tea.3660200506

12

Epistemic Foundations for Conceptual Change

Richard A. Duschl and
María Pilar Jiménez-Aleixandre

Foundational perspectives on conceptual change frameworks have as their roots Piagetian and Kuhnian perspectives on theory change. We have long understood that the conceptual ecology of science learning is complex. However, recent scholarly perspectives (Duschl, 2008; Jiménez-Aleixandre & Erduran, 2008; Lehrer & Schauble, 2006) about "what is science" have challenged extant images of science and science education that stress experimentation and hypothesis testing as their core activity. The proposed alternative is an emphasis on the discourse practices (e.g., argumentation, critiques, tool and theory decision making, research group meetings, peer review) central to scientific reasoning, measuring, and communicating (Duschl & Grandy, 2008; Kelly, McDonald, & Wickman, in press). This new focus on "doing science" in turn raises questions about the design of science-learning environments (Jiménez-Aleixandre, 2008) and how we frame, represent, and teach the nature of science (NOS).

Our contribution to this volume examines recent reviews of research that call for a shift in thinking regarding epistemic goals of science learning (Erduran & Jiménez-Aleixandre, 2008; Kelly et al., in press) and relates this shift to conceptual change notions such as the epistemic status of students' ideas (Jiménez-Aleixandre, 2008). Developing epistemic criteria and evaluating the epistemic status of ideas are viewed as necessary elements in a conceptual ecology of science-learning environments that seek to promote enculturation into scientific cultures and/or achieve NOS learning goals. The recommended shifts are as follows:

- away from a focus on the individual scientist to a focus on social groups or communities of scientists;
- away from a focus on contexts of discovery and justification of conceptual claims to a focus on the development, modification, and evolution of epistemic claims;

This chapter is based on a paper presented at the European Science Education Research Association (ESERA) Conference, Istanbul, Turkey, August–September, 2009. María Pilar Jiménez-Aleixandre's work on epistemic practices is supported by the Spanish Ministry of Science and Innovation, code EDU2009-13890-C02-01.

- away from an exclusive focus on inquiry addressing the fit of concepts in scientific theories to a focus on the tools and technologies that give rise to new methods and practices in building and refining scientific models; and

- away from domain-general "consensus view lists of NOS" to views of NOS that are situated practices associated with the broadening and deepening of the growth of scientific knowledge.

In this chapter, we present exemplary research reports and publications for each of these four shifts and discuss implications for the design of learning environments and curriculum, instruction, and assessment models. Our emphasis is on the inquiry, discourse, and metacognitive practices that promote the development of epistemic criteria and the advancement of learners' images about NOS. One important epistemic practice for doing science is the control of variables strategy (CVS) that has been extensively researched by David Klahr (Klahr, Fay, & Dunbar, 1993; Klahr, Triona, & Williams, 2007) and applied to arguments he has made that direct instruction about CVS is superior to inquiry, discovery, or other forms of minimally guided instructional formats (Klahr, 2009; Klahr & Nigam, 2004). At issue is the extent to which any one or a suite of epistemic practices builds learners' capacities to engage in the construction, critique, and communication of scientific ideas and information. The organization of science education curriculum, instruction, and assessments around (a) core science knowledge, (b) scientific practices (e.g., argumentation discourse, investigative, as well as model building and revision), and (c) learning progressions is a recommendation in the 2007 National Research Council (NRC) research synthesis report, "Taking Science to School: Learning and Teaching Science in Grades K–8," which was written by a committee on which Klahr and Duschl collaborated (Duschl, Schweingruber, & Shouse, 2007).

Toward a Social Epistemic Subject

Science is a social practice, and the processes of knowledge construction, evaluation, and communication take place within given communities. The shift from a focus on the individual scientist or on the individual students to a focus on social groups or communities of scientists is grounded both in science studies, which offer new perspectives about how knowledge is produced (Longino, 1990), and in philosophical approaches (Habermas, 1981; Thagard, 2007). Longino (2008) explained that science is social in different ways. In one sense it is both collaborative, as scientists work in groups, and competitive, as the overall structure is competitive. In another sense, Longino (2008) claimed that knowledge itself is social, as what matters is agreement and disagreement within the scientific community. For Longino, this claim acknowledges the diversity of content and norms found in the contemporary community.

Habermas's (1981) theory of communicative action gives people preeminence over structures, assigning them the potentiality to develop actions directed to social change, a view aligned with critical theory. As Kelly (2008) noted in his discussion about changing the epistemic subject, Habermas's framework involves individual shifts to a social epistemic subject, whereas reason is centered on communicative action and norms for argument are shared, forwarding the goal of rationality through dialogue. Kelly considered two implications of viewing science as a social knowledge for inquiry: the value of a dialogic community supporting inquiry (involving public dialogue about epistemic criteria) and a view of learning commensurate with a social view of inquiry as situated in sociocultural practices.

An instance of research framed in the Habermas perspective is Puig and Jiménez-Aleixandre's (2009) exploration of the interferences between social representations and the competence in using evidence. Puig and Jiménez-Aleixandre examined the influence of the sociocultural construct of human "race" on the evaluation of evidence related to the influence of environment on the expression of genes in a context in which students are asked to evaluate James Watson's claim about genetics causing Black people to be less intelligent than White people. Jiménez-Aleixandre and Puig (in press) argued for a new characterization of critical thinking that includes both a commitment to evidence and a disposition to criticize science that is used to justify social inequalities or social policy, that is, a disposition that may involve developing an independent opinion that challenges one's own community or group.

A complementary perspective by Thagard (2007) posited that coherence, truth, and explanatory coherence of scientific explanations are achieved through the cognitive and social processes in which theories broaden and deepen over time by accounting for new facts and providing explanations of why the theory works. Recent research reviews (Duschl, 2008; Duschl & Grandy, 2008; Duschl et al., 2007; Ford & Forman, 2006; Lehrer & Schauble, 2006) and research studies on science learning (Ford, 2008a, 2008b; Lehrer, Schauble, & Lucas, 2008; Smith, Wiser, Anderson, & Krajcik, 2006) have maintained that the same broadening and deepening practices that are based on a set of improving and refining tenets within a community of investigators ought to hold for teaching and learning practices in science-learning environments.

Toward a Focus on the Development, Modification, and Evolution of Epistemic Claims

Argumentation studies constitute one instance of the current emphasis on the cognitive and discursive practices of scientific communities. Argumentation focuses on the process of knowledge evaluation, with the use of evidence being central in this process (Jiménez-Aleixandre, 2008). The question is: How can we support students' engagement in argumentation? To help to answer this question, Jiménez-Aleixandre noted that Posner, Strike, Hewson, and Gertzog (1982) were first in claiming that the students were the ones who had to decide whether the conditions for conceptual change were met, that is, whether the epistemic status, or in Posner et al.'s terms, the intellectual status of their own ideas included being intelligible, plausible, fruitful, etc., or not. Students' reflection about their ideas and their learning is a relevant component of environments designed to promote epistemic practices, such as argumentation.

Jiménez-Aleixandre (2008) suggested paying attention to six underlying design principles of learning environments whose goal is to promote argumentation. Figure 12.1 highlights these principles as the roles of students, teacher, curriculum, assessment, metacognition, and communication, all revolving around knowledge evaluation.

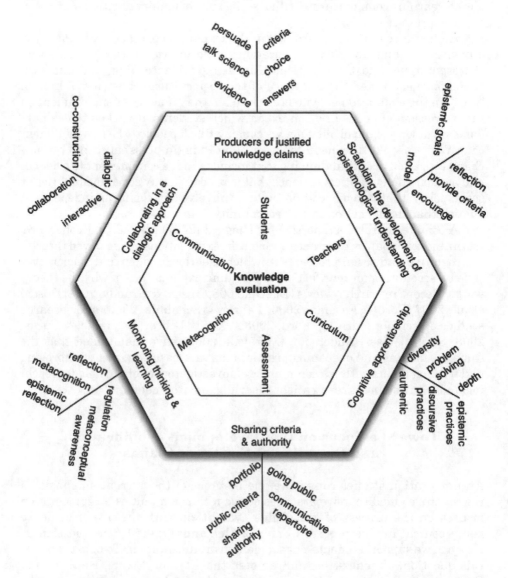

Figure 12.1.   Summary of design principles for argumentation learning environments. From *Argumentation in Science Education: Perspectives From Classroom-Based Research* (p. 96), by S. Erduran and M. P. Jiménez-Aleixandre, 2008, Dordrecht, the Netherlands: Springer. Copyright 2008 by Springer Science + Business Media. Reprinted with permission.

From these six principles, we discuss one aspect related to the curriculum: the design of tasks in order to produce a diversity of outcomes to involve students in considering a plurality of explanations. It needs to be noted that, for some tasks and phenomena, it may be the case that only one explanation is aligned with the scientific view; the meaning of plurality is the existence of other potential explanations (historical or related to students' alternative ideas). Diversity is grounded in a view of knowledge as socially constructed through challenges brought about by differences in perspective (Pea, 1993). This diversity supports the evaluation of alternatives and students' engagement in argumentation. As Longino (2008) indicated, the view of knowledge as social implies acknowledgement of plurality and diversity.

What we mean by diversity is not just more than one explanation or outcome. Proposals, solutions, or alternatives generated have, as a consequence of design, different epistemic statuses, and these can undergo modifications along the argumentation process. Different epistemic statuses mean, for instance, more or less plausible, true, believable, acceptable (Baker, 2002); these epistemic statuses are modified through argumentation. For Baker (2002), there is a second way in which the epistemic statuses of proposals can be modified, by transforming their meaning through discursive operations, such as negotiations.

To consider which dimensions in the task, teacher strategies, classroom climate, or a combination of these may promote their argumentation competencies, Jiménez-Aleixandre, López, and Erduran (2005) framed the question using Toulmin's (1972) notion of *intellectual ecology,* which he defined as coexisting ideas and features of the social or physical situation that provide a range of opportunities for intellectual innovation. Jiménez-Aleixandre et al. proposed four intertwined dimensions in this classroom intellectual ecology: (a) pedagogical (classroom climate and teacher's strategies); (b) cognitive and metacognitive (including students' reflections about their own learning processes); (c) communicative (as representational modes); and (d) social interactions, which are summarized in Figure 12.2.

Jiménez-Aleixandre et al. (2005) examined the quality of fourth-grade (9- to 10-year-old) students' oral arguments by means of a revised version of Erduran, Simon, and Osborne (2004). The original instrument has a focus on rebuttals, and the revised version added a focus on warrants developed by Jiménez-Aleixandre and her colleagues in Santiago de Compostela. It needs to be noted that this notion of rebuttal means a challenge to the evidence (data or warrant) of the opponent, which is different from the meaning given in Toulmin's (1958) argument pattern. The quality of the students' arguments in five sessions of a 10-day teaching sequence was high: 34 of the 67 arguments contain rebuttals, and 33 do not. In other words, about half of the arguments are placed in Categories 5 or 4 of the coding scheme. The students were not explicitly taught argumentation, so it is suggested that the sustained enculturation in this particular school and classroom culture provided the adequate environment for argumentative competencies to develop. The intellectual ecology represented in Figure 12.2 is an attempt to capture different dimensions in this fourth-grade classroom environment.

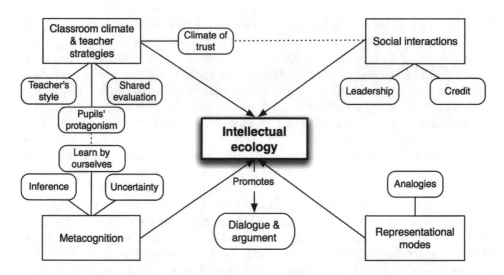

Figure 12.2.   Dimensions in the intellectual ecology of the classroom. From *Argumentative Quality and Intellectual Ecology: A Case Study in Primary School* by M. P. Jiménez-Aleixandre, M. P. López, and S. Erduran, April, 2005. Paper presented at the National Association for Research in Science Teaching annual meeting, Dallas, TX. Reprinted with permission.

Toward a Focus on Tools/Technologies and Methods/Practices in Building/Refining Models

Developments in scientific theory coupled with concomitant advances in material sciences, engineering, and technologies have given rise to radically new ways of observing nature and engaging with phenomena. At the beginning of the 20th century, scientists were debating the existence of atoms and genes; by the end of the century, they were manipulating individual atoms and engaging in genetic engineering. These developments have altered the nature of scientific inquiry and greatly complicated our images of what it means to engage in scientific inquiry and conceptual change. Where once scientific inquiry was principally the domain of unaided sense perception, today scientific inquiry is guided by highly theoretical beliefs that determine the very existence of observational events (e.g., neutrino capture experiments in the ice fields of Antarctica).

One of the important findings from the science studies literature is that not only does scientific knowledge change over time, but so too do the methods of inquiry and the criteria for the evaluation of knowledge change. The accretion growth model of scientific knowledge is no longer tenable. Nor is a model of knowledge growth that appeals to changes in theory commitments alone (e.g., conceptual change models). Changes in research programs that drive the growth of scientific knowledge also can be due to changes in methodological commitments or goal commitments (Duschl & Grandy, 2008). Science studies examining contemporary science practices recognize that both the conceptual frameworks and the methodological practices of science have changed over time.

Changes in methodology are a consequence of new tools, new technologies, and new explanatory models and theories that, in turn, have shaped and will continue to shape scientific knowledge and scientific practices.

Similarly, the dialogical processes of theory development and of dealing with anomalous data occupy a great deal of time and energy on the part of scientists. Importantly, the journey involved in the growth of scientific knowledge reveals the ways in which scientists respond to new data, to new theories that interpret data, or to both. Klahr's contributions to cognitive reasoning in CVS contexts contributed to the dialogical processes regarding development of assessment models of students' learning. Thagard (2007) eloquently elaborated on the dynamics of these practices as they relate to achieving explanatory coherence. Advancing explanatory coherence, he argued, involves theories that deepen and broaden over time by respectively accounting for new facts and providing explanations of why the theory works. These general notions of theory refinement, articulation, deepening, and broadening are missing when we examine domain-general learning strategies like CVS or the "consensus view lists" of NOS (for discussions on measuring NOS, see Duschl & Grandy, 2008; and Duschl & Hamilton, 2011).

In very broad brushstrokes, 20th-century developments in science studies can be divided into three periods. In the first, logical positivism's emphasis on mathematical logic and the hypothetico-deductive method was dominant. Logical positivist views of science held the following assumptions:

- There is an epistemologically significant distinction between observation language and theoretical language that can be made in terms of syntax or grammar.
- Some form of inductive logic would be found that would provide a formal criterion for theory evaluation.
- There is an important dichotomy between contexts of discovery and contexts of justification.

In the 1950s and 1960s, the second period, various writers questioned these and other fundamental assumptions of logical positivism and argued for the relevance of historical and psychological factors in understanding science. Thomas Kuhn introduced the conception of paradigm shifts in the original version of *The Structure of Scientific Revolutions* (Kuhn, 1996) and then revised it in the postscript to the 1970 second edition, introducing the concept of a *disciplinary matrix*. In this disciplinary-matrix view of science, theories play a central role but share the stage with other elements of science, including a social dimension of values and judgments. Although Kuhn saw the scientific communities as essential elements in the cognitive functioning of science, his early work did not present a detailed analysis.

The most recent movements and the third period of the 20th-century philosophy of science can be seen as filling some of the gaps left by Kuhn's undoing of the basic tenets of logical positivism. This movement

- emphasizes the role of models and data construction in the scientific practices of theory development;

- sees the scientific community, and not the individual scientist alone, as an essential part of the scientific process; and
- sees the cognitive scientific processes as a distributed system that includes instruments, forms of representation, and commonly accepted systems for communication and argument.

The contemporary understanding of NOS is the recognition that most of the theory change that occurs in science is not final theory acceptance, but improvement and refinement of a theory (Duschl & Grandy, 2008). What occurs in science is not predominantly the context of discovery or the context of justification as the logical positivists proposed, but the context of theory development and of conceptual modification.

Consideration for both the insights and limitations of logical positivism and early "Kuhnian" responses to logical positivism have expanded our perspectives about NOS, the growth of scientific knowledge, and the goals and limitations of science (for a comprehensive review, see Zammito, 2004). The seven tenets of science proposed by Duschl and Grandy (2008) characterize how the received view of the first period has shifted. The revised tenets reflect the philosophical debates that have emerged since the introduction of Thomas Kuhn's (1996) seminal work, *The Structure of Scientific Revolution,* and, it is important to note, from the postscript to the second edition. In Thagard's (2007) terms, there is no deepening or broadening of explanatory truths over time.

Table 12.1 presents the seven "traditional tenets from logical positivism" headings in column one. Columns two, three, and four respectively present brief descriptions of the "received NOS views," the "reasons for revision," and the "revised NOS views." The table's rows and columns are organized to highlight the reactions, objections, and insights that the seven tenets raised. For each tenet, the contrast between the "traditional" and the "revised" views for NOS is presented. Reading down the traditional "received NOS views" column paints a picture of the commitments held by the logical positivists. Reading down the "revised NOS views" column reveals commitments from those adhering to naturalized philosophical views. The "revised NOS view" stresses the dialogic and dialectical processes/practices of science and does so with respect to conceptual (theories and models) as well as methodological (tools and technologies) changes in scientific inquiry.

The points from the seven tenets in Table 12.1 are placed in an order below that (a) reflects the improvement and refinement practices of scientific inquiry and (b) provides a basis for an expanded scientific method beyond the five-step testing of a hypothesis:

- The bulk of scientific effort is not theory discovery or theory acceptance but theory improvement and refinement.
- Research groups or disciplinary communities are the units of practice for scientific discourse.
- Scientific inquiry involves a complex set of discourse processes.
- The discourse practices of science are organized within a disciplinary matrix of shared exemplars for decisions regarding the (a) values, (b) instruments, (c) methods, (d) models, and (e) evidence to adopt.

Table 12.1. Nature of Science Seven Tenets

Traditional tenet from logical positivism	Received NOS views	Reasons for revision	Revised NOS views
1. There is an important dichotomy between contexts of discovery and contexts of justification.	Logical positivism's focus was on the final products or outcomes of science. Of the two endpoints, justification of knowledge claims was the only relevant issue. How ideas, hypotheses, and intuitions are initially considered or discovered was not relevant.	Theory-change advocates value understanding how the growth of knowledge begins. Perhaps the most important element Kuhn and others added is the recognition that most of the theory change is not final theory acceptance, but improvement and refinement.	The bulk of scientific inquiry is neither the context of discovery nor the context of justification. The dominant context is theory development and conceptual modification. The dialogical processes of theory development and of dealing with anomalous data occupy a great deal of scientists' time and energy.
2. The individual scientist is the basic unit of analysis for understanding science.	Logical positivists believed scientific rationality can be entirely understood in terms of choices by individual scientists.	Kuhn's inclusion of the scientific community as part of the scientific process introduced the idea of research groups or communities of practice as being the unit of scientific discourse. This shift from individual to group produced negative reactions from many philosophers. Including a social dimension was seen as threatening the objectivity and rationality of scientific development. Teams of scientists engage in investigations.	Scientific rationality can be understood in terms of dialogic processes taking place as knowledge claims and beliefs are posited and justified. Scientific discourse is organized within a disciplinary matrix of shared exemplars, for example, values, instruments, methods, models, evidence.

(continued)

Table 12.1. Nature of Science Seven Tenets (*Continued*)

Traditional tenet from logical positivism	Received NOS views	Reasons for revision	Revised NOS views
3. There is an epistemologically significant distinction between observational and theoretical (O/T) languages based on grammar.	Logical positivism focused on the application of logic and on the philosophy of language to analyze scientific claims. Analysis void of contextual and contingent information produces a grammar that fixes criteria for observations.	The O/T distinction debate showed that our ordinary perceptual language is theory laden, what we see is influenced by what we believe. New theories leading to new tools and technologies greatly influenced the nature of observation in science and the representation of information and data.	What counts as observational shifts historically as science acquires new tools, technologies, and theories. Science from the 1700s to the present has made a transition from a sense perception dominated study of nature to a tools, technology, and theory driven study of nature.
4. Some form of inductive logic would be found that would provide a formal criterion for theory evaluation.	There exists an algorithm for theory evaluation. Given a formal logical representation of the theory and data, the algorithm would provide the rational degree of confirmation the data confer on the theory.	Seeking an algorithm for a rational degree of confirmation is hopeless. Scientists working with the same data can rationally come to differing conclusions about which theory is best supported by given evidence. There is ongoing debate about how much variation is rational and how much is influenced by other factors.	Dialogue over the merits of competing data, models, and theories is essential to the process of refining models and theories as well as accepting or rejecting them.

| 5. Scientific theories can most usefully be thought of as sets of sentences in a formal language. | Logical positivists advocated the position that theories are linguistic in character and could be described with deductive-nomological procedures. | Model-based views about the nature of science embrace, where hypothetical-deductive science does not, the dialogic complexities inherent in naturalized accounts of science. Scientific representations and explanations take many different forms: mathematical models, physical models, diagrams, computation models, etc. | Modern developments in science, mathematics, cognitive sciences, and computer sciences have extended the forms of representation in science well beyond strictly linguistic and logical formats. One widespread view is that theories should be thought of as families of models, and the models stand between empirical/conceptual evidence and theoretical explanations. |
| 6. Different scientific frameworks within the same domain are commensurable. | Logical positivists sought to establish criteria that supported the claim that there are normative dimensions to scientific inquiry. The growth of scientific knowledge is a cumulative process. | Science communities are organized within disciplinary matrices. Shared exemplars help to define science communities. Scientific frameworks on different sides of a revolutionary change are incommensurable. Hypothesis testing takes place within more complex frameworks requiring more nuanced strategies for representing and reasoning with evidence. | Different scientific frameworks within the same domain share some common ground. But they can disagree significantly on methodology, models, and/or relevant data. The issue is the extent to which knowledge, beliefs, reasoning, representations, methods, and goals from one research domain map to another research domain. The social and epistemic contexts are complex indeed. |

(*continued*)

Table 12.1.   Nature of Science Seven Tenets (*Continued*)

Traditional tenet from logical positivism	Received NOS views	Reasons for revision	Revised NOS views
7. Scientific development is cumulatively progressive.	Logical positivists held that the growth of scientific knowledge is cumulative and continually progressive. Scientists work with common theory choices.	Theory choice is an important dynamic of doing science and it influences how investigations are designed and conducted. On what grounds (e.g., rational vs. irrational) scientists make such choices is a matter for further research and debate.	The Kuhnian view that "revolutions" involve the abandonment of established guiding conceptions and methods challenges the belief that scientific development is always cumulatively progressive. New guiding conceptions inform what counts as an observation or a theory. Such changes reinforce beliefs that all scientific claims are revisable in principle. Thus, we embrace the notions of the "tentativeness" of knowledge claims and the "responsiveness" of scientific practices.

Note.   From *Teaching Scientific Inquiry: Recommendations for Research and Implementation* (p. 322), by R. Duschl and R. Grandy, 2008, Rotterdam, Netherlands: Sense Publishers. Copyright 2008 by Sense Publishers. Reprinted with permission.

- Scientific inquiry has epistemic and social dimensions, as well as conceptual.
- Changes in scientific knowledge are not just in conceptual understandings alone; important advancements in science are also often the result of technological and methodological changes for conducting observations and making measurements.
- What counts as an observation in science evolves with the introduction of new tools, technologies, and theories.
- Theories can be understood as clusters of models in which the models stand between empirical/conceptual evidence and theoretical explanations.
- Theory and model choices serve as guiding conceptions for deciding "what counts" and are an important dynamic in scientific inquiry.
- Rubrics for a rational degree of confirmation are hopeless; dialogue over merits of alternative models and theories are essential for refining, accepting, or rejecting them and are not reducible to an algorithm.

The expanded scientific method recognizes the role of experiment and hypothesis testing in scientific inquiry, but it emphasizes that the results of experiments are used to advance models and build theories. Thus, the expanded scientific method makes a further recognition that the practices of science involve important dialogic and dialectical practices that function across conceptual, epistemic, and social dimensions.

Concluding Remarks

Looking across the six design principles in Figure 12.1 and the seven tenets in Table 12.1, the bold implication is the need to consider developing an enhanced model of what we communicate to students as scientific methods. The expanded scientific method would be inclusive, not exclusive, of the three sequential images of NOS: hypothetico-deductive experiment driven science, conceptual change theory-driven science, and model-based driven science—hence, the significance of the contributions David Klahr has made in his CVS research examining reasoning in hypothetico-deductive experiment conditions. The implication is that science as a practice has cognitive, social, and epistemological dynamics that are critical to engaging in the discourse and dialogical strategies that are at the core of what it means to be doing scientific inquiry.

The enhanced scientific methods perspective would add four "features" that address opportunities to engage in dialogical processes and practices to the five essential features listed by the NRC (2001):

- Learners are engaged by scientifically oriented questions.
- Learners give priority to evidence, which allows them to develop and evaluate explanations that address scientifically oriented questions.
- Learners formulate explanations from evidence to address scientifically oriented questions.

- Learners evaluate their explanations in light of alternative explanations, particularly those reflecting scientific understanding.
- Learners communicate and justify their proposed explanations.

Following are additional features:

- Learners engage in criticism of their own explanations.
- Learners reflect on alternative explanations that may not have a unique resolution.
- Learners formulate appropriate criticisms of others' explanations.
- Learners respond to criticisms from others.

Consider how each of the seven tenets in Table 12.1 framed by the six design principles in Figure 12.1 has implications for the design of school science with an example of how it might be implemented in a classroom.

1. *Contexts of theory development*—Provide opportunities for students to engage in activities involving the growth of scientific knowledge, that is, to respond to new data, to new theories that interpret data, or to both. Use a dialectical orientation to school science to model how science and scientists are being responsive to anomalous data and worthy alternative conceptual frameworks when refining and modifying theory. The responsive label is preferred over saying that scientific claims are at best only tentative, thus avoiding antiscience connotations that scientific claims, being tentative, are unsupported by evidence or scientific reasoning.
2. *Individual/group inquiry*—Use distributed learning models during investigations. Avoid when possible having all students do the same investigation, so that individuals/small groups complete components of an inquiry and then report back to the large group the data and the evidence they obtain. Whole class discussions can then focus on a larger corpus of data and evidence in the development of explanations.
3. *Observation/theory*—Use dialectical processes regarding which theoretical frameworks are being used as guiding conceptions when critiquing or making decisions about what data to collect, what questions to ask, what data to use as evidence, among others.
4. *Theory evaluation*—Engage learners in the development of criteria for theory/explanation evaluation. This process includes making decisions regarding when it is plausible to pursue the development and interrogation of theory. Furthermore, there is the need to have learners consider alternative explanations and participate in dialogical activities that debate and argue the merits/demerits of the alternative models and theories.
5. *Theory language*—Scientific explanations are not strictly linguistic statements. Scientists develop and use physical models, computational models, mathematical models, and iconic models, among others, to explain scientific investigations. So, too, should students be encouraged

to develop and to use model-based approaches in scientific investigations and inquiry.

6. *Shared exemplars*—Provide attention to the theoretical or model-based frameworks that guide scientific inquiry. Establish shared classroom learning goals by organizing curriculum and instruction around the use of core science ideas, driving questions, and immersion units. Establish shared exemplars by requesting students' claims be supported by sources of critical evidence. Develop in students the idea that science is about engagement in theory change, model building, and revision.

7. *Scientific progress*—provide learners opportunities to engage in the examination of alternative explanations and guiding conceptions when developing accounts of phenomena and mechanisms. Allocate room in the curriculum for learners to engage in serious discussions about the criteria that are used to assess and make judgments about knowledge claims.

Future research on science learning and teaching needs to focus more on learning in context. Research is needed on developmental trajectories/progressions that examine learning and reasoning. Such research, although informed by lab studies, must be grounded in the study of learning environments in which student learning is examined in the context(s) of instruction-assisted development with mediation by teachers, educators, parents, or peers. Additional insights for the design of learning environments come from research by Herrenkohl and Guerra (1998); Rosebery, Warren, and Conant (1992); Smith, Maclin, Houghton, and Hennessey (2000); and van Zee and Minstrell (1997). Rosebery et al.'s study spanned an entire school year, whereas Smith et al. followed a cohort of students for several years with the same teacher. Both studies used classroom practices that place a heavy emphasis on (a) requiring evidence for claims, (b) evaluating the fit of new ideas to data, (c) providing justifications for specific claims, and (d) examining methods for generating data. Engle and Conant (2002), reporting on the pioneering "communities of learners" research by Ann Brown (1997), referred to such classroom discourse as "productive disciplinary engagement" when it is grounded in the disciplinary norms and practices for both social and cognitive activity.

The emerging consensus position is to organize and align curriculum, instruction, and assessment and to do so around core knowledge, enduring understandings, and learning progressions. The research agenda is complex given the new images we have of science through naturalized philosophy of science, of capable young learners, of scientific participatory practices being more than doing investigations and conducting inquiry, and of the importance of context when constructing and evaluating scientific knowledge. Here, then, are some of the critical areas for research and development identified in *Taking Science to School* (Duschl et al., 2007, pp. 351–355):

- Research is needed on students' understanding of how scientific knowledge is constructed and how they come to understand and negotiate different knowledge communities.

- More research is needed to further elaborate the interplay between domain-specific and domain-general knowledge over the course of development and to better understand how to leverage these interconnections to inform instructional models.
- Extensive research and development efforts are needed before learning progressions are well established and tested. Longitudinal studies over multiple ages are particularly important to get better understandings of continuities and discontinuities in students' understanding across grades.
- Research is needed to develop a better understanding of whether and how instruction should change with children's development. Research on curriculum materials is a critical area.
- Research on supporting science learning from culturally, linguistically, and socioeconomically diverse students is an area of critical need.

References

Baker, M. (2002). Argumentation interactions, discursive operations and learning to model in science. In P. Brna, M. Baker, K. Stenning, & A. Tiberghein (Eds.), *The role of communication in learning to model* (pp. 303–324). Mahwah, NJ: Erlbaum.

Brown, A. L. (1997). Transforming schools into communities of thinking and learning about serious matters. *American Psychologist, 52,* 399–413. doi:10.1037/0003-066X.52.4.399

Duschl, R. (2008). Science education in 3-part harmony: Balancing conceptual, epistemic and social learning goals. In J. Green, A. Luke, & G. Kelly (Eds.), *Review of research in education* (Vol. 32, pp. 286–291). Washington, DC: American Educational Research Association.

Duschl, R., & Grandy, R. (Eds.). (2008). *Teaching scientific inquiry: Recommendations for research and implementation.* Rotterdam, the Netherlands: Sense.

Duschl, R., & Hamilton, R. (2011). Learning science. In R. Mayer & P. Alexander (Eds.), *Handbook of research on learning and instruction* (pp. 78–107). New York, NY: Routledge.

Duschl, R., Schweingruber, H., & Shouse, A. (Eds.). (2007). National Research Council, Committee on Science Learning, Kindergarten Through Eighth Grade. *Taking science to school: Learning and teaching science kindergarten to eight grade.* Washington, DC: National Academies Press.

Engle, R. A., & Conant, F. C. (2002). Guiding principles for fostering productive disciplinary engagement: Explaining an emergent argument in a community of learners classroom. *Cognition and Instruction, 20,* 399–483. doi:10.1207/S1532690XCI2004_1

Erduran, S., & Jiménez-Aleixandre, M. P. (Eds.). (2008). *Argumentation in science education: Perspectives from classroom-based research.* Dordrecht, the Netherlands: Springer.

Erduran, S., Simon, S., & Osborne, J. (2004). TAPping into argumentation: Developments in the use of Toulmin's argument pattern in studying science discourse. *Science Education, 88,* 915–933. doi:10.1002/sce.20012

Ford, M. (2008a). Disciplinary authority and accountability in scientific practice and learning. *Science Education, 92,* 404–423. doi:10.1002/sce.20263

Ford, M. (2008b). "Grasp of practice" as a reasoning resource for inquiry and nature of science understanding. *Science & Education, 17,* 147–177. doi:10.1007/s11191-006-9045-7

Ford, M., & Forman, E. A. (2006). Redefining disciplinary learning in classroom contexts. *Review of Research in Education, 30,* 1–32. doi:10.3102/0091732X030001001

Habermas, J. (1981). *The theory of communicative action.* Boston, MA: Beacon Press.

Herrenkohl, L., & Guerra, M. (1998). Participant structures, scientific discourse, and student engagement in fourth grade. *Cognition and Instruction, 16,* 431–473. doi:10.1207/s1532690 xci1604_3

Jiménez-Aleixandre, M. P. (2008). Designing argumentation learning environments. In S. Erduran & M. P. Jiménez-Aleixandre (Eds.), *Argumentation in science education: Perspectives from classroom-based research* (pp. 91–115). Dordrecht, the Netherlands: Springer.

Jiménez-Aleixandre, M. P., & Erduran, S. (2008). Argumentation in science education: An overview. In S. Erduran & M. P. Jimenez-Aleixandre (Eds.), *Argumentation in science education: Perspectives from classroom-based research* (pp. 3–27). Dordrecht, the Netherlands: Springer.

Jiménez-Aleixandre, M. P., López, R., & Erduran, S. (2005, April). *Argumentative quality and intellectual ecology: A case study in primary school.* Paper presented at the National Association for Research in Science Teaching annual meeting, Dallas, TX.

Jiménez-Aleixandre, M. P., & Puig, B. (in press). Argumentation, evidence evaluation and critical thinking. In B. Fraser, K. Tobin, & C. McRobbie (Eds.), *Second international handbook of science education.* Dordrecht, the Netherlands: Springer.

Kelly, G. (2008). Inquiry, activity and epistemic practice. In R. Duschl & R. Grandy (Eds.), *Teaching scientific inquiry: Recommendations for research and implementation* (pp. 99–117). Rotterdam, the Netherlands: Sense.

Kelly, G., McDonald, S., & Wickman, P. (in press). Science learning and epistemology. In B. Fraser & K. Tobin (Eds.), *Second international handbook of science education.* Dordrecht, the Netherlands: Springer.

Klahr, D. (2009). "To every thing there is a season and a time to every purpose under the heavens": What about direct instruction? In S. Tobias & T. Duffy (Eds.), *Constructivist instruction: Success or failure* (pp. 291–310). New York, NY: Routledge.

Klahr, D., Fay, A., & Dunbar, K. (1993). Heuristics for scientific experimentation: A developmental study. *Cognitive Psychology, 25,* 111–146. doi:10.1006/cogp.1993.1003

Klahr, D., & Nigam, M. (2004). The equivalence of learning paths in early science instruction: Effects of direct instruction and discovery learning. *Psychological Science, 15,* 661–667.

Klahr, D., Triona, M., & Williams, C. (2007). Hands on what? The relative effectiveness of physical vs. virtual materials in an engineering design project by middle school children. *Journal of Research in Science Teaching, 44,* 183–203. doi:10.1002/tea.20152

Kuhn, T. (1996). *The structure of scientific revolutions* (3rd ed.). Chicago, IL: University of Chicago Press.

Lehrer, R., & Schauble, L. (2006). Cultivating model-based reasoning in science education. In K. Sawyer (Ed.), *The Cambridge handbook of the learning sciences* (371–388). New York, NY: Cambridge University Press.

Lehrer, R., Schauble, L., & Lucas, D. (2008). Supporting development of the epistemology of inquiry. *Cognitive Development, 23,* 512–529. doi:10.1016/j.cogdev.2008.09.001

Longino, H. E. (1990). *Science as a social knowledge.* Princeton, NJ: Princeton University Press.

Longino, H. E. (2008). Philosophical issues and next steps for research. In R. Duschl & R. Grandy (Eds.), *Teaching scientific inquiry: Recommendations for research and implementation* (pp. 134–137). Rotterdam, the Netherlands: Sense.

National Research Council. (2001). *Knowing what students know: The science and design of educational assessment.* Washington, DC: National Academies Press.

Pea, R. (1993). Distributed intelligence and designs for education. In G. Salomon (Ed.), *Distributed cognitions: Psychological and educational considerations* (pp. 47–87). Cambridge, England: Cambridge University Press.

Posner, G. J., Strike, K. A., Hewson, P. W., & Gertzog, W. A. (1982). Accommodation of a scientific conception: Towards a theory of conceptual change. *Science Education, 66,* 211–227. doi:10.1002/sce.3730660207

Puig, B., & Jiménez-Aleixandre, M. P. (2009, August/September). *Use of evidence and critical thinking about determinist claims on race and intelligence.* Paper presented at the European Science Education Research conference, Istanbul, Turkey.

Rosebery, A. S., Warren, B., & Conant, F. (1992). Appropriating scientific discourse: Findings from language minority classrooms. *Journal of the Learning Sciences, 2,* 61–94. doi:10.1207/s15327809jls0201_2

Smith, C., Maclin, D., Houghton, C., & Hennessey, M. G. (2000). Sixth-grade students' epistemologies of science: The impact of school science experience on epistemological development. *Cognition and Instruction, 18,* 349–422. doi:10.1207/S1532690XCI1803_3

Smith, C., Wiser, M., Anderson, C. A., & Krajcik, J. (2006). Implications of research on children's learning for standards and assessment: A proposed learning progression for matter and atomic-molecular theory. *Measurement: Interdisciplinary Research and Perspectives, 4,* 1–98. doi:10.1080/15366367.2006.9678570

Thagard, P. (2007). Coherence, truth, and the development of scientific knowledge. *Philosophy of Science, 74,* 28–47. doi:10.1086/520941

Toulmin, S. (1958). *The uses of argument.* New York, NY: Cambridge University Press.

Toulmin, S. (1972). *Human understanding. Vol. I. The collective use and evolution of concepts.* Princeton, NJ: Princeton University Press.

van Zee, E., & Minstrell, J. (1997). Using questioning to guide student thinking. *Journal of the Learning Sciences, 6,* 227–269. doi:10.1207/s15327809jls0602_3

Zammito, J. H. (2004). *A nice derangement of epistemes: Post-positivism in the study of science from Quine to Latour.* Chicago, IL: University of Chicago Press.

13

Patterns, Rules, and Discoveries in Life and in Science

David Klahr

This chapter includes two relatively distinct reflections on the journey from child to scientist. In the autobiographical part, I describe a series of important events along that path. The autobiographical part is, necessarily, very personal. I reflect on how early events in my life have influenced the way I think and feel about doing science. The second part is about science, in particular, about how the "child as scientist" discovers regularities in the world, encodes and abstracts them, and uses them to make predictions. The broad domain has to do with quantitative development, which happens to be the topic on which I began my career in cognitive development, so that even the second part of this chapter has an autobiographical flavor to it. I will describe an unsolved question about children's thinking and speculate about how it might be investigated in the future. The question comes from the area of children's early numerical thinking, an area in which some challenging questions remain unanswered.

A Child's Path to Science: From Sorting, Surveying, Satellites, and Serendipity at Stanford, to Computer Simulations

The chapters in this volume represent a synthesis of current ideas in cognitive development, scientific reasoning, and science education, much of it based on research initiated in the early 1970s by several of the contributors to this volume, as well as by my collaborators and me. In reading these chapters, I have had the luxury to reflect on personal questions that don't usually arise in the normal day-to-day plying of one's trade. They are questions such as: "What are the forces and experiences in my formative years that profoundly influenced the way I *think* about my research and the way that I *feel* about it?" "What satisfies, gratifies,

My deepest thanks to the organizers and editors of this Festschrift: Jeff Shrager, Kevin Dunbar, and—most of all—Sharon Carver, for the energy, generosity, respect, and affection that they put into the project. I am also indebted to Audrey Russo, the administrative assistant for the symposium, for her creativity, perseverance, enthusiasm, and assistance not only with respect to this chapter but in all my professional activities. Finally, but certainly not least, I offer my thanks and love to my wife for always finding the right balance of curiosity, challenge, and sustenance for both the affective and the cognitive aspects of my life.

motivates, and excites me, and why?" "What happened to me along the way, and how do those events continue to influence me?" Table 13.1 lists the answers to these questions in very brief form; in this section of the chapter, I expand and explain each of them.

Category Formation and Parental Approval: Logic and Love

We would like to think that all parents want to find contexts and activities in which they can show that they love and support their children. But sometimes it takes a little parental ingenuity to find something that the kids are good at and that the parents also value.

My father had been a pretty good athlete in his youth. When I was growing up, he would occasionally show me a photo, taken around 1920, of his high school football team from P.S. 17, in New York. In the photo, standing directly behind my dad at center, stands quarterback Lou Gehrig; he played football long before he became a baseball icon. My dad clearly valued his early comradeship with someone who went on to become a famous and beloved athlete, and it made his interest in sports very strong. He valued athletics, and he certainly would have encouraged and supported me if I had gotten involved in sports. However, I was definitely not the kind of kid whose natural athleticism was evident from the moment one saw him. As my sister often reminded me during my preteen and early teen years, I was chubby, pigeon-toed, nearsighted, timid, and pretty uncoordinated. This physique certainly did not bode well for my ever making my dad proud of my performance on the local Little League team. But my dad was very ingenious in finding something for me to do that (a) I was good at and (b) he really valued. And that activity had, I believe, a profound impact on my love of science.

Throughout my childhood in Connecticut, my parents owned and operated the Stamford Watch Hospital, a small mom-and-pop jewelry and watch repair business where, according to their newspaper and radio ads, "the sick always recovered." In those days—several years before quartz crystals resonating at 2^{15} Hz replaced the delicate hairspring balance wheels that ticked and tocked—watches were mechanical devices consisting of gears, levers, springs, bearings, and other delicate moving parts that needed to be wound daily and cleaned, oiled, and adjusted every year or so. After my dad would clean and repair a watch, he would have to let it run for a couple of days to make sure it kept accurate time. But a single winding of the watch lasted for only about 24 hours before the watch would come to a stop, so he had to wind them daily. This schedule meant that, even on Sundays and holidays, he had to go to the store to adjust and wind all the watches that were being checked.[1] On many occasions I would accompany him. There was little for me to do during the hour or so that it took

---

[1]Clearly, this, and many other, aspects of my parents' life as shopkeepers meant that their work was never done. Perhaps this model was another kind of early influence on my own career, one that I hadn't recognized until writing this chapter. There is no doubt that academic life includes an unrelenting set of time-urgent demands that blur the line between "working hours" and "nonworking hours"—demands that I, and all of my successful colleagues, seem to have accepted and integrated into our lives.

Table 13.1. Personal Shaping Forces, Contexts, and Lessons Learned

Career point	Topic	Context	Forces	Lesson learned
Preteen	Category formation and parental approval: logic and love	Helping my father in his business by sorting watch parts	Parental approbation and appreciation	Classification requires creativity. I can do it. It is valued.
Teen and college	Abstract representations of reality: surveys and maps	After-school job as surveyor's assistant	Intellectual appreciation of "real-world" measurement process	Measurement processes abstract, refine, simplify, but also create knowledge
Postcollege	Knowledge-driven search trumps trial and error	Programmer at NORAD, tracking satellites and missiles	Complex computations on limited computing devices	Advances arise from ingenious problem formulations, not brute force computation.
Early grad school	Serendipity at Stanford	Summer conference on "Learning and the Educational Process" at Stanford	Exposure and introduction to an entirely new set of problems: Piaget's theory of cognitive development	"Secret weapons" can be brought to bear on well-established problems.

NORAD = North American Aerospace Defense Command.

him to wind, check, and adjust all of the current patients in the Stamford Watch Hospital, but he was very clever. He found a way to keep me occupied, to be of use to him, and to feel good about being useful. Although I did not realize it at the time, that experience had an enduring impact.

My father would collect all the excess watch parts on his workbench: an accumulated pile of pushpins, stems, crowns, springs, hands, bearings, and gears. He would put the pile into an empty cigar box, seat me at a table in the back of the store, dump the pile on the table, spread it out, hand me a couple of plastic boxes partitioned into a grid of little compartments, and say "sort this stuff." Then he would go to wind and adjust a few dozen "recovering" watches, leaving me to organize the items so that when he needed a specific part he could find it quickly.

As you might imagine, mapping the multidimensional space that these items occupied into the two-dimensional grid provided by the plastic boxes was a fascinating challenge. Should it be organized by material, by function, by size, by shape? Which should be the primary criterion; which the secondary? I used all kinds of different schemes, changing them from one month to the next. When I was finished, I would proudly present the sorted and categorized collection to my father, describing the latest organizational scheme that I had used.

He always seemed pleased. He would take my sorted assemblage and place it on his workbench, thereby acknowledging that my efforts had, indeed, been useful to him. During the next week or so, it was very gratifying for me to come into the store and see my little arrangement at his right-hand side on the work-bench. My father was not a clinical psychologist; in fact, he may have never even heard the term. Moreover, in that era, and particularly in my family, one simply did not talk about self-esteem, parental approval, self-efficacy, or anything more "psychological" than being in a good mood or a bad mood. But my father was very wise because he had invented a way to give me an opportunity to discover that the product of my thinking—of my ability to create schemes for classifying and organizing—could be of value and practical use to him and, indirectly, to the entire family, because it was of use to the business. This experience had a deep impact on my psyche, though I did not realize it at the time. I certainly could not have articulated what was happening here, that it was something quite wonderful: cognition, invention, problem solving, and precision rewarded by love, approval, and practical utility!

I have been somewhat of a compulsive sorter ever since. In my personal life, it's my tools, my photos, my books, my children's toys; I'm always arranging and rearranging them. Of course, the kinds of cognitive processes that support my little "classification obsession" are essential to the way that we function as scientists. A fundamental part of our work is to categorize, classify, and sys-tematically present our results. Thus, even 60 years later, this early formative experience in my father's shop—one that engaged both my intellect and affect—still serves as a source of my enjoyment and satisfaction as a scientist.

Abstract Representations of Reality: Surveys and Maps

The moral of this next story is that when we measure, record, and analyze some-thing in the real world, we create knowledge, but that knowledge is inherently approximate and intentionally abstract. The abstraction process is elegant, and the approximation process is unavoidable. Moreover, participating in both processes can be deeply satisfying, as they were for me when I first experienced them. As in the first example, this resonance is something that I did not realize when I first encountered it, but that, as I reflect on the deeper forces that have kept me on the path of science, seems to have been very important.

When I was in high school and college, I worked after school, and for a couple of summers, as a surveyor's assistant. We did property surveys, ran lines for new roads and sewers, collected data for boundary disputes, surveyed the scenes of traffic accidents, and did all the other sorts of things done by survey crews with their tripods, transits, and plumb bobs.

A typical job might be one in which we were hired to make a property map. We would arrive with our beat-up Willys Jeep, and I would take the transit out of its box, set it on the tripod, and get the steel measuring tape. My job was to schlep the equipment, hold the "rod" for the guy looking through the transit, cut through brush so as to create a line of sight for the surveyor and his transit, and to do other grunt work. But I watched what these guys did, and I was fascinated. From the transit they would read, as accurately as possible from the vernier scale on the circumference of the transit base, the exact angle, to minutes and seconds of arc, of each turn of the transit to the next survey point. Then they would measure the distance from one point in the ground to another (e.g., a corner of the lot, an edge of the house or the driveway) with a 100-ft steel measuring tape, as one of us held a plumb bob as closely as possible over a survey point in the ground, and we would pull the tape taut to a prespecified load on a small spring-tension measuring device, so that we knew, for example, that we had exactly 10 lb of horizontal force to control for the catenary sag in the tape.

For each measurement, the survey chief would carefully pencil an entry into his battered field book. (No computers in those days!) Only later did I realize that no matter how hard we tried or how careful we were, there was always some error: in reading the vernier scales on the transit; or in locating the plumb bob precisely over a survey point in the ground; or in measuring distances, even with a steel tape and the tension corrections. Of course, I knew that the stuff we did in science lab in school was always full of errors, but I thought of error as a kind of mistake rather than an inherent aspect of measurement. The important lesson I learned, but surely never explicitly articulated, in my surveying days was that error is unavoidable in science.

But there was a more important lesson, and it was more abstract, and, for me, more profound. Once we returned to the office, I would watch as the information from the field book was transformed into a map, with the help of straightedge and compass. The challenge was to start at a specific point on the paper and then draw straight lines and intersecting angles at scale, such that they would correspond to the real-world angular and linear measurements. The Holy Grail in this endeavor was to get the end point of the final line on the paper to end precisely on top of the start point of the first line. This "closing the survey" resulted in a lot of satisfaction and pride among the survey crew.

As I observed this process, I was fascinated with the way in which all of our efforts in the field, in the real world, with stumps and bumps, rocks and buildings, and briars and mud, would be transcribed from the field books into maps, in which the physical properties had been transformed into a symbolic abstraction. Much was lost, but *what was essential for the purposes of the survey had been retained.* Moreover, *some knowledge existed in the abstractions that did not exist in the real world.* The distances, angles, elevations, and contour lines all culminated in a succinct simplification that revealed new relations among the elements.

Isn't that what do we do as psychologists? We might be studying scientific reasoning or problem solving, language acquisition or number concepts, but in all cases, we extract from the richness of each individual case only what is of interest to us, and we leave the rest behind. In the kind of work with which I am most familiar, the primary yield from many hours of data collection with many children is a spreadsheet, with columns for the various conditions and measurements and rows for the children. That is, each child's response to our challenges becomes a row in a spreadsheet. That's all that's left. That's all we want to examine. We have retained what's essential for our purposes and discarded the rest: the children's voices, smiles, cute behaviors, funny but irrelevant comments, and so on. We go from 50 children to 50 rows in a spread-sheet, and then we abstract again. We take the data, we pour it into our statistics package, and we aggregate and simplify even further in order to tell our story. We present effects, contrasts, and d' values. By selective simplification, we have created a new entity, a new kind of knowledge, that did not exist until we did those transformations. The point of this lesson is the direct analogy between the translation from the physical world to the surveyor's field notes to the final map, on the one hand, and from the real children, to our data sheets and our extracted statistical models, on the other.

In hindsight, I realize that I found this surveying process so interesting, challenging, and satisfying because the job came with two powerful affective components. First, it had high prestige among my nerdy friends because I had been chosen for the position—ahead of my classmates—on the basis of my physics teacher's recommendation of me as technically competent and reliable. Second, it had high status, even more broadly, because surveying was associated with macho construction jobs, with being outdoors, and with working under severe, and occasionally somewhat dangerous, conditions. So the affective aspect was tremendously fulfilling, and the intellectual part is strongly associated with what we do as researchers. That is, the process of doing research is just like what used to happen in my surveying days when we would go from the survey in the damp, muddy, buggy field to the map or blueprint based on the survey. I'm convinced that my early affective and cognitive experiences as a sur-veyor's assistant gave me a deeply embedded, although unarticulated, under-standing of and attachment to both the elegance and limitations of the research process.

Knowledge-Driven Search Trumps Trial and Error

In graduate school, I began to learn about formal models of problem solving and decision making, and about the profound difference in efficiency of knowledge-driven search over trial-and-error search. I also discovered that I had already had a personal experience in which I had seen this contrast in action—a personal experience that, when I eventually encountered a formal description of it, really rang a bell.

My first job after graduating from college was as a computer programmer for Wolf Research and Development Company, a very small company in Boston that had several air force contracts involving computer programming. My first assignment was to work on what we then called "an adaptive program" but which today would look like some pretty simple machine learning work. That was the sort of thing that had attracted me to the job, because my senior thesis at MIT involved a primitive bit of artificial intelligence—writing a program that learned how to play the game Nim by watching an expert play it.[2] However, Wolf also did a lot of bread-and-butter work that was mainly taking data in one format and converting it to another, for example, taking readings from a radar set based on azimuth, elevation, and distance from the radar site and converting them to latitude and longitude. The tasks were pretty straight-forward conceptually; however, in those days of millisecond machines with only 2,000 words of memory, even these mundane tasks took a lot of ingenuity. After I had been at Wolf for a year or so, they landed a big contract with the North American Aerospace Defense Command (NORAD) in Colorado Springs, and being young, single, and eager to travel, I jumped at the chance to move west to work on the project.

As anyone over 50 will recall, these were very serious and crazy times. We were engaged in a cold war with the U.S.S.R., and the fundamental military strategy was called mutually assured destruction, or MAD. And mad it was. The basic idea was for each side to guarantee that if one side attacked the other side would immediately counterattack. Each side knew that it could not intercept the other's nuclear-armed intercontinental ballistic missiles, but each also knew that it could launch enough missiles of its own to destroy the initial attacker, even while being destroyed itself. So nobody wins, and everybody loses. NORAD played a key role in this astoundingly insane zeitgeist because its job was to determine whether anything coming over the horizon was a missile. This decision might not seem to have been much of a challenge because the United States had enormous radars—approximately the size of a football field tipped on its side—sitting in Alaska, Turkey, and England, pointed toward Russia, scanning the horizon.

However, there *was* a problem, because even in the early 1960s a lot of objects—ranging from exploded rocket boosters to actual nuts and bolts—were coming over the horizon every hour, and they were all harmless. Even then, there were many objects in near earth orbit.[3] So the big radars peering over the horizon were seeing a lot of moving objects and sending the signals of their tracks to NORAD, at which point our computers would try to determine whether any of these were in a ballistic trajectory—indicating that the Russians had launched

---

[2]When you tire of reading this chapter, try this: http://www.archimedes-lab.org/game_nim/nim.html#
[3]Today there are an estimated 20,000 objects at least as large as an apple, and perhaps half a million smaller objects, in near earth orbit. In fact, Vanguard I, launched in 1958, is still in earth orbit. These objects pose an ever-increasing danger to space missions.

their missiles—or in an orbital trajectory, indicative of harmless pieces of metal circling the earth. These computations had to be completed quickly because it takes only about 15 minutes for a nuclear-armed ICBM to get from launch to target. They also had to be done correctly because a false negative meant the end of New York or Washington or our building in Colorado Springs![4] A false positive meant the end of civilization.

The basic computational problem was to match the "track" of the sighted object to either a ballistic or an orbital trajectory. For a single object, this would not have been much of a challenge, even with the existing computational power. But, as noted above, there were many objects and thus many tracks to compute— long before the days of parallel computers. Of course, we did not have much computational power, certainly not by today's standards. NORAD's state- of-the-art computer was the Philco 2000: 32K memory, a 1M disk, and 22K multiplications per second. (The nontechnical reader might think of it this way: Your cell phone has about 2,000 times as much memory as the computer at the heart of the defense system of the so-called free world in the 1960s.)

The programming teams tried various clever ways to do this discrimination as efficiently as possible. Of course, it was all in assembler code, so it was very labor intensive. *And then someone had a brilliant idea.* So brilliant, and so obvi- ous, that it made a deep impression on me. *Instead of treating each observation as something totally unknown, make use of what you already know.*

You know that object X is in orbit, and that means you can predict exactly where and when it should come over the horizon in about 90 minutes. Rather than treat each sighting as if you know nothing, once you know what you are looking at on the horizon *now,* just revise its orbital path a bit and *predict* where it should show up the next time around—and you have plenty of time to do it. If, when you look at the first few blips that you think are object X, and those blips fit the prediction, then you are done with that guy—and all the data associated with that sighting—for another 90 minutes. You just have to make a slight revision to the known orbit. If it's *not* there, then it blew up or disintegrated on its last trip around. And that leaves you lots of computational power to focus on the remaining unexpected blips on the horizon. Simple and elegant: *Knowledge trumps brute-force computation.* Theory-guided search is the way to go!

I wish I'd thought of that, but I didn't. However, I never forgot the lesson. Always ask yourself, "What do I already know?" before starting a complicated search. To put it in terms that Kevin Dunbar, Anne Fay, Chris Schunn, and I used in our work on scientific reasoning (Klahr, Fay, & Dunbar, 1993; Schunn & Klahr, 1992, 1996), your location in the hypothesis space should guide your search in the experiment space. Little did I know at the time that my experi- ence of peering into real space would influence my research in cognitive spaces. Even today, with all of the incredible computing power available to us, the big advances in computer science come from ingenious formulations of problems, rather than from brute-force computation.

---

[4]When I worked at NORAD, it had not yet moved into the "hard site," hundreds of feet underground in Cheyenne Mountain. Our building was called a "soft site."

Serendipity at Stanford

So much for introspections on early influences. But while I have been focusing on the ways in which specific aspects of my varied experiences have contributed to the attraction and satisfaction of my career as a scientist, I have yet to explain how, given my engineering and programming background, I became a particular kind of scientist—one with an interest in cognitive and developmental psychology. That requires one more personal anecdote, about an event that was truly transformative—and entirely serendipitous, for it redirected me from one kind of scientific career to another.

The first step on the path to that event was made in fall 1962, when I left the lovely town of Colorado Springs, nestled at the foot of Pikes Peak, and drove to smoky Pittsburgh in my hot little TR3 sports car, to enter a PhD program in organizational behavior in the Graduate School of Industrial Administration (GSIA) at Carnegie Tech (now called the Tepper School of Business at Carnegie Mellon University). I had been attracted to that program because Herb Simon and Allan Newell were at Carnegie Tech as central players in what came to be called "the cognitive revolution" in the late 1950s and early 1960s; GSIA seemed an ideal place to pursue my long-standing interest in doing intelligent things with computers.

After a couple of years of courses in organization theory, economics, and management decision making in a PhD program that Newell and Simon called "Systems and Communication Sciences" (the precursor to what became Carnegie Mellon's School of Computer Science), I had just begun to formulate my dissertation topic on using multidimensional scaling techniques (Kruskal, 1963) to characterize the decision-making process of college admissions officers (Klahr, 1969a). But I was still doing background reading and not fully engaged in the work.[5] Along the way, I had learned how to program in one of the then-novel list-programming languages, called IPL-V.[6]

Thus, in spring 1965, when I was about halfway through my graduate program in GSIA, I happened to be schmoozing with one of the GSIA faculty, Walter Reitman.[7] I asked him what his summer plans were, and he told me he was going to a 6-week summer conference at Stanford.

"Sounds nice," I said.

"Want to come?" he asked. "I could use a teaching assistant on how to construct cognitive models in IPL-V."

---

[5]However, I was sufficiently interested in multidimensional scaling to publish a paper on the topic that became one of my most widely cited, even though I never did another psychometric paper (Klahr, 1969b).

[6]This was Carnegie Tech's competitor with MIT's LISP. Although IPL preceded LISP by a couple of years, LISP went on to completely dominate AI programming. Nevertheless, IPL was the language in which many of the landmark programs in AI (EPAM, the Logic Theorist, and the early chess programs) were created.

[7]Reitman was a true innovator who challenged the seriality of the Newell and Simon approach to cognition by proposing a radically different computational architecture that he called "Argus," inventing, in effect, connectionist computational concepts 20 years before the beginning of PDP modeling (Reitman, 1964, 1965). He was also the founding editor of the journal *Cognitive Psychology* in 1970.

It didn't take a lot of thought before I agreed. The idea of 6 weeks at Stanford sure sounded nicer than another hot summer in smoky and sooty Pittsburgh, so off I went.

The Conference on Learning and the Educational Process, sponsored by the Social Science Research Council, was decades ahead of its time. Its goal was "to stimulate the thought of any person seriously interested in research approaches to the problems in education" (Krumboltz, 1965, p. ix). From my perspective, it more than achieved its goals because it certainly stimulated my thought, and I was not even interested in "research approaches to the problems in education" at the time! To be honest, I was just looking for a pleasant summer in the Bay Area. Suddenly I was thrown into an intense, highly interactive, richly debated conversation with many of the giants (or giants-to-be) in the field: Robert Gagné, Richard Atkinson, Lee Cronbach, Daniel Berlyne, Jerry Kagan, John Carroll, Bob Glaser, David Premack, Hiroshi Azuma, John MacNamara, and Richard Snow,[8] among others. Not that I knew they were giants—remember, I was coming from a background first in engineering, then organizational behavior, with no connection whatsoever to what we now call the *education sciences*— but I was certainly dazzled by the clarity of their thought, the richness of the problems they were discussing, and the importance of the challenges they were addressing. I have remained interested in cognition and instruction ever since (Klahr, 1976; Carver & Klahr, 2001). In fact, I view the Stanford conference as the intellectual precursor of the predoctoral training program in the education sciences that my colleagues and I created at Carnegie Mellon half a dozen years ago.[9] But the really profound influence of the Stanford conference was not that it stimulated my interest in educational research but, rather, that it turned me toward a career of research on cognitive development.

Here is how it happened. Two or 3 days into the conference, I initiated a conversation after dinner with a cheerful young Scotsman who had recently completed his PhD in education from the University Warwick in England. His name was Iain Wallace,[10] and he opened the conversation with the kind of thing that one does at such conferences.

"What do you do?" he asked.

I replied, in what I regretfully admit was probably a cocksure tone, "Oh, I write complex computer models of thinking and problem solving," and then I launched into an extensive discourse on all the wonderful things going on at Carnegie Tech. I went on for about an hour, at which point I dimly recalled that the conventions of social discourse suggest that, in this sort of situation, you should ask other people what *they* do.

Klahr:	Oh, and what do you do?
Wallace:	Well, I'm a Piagetian.
Klahr:	What's that?
Wallace:	What do you mean, "What's that?"
Klahr:	What's a Piagetian?

---

[8]I estimate that the correlation between a reader's age and the number of recognized names on this list is > .9.

[9]http://www.cmu.edu/pier/

[10]Actually, John Gilbert Wallace, but "Iain" to friends and family.

Wallace: Oh, someone who studies Piaget.
Klahr: Who? Who's Piaget? Isn't there a watch brand called "Piaget"?

They say ignorance is bliss, but such unadulterated ignorance is rare, and I sure had a pure form of it with respect to Piaget and cognitive development at the start of the summer of 1965!

Undaunted, and quite eloquently, Iain began. He told me who Piaget was and the problems that he was addressing. I learned that Piaget was interested in cognitive structures. I learned about his ingenious empirical studies with young children (often his own children!). As I listened to Iain's lucid articulation of the fascinating set of phenomena, questions, procedures, and proposed solutions that make up Piaget's "genetic epistemology," I learned that Piaget had formulated his stage theory in the context of a kind of modified algebraic representation and that his fundamental interest was in cognitive change and dynamic processes. It occurred to me that perhaps Piaget was using an inadequate formalism with which to cast his theory. I said to Iain, "But algebra is the wrong language, because it's static, and computational models are expressed in a dynamic language. Wouldn't it be interesting to try to formulate computational models of the kind of phenomena that Piaget studies: number conservation, class inclusion, and transitivity? Perhaps you and I could collaborate on a project in which we applied 'the Carnegie Tech approach' to problems of cognitive development."

He agreed, and during the remaining weeks of the conference, we began to formulate plans for finding a way for the two of us to collaborate. For me, this was not easy because I was still on a career track headed toward a faculty position in the decision-making territory of the business school world, which was not exactly a hotbed of interest, support, or activity in computational models of number conservation. The challenge for me was to find some funding agencies that would support this new passion of mine, for which I had no track record. This process took a while, and in the meantime the inertia of my PhD training kept me on the B-school track. I completed my PhD and took my first position as an assistant professor at the University of Chicago, where I taught some courses in organizational behavior in the business school and others on the newly emerging field of artificial intelligence in the math department.[11]

For several years, I tried to get funding from different agencies that would allow me to shift from organizational behavior to start collaborating with Iain Wallace on cognitive development research. After several disappointments, we got lucky. In 1968, Wallace secured funds from the British Social Science Research Council for me to spend a semester with him at the newly founded University of Stirling, and I managed to get a Fulbright Teaching Fellowship to teach the following semester at the newly formed London School of Business, which solved the proximity problem.[12]

---

[11]In the early days of cognitive science, universities did not know where to put such topics. Some chose psychology departments, some chose electrical engineering (after all, computers had power supplies and transistors, didn't they?), and some chose mathematics departments.

[12]Of course, Stirling, Scotland, and London, England, are not exactly in one another's backyards, and there was no Internet yet, but for us, this was close enough to continue our projects via several long weekends of collaboration in London or Stirling.

At this point, a slight digression on organizational climate is in order. It was not coincidental that both of the institutions where I spent my first full year collaborating with Wallace were new organizations, quite open to faculty with nontraditional research interests. Perhaps the message for young faculty is that if you want to shift fields a little bit, you should look for an innovative institutional context and be willing to take some risks. Also, be prepared to ignore your more conservative colleagues. I know that when, as an assistant professor in my second year at the University of Chicago Business School, I told colleagues that I was planning to take a year off and go to Scotland and England to do research on children's thinking, typical responses went more or less like this: "That's the stupidest thing I can imagine. You haven't even been reviewed for reappointment yet and you're already leaving, you're already changing fields, you don't have a track record, and you've only published a little bit in your own field. What's the matter with you? Are you nuts?"

Perhaps. But it didn't matter, because while I was still in Scotland, I got a letter from Richard Cyert, then dean at GSIA (who later became one of Carnegie Mellon University's most influential and respected presidents). Dick, who had been briefed by Herb Simon[13] on how to phrase the job offer, said, "We think that cognitive psychology knows enough now that we could start to engineer better education in business school, so we would like you to come back and be GSIA's 'learning engineer.' Your challenge would be to take what we know about learning and forgetting and memory and problem-solving and get the faculty who teach accounting and economics and marketing to use the results of this emerging discipline of cognitive science to improve their courses."

I replied, "That's very interesting, but I really want to do developmental psychology also, so here's the deal. Suppose I make the 'learning engineering' work my teaching load, while my research focus would be on cognitive development, and I would have a joint appointment in psychology."

And they said, "Okay. Come back." That explains how I became a faculty member, and in fact a department head for 10 years, in a world-class department of psychology without ever getting either an undergraduate or a graduate degree in psychology!

Lest this sound just a little too smug, I need to acknowledge the incredible luck that seemed to embrace me at each fork in my meandering path. An important manifestation of that luck is what Herb Simon called "a secret weapon." He once told me that to break into a well-established field from outside you had to have a secret weapon. I was particularly lucky because I had two secret weapons. One was computer modeling. As I noted earlier, I happened to stumble into one of the few places in the world that were beginning to develop and exploit computer languages for formulating complex theories of cognition, and acquiring that skill several years before it became widely disseminated certainly gave me what economists call a "comparative advantage." My other secret weapon was Iain Wallace: a colleague well trained in cognitive development, and a tremendously creative, energetic, and original thinker.

---

[13]Simon's substantial influence on my life occurred at this and several other crucial points, all of which are described elsewhere (Klahr, 2004).

For the next 10 years or so, Iain and I continued our collaboration in various places: in Scotland, in Pittsburgh, and in Australia. We created production system models for children at different stages of class inclusion, quantification, conservation, and transitivity. Eventually our interests and careers took us in different but similar directions. Wallace became a dean of education, and then a provost, at a couple of Australian universities. I moved from a focus on cognitive development to more of a problem-solving and scientific-reasoning focus, expanding to adults and to educational issues.

I feel very fortunate to have had these two secret weapons. I am convinced that they had more to do with my rapid and successful entry into the field of cognitive development than any extraordinary intellectual skills on my part. There is no false modestly here because I certainly am aware that I have the requisite smarts and energy to have had a reasonably productive career as an academic in one or another modestly technical area of cognitive science or management science. But the comparative advantage of entering psychology just as the cognitive revolution was gathering its full momentum and of having mastered the requisite computational skills to cast developmental theory in the form of computational models (cf. Klahr & Wallace, 1970a, 1970b) gave my work a kind of instant recognition, that was, in my opinion, well beyond any sort of extraordinary effort or creativity on my part. I was both pleased and confused by all of this. In fact, when I received an invitation to give a talk at the Minnesota Symposium on Child Development in 1971, I did not have a clue about who the people were who invited me (Anne and Herb Pick, two of the most prominent developmentalists of that era), and when I attended the symposium, I spent a couple of somewhat awkward days there because I did not know a single person, not having come through the normal professional socialization process of a developmental psychology graduate student. However, the appearance of my paper in a very high-prestige symposium volume gave our work even more legitimacy and influence (Klahr, 1973).

I think that these shaping forces and contexts provide at least a partial explanation for why I did what I did and why I do what I do, although I certainly did not view them at the time in the way I have just described them. Only time puts these significant influences into perspective.

Children's Path to Number Conservation: Series Completion, Subitizing, and Statistical Learning

In this part of the chapter, I make a transition from autobiography to a scientific question. I focus on a fascinating puzzle about *number conservation*—a topic in cognitive development that used to be studied intensively (by several of the authors of other chapters in this volume, in fact) and that was ultimately abandoned by all of us as we moved on to other topics without having answered one of its most challenging questions. The puzzle is, "How do children acquire empirical evidence about number conservation?" This discussion has three parts. First, I describe the problem. Next, I summarize a theoretical account of how children acquire the knowledge elements that enable them to understand number conservation. This account draws heavily on a theoretical paper that I wrote 25 years ago (Klahr, 1984), a paper that made some claims that, at the time, could not be tested by either the empirical tools or the theoretical models available. Finally, I suggest that recent advances in our research methodologies and theories, including several represented in this volume, make it possible to return to that topic in order to really understand it.

As shown in Figure 13.1, there was a substantial amount of research on the general topic of number conservation in the early 1970s, but it dropped precipitously through the early 1990s. However, recent years have seen a resurgence of research on the development of quantitative concepts, with number conservation at the core of that interest. As I argue below, much of this activity has been stimulated by the theoretical and methodological advances in our field.

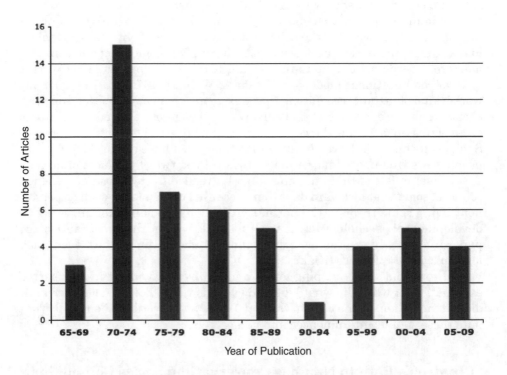

Figure 13.1. Number of papers published in *Child Development, Cognitive Psychology, Cognitive Science, Cognition, Cognition & Instruction, Cognitive Development, Developmental Psychology, Developmental Science, Journal of Experimental Child Psychology, Journal of Cognition & Development, Journal of Genetic Psychology, Psychology Bulletin,* and *Psychology Review,* with the words *Acquisition of conservation, Acquisition of number conservation, Conception of number, Conservation acquisition, Conservation learning, Conservation of discontinuous quantity, Conservation of number, Conservation of quantity, Conservation skills, Development of number, Inducing conservation, Number concept, Number concepts, Number conservation, Number development, Number invariance, One-one-correspondence, Quantitative invariance, Quantity conservation, Reasoning about number, Subitizing, Training conservation,* or *Transfer of conservation* in their title or abstract during each 5-year period from 1965 to 2009.

What Knowledge Elements Does Number Conservation Comprise?

If a set contains a certain number of discrete items, and if they undergo transformations such as spreading, rotating, compressing, or transposing, then the number of items does not change. That is, the types of physical actions just listed (aka *number conserving transformations*) are all *invariant with respect to number*. However, if you remove, eat, add, subtract, or vaporize one or more items, then the number of items in the set does change. The second group of actions (aka *number changing transformations*) is *not* invariant with respect to number. This distinction is so obvious to any normal adult that it seems a bit pedantic to even state it. However, it is not a piece of knowledge that young children have. Even since Piaget's time, tens of thousands of preschool children around the world have sat across tables from developmental psychologists and then have been (a) presented with arrays containing a small number of objects, (b) asked to quantify the amounts in each collection, and/or asked to determine their relative numerosity, (c) observed as one or both arrays was subjected to one or more of the types of transformations just listed, and finally (d) asked to make a statement about the relation between the initial number of set elements and the final number or between the transformed set and the untransformed set.

The specific attributes of this canonical procedure vary along several dimensions: one set or two; the number of objects; whether one set had more, less, or the same number as the other set; the type of transformation; the spatial layout of the arrays; the heterogeneity or homogeneity of the objects; the semantic relations between one set and another (e.g., all pennies in both sets, or eggs in one set and egg cups in the other); and so on. For example, Figure 13.2 shows a set of typical variants of the type studied by many conservation researchers to explore the relation between physical arrangement, type of transformation, and set size. In Task 1, the two arrays start the same with respect to number, length, and density. Then array B is compressed, reducing its length and increasing its density but not changing number. Finally, the child is asked to judge the relative numerosity of sets A and B′. In Task 3, array A starts out with less numerosity, length, and density than array B; B is then compressed so that it is denser and equal in length to A. Again, the child is asked to judge the relative numerosity of the two sets. The wording of the final question is yet another variable in this type of research. The experimenter could ask a vague question, such as, "Which collection is bigger?" to which the child might respond on the basis of length rather than number; or the question might be more focused on number—albeit still a bit vague—such as, "Are there more here, or here?"; or the question could be even more explicit about the fact that it is number, rather than length or density, that is the focal dimension, as in "Which set has more items?" or "Who has more cookies to eat?" But this study is just one of many, and the size of the experiment space (Klahr, 2000) here has sustained a small industry of developmentalists and produced a vast empirical base about the conditions under which children appear to understand the difference between number-preserving transformations and number-changing transformations.

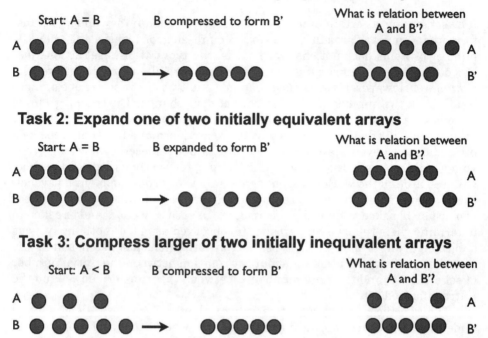

Task 1: Compress one of two initially equivalent arrays

Start: A = B   B compressed to form B'   What is relation between A and B'?

Task 2: Expand one of two initially equivalent arrays

Start: A = B   B expanded to form B'   What is relation between A and B'?

Task 3: Compress larger of two initially inequivalent arrays

Start: A < B   B compressed to form B'   What is relation between A and B'?

Figure 13.2.   Typical conservation tasks.

From the perspective of any typical adult, all of these variants might seem irrelevant. All I need to tell you about one of these experimental manipulations is the initial relation and the type of transformation. If sets A and B start with an equal number of objects, and I tell you that I moved the items in set B closer together, you know that A and B have remained numerically equivalent. If I tell you that I ate one of the cookies in set A, you know that set A is now smaller than set B. You need not look at the final collections to determine their relative size. Why? Because you know that compression has no effect on number and eating does. To reiterate this crucial point: A child who *fully* understands conservation need know only the *initial state* and *transformation type*. There is no need to encode the final arrays because transformational types uniquely determine the outcome.[14]

In her pathbreaking study of children's conservation knowledge, Gelman (1972) demonstrated that 4-year-olds were surprised when what they expected to be quantity-preserving transformations—Gelman called them *number irrelevant transformations*—yielded apparent changes in quantity (because the experimenter was doing "magic tricks" with the objects).

---

[14]Ah yes, the reader will interject, "But what about ambiguous cases, such as where one set starts larger than the other and the transformation is quantity changing? Without exact numerical information about the *size* of the transformation, the outcome is ambiguous." Granted, but not crucial to the argument here.

> As the magic experiments demonstrate, when children reason about numerosity they recognize the existence of a large class of transformations (manipulations) that can be performed on a set without altering the numerosity of the set. When called upon to explain unexpected spatial rearrangements, color changes, and item substitutions, they postulate transformations which have no effect on numerosity, such as lengthening and substitution. When probed, children typically make statements showing that they realize that these transformations do not affect numerosity. (Gelman, 1972, p. 82)

In fact, by first grade, most children have a robust understanding of the difference between the types of physical transformations that do and do not change the number of objects in a set. The crucial question is, *how* do children learn this? How do children come to classify one class of physical actions in the world as quantity-preserving transformations and another class as quantity-changing transformations? Clearly, there is no direct tutelage, unless the children happen to be unfortunate enough to have developmental psychologists as parents![15]

How Do Children Learn to Distinguish Between Quantity-Preserving and Quantity-Changing Transformations?

To classify the vast range of physical transformations that can be applied to small sets of discrete objects, children need three types of cognitive capacities. First, they need to be able to detect simple temporal patterns and make predictive extrapolations from them. Second, they need to be able to reliably quantify small collections of discrete objects. Third, they need to be able to parse the continuous flow of observed physical transformations in the environment into discrete temporal units having a beginning and an end. In the following paragraphs, I summarize evidence supporting the view that children have the first two of these capacities, and I suggest some new research paradigms that could be used to discover how and when they acquire the third capacity. The autobiographical tone of the first part of this chapter continues, albeit in the background, in the following discussion.

CHILDREN'S ABILITY TO DETECT AND EXTRAPOLATE SEQUENTIAL REGULARITIES. My first developmental psychology publication (Klahr & Wallace, 1970a), begins as follows:

> The ability to detect environmental regularities is a cognitive skill essential for survival. Man has a propensity to seek and a capacity to find serial patterns in such diverse areas as music, economics, and the weather. Even when no true pattern exists, humans attempt to construct one that will enable them to predict the sequence of future events. (p. 243)

---

[15]And here I must thank my children (Anna, Joshua, Sophia, and Benjamin) for being willing and long-suffering sources of ideas and insights during their childhood as I subjected them to this and other forms of probes, tests, challenges, and observations—even to the point of publishing some of their behavior (Klahr, 1978). And to the extent that they thought that either Dad or they were a little odd, my apologies.

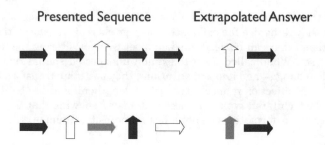

Figure 13.3. Series completion problems of the type used by Klahr and Wallace, 1970(a). In the first problem, the orientation pattern is: *right, right, up,* and the correct extrapolation is *up, right.* The color pattern is synchronized with the orientation pattern: *black, black, white.* In the second problem, orientation has a cycle of only two, *right, up,* but color has a cycle of three: *black, white, gray.* Thus, the extrapolation requires the creation of a novel object (*gray up*). From "The Development of Serial Completion Strategies: An Information Processing Analysis," by D. Klahr & J. G. Wallace, 1970, *British Journal of Psychology, 61,* pp. 243–257. Copyright 1975 by Elsevier Limited. Reprinted with permission.

The question we addressed was whether or not 5-year-old children could solve series completion problems. Adults' well-established ability to identify and extrapolate letter series completion problems had been modeled in a computer program (Simon & Kotovsky, 1963),[16] and our goal was to construct a computational model that could account for children's ability to solve the same general class of problems. Because we did not want to use problems that required children to have mastered the alphabet, we used a set of problems that varied in the color and orientation of simple objects, and that sometimes demanded decomposition and then reconstruction of problem attributes in order to extrapolate patterns such as those shown in Figure 13.3.

Our investigation revealed not only that children could detect and extrapolate simple holistic patterns (e.g., the one shown in Figure 13.3) but also that they could decompose the dimensions of the objects and detect and extrapolate the pattern for those dimensions.[17] That is, for problems similar to the one shown in Figure 13.3, they could isolate the color pattern from the orientation pattern and then recombine them in predicting the extrapolated item. Forty years later, the investigation of developing pattern induction capacity in children, even in infants, has become a very active research area, particularly in studies of early language acquisition (cf. Marcus, Vijayan, Rao, & Vishton, 1999; Saffran & Thiessen, 2003). There is no question that even very young children can detect, encode, and extrapolate temporal sequences of visual and auditory input.

---

[16]This paper should be inducted into in the "Unheralded Landmark Papers Hall of Fame." It is the first published paper in which a theory of human performance was evaluated by directly comparing the time it took a computer model and humans to solve a set of problems that varied in difficulty. To the best of my knowledge, it has never been fully appreciated as such.

[17]These are but one of a wide range of different types of inductive problems, recently classified by Kemp and Jern (2009).

QUANTIFICATION OF SMALL SETS BY SUBITIZING. Can children reliably and accurately quantify small collections of discrete objects? The literature on children's quantification abilities has identified three types of processes that are involved in encoding sets of objects and producing some kind of internal knowledge element corresponding to the size of the set: subitizing, counting, and estimation. An important developmental question is whether or not children can consistently encode sets of one, two, or three objects, before they have learned much about counting or estimation.

Evidence for subitizing as an early acquired and distinct process was reported in Chi and Klahr (1975). Adults and children were presented with random dot patterns and asked to say, as fast as they could, how many were in the pattern. The results, shown in Figure 13.4 (left panel), show a sharp discontinuity between the reaction times for three and four items, for both children and adults. One possible alternative interpretation of these results is that they are based on a set of learned patterns, in which more objects simply allow a large number of possible canonical patterns. Thus one dot is unique, two dots always form a line, three dots always form either a triangle or a line, but four and more dots suddenly allow a much larger set of such forms. However, a little known, but quite important, refutation of this interpretation was provided in a study by Akin and Chase (1978). They presented adults with complex block patterns and asked them to quantify the number of blocks as fast as possible. The results,

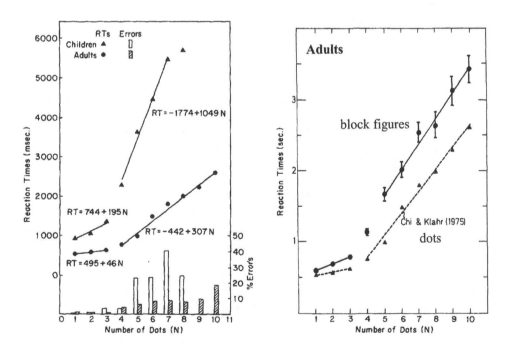

Figure 13.4. Subitizing and counting RT curves. From "Span and Rate of Apprehension in Children and Adults," by M.T. Chi & D. Klahr, 1975, *Journal of Experimental Child Psychology, 19,* pp. 434–439. Copyright 1975 by Elsevier Limited. Reprinted with permission.

shown in Figure 13.4 (right panel), reveal the same abrupt change in reaction time between three objects and four objects, but these results cannot be explained by the "canonical pattern" interpretation described above.

The question about whether subitizing—quantification of small arrays—is distinct from processes such as counting and estimation that produce internal representations of set size was a hot topic in the 1970s and, in fact, remains contentious (Gallistel, 2007; Hannula, Räsänen, & Lehtinen, 2007; Le Corre & Carey, 2007; Piazza, Mechelli, Butterworth, & Price, 2002). My initial view (Klahr & Wallace, 1976) was that subitizing is indeed a distinct and early acquired—perhaps innate—quantification process. In the early years of the debate, evidence supporting one view or another was based on the behavioral measures available at the time, but in recent years some very sophisticated brain-imaging techniques have been used to address the question, with some impressive results supporting the "subitizing is special" position.

For example, Piazza, Giacomini, Le Bihan, and Dehaene (2003) used functional magnetic resonance imaging techniques to measure the activity of attention-related regions of the brain in a task in which adult subjects were asked to say, as rapidly as possible, the number of items in a series of displays consisting of from one to seven randomly distributed items. They found a distinctively different pattern of activation between quantifying one to three items and quantifying four to seven items. Their interpretation of these blood-oxygen-level-dependent responses and reaction time data is that different regions of the brain are activated for the higher numbers (i.e., when counting, as opposed to subitizing, is occurring). Based on this evidence and similar converging results, Dehaene (2009) concluded:

> Although we currently have very little idea of how this system is organized at the neural level, it seems clear that a very quick and automatic grasp of the numerosities 1, 2, and 3 is part of the human intuition of numbers. (p. 244)

PARSING AND SEGMENTATION OF PHYSICAL ACTIONS. At this point, I have argued (a) that children can detect, encode, and predict sequential regularities, and (b) that subitizing is a distinct process used to rapidly quantify small collections of discrete objects without counting. The next question that needs to be addressed is how children parse continuous actions in the world so that they can categorize actions that transform collections in ways that do or do not change their numerical amount. The answer to this question has two parts. The first part will demonstrate that—for small values of N—young children can reliably distinguish quantity-changing transformations from quantity-preserving changes. The second part will have to explain *how* such transformations are learned—that is, how a specific combination of physical actions, usually executed by a human hand, gets to be encoded as one type or another of quantity relevant transformations.

Evidence on the first part of the question is currently controversial. Some reports claim that 5-month-old infants can discriminate addition from subtraction transformations (Wynn, 1992, 1998), while others claim that such competence develops slowly over the first 4 or 5 years of life (Clearfield & Mix, 1999; Huttenlocher, Jordan, & Levine, 1994; Starkey, 1992; Vilette, 1996) and that Wynn's results are based on methodological artifacts (Cohen, 2002; Cohen & Marks, 2002). There is no question that by the time children are 4 or 5 years old, they expect what adults would call an "addition transformation" to *increase* the number of objects in a set, a "subtraction" one to *decrease* the number, and a "simple rearrangement" to leave the number unchanged. However, the specific age of acquisition is not important unless one wants to argue that this discrimination ability is innate. What *is* important is how transformational classes are learned.

What Needs to Be Known to "Pass" a Conservation Test?

I address the question in two main parts. First, I describe the kinds of knowledge components required to "do" conservation and the kinds of precursor knowledge components that contribute to full-fledged "conservation acquisition." Although these conservation tasks appear simple, they actually have layer upon layer of complexity that requires the careful articulation of different aspects of the task, so that some unambiguous notation is necessary in the following exposition. After describing my notation, I suggest an account of how the child acquires those knowledge components.

KINDS OF KNOWLEDGE REQUIRED. In Figure 13.5, I introduce some notation for the classic version of the conservation-of-number task in which the child observes two distinct collections of discrete objects and is asked to quantify them (e.g., "How many here?" and "How many there?").

1. $Q_i(X) \longrightarrow x_i$ $Q_i(Y) \longrightarrow y_i$ A quantification operator encodes the external collection (X) and produces an internal symbol indicating the <u>amount</u> and the <u>type of quantifier</u> that produced that symbol. Ditto for external collection Y.

1a. $Q_s(X) \longrightarrow x_s$ $Q_s(Y) \longrightarrow y_s$ In this case, the operator is Subitizing.

2. $(x_s = y_s) \longrightarrow (X \overset{Q}{=} Y)$ If the subitizing symbols from the two collections are the same, then you know that those external collections are quantitatively equivalent.

3. $T_p(Y) \longrightarrow (Y')$ Collection Y undergoes a "perceptual" transformation (i.e., NOT T_+ or T_-)

4. $\{X \overset{Q}{=} Y\} \ \& \ T_p(Y) \longrightarrow (Y') \Longrightarrow \{X \overset{Q}{=} Y'\}$ Now you know that If two collections are initially quantitatively equivalent, and one undergoes a perceptual transformation (from Y to Y') then you know that collection X is quantitatively equivalent to collection Y'.

Figure 13.5. Processing Steps for Equivalence Conservation.

Step 1 shows the following: Some kind of quantification process, Q_i, operates on the first external set (set X). The subscript on Q_i indicates that the analysis is intended to cover any of the three types of quantification operators, counting—Q_c, subitizing—Q_s, or estimation—Q_e. That operator encodes collection X and produces some internal quantitative representation of how much X is there, when quantified by operator Q_i. That *internal* representation of that amount is x_i. Step 1a is more specific. It shows the notation for a case in which the child subitized collection X, thereby producing an internal knowledge element that represents the size of set X, as determined by the subitizing process. A similar process would occur for collection Y.

Step 2 is a production (Klahr, Langley, & Neches, 1987; Newell, 1990) in which the condition side is a test for whether the two internal quantitative symbols for the two collections are equivalent. If they are, then the inference is made that the *external* collections, from which the two *internal* symbols were derived, are quantitatively equivalent.

At this point, the first phase of the conservation procedure has been encoded, and the initial quantitative equivalence of two collections has been established. Next, we come to the modification—or "transformation"—of one of the collections. Here I introduce three kinds of generic transformations: those that increase quantity, those that decrease it, and those that preserve it. The notation is simply T_+, T_-, and T_p, respectively. The origins of the system's knowledge about how to encode and represent the observed or enacted physical actions into one of these three classes are described below; it is, in fact, the key to the whole account of conservation acquisition being described here.

In Step 3, since we are modeling conservation rather than nonconservation in this example, we use a quantity-preserving transformation on one of the collections that yields a transformed version of that collection. The notation for Step 3 indicates that a quantity-preserving transformation (T_p) was applied to collection Y, yielding collection Y'. (Think: "The set of three objects was spread out.")

Finally, in Step 4, we get to "the" conservation rule. This one says, in effect, "If you know that two collections were initially equal, and that one of them underwent a quantity-preserving transformation, then you know that the quantity of the transformed collection is still equal to the untransformed one."

This final knowledge element is essential for fully understanding conservation because it means that the system does not have to requantify the transformed collection in order to make a judgment about the relative magnitude of collections X and Y. To be concrete: If you put three cookies in a box, shut the box, and move it from you right hand to your left, you would know for sure that there are three cookies in that box because hand shifting is a quantity-preserving transformation.

While this decomposition may seem belabored, it suggests that young children have quite a bit to learn before they can pass conservation tests, and it may explain the otherwise surprising cases in which they have not yet acquired all of the necessary knowledge to do so. Piaget was the first to demonstrate that even when children count the same number in two collections, it does not mean they see them as quantitatively equivalent.

> Aud . . . counts eight pennies, says that he will be able to buy eight flowers, makes the exchange, and then cannot see that the sets are equivalent:

"There are more, because they're spread out." These cases clearly show that perception of spatial properties carries more weight than even verbal numeration. (Piaget, 1952, p. 59)

The extent to which children have this kind of knowledge, how they got it, in what contexts, for which materials and what range of numbers, and whether it could be trained, accelerated, and so on, occupied much of the field of cognitive development for about twenty years toward the end of the last century. Indeed, several of the authors in this volume, myself included, established their careers by exploring these issues.

How Are the Elements of a "Conservation Rule" Acquired? Let us assume that the cognitive system has the capacity to parse, encode, and store for further processing the temporal sequences of external quantities and actions upon them. For example, in a data structure that Wallace and I called a *specific consistent sequence,* a set of objects within the subitizing range is encoded, a specific physical transformation is observed and encoded, the collection is requantified, and the resulting quantitative symbols—generated by that particular quantification operator—are compared and tagged as being either the same or different. The assumption is that, at the outset, transformations are encoded as quantity preserving or quantity changing, and only later are the latter types of transformations further discriminated as either addition or subtraction transformations. We called these types of knowledge elements *specific* because at this point, all that the system knows, in effect, is that in one case, if you picked up three coins you still had three coins, and in another case, if you push two dolls together you still have two dolls. There is no generalization here across number, transformation, or objects.

Over time, and with many such sequences, the system starts to generalize. For example, Figure 13.6a shows a situation in which the system has encoded the fact that for a specific quantity (two items) and a specific physical transformation (spreading), the initial and final internal quantitative representations are the same. So it learns, in effect, that "spreading doesn't change twoness."

Eventually, as shown in Figure 13.6b, the system might discover that spreading doesn't change any of the types of quantitative symbols that subitizing is capable of producing. In other words, it will have discovered that spreading is a quantity-preserving transformation, at least with respect to small collections of discrete objects. Ultimately, the system will discover, through this process of abstraction and generalization, that there are a class of quantity-preserving transformations and another class of transformations that either increase or decrease quantity.

At this point, the system has sufficient knowledge about the relation between subitized quantities and transformations *that it doesn't have to do any requantification in order to make an inference about relative quantity, given initial quantity and the transformational type.* This knowledge is compactly represented in the following production:

$$(_{o}x_{s}) \; [T_{p}(X) \rightarrow X'\,] \rightarrow {}_{o}x_{s} = {}_{n}x_{s}$$

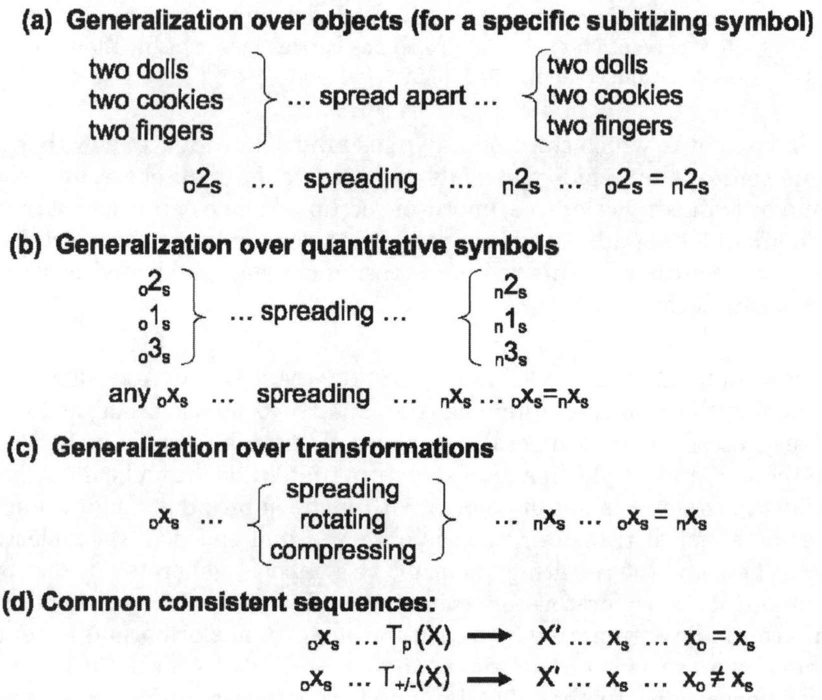

(a) Generalization over objects (for a specific subitizing symbol)

$$\left.\begin{array}{l}\text{two dolls}\\\text{two cookies}\\\text{two fingers}\end{array}\right\} \ldots \text{spread apart} \ldots \left\{\begin{array}{l}\text{two dolls}\\\text{two cookies}\\\text{two fingers}\end{array}\right.$$

$$_o2_s \ldots \text{spreading} \ldots _n2_s \ldots _o2_s = _n2_s$$

(b) Generalization over quantitative symbols

$$\left.\begin{array}{l}_o2_s\\_o1_s\\_o3_s\end{array}\right\} \ldots \text{spreading} \ldots \left\{\begin{array}{l}_n2_s\\_n1_s\\_n3_s\end{array}\right.$$

$$\text{any } _oX_s \ldots \text{spreading} \ldots _nX_s \ldots _oX_s = _nX_s$$

(c) Generalization over transformations

$$_oX_s \ldots \left\{\begin{array}{l}\text{spreading}\\\text{rotating}\\\text{compressing}\end{array}\right\} \ldots _nX_s \ldots _oX_s = _nX_s$$

(d) Common consistent sequences:

$$_oX_s \ldots T_p(X) \longrightarrow X' \ldots x_s \ldots x_o = x_s$$

$$_oX_s \ldots T_{+/\text{-}}(X) \longrightarrow X' \ldots x_s \ldots x_o \neq x_s$$

Figure 13.6. Examples of Generalization Over Timeline Entries for (a) Objects, (b) Quantitative Symbols, and (c) Transformations, Produce (d) Common Consistent Sequences.

This production says that

> *if* you know the initial quantify of a subitizable collection X (the "old" collection), *and* you observed and encoded a quantity preserving transformation (T_p) on that collection, producing a "new" collection (X'), *then* you know, without further encoding, that the appropriate quantitative symbol for representing that quantity is the same as the previous one ($_oX_s = _nX_s$).

The system gets to this state by eliminating the redundancy inherent in all the processing so far, and it creates a rule that the initial state and the transformational class are sufficient to form an expectation—a prediction, if you will, about what the resultant quantity will be. At this point, the system has "acquired" conservation of quantity.

ON THE BASIS OF WHAT EVIDENCE IS INFORMATION ABOUT TRANSFORMATIONAL CLASSES NOTICED, ENCODED, AND ABSTRACTED? The account presented here puts the burden of acquiring conservation on children's ability to encode and classify physical transformations from the ongoing perception, encoding, storage, and classification of a huge, complex, and semicontinuous stream of visual input. How can we, as developmental scientists, gather information about how this happens? How can we document the way that children discover transformational classes in the world of continuous action sequences? I believe the answer lies in a converging portfolio of novel and powerful methodological and theoretical developments in our field: (a) statistical learning models, (b) research paradigms for discovering event segmentation capacities in adults and children, and (c) in vivo recording of children's observations of quantity-relevant physical transformations in the natural environment. In the following sections, I briefly describe each of them.

Statistical Learning. In the past dozen years or so, developmental psychologists have used statistical learning theory (Thiessen, 2009) to account for the way that infants encode auditory input generated by adult speech. The core idea is that there are reliable featural regularities in the continuous stream of sounds that allow the cognitive system to distinguish transitional probabilities for sequences *within* words from the transitional probabilities *between* words, and that infants can detect and use those statistical relationships between neighboring speech sounds to segment words (cf. Thiessen & Saffran, 2007).

Do similar statistical processing mechanisms operate on visual input? More specifically, can children extract the same kind of statistical regularities from the continuous stream of physical actions they observe in the world, into classes of quantity-changing and quantity-preserving transformation? Can they derive quantitative regularities from those transformational classes? A dozen years ago, no one knew for sure. For example, at the conclusion of one of their pioneering papers on this topic, Saffran, Aslin, and Newport (1996) wrote, "It remains unclear whether the statistical learning we observed is indicative of a mechanism specific to language acquisition or of a general learning mechanism applicable to a broad range of distributional analyses of environmental input" (p. 1928). Clearly, if statistical learning mechanisms *are* sufficiently general to be independent of specific sensory modes and time scale of speech perception and segmentation, then they might be able to account for detection and segmentation of the encoding of dynamic action sequences observed by the child.

Event Segmentation. The key to statistical learning is to appropriately process transitional probabilities between sequential events, and that requires an additional capacity: the segmentation of a continuous input steam into a series of discrete events. Evidence for the existence of that capacity is well established, not only in adults (Zacks, 2004; Zacks, Kumar, Abrams, & Mehta, 2009) but also in infants (Baldwin, Baird, Saylor, & Clark, 2001). Moreover, about 10 years after Saffran and colleagues' work on speech segmentation, they directly addressed the issue of how human action sequences are segmented into discrete events (Baldwin, Andersson, Saffran, & Meyer, 2008). Their study was motivated by the fact that

> existing findings indicate that skill at detecting action segments plays a key role in processing of dynamic human activity . . . [but] . . . the available findings have provided little insight into the specifics of how observers of dynamic action identify relevant action segments within a continuous behavior stream. That is, the mechanisms enabling adults to extract segments from a continuous flow of activity have not been known. (Baldwin et al., 2008, p. 1384)

To address this question, Baldwin et al. presented adults with sequences of novel and arbitrary actions that included mixes of high and low transition probabilities within and between segments (analogous to the research using artificial speech sounds with infants) to see whether their participants could distinguish between them (as in infant speech research). Their results show that "adults can discover sequential probabilities within dynamic intentional activity that support extraction of higher-level action segments" (Baldwin et al., 2008, p. 1401).

My earlier account of how transformational classes might be learned rests on the assumption that children can parse continuous physical actions relating to quantitative transformations into coherent units, and that they can associate those units with pre- and post-transformational quantification encodings. The research on event segmentation provides clear evidence for the tenability of these assumptions. I have also argued that statistical learning theory suggests a plausible account of how the stream of visual input from quantity-relevant transformations might be segmented. An important aspect of statistical learning theory that is relevant for the kind of event segmentation I am proposing is that "many of the relations infants and adults learn involve regularities between elements that are not immediately adjacent" (Thiessen, 2009, p. 37). Thus, while the purported regularities between transformations and quantification are likely to be distributed over other events, statistical learning processes could, in principle, detect and encode them. The remaining question is how developmental researchers can obtain the necessary data to further explore these claims.

In Vivo Recoding of Transformations. What in the world do babies and young children see with respect to quantitatively relevant action sequences? How can we discover what they see? Can we collect a corpus of everyday action encodings and then determine whether statistical learning theory can provide a plausible account of how those encodings are processed to extract quantitative transformations? Is there sufficient signal in the noise to accomplish the classification of transformations with respect to their effect on small quantities (within the subitizing range)?

To answer these questions, we need to extend and apply data collection paradigms that are just beginning to be developed. Put simply, if we want to know what kinds of information infants and young children encounter in the environment and what they do with it, then we need to see what they see as they encounter the real world. That is, we need to do in vivo research on children's encounters with quantitative aspects of the physical world. In vivo recording of human behavior has already proven informative in a wide range of complex human activities, ranging from observation of real scientists making real discoveries (Dunbar, 1999, 2002) to infant motor behavior (Adolph et al., 2011) to intelligent tutors generating enormous databases as hundreds of thousands of students make second-to-second choices while using educational software (Baker, Corbett, & Koedinger, 2004; Romero & Ventura, 2007).

Cicchino, Aslin, and Rakison (2011) showed how recording infants' in vivo behavior can inform the theory described earlier. Using a head-mounted camera, they generated a continuous record of what was in the baby's field of view (but not necessarily what the eyes were attending to) and categorized the babies' in vivo experiences. They found that when adults are in the baby's field of view, they are typically acting as causal agents, and babies are unlikely to observe much self-propelled action. Although Cicchino et al. did not focus on the kind of quantitative transformations that are important for the theory I have been proposing, it seems that most of the important transformational classifications will come from situations in which adults are indeed the agents of change with respect to small quantities.

The opportunity for in vivo research on what children see in the natural world (as opposed to the psychologist's laboratory) has been substantially facilitated by the recent development of a sophisticated but very lightweight eye tracker that can be mounted on infants' heads as they negotiate their everyday environment—rather than sitting strapped into seats in the researcher's lab—to reveal exactly where in the scene the baby is looking (Franchak, Kretch, Soska, & Adolph, 2010). In the first publication on this new technology, Franchak et al. (2010) reported a very high proportion of infants' fixations being directed to the manipulation of objects in mothers' hands. While this study was not designed to focus on quantification or on quantity-related transformations, it is clear that such studies could be mounted. It is this level of dense data recording that will enable us to collect the necessary information about the frequency, reliability, and grain size of children's exposure to the kinds of data necessary to assess the hypothesized processes sketched in Figure 13.5.

Conclusion

This chapter is an odd bird, being a mix of two things that scientists are trained to avoid: excessive personalization and highly speculative theorizing. Nonetheless, I hope that the reader has found the final product interesting. I hope that the first part motivates readers to think about their own emotional attraction to their work and about the developmental paths to their current identification as researchers. I also hope that some readers have found my scientific speculations in the final part of the chapter sufficiently intriguing to encourage them to expand and implement the suggestions made here about how to advance our understanding of quantitative development. At the same time, I view the diverse contributions to this volume as fodder for my future scientific work, particularly as I now better understand the diverse ways that conversations and observations in the informal social world have and will shape my theory, research, and practice related to cognitive development, scientific reasoning, and science education.

References

Adolph, K. E., Cole, W. G., Komati, M., Garciagirre, J. S., Badaly, D., Lingeman, J. M., . . . Sotsky, R. B. (2011). How do you learn to walk? Thousands of steps and hundreds of falls per day. Manuscript in revision.

Akin, O., & Chase, W. (1978). Quantification of three-dimensional Structures. *Journal of Experimental Psychology: Human Perception and Performance, 4,* 397–410. doi:10.1037/0096-1523.4.3.397

Baker, R., Corbett, A., & Koedinger, K. (2004, August/September). Detecting student misuse of intelligent tutoring systems. In J. C. Lester, R. M. Vicari, & F. Paraguançu (Eds.), *Lecture Notes in Computer Science: Vol. 7. Intelligent Tutoring Systems* (pp. 531–540). Proceedings of the 7th International Conference, ITS, Maceió, Alagoas, Brazil.

Baldwin, D., Andersson, A., Saffran, J., & Meyer, M. (2008). Segmenting dynamic human action via statistical structure. *Cognition, 106,* 1382–1407. doi:10.1016/j.cognition.2007.07.005

Baldwin, D. A., Baird, J. A., Saylor, M., & Clark, M. A. (2001). Infants parse dynamic action. *Child Development, 72,* 708–717. doi:10.1111/1467-8624.00310

Carver, S. M., & Klahr, D. (Eds.). (2001). *Cognition and instruction: 25 years of progress.* Mahwah, NJ: Erlbaum.

Cohen, L. B., & Marks, K. S. (2002). How infants process addition and subtraction events. *Developmental Science, 5,* 186–201. doi:10.1111/1467-7687.00220

Chi, M. T., & Klahr, D. (1975). Span and rate of apprehension in children and adults. *Journal of Experimental Child Psychology, 19,* 434–439. doi:10.1016/0022-0965(75)90072-7

Cicchino, J. B., Aslin, R. N., & Rakison, D. H. (2011). Correspondences between what infants see and know about causal and self-propelled motion.. *Cognition, 118,* 171–192.

Clearfield, M. W., & Mix, K. S. (1999, April). *Infants use contour length—not number—to discriminate small visual sets.* Poster presented at the biennial meeting of the Society for Research in Child Development, Albuquerque, NM.

Cohen, L. B. (2002). Extraordinary claims require extraordinary controls. *Developmental Science, 5,* 210–212. doi:10.1111/1467-7687.00222

Cohen, L. B., & Marks, K. S. (2002). How infants process addition and subtraction events. *Developmental Science, 5,* 186–201. doi:10.1111/1467-7687.00220

Dehaene, S. (2009). Origins of mathematical intuitions: The case of arithmetic. *The year in cognitive neuroscience 2009. Annals of the New York Academy of Sciences, 1156,* 232–259. doi:10.1111/j.1749-6632.2009.04469.x

Dunbar, K. (1999). *The scientist. In vivo: How scientists think and reason in the laboratory.* In L. Magnani, N. Nersessian, & P. Thagard, P. (Eds.), *Model-based reasoning in scientific discovery* (pp. 89–98). New York, NY: Kluwer/Plenum.

Dunbar, K. (2002). Science as category: Implications of in vivo science for theories of cognitive development, scientific discovery, and the nature of science. In S. Stich, P. Carruthers, & M. Siegal (Eds.), *Cognitive models of science* (pp. 154–170). New York, NY: Cambridge University Press.

Franchak, J. M., Kretch, K. S., Soska, K. C., & Adolph, K. E. (2011) Head-mounted eye-tracking: A new method to describe the visual ecology of infants. *Child Development, 82,* 1–13.

Gallistel, C. R. (2007). Commentary on Le Corre & Carey. *Cognition, 105,* 439–445. doi:10.1016/j.cognition.2007.01.010

Gelman, R. (1972). Logical capacity of very young children: Number invariance rules. *Child Development, 43,* 75–90. doi:10.2307/1127873

Hannula, M. M., Räsänen, P., & Lehtinen, E. (2007). Development of counting skills: Role of spontaneous focusing on numerosity and subitizing-based enumeration. *Mathematical Thinking and Learning, 9*(1), 51–57.

Huttenlocher, J., Jordan, N. C., & Levine, S. C. (1994). A mental model for early arithmetic. *Journal of Experimental Psychology: General, 123,* 284–296.

Kemp, C. & Jern, A. (2009, August). A taxonomy of inductive problems. *Proceedings of the 31st Annual Conference of the Cognitive Science Society.* Austin, TX.

Klahr, D. (1969a). Decision making in a complex environment. *Management Science, 15,* 595–618. doi:10.1287/mnsc.15.11.595

Klahr, D. (1969b). Statistical significance of Kruskal's nonmetric multidimensional scaling technique. *Psychometrika, 34,* 190–204.

Klahr, D. (1973). An information-processing approach to the study of cognitive development. In A. Pick (Ed.), *Minnesota symposia on child psychology* (Vol. 7, pp. 141–177). Minneapolis: University of Minnesota Press.

Klahr, D. (Ed.). (1976). *Cognition and instruction.* Hillsdale, NJ: Erlbaum.

Klahr, D. (1978). Goal formation, planning, and learning by pre-school problem solvers, or: "My socks are in the dryer." In R. S. Siegler (Ed.), *Children's thinking: What develops?* (pp. 181–212). Hillsdale, NJ: Erlbaum.

Klahr, D. (1984). Transition processes in quantitative development. In R. Sternberg (Ed.), *Mechanisms of cognitive development* (pp. 102–139). San Francisco, CA: Freeman.

Klahr, D. (2000). *Exploring science: The cognition and development of discovery processes.* Cambridge, MA: MIT Press.

Klahr, D. (2004). Encounters with the force of Herbert A. Simon. In M. Augier & J. G. March (Eds.), *Models of a man: Essays in memory of Herbert A. Simon* (pp. 433–450). Cambridge, MA: MIT Press.

Klahr, D., Fay, A. L., & Dunbar, K. (1993). Developmental differences in experimental heuristics. *Cognitive Psychology, 25,* 111–146. doi:10.1006/cogp.1993.1003

Klahr, D., Langley, P., & Neches, R. (Eds.). (1987). *Production system models of learning and development.* Cambridge, MA: MIT Press.

Klahr, D., & Wallace, J. G. (1970a). The development of serial completion strategies: An information processing analysis. *British Journal of Psychology, 61,* 243–257. doi:10.1111/j.2044-8295.1970.tb01241.x

Klahr, D., & Wallace, J. G. (1970b). An information processing analysis of some Piagetian experimental tasks. *Cognitive Psychology, 1,* 358–387. doi:10.1016/0010-0285(70)90021-6

Klahr, D., & Wallace, J. G. (1976). Cognitive development: An information processing view. Hillsdale, NJ: Erlbaum.

Krumboltz, J. D. (Ed.). (1965). *Learning and the educational process.* Chicago, IL: Rand McNally.

Kruskal, J. B. (1964). Multidimensional scaling by optimizing goodness of fit to a nonmetric hypothesis. *Psychometrika, 29:* 1–27.

Le Corre, M., & Carey, S. (2007). One, two, three, four, nothing more: An investigation of the conceptual sources of the verbal counting principles. *Cognition, 105,* 395–438. doi:10.1016/j.cognition.2006.10.005

Marcus, G. F., Vijayan, S., Rao, S. B., & Vishton, P. M. (1999, January 1). Rule learning by seven-month-old infants. *Science, 283,* 77–80. doi:10.1126/science.283.5398.77

Newell, A. (1990). *Unified theories of cognition.* Cambridge, MA: Harvard University Press.

Piaget, J. (1952). *The child's conception of number.* London, England: Routledge & Kegan Paul.

Piazza, M., Giacomini, E., Le Bihan, D., & Dehaene, S. (2003). Single-trial classification of parallel pre-attentive and serial attentive processes using functional magnetic resonance imaging. *Proceedings of the Royal Society, of London. Series B: Biological Sciences, 270,* 1237–1245. doi:10.1098/rspb.2003.2356

Piazza, M., Mechelli, A., Butterworth, B., & Price, C. (2002). Are subitizing and counting implemented as separate or functionally overlapping processes? *NeuroImage, 15,* 435–446. doi:10.1006/nimg.2001.0980

Reitman, W. R. (1964). Heuristic decision procedures, open constraints, and the structure of ill-defined problems. In M. W. Shelly & G. L. Bryan (Eds.), *Optimality and human judgment* (pp. 282–315). New York, NY: Wiley.

Reitman, W. R. (1965). *Cognition and thought.* New York, NY: Wiley.

Romero, C., & Ventura, S. (2007). Educational data mining: A survey from 1995 to 2005. *Expert Systems with Applications, 33,* 135–146. doi:10.1016/j.eswa.2006.04.005

Saffran, J. R., Aslin, R. N., & Newport, E. L. (1996, December 13). Statistical learning by 8-month-old infants. *Science, 274,* 1926–1928. doi:10.1126/science.274.5294.1926

Saffran, J. R., & Thiessen, E. D. (2003). Pattern induction by infant language learners. *Developmental Psychology, 39,* 484–494. doi:10.1037/0012-1649.39.3.484

Schunn, C. D., & Klahr, D. (1992, July–August). Complexity management in a discovery task. *Proceedings of the Fourteenth Annual Conference of the Cognitive Science Society.* Indiana University, Bloomington.

Schunn, C. D., & Klahr, D. (1996). The problem of problem spaces: When and how to go beyond a 2-space model of scientific discovery. In *Proceedings of the 18th Annual Conference of the Cognitive Science Society* (pp. 25–26). University of California, San Diego.

Simon, H. A., & Kotovsky, K. (1963). Human acquisition of concepts for sequential patterns. *Psychological Review, 70,* 534–546.

Starkey, P. (1992). The early development of numerical reasoning. *Cognition, 43,* 93–126. doi:10.1016/0010-0277(92)90034-F

Thiessen, E. D. (2009). Statistical learning. In E. Bavin (Ed.), *Cambridge handbook of child language* (pp. 35–50). Cambridge, England: Cambridge University Press.

Thiessen, E. D., & Saffran, J. R. (2007). Learning to learn: Acquisition of stress-based strategies for word segmentation. *Language Learning and Development, 3,* 75–102.

Vilette, B. (1996). De la "proto-arithmetiques" aux connaissances additive et soustractives [From "proto-arithmetic" to additive and subtractive knowledge]. *Revue de Psychologie de l'Education, 3,* 25–43.

Wynn, K. (1992, August 27). Addition and subtraction in human infants. *Nature, 358,* 749–750. doi:10.1038/358749a0

Wynn, K. (1998). Psychological foundations of number: Numerical competence in human infants. *Trends in Cognitive Science, 2,* 296–303.

Zacks, J. (2004). Using movement and intentions to understand simple events. *Cognitive Science: A Multidisciplinary Journal, 28,* 979–1008. doi:10.1207/s15516709cog2806_5

Zacks, J. M., Kumar, S., Abrams, R. A., & Mehta, R. (2009). Using movement and intentions to understand human activity. *Cognition, 112,* 201–216. doi:10.1016/j.cognition.2009.03.007

Index

About the Editors

Sharon M. Carver, PhD, is a developmental psychologist who serves as a teaching professor at Carnegie Mellon University and the director of the Psychology Department's early childhood laboratory school, The Children's School. With David Klahr, she codirects the university's doctoral Program in Interdisciplinary Education Research (PIER). Dr. Carver earned an AB in psychology from Princeton University and a PhD in psychology from Carnegie Mellon University, where her advisor was David Klahr. Dr. Carver's research focus is on the explicit specification of learning goals, the alignment of instruction and assessment with those goals, and the application of diverse teaching strategies to facilitate transfer. She seeks to enhance the reciprocal impact of theory and research in multiple disciplines to strengthen the learning of children, educators, families, university students, and researchers.

Jeff Shrager, PhD, is a consulting associate professor of symbolic systems at Stanford University, and chief technological officer of CollabRx, Inc., a biomedical informatics startup. A computational psychologist of science, Dr. Shrager seeks to understand how science works and to build human–computer networks that facilitate scientific discovery. Dr. Shrager holds degrees in computer science and cognitive and developmental psychology from The University of Pennsylvania and Carnegie Mellon University, respectively, and has conducted research in cognitive and developmental neuroscience, informal science education, scientific computing, human learning, artificial intelligence, molecular microbial marine biology and genomics, nonlinear mathematics, and many other areas.